赖世雄经典英语语法

新版

A Guide to English Grammar

赖世雄◎著

外文出版社
FOREIGN LANGUAGES PRESS
全国百佳出版社

图书在版编目（CIP）数据

赖世雄经典英语语法：新版 / 赖世雄著. -- 北京：外文出版社，2019.5（2020重印）
（赖世雄优能英语）
ISBN 978-7-119-12028-7

Ⅰ. ①赖… Ⅱ. ①赖… Ⅲ. ①英语－语法－自学参考资料 Ⅳ. ①H314

中国版本图书馆CIP数据核字(2019)第093812号

选题策划：蔡　箐　　叶　俭
特约编辑：贾志敏　　王　艳
责任编辑：李春英
装帧设计：柏拉图
印刷监制：秦　蒙
出版发行：外文出版社有限责任公司
地　　址：中国北京西城区百万庄大街24号　　邮政编码：100037
网　　址：http://www.flp.com.cn
电子邮箱：flp@cipg.org.cn
电　　话：（010）008610-68320579（总编室）
（010）008610-68995852（发行部）
（010）008610-68996183（投稿电话）
印　　制：北京华创印务有限公司
经　　销：新华书店 / 外文书店
开　　本：880 mm×1230 mm　　1/32
印　　张：16.75
字　　数：650 千字
版　　次：2020 年 2 月第 1 版第 3 次印刷
书　　号：ISBN 978-7-119-12028-7
定　　价：49.00 元

序

我们大家都知道英语语法的重要性。有了扎实的语法基础，我们才能看懂复杂艰涩的结构，才能写出并说出正确的句子。问题是：我们学了多年的英语，一提到语法就头痛、心生畏惧，甚至因此心灰意冷，不再想继续学英语。究其原因何在?

原来是，传统的语法书一味守着八大词类，以切割的方式讲解。其结果是，我们只知道一大堆词性及专业术语，却不知一个简单句子的基本结构是什么，真有一种见树不见林、完全没有头绪的感觉。

我个人就深受这些错误学习方式的毒害，中学时代的我英语成绩曾得过 7 分。直至我日后以自我摸索的方式自学苦读英语，才逐渐了解学习语法的正确方式。因此这套语法丛书就是根据我多年学习英语的经验编写而成。本书有下列特点：

从单词造句出发：扬弃传统的八大词类分项解说，让读者立即认识主语及动词，明了单词造句的基本原则。

细谈连词的用法：使读者明白连词及关系词的用法，进而熟悉并列句以及复合句的造句方式。

详解非谓语动词：使读者了解分词、不定式、动名词的形式及用法，完全掌握分析句子结构的能力。

本书涵盖所有有关语法的重点，除了上述重点以外，举凡时态、虚拟语气、副词、反意疑问句等，无不包括在内。本书也增添了介词及复合形容词的内容，均采用条列式重点解说，解说文字浅显易懂，每章习题更有详解，极利于欲把英语语法彻底学好的人士学习。本书可说是市场上最容易学习、也最容易吸收的最佳英语语法参考书，值得亲爱的读者细细品味。

另外，应广大读者的强烈要求，此次改版升级特别增加了我本人录制的广播教学音频。这套讲解音频早年在中央人民广播电台广播时就颇受读者欢迎。广播教学模式除了讲解书里的知识要点外，更是即兴衍生出很多新的知识点，所以比书籍内容更加活泼有趣，十分适合搭配学习。不过大家需要注意的是，广播教学强调的是语法的宏观掌握，采用了点拨式的讲解模式，而不是对照着书本原封不动地讲解，所以读者在听的过程中不要生硬地和书本逐页对应，而是要从宏观的角度，以更大的格局来领悟语法的体系，达到水到渠成的效果，这才是我录制教学音频的初衷。在讲解过程中，我偶尔会脱离书本的例句，即兴造出一些更加有趣的例句来调动大家的热情，达到快乐学习的效果。另外，《赖世雄经典英语语法》在一版再版的过程中，书中的不少例句也进行了与时俱进的修改和增补，所以你听到的句子可能和书上的例句不是一模一样，但正是因为如此，语法的学习反而充满了乐趣，因为你不仅吸收了双倍的知识，更感受到了严谨语法的别样趣味。

最后祝大家学习愉快！

赖世雄

于台北常春藤

目录

第四章　非谓语动词

第五章　助动词及易用错的动词

第一章　句子的形成

概述

1. 任何一个句子一定由主语（subject，简写成 S）及动词（verb，简写成 V）组成。

例: John works hard.
S V
（约翰工作很努力。）

He plays the piano well.
S V
（他钢琴弹得很好。）

Mary seems to be fond of learning English.
S V
（玛丽似乎喜欢学英语。）

2. 有时主语可以省略，而形成祈使句。这种祈使句句首为原形动词，之前省略了 You should（你应当）。

例: Work hard. = (You should) work hard.
原形V
（努力工作。）

Be quiet. = (You should) be quiet.
（安静。）

注意

祈使句变成否定形式时，要在原形动词前加 Don't。

例: Don't fool around.
（别游手好闲。）

Don't be silly.
（别傻了。）

第一节　可做主语的词类

一般所见到的结构中，通常是以名词做主语，但除了名词以外，还可用代词、动名词或不定式短语、名词性从句、名词短语、表距离的地点副词短语等做主语。兹介绍如下：

1. 名词做主语：

例：The child is apt to tell lies.
（这孩子喜欢说谎。）

Gold is of much value.
（黄金很值钱。）

2. 代词做主语：

例：He always keeps his promise.
（他总是信守承诺。）

It is a lot of fun to climb mountains.
（爬山蛮好玩的。）

3. 动名词或不定式短语做主语：

动词绝不可直接当主语，一定要变成动名词或不定式短语，如此才可视为名词的对等语，做主语用。

例：See him makes me angry. (×，See 为动词)
→ Seeing him makes me angry. (✓，Seeing 为动名词)
（看到他就令我生气。）

See him is my purpose of coming here. (×，See 为动词)
→ To see him is my purpose of coming here. (✓，To see 为不定式短语)
（我来这儿是为了看他。）

a. 动名词做主语

用动名词做主语，通常用以表示已知的事实或曾经做过的经历。

试译下列句中的主语：

集邮是他的爱好之一。

____

由“爱好”一词得知，此处的“集邮”乃是一种经历。
故应用动名词短语 Collecting stamps，而成：
Collecting stamps is one of his hobbies.

再译下列句中的主语：

听音乐使我快乐。

____

由“使我快乐”得知，“听音乐”是说话者曾经做过的事，故仍用动名词短语 Listening to music 做主语，而成：

Listening to music makes me happy.

b. 不定式做主语

用不定式做主语时，通常表示一种意愿、目的或未完成的事。

试译下列句中的主语：

出国留学是我最大的愿望。

____

由“愿望”一词得知此处的“出国留学”乃是一种意愿或尚未做的事，故应以不定式短语 To study abroad 当主语，而成：

To study abroad is my greatest desire.

再译下列句中的主语：

到日本游玩是我今年的计划。

____

由“计划”一词得知说者尚未到过日本游玩（go to Japan for a visit），故此处应使用不定式短语 To go to Japan for a visit 做主语，而成：

To go to Japan for a visit is my plan for this year.

注意:

1) 不定式或动名词短语做主语时，往往会形成主语太长的现象，故通常均用代词 it 做形式主语，置于句首，而将真正主语（亦即不定式或动名词短语）移至句尾。动名词短语移至句尾时，通常改为不定式短语。

例: Collecting stamps is one of his hobbies.

= It is one of his hobbies to collect stamps.

形式主语　　　　　　　真正主语

Listening to music makes me happy.

= It makes me happy to listen to music.

形式主语　　　　　　　真正主语

To study abroad is my greatest desire.

= It is my greatest desire to study abroad.

形式主语　　　　　　　真正主语

2) 有时我们亦可见到被 it 代替的动名词短语移至句尾时，仍保留动名词形态而不变成不定式短语。但此种用法并不普遍，初学语法者宜尽量避免。

例: It is interesting to learn English. (佳)

It is interesting learning English. (可)

（学英语很有趣。）

3) 下列句型则属例外情形，it 要代替动名词短语，不可使用不定式短语：

It is no use + 动名词短语.

例: It is no use crying over spilt milk.

（覆水难收。）

It is no use asking him for help.

（向他求救是没有用的。）

注意

It is no use + 动名词短语.

= It is useless + 不定式短语.

= It is of no use + 不定式短语.

= There is no use / sense / point + in + 动名词短语.

例: It is useless to cry over spilt milk.

= It is of no use to cry over spilt milk.

= There is no use in crying over spilt milk.

（覆水难收。）

4. 名词性从句做主语：

a. 从事翻译时，我们会碰到类似这样的句子：

他不学习令我生气。

这个句子的主语虽然是“他不学习”，但若译成 He doesn't study 则大错特错。

He doesn't study makes me angry. (×)

因为 He doesn't study 是句子。所谓句子，就是一开头就是主语的结构（此处的 He 就是主语）。句子绝不能当主语，一定要变成名词性从句方可做主语。

故本句的正确译法应为：

That he doesn't study makes me angry. (✓)

名词性从句

b. 名词性从句的种类：

名词性从句包括宾语从句、主语从句、表语从句、同位语从句。
名词性从句一共有三种：

1) that 从句
2) whether 从句
3) 疑问词所引导的从句

分项说明如下：

1) that 从句

任何一个主语起首的句子前面冠以 that，即成 that 从句。

He doesn't believe my words. (句子)
→ that he doesn't believe my words (名词性从句)
（他不相信我说的话）

He enjoys dancing. (句子)
→ that he enjoys dancing (名词性从句)
（他爱跳舞）

There is a lot of work to do. (句子)
→ that there is a lot of work to do (名词性从句)
（有很多工作要做）

2) whether 从句

本从句是由可用 yes / no 回答的问句变化而成，这种可用 yes / no 回答的问句称为一般疑问句。

a) 问句有 be 动词时：

主语与 be 动词还原，前面冠以 whether。

例:Is he happy?
→ whether he is happy
（他是否快乐）

b) 问句有一般助动词（can、will、may、should、ought to、must、have）时：

主语与助动词还原，前面冠以 whether。

例:Can he do it?
→ whether he can do it
（他是否能做这件事）

Has he done it?
→ whether he has done it
（他是否已做好此事）

c) 问句有 do、does、did 等助动词时：

主语与助动词还原，再将 do、does、did 去掉，后面的动词依人称和时态变化。

例：Did he come? (疑问句)

→ whether he did come

came

（did 为一般过去时，故 come 改为过去式 came）

→ whether he came (名词性从句)

（他是否来了）

Does he like it? (疑问句)

→ whether he does like it

likes

（does 为第三人称单数一般现在时，故 like 改为 likes）

→ whether he likes it (名词性从句)

（他是否喜欢它）

3) 疑问词从句：

本从句是由疑问词（when、what、how、where、why）等引导的问句变化而成，这种由疑问词引导的问句称为特殊疑问句。

a) 问句有 be 动词时：

主语与 be 动词还原，前面保留疑问词。

例：What is he doing? (疑问句)

→ what he is doing (名词性从句)

（他正在做什么）

b) 问句有一般助动词时：

主语与助动词还原，前面保留疑问词。

例：Where can he find it? (疑问句)

→ where he can find it (名词性从句)

（他在哪里能找到它）

c) 问句有 do、does、did 等助动词时：

主语与助动词还原，前面保留疑问词，再将 do、does、did 去掉，动词依人称和时态变化。

例：What did he write? (疑问句)

→ what he did write

wrote

（did 为一般过去时，故 write 改为 wrote）

→ what he wrote (名词性从句)
（他写什么）

When did he come? (疑问句)
→ when he did come
came
（did 为一般过去时，故 come 改为 came）
→ when he came (名词性从句)
（他何时来）

How does he do it? (疑问句)
→ how he does do it
does
（does 为第三人称单数一般现在时，故 do 改为 does）
→ how he does it (名词性从句)
（他怎么做这件事）

注意
who、what、which（哪一个）为疑问代词，若在问句中做主语，变成名词性从句时，结构不变。

例: Who came here? (疑问句)
主语
→ who came here (名词性从句)
（谁来这儿）

What happened last night? (疑问句)
主语
→ what happened last night (名词性从句)
（昨晚发生什么事）

Which was bought? (疑问句)
主语
→ which was bought (名词性从句)
（哪个被买走）

C. 名词性从句的功能

我们已知，名词性从句乃由句子或问句变化而成，和动名词或不定式短语一样，名词性从句也要被视为名词。由于具有名词的特性，故可做主语、宾语或在 be 动词之后做表语。

1) 名词性从句做主语：

例: That honesty is the best policy is a proverb (which) we should always keep in mind.
（主语：That honesty is the best policy）
（"诚实为上策"是一句我们应时刻谨记在心的箴言。）

Where he lives is still in doubt.
（主语：Where he lives）
（他住哪里仍不确定。）

Whether he can do it remains to be seen.
（主语：Whether he can do it）
（他能胜任与否仍有待观察。）

注意

一如动名词或不定式短语，名词性从句做主语时容易造成主语太长的现象，因此亦可用形式主语 it 代替，置于句首，而被代替的名词性从句则置于句尾。

故上列各句可改写为：

It is a proverb we should always keep in mind that honesty is the best policy.
It is still in doubt where he lives.
It remains to be seen whether he can do it.

2) 名词性从句做及物动词的宾语：

*及物动词在英语中称作 transitive verb，简写为 vt.；宾语则称作 object，简写为 o.。

例: I know that he will go abroad in the near future.
（vt.：know；o.：that he will go abroad in the near future）
（我知道他最近即将出国。）

I wonder whether he has finished the work.
（vt.：wonder；o.：whether he has finished the work）
（我想知道他是否已做完这份工作。）

I don't know how he'll handle it.
（vt.：know；o.：how he'll handle it）
（我不知道他将如何处理这件事。）

3) 名词性从句做介词的宾语：

＊介词在英语中称作 preposition，简写成 prep.。

a) 此时仅能用 whether 从句或疑问词引导的名词性从句做宾语。that 从句不可做介词的宾语。

例:I am worried about whether he can do it.

prep. o.

（我很担心他是否能做这件事。）

I'm curious about how he'll cope with the problem.

prep. o.

（我很好奇他将如何应付这问题。）

I am sure of that the team has won the game. (×)

prep. o.

b) 遇有介词，且非要使用 that 从句时，其补救方法如下：

(1) 介词 + the fact + that 从句

如此，就可用 the fact 做介词的宾语，而 that 从句就成了 the fact 的同位语。

例: I am sure of the fact that the team has won the game.

prep. o. 同位语

（我确定这一队赢了这场比赛。）

I am worried about the fact that he doesn't study.

prep. o. 同位语

（我担心他不学习。）

(2) 保留介词，不加 the fact，但介词之后的 that 从句要做下列变化：

第一步：除去 that；

第二步：that 后的主语变成所有格；

第三步：动词变成动名词。

例: I am worried about ~~that~~ ~~he~~ ~~plays~~ around all day.

prep. his playing

→ I am worried about his playing around all day.

prep.

（我为他整天游手好闲而担心。）

注意:

(a) that 从句若有助动词 do、does、did 时，去掉即可。

例: I am worried about that he doesn't study.
prep. his not studying

→ I am worried about his not studying.
prep.

(b) that 从句若有助动词 will 或 would 时，去掉即可。

例: I am sure of that the team will win the game.
prep. the team's winning

→ I am sure of the team's winning the game.
prep.

（我确信这一队会赢得这场比赛。）

(c) 从句若有以下助动词时，做下列变化：

may → be likely to

can → be able to

再将 be 动词变成动名词 being。

例: I am happy about that he may come. (×)
prep.

→ I am happy about that he is likely to come.
prep. his being

→ I am happy about his being likely to come.
prep.

（我很高兴他可能会来。）

I am sure of that he can do it. (×)
prep.

→ I am sure of that he is able to do it.
prep. his being

→ I am sure of his being able to do it.
prep.

（我确定他能做这件事。）

(3) be + adj. + that 从句：

也就是去掉介词，将 that 从句放在形容词后面，做其宾语。

例: I am worried about that he plays around all day.

→ I am worried that he plays around all day.
adj. 宾语从句

I am sure ~~of~~ that the team has won the game.

→ I am sure that the team has won the game.

adj.　　　　宾语从句

注意:

a) 以上三种用法中以 (1)、(3) 最为普遍，但 (2) 则是常考的一种句型，同学们宜牢记。

b) 有时介词之后亦可直接接 that 从句，而不需 the fact，形成惯用语，同学们亦应牢记。

in that = because　　因为

例:He is talented in that he can speak five different languages.

（他很有才华，因为他能说五种语言。）

except that　　只可惜；除了……

例:He is nice except that sometimes he lies.

（他人很不错，只可惜有时会说谎。）

notwithstanding that　　尽管

= despite the fact that

= in spite of the fact that

例:Notwithstanding that he is nice, I don't like him.

= Despite the fact that he is nice, I don't like him.

prep.

= In spite of the fact that he is nice, I don't like him.

（尽管他人好，我却不喜欢他。）

5. 名词短语做主语：

名词短语是由“疑问词 + 不定式短语”组成。

a. 疑问副词

where to live	住哪里
whether to try again	是否再试一次
when to talk to him	什么时候和他谈
how to do it	如何做那事

b. 疑问代词

what to do	做什么
whom to see	看谁

which to buy　　　　买哪一个
whom to talk to　　　与谁谈

注意:

1) 疑问副词形成的名词短语中，疑问副词因为是副词的性质，故不做不定式短语中及物动词的宾语。但疑问代词形成的名词短语中，疑问代词因具名词的性质，故一定要做不定式短语中动词或介词的宾语。故 what、whom、which 在上列名词短语中，分别作 do、see、buy、to（介词）的宾语。

2) 名词短语因具名词性质，故亦可做主语，是由名词性从句化简而成。

例: Where to meet him is not decided yet.
= Where we should meet him is not decided yet.
（在哪里见他还未决定。）

How to handle the problem depends on how much money we can collect.
= How we can handle the problem depends on how much money we can collect.
（我们如何处理这问题要视我们能募集到多少钱而定。）

6. 表距离的地点副词短语做主语：

from + 地点名词 + to + 地点名词

此为表距离的地点副词短语，亦可做主语，与单数的 be 动词连用。

例: From Shanghai to Beijing is about 1000 kilometers.
（从上海到北京大约 1000 公里。）

上面例句中，主语亦可用 it 代替，而形成下列结构：

It is about 1000 kilometers from Shanghai to Beijing.

第二节　动词的种类及其用法

概述

在前面的一节中，我们已为大家介绍主语的种类及其用法。在本节中，我们要谈谈动词的种类及用法。如此我们就可了解单句的结构。

如果说主语是一个人的脑袋，动词便可说是他的心脏，而其他修饰语如形容词、副词等，则可说是他的四肢。如果心脏一停，则身体的其余各部分自然也就失去作用。由此可知动词的重要性。

但一般语法书在谈论动词时，不是用过多的抽象定义，就是过于繁琐，以至许多同学学了多年语法之后仍对动词不甚了解。本节针对此一毛病，以不同于传统的解说方式，探讨与动词有关的所有重点。只要同学们耐心看下去，一定会豁然开朗。

1. 动词（verb）基本上可分为五大类：

a. 完全不及物动词：
（complete intransitive verb，简写：c. vi.）

b. 不完全不及物动词：
（incomplete intransitive verb，简写：i. vi.）

c. 完全及物动词：
（complete transitive verb，简写：c. vt.）

d. 不完全及物动词：
（incomplete transitive verb，简写：i. vt.）

e. 授予动词：
（dative verb，简写：d.v.）

英语中基本句型就是按此五大动词分类。

2. 如何判断完全不及物动词：

最好的判断方法就是查词典。但在考试时，我们总不能带词典进入考场嘛，因此在没有词典帮助的情况下，我们可采用下列方法自己判断：

我 ____________ 他。（主动）

他被我 ____________。（被动）

在上列的空格中，我们可以任意放入一个英语动词，翻成中文后，意思若无毛病，就是及物动词，否则就是不及物动词。

例: kill　　杀

我 kill 他。

他被我 kill。

由此得知“我杀了他。”“他被我杀了。”，语意无毛病，即可得知 kill 为及物动词。

例: dance　　跳舞

我 dance 他。

他被我 dance。

由此得知“我跳舞他。”“他被我跳舞。”，语意有毛病，即可得知 dance 乃不及物动词。

当然，“我 ______ 他。”或“他被我 ______。”中的主语、宾语可任意变换，以符合文意。

例: do　　做

约翰 do（做）事情。

事情被约翰 do（做）。

根据上述 do 是及物动词。

由此得知，我们很容易判断动词是否为及物或是不及物。

及物动词:

kill	杀	enjoy	喜欢
do	做	love	爱
make	制造	hate	恨
produce	生产	……	
notice	注意		

不及物动词:

dance	跳舞	study	学习
happen	发生	live	生活
run	跑步	……	
sing	唱歌		

3. 兼做及物与不及物动词之常用动词:

有些动词有两个或两个以上的意思，套用上述方法，可以判断出有些动词有时可当及物动词，有时亦可当不及物动词。此类动词在英语中为数不少，同学们在平日的阅读中就应当注意。兹列举常用的动词提供参考:

sing	vt. 唱（一首歌）	vi. 唱歌
run	vt. 经营（工厂）	vi. 跑步
study	vt. 研究（问题）	vi. 学习
kill	vt. 杀死（某人）	vi. 杀人

4. 不及物动词可做及物动词，用同系名词做其宾语：

有些不及物动词可变成及物动词，以同系名词做其宾语。

例: **dream**　vi. 做梦
vt. 做（梦）
dream a terrible dream
（做一个可怕的梦）

live　vi. 生活
vt. 过（生活）
live a happy life
（过着快乐的生活）

smile　vi. 微笑
vt. 露出（微笑）
smile a bright smile
（露出欢快的微笑）

laugh　vi. 笑
vt. 展开（大笑）
laugh a hearty laugh
（开怀大笑）

sigh　vi. 叹气
vt. 叹（气）
sigh a deep sigh
（深深地叹一口气）

sleep　vi. 睡觉
vt. 睡（觉）
sleep a sound sleep
（睡了一个安稳觉）

5. 完全及物动词与完全不及物动词：

由上我们已得知，完全及物动词和完全不及物动词的判断方法。在此，我们就为此两种动词定下明确的定义：

a. 完全及物动词

即加了宾语后，意思才很完全的动词。

例: He killed her.
vt.
（他杀了她。）

b. 完全不及物动词

即不需加宾语，意思就很完全的动词。

例: He laughed.
vi.
（他笑了。）

6. 完全及物动词出现的形态：

a. 主语 + 及物动词 + 宾语

例: He wrote a book.
S vt. o.
（他写了一本书。）

b. 主语 + be 动词 + 及物动词的现在分词 + 宾语

本句型用以表示某动作正在进行的主动状态。

例: He was writing a book.
S be 动词 现在分词 o.
（他正在写一本书。）

c. 主语 + be 动词 + 过去分词（past participle，简称 p.p.）

本句型用以表示被动的概念。

例: The book was written by him.
S be 动词 p.p.
（这本书是他写的。）

d. 主语 + be 动词 + being + 过去分词

本句型用以表示某动作正在进行的被动状态。

例: A book was being written by him.
S be 动词 现在分词 p.p.
（有一本书正被他撰写中。）

7. 完全不及物动词出现的形态：

a. 主语 + 不及物动词

例: Something happened.

S　　vi.

（有事情发生了。）

b. 主语 + be 动词 + 不及物动词的现在分词

本句型用以表示某动作正在进行的状态。

例: Something was happening.

S　be 动词　现在分词

（有事情正在发生。）

Something was happened. (×)

＊happened 是不及物动词，故无被动语态。

注意:

1) 完全不及物动词，就是意思很完全的不及物动词。这个动词置于主语之后，可单独存在，之后不须加任何词类意思就很完全。

例: Something happened.

（有事情发生了。）

＊happened（发生）意思完全，故之后不需加名词或形容词以补充其意思的不足。

He died.

（他死了。）

＊died 是完全不及物动词，意思完整，故可单独存在，不须接名词或形容词等词类，以补充其意思的不足。

2) 但完全不及物动词之后，可接副词（adverb，简写成 adv.）或副词对等语（如介词短语、状语从句等），以修饰该动词。

例: Something happened yesterday.

vi.　adv.

（昨天有事情发生。）

He died in an accident.

vi.　介词短语

（他死于一场意外。）

He left because he didn't want to see Mary again.

vi.　状语从句

（他走了，因为他不想再见到玛丽。）

8. 不完全不及物动词：

这类动词（简写成 i. vi.即系动词）意思不完全，因而无法单独存在，之后要接名词、形容词或名词对等语（如代词、动名词、不定式、名词性从句、名词短语等），以补充其意思的不足。我们称作表语（subjective complement，简称s.c.）。

例: He looks happy.

S　i. vi.　adj.

（他看起来很快乐。）

He became a good student.

S　i. vi.　n.

（他变成好学生了。）

My trouble is that I have no money.

S　i. vi.　名词性从句

（我的困难就是没钱。）

He is in danger now.

S　i. vi.　介词短语

（他正处于危险中。）

9. 不完全不及物动词的判断方法：

我 ____________________ 他。

他被我 ____________________。

兹以 become 作示范：

a. 先将 become（变成）置于上列两空格中，得知

我变成他。

他被我变成。

第一句语意尚可，也合乎中文语法，但第二句就不合语意也不合乎中文语法，故得知 become 是不及物动词。

b. 确知 become 为不及物动词后，即可利用完全不及物动词的造句法，形成下列句型：

主语 + vi.

主语 + be动词 + vi. 的现在分词

将 become 套入上列句型中，即成：

He became（他变成）

He was becoming（他正变成）

c. 但由中文的翻译得知：“他变成”或“他正变成”。

这两句的语意均不完全，故知 became 是意思不完全的不及物动词，不能单独存在，之后要接补充语，如此句意才完全，故下列两句的 became 之后有补充语，句意完全，属正确的句子。

例: He became happy.
S s.c.
（他变得快乐了。）

He became a good boy.
S s.c.
（他变成好孩子了。）

10. 不完全不及物动词的种类及其表语的用法：

以下赖老师将不完全不及物动词分成六大类，从 a.~f. 逐一说明。

a. be 动词

be 动词之后可用名词（含名词对等语，如名词性从句、名词短语、动名词、不定式等）或形容词（含做形容词的现在分词、过去分词、介词短语、地点副词或地点副词短语等）做表语。

> **注意**
> 用名词做表语时，be 动词译成“是”；用形容词做表语时，be 动词不必译出；用地点副词或地点副词短语做表语时，be 动词译成“在”。

＊be 动词之后有十一种表语：

1) 名词：

例: He is a great hero. (is 译成“是”)
（他是大英雄。）

2) 名词性从句：

例: The trouble with me is that I lack money. (is 译成“是”)
（我的麻烦是缺钱。）

The problem is whether he can join us. (is 译成“是”)
（问题是他是否能加入我们。）

3) 名词短语：

例: The question is when to set out.（is 译成“是”）
（问题是何时出发。）

4) 做名词用的动名词短语：

例: My hobby is collecting stamps. (is 译成“是”)

（我的爱好是集邮。）

5) 做名词用的不定式短语：

例: My purpose here is to see him. (is 译成“是”)

（我来这里的目的是要见他。）

6) 形容词：

例: She is beautiful. (is 不必译出)

（她很美。）

7) 做形容词用的现在分词：

例: The story is interesting. (is 不必译出)

（这故事真有趣。）

8) 做形容词用的过去分词：

例: I am interested in the story. (am 不必译出)

（我对这故事感兴趣。）

9) 做形容词用的介词短语：

此类介词短语由“of + 抽象名词”形成。

例: The book is | of great value. / valuable. | (is 不必译出)

（这本书很有价值。）

The machine is | of no use. / useless. | (is 不必译出)

（那部机器毫无用处。）

10) 地点副词：

例: She is there. (is 译成“在”)

（她在那儿。）

They are upstairs. (are 译成“在”)

（他们在楼上。）

Is he home now?

（他现在在家吗？）

11) 地点副词短语：

本短语由“介词＋地点名词”形成。

例: She is in town. (is 译成“在”)
（她人在城里。）

They are at home now. (are 译成“在”)
（他们现在在家。）

She is in danger. (is 译成“在”)
（她有危险。）

注意:

a) be 动词之后的现在分词有两种词性：

一做形容词，一做动词进行时的现在分词。换言之，同学们遇到 V-ing；可译成“……的”时，就是做形容词的现在分词，否则就是表“进行状态”的现在分词，要译成“正在……”，而不视为形容词。

例: The girl is charming.
（这女孩很迷人。）

＊charming 可译成“迷人的”，故此处为形容词。

句型分析如下：

The girl　is　charming.
(1)　(2)　(3)

(1) 主语
(2) be 动词
(3) 现在分词，做形容词，当表语。

The girl is singing.
（这女孩在唱歌。）

＊singing 不可能译成“唱歌的”，而是由完全不及物动词 sing 转变成的现在分词，置于 be 动词之后，表进行的状态，译成“正在唱歌”。句型分析如下：

The girl　is singing.
(1)　(2)

(1) 主语
(2) 完全不及物动词 sing 的进行时

注意:

以上句子不可分析成：

The girl　is　singing.
主语　i. vi.　现在分词做形容词用 (×)

了解上述结构分析后，可知道下列句子的结构应分析如下：

The girl is bathing.

主语　完全不及物动词的进行时

（这女孩正在洗澡。）

而非：

The girl is bathing.

主语　i. vi.　现在分词做形容词用 (×)

b) be 动词之后的过去分词亦有两个词性：

一做形容词，可译成“感到……的”；一做及物动词的被动语态，译成“被……”，而不视为形容词。

例: The man is tired.

（这个人很累。）

* tired 可译成“感到累的”，故此处为形容词。

句型分析如下：

The man is tired.

(1)　(2)　(3)

(1) 主语

(2) be 动词

(3) 过去分词，做形容词，当表语。

再看下例：

例: The man was killed.

（这男的被杀了。）

* killed 不能译成“感到杀的”，而要译成“被杀”，故 killed 为完全及物动词的被动语态。

句型分析如下：

The man was killed.

主语　及物动词 kill 的一般过去时被动语态

c) 比较下列两句中 washing 的词性：

He is washing the car.

现在分词

His job is washing cars.

动名词

注意

be 动词之后出现 V-ing 时，该 V-ing 有时是现在分词，有时却是动名词，一般语法书总是交代不清，弄得同学们一头雾水。常有些同学们就因此而放弃学语法，以至英语越来越退步。

在这儿，赖老师告诉你两个简单的方法：

方法 1：

V-ing 之前的 be 动词可译成“正在”时，该 V-ing 就是现在分词。

例: He is washing the car.

（他正在洗车。）

故 washing 为现在分词。

V-ing 之前的 be 动词可译成“是”时，该 V-ing 就是动名词。

His job is washing cars.

（他的工作正在洗车。）(×)

（他的工作就是洗车。）(√)

由上得知，本句中的 washing 非现在分词，而是动名词，置于 be 动词之后，作表语。

方法 2：

若同学们觉得方法 1 有点难时，可试试这个方法：

be 动词之后的 V-ing 可与主语互换时，该 V-ing 就是动名词；若不能互换时就是现在分词。

例: He is washing the car.

（他在洗车。）

→ Washing the car is he. (×)

（洗车就是他。）

故本句中的 washing 为现在分词。

例: His job is washing cars.

（他的工作是洗车。）

→ Washing cars is his job. (√)

（洗车是他的工作。）

故本句中的 washing 是动名词，具有名词的功能，既可做表语，亦可做主语。

b. become（变成）

become 可用任何名词、形容词或可做形容词用的现在分词或过去分词（即可以译成“……的”之类的分词）做表语。

例: He became angry.

形容词

（他生气了。）

You'll become a good student if you study hard.

名词

（如果你用功，就可成为好学生。）

She is becoming more and more charming.
形容词
（她越来越迷人。）
*charming 可译成“令人着迷的”，故可做形容词使用。

After failing, he became depressed.
形容词
（失败后，他变得意志消沉。）
*depressed 可译成“感到消沉的”，故可做形容词使用。

c. turn（变成）

turn 通常只用形容词做表语，而且所能使用的形容词多与颜色或情绪有关。

例: His face turned pale when he heard the news.
形容词
（听到那消息时，他脸色变得苍白起来。）

The leaves were turning yellow.
形容词
（树叶变黄了。）

His face turned red with anger when he saw Mary.
（看到玛丽时，他气得脸都红了。）

She turned beautiful. (×)
→ She became beautiful. (√)
（她变漂亮了。）
*beautiful 不是与颜色或情绪有关的形容词，故不可在 turn 之后做表语。

注意
turn 亦可用以表示转业，通常与名词连用，形成复合词，做形容词用。

例: Mr. Johnson is a soldier-turned farmer.
（约翰逊先生是个军人转业的农民。）

d. get（变成）

get 通常用表“生气”或“激动”的形容词做表语。若用其他形容词时，宜用 become。

例: He got mad.
形容词
（他生气了。）

She got beautiful. (×)
→ She became beautiful. (√)
（她变漂亮了。）

Things have got good. (×)
→ Things have become good. (√)
（事情变好了。）

注意:

1) 若 get 用于进行时的结构中，之后可接任何形容词的比较级形态做表语。即：be getting more and more + 任何形容词

例: She is getting more and more beautiful.
（她越来越美丽。）

Things are getting better and better.
（事情越来越顺利。）

2) | get / be | + p.p.（被动语态）

本句型表“被……”之意。get 等于 bc 动词，不可译成“变成”。

*p.p. 为 past participle 的缩写，即“过去分词”。

例: He got killed in the accident.
= He was killed in the accident.
（他在车祸中丧生。）

If you are not careful, you'll | get / be | hurt.
（你如果不小心点，就会受伤。）

e. seem 似乎

= appear

seem 之后用不定式短语做表语。

例: He seems to know it. (√)
He seems knowing it. (×)
（他似乎知道此事。）

但在 seem to be + 名词/形容词结构中，to be 可省略，直接用名词或形容词做表语。

例: He seems to be happy.
形容词

= He seems happy.
（他似乎很快乐。）

He seems to be a nice man.

名词

= He seems a nice man.

（他似乎是个好人。）

f. 感官动词

感官动词一共有五个，一律译成“……起来”，之后一律用形容词（或可做形容词用的分词）做表语。

look	（看起来）	+ 形容词
sound	（听起来）	
smell	（闻起来）	
taste	（尝起来）	
feel	（感觉起来，感到）	

例: His idea sounds good.

形容词

（他的主意听起来不错。）

The food smells good.

形容词

（这食物闻起来很香。）

I feel tired now.

形容词

（我现在觉得很疲倦。）

It looks interesting.

形容词

（它看起来很有趣。）

注意:

1) 感官动词后绝不可用名词做表语，若要与名词连用时，须采用下列句型：

look	+ like + 名词
sound	介词
smell	
taste	
feel	

*like 为介词，译成“像”，之后的名词为其宾语。

例: It sounds a good idea. (×)

→ It sounds like a good idea. (✓)

（听起来像是个好主意。）

That material feels like silk. (✓)
名词
（那料子摸起来像丝。）

The food tastes like fish. (✓)
名词
（这食物尝起来像鱼肉。）

2) feel like + 名词　　感觉像……
feel like + 动名词　　想要……

例: When Jane said she would marry me, I felt like a newborn baby.
名词
（当简说她要嫁给我时，我觉得我就像个新生儿一样。）

I feel like taking a walk today.
动名词
= I would like to take a walk today.
（我今天想散散步。）

I feel like to take a walk today. (×)
I would like taking a walk today. (×)

3) feel、taste、smell 亦可当完全及物动词，可用名词做宾语。此时 feel、taste、smell 的意思均有改变。

feel（摸） taste（尝） smell（闻）	+ 名词

例: The doctor felt my forehead and said I had a fever.
vt.　n. 作宾语
（医生摸我的额头说我发烧了。）

Don't taste that food; it has spoiled.
vt.　n. 作宾语
（别尝那食物，它已经馊了。）

He smelled something burning.
vt.　n. 作宾语
（他闻到有东西烧焦了。）

4) look 与介词连用时，可形成短语动词，视为及物动词。如：
look into = investigate　vt.　调查

look over = examine　vt. 检查
look at　= watch　vt. 看
此时，就要用副词修饰这些短语动词。

例: He looked at me happily.
副词
（他愉快地看着我。）

He looked into the case carefully.
副词
（他仔细地调查这件案子。）

注意
上列句中的副词经常会置于 look 与介词之间，而成：
He looked happily at me.
He looked carefully into the case.

赖老师之所以举这些例子，是因为有些同学没弄明白，一见到 look 就以为一定是感官动词，于是就置形容词于其后，而成：
He looked happy at me. (×)
He looked careful into the case. (×)

注意
look 之后有介词时，look 就不是感官动词，而与该介词形成短语动词（如 look into / look at），一定要用副词修饰，而非以形容词修饰。

11. 不完全不及物动词的重要相关短语：

其他常用的不完全不及物动词及有关重要例句列举如下，同学们一定要背起来哦！

例: John fell ill and couldn't attend school today.
形容词
（约翰病了，因此今天无法上学。）
＊此处 fell 是 fall 的过去式，表“变成”。

He soon fell asleep.
形容词
（他很快就睡着了。）
＊此处 fell 亦是 fall 的过去式，表“变成”。

Provisions ran short.

形容词

（粮食不足了。）

I don't know how he came to be so popular.

（我不知道他怎么会变得如此受欢迎。）

*此处 came to be 相当于 gradually became（渐渐变成）。

The document proved to be a forgery.

（这份文件证实是伪造的。）

12. 完全及物动词：

稍早赖老师提到，完全及物动词就是加了宾语后意思很完全的动词，有主动及被动两个语态。在此，我们要与大家讨论主动语态。至于被动语态，我们则将在语态的专篇中再讨论。

完全及物动词在主动语态中，用法极为简单，句型如下：

主语 + 完全及物动词 + 宾语（object，简称 o.）

例：Peter loves music.

S vt. o.

（彼得喜爱音乐。）

They want to go dancing.

S vt. o.

（他们想去跳舞。）

He thinks that the book is good.

S vt. o.

（他认为这本书很好。）

13. 完全及物动词的用法：

完全及物动词的宾语，有名词、代词、不定式、动名词、名词性从句及名词短语等。同学们稍加注意，就可发现这些词类、短语或从句均有名词的特性，故亦可用做主语。

a. 名词当及物动词的宾语

例：He didn't buy that car.

vt. o.

（他没有买那辆车。）

b. 代词当及物动词的宾语

例：I don't like John. In fact, I hate him.

vt. o.

（我不喜欢约翰。事实上，我讨厌他。）

c. 不定式当及物动词的宾语

这些动词皆有表示某种愿望、企图之意，常用的此类动词如：want（想要）、hope（希望）、desire（想要）等。

例: I want to see him now.
vt. o.
（我现在就要见他。）

I hope to study abroad someday.
vt. o.
（我希望有一天能出国留学。）

d. 动名词当及物动词的宾语

并非所有及物动词均可用动名词做宾语。常以动名词做宾语的动词有下列几个：

例: He **considered** studying abroad.
vt. o.
（他考虑出国留学。）

I once **imagined** going on a date with him.
vt. o.
（我曾想象和他去约会。）

I just can't **fancy** getting along with them.
vt. o.
（我无法想象我会和他们相处得来。）

He **risked** doing it.
vt. o.
（他冒险做这事。）

I **avoided** seeing him again.
vt. o.
（我避免再见到他。）

He **escaped** being killed in the accident.
vt. o.
（他在那次意外中幸免于难。）

They **suggested** putting off the game.
vt. o.
（他们建议将比赛延期。）

He **recommended** traveling abroad.
vt. o.
（他建议去国外旅行。）

I **enjoy** dancing.
vt.　o.
（我喜欢跳舞。）

I **resent** having to do so much work.
vt.　o.
（我讨厌要做这么多工作。）

I **practiced** playing the piano.
vt.　o.
（我练过钢琴了。）

He | **stopped** / **quit** | smoking.
vt.　o.
（他戒烟了。）

Would you **mind** opening the window for me?
vt.　o.
（你介意为我打开窗户吗？）

注意:

1) resist V-ing　抗拒……
refuse to V　拒绝……

例: I **refused to do** it.
（我拒绝做此事。）

I couldn't **resist having** some more ice cream.
（我忍不住要再吃些冰淇淋。）

2) expect to V　期望……
= anticipate V-ing

例: I **expect to travel** around the world with him.
= I **anticipate traveling** around the world with him.
（我期望和他一起环游世界。）

3) stop V-ing　停止……
= quit V-ing
= cease | V-ing / to V |

例: He **stopped writing** after he got married.
（他结婚后就不再写作了。）

He decided to **quit smoking**.
（他决定戒烟。）

They **ceased** | **to work** / **working** | at exactly 5:00 p.m.
（他们下午 5 点整停工。）

> **注意**
> stop to V　　停下来而去……

例: He **stopped to talk** to me when he saw me.
= He **stopped** (what he was doing) **to talk** to me when he saw me.
（他看见我时，便停下来和我说话。）

4) **continue**（继续）、**start**（开始）、**begin**（开始）、**like**（喜欢）、**love**（爱）、**hate**（恨），可用不定式或动名词做宾语，意思不变。

例: He continued | **trying** / **to try** | his luck at the casino.
（他继续在赌场里碰运气。）

They started | **building** / **to build** | the house.
（他们开始建这栋房子。）

I | **like** / **love** / **hate** | **listening** / **to listen** | to music.
（我喜欢/爱/厌恶听音乐。）

e. 名词性从句当及物动词的宾语

稍早我们已为同学们介绍名词性从句的形成方式、种类及其功能，再提醒一下，名词性从句有三种：

1) that 引导的名词性从句
that he can't do it　　（他不能做此事）

2) whether 引导的名词性从句
whether he will come　　（他是否会来）

3) 疑问词引导的名词性从句
when he will do it　（他何时做）
what he is doing　（他正在做什么）
how he'll handle it　（他如何处理此事）

注意
为了方便记忆，我们可将名词性从句记成“戴慧怡”。
戴：即 that 之讹音
慧：即 whether 第一音节之讹音
怡：即疑问词从句“疑”之同音字

由于名词性从句具有名词的功能，故亦可做及物动词的宾语。

例: I believe that he is a man of his word.
vt.（believe）　o.（that he is a man of his word）
（我相信他是个言而有信的人。）

I wonder whether he can do it.
vt.（wonder）　o.（whether he can do it）
（我不知道他是否能够做此事。）

I don't know where he lives.
vt.（know）　o.（where he lives）
（我不知道他住哪里。）

注意:

1) that 从句做及物动词的宾语时，名词性从句连词 that 通常予以省略。

例: They feel (that) it is impossible to win the game.
vt.（feel）　o.（(that) it is impossible to win the game）
（他们觉得不可能赢这场比赛。）

He thinks (that) the book is worth reading.
vt.（thinks）　o.（(that) the book is worth reading）
（他认为这本书值得一读。）

2) whether 从句做及物动词的宾语时，名词性从句连词 whether 亦可被 if 取代。

例: I don't know **whether** the typhoon will come.
vt.（know）

= I don't know **if** the typhoon will come.
（我不知道台风是否会来。）

I doubt **whether** the man is competent enough to handle it.

vt.

= I doubt **if** the man is competent enough to handle it.

（我不知道这个人是否有足够的能力处理此事。）

但 whether 从句若做主语、介词的宾语或 be 动词后的表语时，whether 不可被 if 取代。

a) whether 从句做主语：

例: **Whether** he can go is not yet known. (✓)

S

（他是否能去还不知道。）

If he can go is not yet known. (×)

S

但: It is not yet known whether he can go. (✓)

= It is not yet known if he can go. (✓)

b) whether 从句做介词的宾语：

例: He is worried about **whether** he can pass the exam. (✓)

介词 宾语

（他很担心是否能通过这次考试。）

He is worried about **if** he can pass the exam. (×)

c) whether 从句做 be 动词后的表语：

例: The problem is **whether** he has enough money for the trip. (✓)

be 动词 表语

（问题在于他是否有足够的钱旅行。）

The problem is **if** he has enough money for the trip. (×)

f. 名词短语（形成方式见第一节第 5 项）当及物动词的宾语

例: I know how to handle the problem.

vt. o.

（我知道如何处理这问题。）

I don't know whom to talk to.

vt. o.

（我不知道该向谁说。）

14. 不完全及物动词：

不完全及物动词（incomplete transitive verb）仍属一种及物动词，但此类动词加了宾语之后，意思并不完全，需要加补语（complement），以补充意思之不足。

茲以 make 为例：

a. make 做“制造”或“做”解时，为完全及物动词。

例：He made a kite. (✓)
完全vt. o.
（他做了一个风筝。）
＊本句意思完整，故无需补语。

b. 但 make 若做“使”或“叫”解时，则为不完全及物动词。

例：He made Mary. (×)
不完全vt. o.
（他使玛丽。）
＊本句意思不完全，故需补语。

He made Mary happy. (✓)
不完全vt. o. o.c.
（他使玛丽快乐。）
＊happy 为形容词，此处做宾语补语，使句子完整。

＊o.c. 是 objective complement 的缩写，表“宾语补语”。“表语”则称作 subjective complement，简写成 s.c.。

例：He made Mary. (×)
不完全vt. o.
（他叫玛丽。）
＊本句意思不完整（未说明“他叫玛丽如何”），故需补语。

He made Mary clean the window. (✓)
不完全vt. o. o.c.
（他叫玛丽擦窗户。）
＊clean 为原形动词，连同 the window 一起做宾语补语，使句意完全。

15. 不完全及物动词的分类及用法：

不完全及物动词使用起来稍嫌复杂。为了方便同学们记忆，赖老师特别加以分类，叙述如下，希望同学们一定要牢记：

a. 使役动词

1) 叫……

make / have ＋宾语＋原形动词（做补语）

例：I made him wash the car.
o. o.c.
（我叫他洗车。）

I had John report to me.
　　　o.　　o.c.
（我叫约翰向我报到。）

注意:

a) get 亦可表“叫……”之意，但只能用不定式短语做宾语补语，句型如下：
get sb to V　　叫某人……

例:I got him to wash the car. (✓)
　　　o.　　o.c.
（我叫他洗车。）

I got him wash the car. (×)
　　　o.　　o.c.

b) make 可使用于被动语态中，但 have 及 get 则不可。

主动语态：

例:I | made / had (vt.) | him wash the car.
　　　　　　　　　　o.　　o.c.

= I got him to wash the car.
　vt.　o.　　o.c.

（我叫他洗车。）

上列第一句的 wash the car 及第二句的 to wash the car 均修饰宾语 him，故为宾语补语。

被动语态：

例:He was made to wash the car.
　S　　　　　　　s.c.

（他被要求洗车——也照做了。）

变被动语态时，原形动词 wash 就要变成不定式短语 to wash，而成 to wash the car。

例:He was | had / got | to wash the car. (×)

＊have、get 无被动用法。

2) 让……

此时使用 let，句型如下：

a) let + 宾语 + 原形动词（做宾语补语）

例:I let him wash the car.

o. o.c.

（我让他洗车。）

I let Peter try it.

o. o.c.

（我让彼得试试看。）

b) let + 宾语 + 做副词用的介词（in、out、down）

例:He let me in.

o. o.c.

（他让我进来。）

Don't let him out.

o. o.c.

（别让他出去。）

His performance let me down.

o. o.c.

（他的表演令我失望。）

注意:

(1) 上述介词由于其后无宾语，可单独存在做副词用，因此称为介副词。与地点副词（如 there、here、home）一样，介副词可做 be 动词之后的表语。

例: He is in. (介副词)
（他在家。）

He is out. (介副词)
（他出去了。）

He is there. (地点副词)
（他在那里。）

He is here. (地点副词)
（他在这里。）

He is home. (地点副词)
（他在家里。）

He is downtown. (地点副词)
（他在城里。）

He is in the house. (地点副词短语)
（他在房子里。）

(2) 但在 let 之后，只能用介副词做补语，而不可用地点副词做补语。

例: He let me in. (✓)
（他让我进去。）

He let me there / here / home. (×)

(3) let 之后若用原形动词做补语，变被动语态时，该原形动词要变成不定式短语。然而此用法已不多见。

例: I let him wash the car. (✓)
o. o.c.

→ He was let to wash the car. (罕，老美绝不会有此说法)
S s.c.

3) 强迫 / 要求 / 怂恿 / 催促……

此类动词 + 宾语 + 不定式短语（做宾语补语）

例: I forced him to recite the lesson.
o. o.c.
（我强迫他背这课。）

I asked him to write the letter.
o. o.c.
（我要求他写这封信。）

I encouraged him to work harder.
o. o.c.
（我鼓励他更努力些。）

He compelled (= forced) me to do it against my will.
o. o.c.
（他强迫我做违反意愿的事。）

He told me to finish the work by ten.
o. o.c.
（他叫我 10 点钟以前做完这项工作。）

此类动词尚有许多个，兹将常出现的此类动词列举如下：
push one to...　　（催促某人去……）
seduce one to...　　（勾引某人去……）
entice one to...　　（引诱某人去……）
expect one to...　　（期望某人去……）
want one to...　　（要某人去……）

此类动词变被动语态时，仍用不定式短语做补语。

例: I asked him to write the letter.
o.　o.c.
（我请求他写这封信。）

→ He was asked to write the letter.
S　s.c.
（他被请求写这封信。）

在第二句中，由于 to write the letter 修饰主语，故称主语补足语。

4) 使……成为

此类动词只有 make 一个，加了宾语之后，要用形容词或名词做补语，句型如下：

主语 + make + 宾语 + 形容词 / 名词 （做宾语补语）

例: His teacher made him a good student.
o.　o.c.（名词做宾语补语）
（他的老师使他成为好学生。）

The trip made him happy.
o.　o.c.（形容词做宾语补语）
（这次旅行使他很愉快。）

由于 make 之后的宾语可直接接名词或形容词做补语，故不必造成下列的句子：

例: His teacher made him become a good student. (×)
The trip made him be happy. (×)

b. 知觉动词

此类动词有三类：
看：see、observe（观察）、watch（看）、look at（注视）、notice（注意）
听：hear、listen to
感觉：feel

1) 此类动词可做完全及物动词，加了宾语之后无须另加补语。

例: Did you see him?
vt. o.
（你看见他没有？）

He was listening to music.
vt. o.
（他正在听音乐。）

I felt a pain in my back.
vt. o.
（我觉得背痛。）

2) 但此类动词亦可做不完全及物动词，加了宾语之后，须另加宾语补语。用法如下：

a) 表事实时，用原形动词做补语，译成“……了。”

例: I saw him dance.
o. o.c.
（我看见他跳舞了。）

I heard him sing.
o. o.c.
（我听见他唱歌了。）

I felt him move.
o. o.c.
（我感觉到他动了。）

b) 表进行状态时，用现在分词做补语，译成“……正在……。”

例: I saw him dancing when I walked in.
o. o.c.
（我进来时，看见他正在跳舞。）

As I pushed the door open, I heard him singing.
o. o.c.
（我推开门时，听见他正在唱歌。）

When the doorbell rang, I felt my legs trembling.
o. o.c.
（门铃响时，我感觉到我的双腿正在发抖。）

c) 表被动状态时，要用过去分词做补语，译成“……被……。”

例:I saw him killed.

o.　o.c.

（我看见他被杀死了。）

I heard the door closed.

o.　　o.c.

（我听见门被关上了。）

I felt myself lifted.

o.　o.c.

（我感觉到自己被举起来了。）

> **注意**
> 以上三种补语变被动语态时，除原形动词要变成不定式短语之外，其余不变。

例:I saw him do it.

→ He was seen to do it.

（我看见他做那件事。）

I saw him dancing.

→ He was seen dancing.

（我看见他正在跳舞。）

I saw the dog run over by a car.

→ The dog was seen run over by a car.

（我看见那只狗被车辗过。）

C. 任命动词

此类动词多表“选举”、“指派”之意，其宾语之后接表职位的名词做补语，通常该名词之前要省略冠词。此类动词常用的有：

elect（选举）、assign（指派）、appoint（任命）。

例: We elected him chairman of the committee.

o.　o.c.

（我们选他为委员会主席。）

The colonel assigned him platoon leader.

o.　　o.c.

（上校指派他为排长。）

d. 认定动词

此类动词均表“视……为”之意，加了宾语之后，用名词或形容词做宾语补语。

1) 与介词连用者：

例: We regard / look upon / think of / see / view him as a genius.

(him = o.; as a genius = o.c.)

（我们都把他视为天才。）

I mistook the long-haired boy for a girl.

(the long-haired boy = o.; for a girl = o.c.)

（我误将那长发的男孩视作女孩。）

2) 与 to be 连用者：

例: We consider / deem / think him to be a genius. / to be nice.

(him = o.; to be a genius / to be nice = o.c.)

（我们认为他是天才/人很好。）

*唯 to be 可予省略，而成：

We consider / deem / think him a genius. / nice.

注意:

a) 一般介词之后只能用名词、代词或动名词做宾语。

例:I am sick of his rude attitude.

(of = prep.; attitude = n.)

（我很讨厌他粗鲁的态度。）

I am sick of associating with him.

(of = prep.; associating = 动名词)

（我讨厌与他为伍。）

但表“视……为”的动词与 as 或 for 连用时，它们之后除可接名词外，亦可直接接形容词做补语。

例:I regard his behavior as inappropriate.

(as = prep.; inappropriate = adj.)

（我认为他的行为不当。）

John works hard, so I take it for granted that he'll be successful someday.
prep. p.p.作 adj.
（约翰很努力，因此他总有一天会成功，我认为这是理所当然的事。）

b) think、believe、find、deem、consider 这五个动词做不完全及物动词时，不得直接用不定式短语做宾语，一定要用形式宾语 it 取代。此时 think 译成“认为……是……”、deem 译成“认为……是……”、consider 译成“认为……是……”。

句型如下：

主语 + think / believe / find / deem / consider + it + 宾语补语 (n. 或 adj.) + to V
（it：形式宾语；to V：真正宾语）

例: I think to climb mountains fun. (×)
S 不完全 vt. o. o.c.
→ I think it fun to climb mountains. (✓)
形式宾语 o.c. (adj.) 真正宾语
（我认为爬山是很有趣的——我认为爬山很有趣。）

同理:

I find it necessary to do the work.
形式宾语 o.c. (adj.) 真正宾语
（我发觉做这件事是有必要的——我发觉做这事有必要。）

I believe it worthwhile to study hard.
形式宾语 o.c. (adj.) 真正宾语
（我相信用功是值得的——我相信用功很值得。）

I deem it an honor to give this speech.
形式宾语 o.c. (n.) 真正宾语
（我认为能做这次演讲是一项荣誉——我很荣幸能做这次演讲。）

但 find、believe、think、deem、consider 亦可做完全及物动词，此时要用 that 引导的名词性从句做宾语。此时 find、believe、think、deem、consider 分别译成“发现”、“相信”、“认为”、“认为”、“认为”。

例:I think that it is interesting to climb mountains.
S 完全vt. o.
（我认为爬山很有趣。）

I believe that it is worthwhile to study hard.
S 完全vt. o.
（我相信用功是值得的。）

由于 that 从句做及物动词的宾语时，that 可省略，因此上列二例亦可改为：

I think it is interesting to climb mountains.

I believe it is worthwhile to study hard.

现在我们便可清楚得知下列两种结构虽不一样，但表达的意思却完全相同。

不完全及物动词：

I think it interesting to climb mountains.

*think 译成"认为……是……"。

I believe it worthwhile to study hard.

*believe 译成"相信……是……"。

完全及物动词：

I think (that) it is interesting to climb mountains.

*think 译成"认为"。

I believe (that) it is worthwhile to study hard.

*believe 译成"相信"。

c) make 表"使……成为……"时，亦为不完全及物动词，其后不得用不定式短语做宾语，一定要用形式宾语 it 取代。

句型如下：

主语 + make + it + 宾语补语（n. 或 adj.）+ to V
形式宾语 真正宾语

例:He made it a rule to get up early.
不完全vt. 形式宾语 宾语补语 (n.) 真正宾语
（他有早起的习惯。）

*make it a rule to V 把……变成习惯
= make it a habit to V

Hard work made it possible for him to win the honor.
不完全vt. 形式宾语 宾语补语 (adj.) 真正宾语
（努力工作使他有可能赢得此荣誉。）

d) find、believe、think、deem、consider 做不完全及物动词时，亦不得直接用 that 引导的名词性从句做宾语，一定要用形式宾语 it 取代。

例:I find that he sings so well wonderful. (×)

→ I find it wonderful that he sings so well. (√)

形式宾语 o.c. 真正宾语

（我发现他歌唱得这么好真是太棒了。）

同理:

I believe it necessary that he should work hard.

不完全 vt. 形式宾语 o.c. (adj.) 真正宾语

（我相信他努力是有必要的——我相信他必须努力。）

The difficulty of the job made it necessary that he should do it with care.

不完全vt. 形式宾语 o.c. (adj.) 真正宾语

（该工作的困难性使得他小心去做是有必要的——该工作的困难性使得他有必要小心去做。）

e. 转变动词

此类动词均表“使……变成……”之意，常用的有 change 与 turn 两个。通常要与介词 into 连用。

例: The experience turned / changed him into a good student.

（这个经历使他变成好学生了。）

f. 其他重要的不完全及物动词

例: They set him free.

不完全vt. o. o.c. (adj.)

（他们释放了他。）

I painted the door green.

不完全vt. o. o.c. (adj.)

（我将门漆成绿色。）

The sight struck him dumb.

不完全vt. o. o.c. (adj.)

（该景象使他目瞪口呆。）

The baby cried itself to sleep.

不完全vt. o. o.c. (介词短语)

（小宝宝哭着睡着了。）

*小宝宝（baby）因为头发稀疏兜着尿片，看不出是男是女，故用代词 it、itself 代替。若已知小宝宝的性别，当然就可使用 he、himself、him、she、her、herself 等代词了。

His assistance will render (= make) success certain.
不完全vt. o. o.c. (adj.)
（他的协助将使成功在握。）

The misfortune nearly drove him mad.
不完全vt. o. o.c. (adj.)
（那次不幸的遭遇几乎使他发疯。）

They named the baby Tom.
不完全vt. o. o.c. (n.)
（他们给小宝宝取名为汤姆。）

They call him a liar.
不完全vt. o. o.c. (n.)
（他们叫他骗子。）

Don't leave the door open.
不完全vt. o. o.c. (adj.)
（别让门敞开着。）

You must keep your teeth clean.
不完全vt. o. o.c. (adj.)
（你一定要让你的牙齿保持干净。）

I want the job done no later than five.
不完全vt. o. o.c. (过去分词做形容词用)
（我要这项工作在 5 点以前做完。）

Help me (to) find my watch.
不完全vt. o. o.c. (不定式短语做宾语补语)
（帮我找我的表。）

*help 之后接了宾语，再以不定式短语做宾语补语时，to 可予省略。

16. 授予动词：

授予动词（dative verb，简写成 d.v.）为及物动词的一种，只是接两个宾语。第一个宾语叫做间接宾语（indirect object，简写成 i.o.），表授予的对象；第二个宾语叫直接宾语（direct object，简写成 d.o.），表授予的东西。

例: I will give you this watch.
d.v. i.o. d.o.
（我要送你这块表。）

Please lend me your book.
d.v. i.o. d.o.
（请把你的书借我。）

I bought him a car.
d.v. i.o. d.o.
（我给他买了辆车。）

I asked him a question.
d.v. i.o. d.o.
（我问了他一个问题。）

以上结构中，you、me、him 均为间接宾语，this watch、your book、a car、a question 均为直接宾语。然而同学们一定会问，为何要做如此分类呢？赖老师这样告诉你：拿第一句来说吧，中文译为："我要送你这块表。"说这句话的人，手中一定先拿着表，然后再送给对方。故 this watch 先被接触，称为直接宾语，而 you 则后被接触，称为间接宾语。我们再以第四句加以说明。本句译为："我问了他一个问题。"我们想一想：与"我"先接触的是"问题"，因为"我"一张口，"问题"就随着声音跑了出来，然后才传达给"他"。故 a question 为直接宾语，而 him 则为间接宾语。

17. 间接宾语与直接宾语倒置原则：

若间接宾语与直接宾语位置颠倒时，就需要另加介词 to、for 或 of。

a. 表"给予"的概念，要用 to。

例: I gave him the book.
= I gave the book to him.
d.o. prep. i.o.
（我给他这本书。）

I sent him the letter.
= I sent the letter to him.
d.o. prep. i.o.
（我寄这封信给他。）

I told him the story.
= I told the story to him.
d.o. prep. i.o.
（我讲这个故事给他听。）

I teach them English.
= I teach English to them.
d.o. prep. i.o.
（我教他们英语。）

b. 表“代劳”的概念，要用 for。

例: I bought him the book.

= I bought the book for him.

d.o. prep. i.o.

（我为他买了这本书。）

> **理由**
> “我”到书店为他买本书，因此“我”出了劳力。

例: I made him a chair.

= I made a chair for him.

d.o. prep. i.o.

（我替他做了一把椅子。）

> **理由**
> “我”出了劳力制做一把椅子，故介词要用 for 表示为他代劳之意。

c. 表“从……中”的概念，要用 of。

例: I asked him a question.

= I asked a question of him.

d.o. prep. i.o.

（我问他一个问题。）

> **理由**
> 此处的 of，等于 from 之意，但使用时，仍以 of 为宜。凡表“要求”的动词均属此用法 。

例: I didn't expect much of him.

d.o. i.o.

（我对他不抱很大的期望。）

He required nothing of me.

d.o. i.o.

（他对我毫无所求。）

He demanded little of me.

d.o. i.o.

（他对我几乎无所求。）

只是使用此三个动词时，不得像 ask 一样，可将间接宾语置于前面。

例: I didn't expect him much. (×)
　　i.o.　d.o.

He required me nothing. (×)
　　i.o.　d.o.

He demanded me little. (×)
　　i.o.　d.o.

18. 与 of 连用的授予动词:

下列动词亦与 of 连用，但是与上述不同的是，of 之后是以表“东西”的名词为宾语，而非以表“对象”的名词为宾语，同学们务必牢记。

a. rob　抢夺

例: He robbed my money. (×)

→ He robbed me of my money. (✓)
　　对象　东西

（他抢了我的钱。）

My money was robbed. (×)

→ I was robbed of my money. (✓)

（我的钱被抢了。）

b. deprive　剥夺（权利）

例: The court deprived all his civil rights. (×)

→ The court deprived him of all his civil rights. (✓)
　　对象　东西

（法院剥夺了他的公民权利。）

All his civil rights were deprived. / stripped. (×)

→ He was deprived / stripped of all his civil rights. (✓)

（他被剥夺了公民权利。）

c. relieve　解除（职务、指挥权等）

例: The captain relieved the platoon leader of his command.

（连长解除了排长的指挥权。）

d. rid　解除，摆脱

例: I cannot rid myself of the painful memory.

= I cannot get rid of the painful memory.

（我无法摆脱这段痛苦的回忆。）

> **注意**
>
> rid 三态同形。rid myself of 中的 rid 是动词，表“使脱离”；get rid of 中的 rid 是过去分词，相当于形容词，表“脱离的”，get 相当于 be，但 get rid of（摆脱）表“动作”，而 be rid of（已摆脱）则表“状态”。

比较:

I'll get rid of those chores.

（我要摆脱那些杂务。）

I'm glad to be rid of those chores.

（我很高兴摆脱了那些杂务。）

e. break　戒除

例: You should break / rid yourself of the bad habit of smoking.

（你应该戒除抽烟的恶习。）

不过上句亦可写成：

You should break the bad habit of smoking.

f. cure　治愈

例: The doctor cured him of his disease.

（医生治好了他的病。）

不过上句亦可写成：

The doctor cured his disease.

19. 表“提供”的授予动词：

常用的此类动词有 offer、provide、supply、furnish、present 等。除 offer 以外，其余要与介词 with 连用。

例: He offered me (i.o.) all I needed (d.o.).

= He provided / supplied / furnished me with all I needed.

（他提供我所需要的东西。）

He | provided / supplied / furnished | me all I needed. (×)

注意:

a. He offered me all I needed.
= He offered all I needed to me.
He provided me with all I needed.
= He provided all I needed for me.

b. offer 除表“提供”外，亦表“愿意、主动提议”，此时接不定式短语做宾语，句型如下：

offer to V　　愿意……
= be willing to V

例: After he heard of my situation, he offered to help me.
（当他听说我的情况后，便自愿帮助我。）

c. present（赠予）的用法与 provide 相似，不同的是将间接宾语置于句尾时，要与介词 to 连用。

例: He presented me with a watch.
　　　　　　　　i.o.　　d.o.
= He presented a watch to me.
　　　　　　　　d.o.　　i.o.
（他送我一块表。）

20. 其他补充要点：

a. 在第 16 项中，我们已为同学们介绍过，表“给予”的概念，要与 to 连用。

例: I gave him a book.
= I gave a book to him.
（我给他一本书。）
I wrote him a letter.
= I wrote a letter to him.
（我给他写了一封信。）

但：explain（解释）、introduce（介绍）、propose（提议）、recommend（建议）、express（表示）等动词，不论间接或直接宾语的位置是否颠倒，均要与 to 连用。

例: He explained me the reason. (×)

→ He explained the reason to me. (√)
d.o. i.o.

= He explained to me the reason. (少用)

（他向我解释理由。）

He introduced me the girl. (×)

→ He introduced the girl to me. (√)
d.o. i.o.

= He introduced to me the girl. (少用)

（他把那位女孩介绍给我。）

He recommended me the method. (×)

→ He recommended the method to me. (√)
d.o. i.o.

= He recommended to me the method. (少用)

（他建议我用这个方法。）

He proposed the committee a motion. (×)

→ He proposed a motion to the committee. (√)
d.o. i.o.

= He proposed to the committee a motion. (少用)

（他向委员会提了一个提议。）

b. 比较下列两句的不同:

例: I took a picture of him.

（我拍了一张他的照片。—— 照片里有他的影像。）

I took a picture for him.

（我为他拍了一张照片。—— 我代替他来拍照，照片中是别的影像，而非他的影像。）

第三节　结　论

1. 五大句型：

从动词的分类我们已得知，动词一共有五种：

a. 完全不及物动词

b. 不完全不及物动词

c. 完全及物动词

d. 不完全及物动词

e. 授予动词

再根据此五类动词，演绎成英语的五大类句型：

第一句型：

主语 + 完全不及物动词

例：He fainted.
完全 vi.
（他昏倒了。）

He slept.
完全 vi.
（他睡觉了。）

He went away.
完全 vi. adv.
（他离开了。）

He went to the station.
完全 vi. 介词短语做 adv.
（他去车站了。）

第二句型：

主语 + 不完全不及物动词 + 表语

例：He is good.
不完全 vi. adj. 做表语
（他人很好。）

He looks happy.
不完全 vi. adj. 做表语
（他看起来很愉快。）

第三句型：

主语 + 完全及物动词 + 宾语

例: He ate it.
完全 vt. o.
（他吃了它。）

He wants to do it.
完全 vt. 不定式短语，做“意愿”动词的宾语
（他要做此事。）

He knows that he is wrong.
完全 vt. 名词性从句做宾语
（他知道他错了。）

I wonder when he'll come.
完全 vt. 名词性从句做宾语
（我不知道他何时会来。）

They enjoy dancing.
完全 vt. 动名词做宾语
（他们喜爱跳舞。）

I don't know how to do it.
完全 vt. 名词短语做宾语
（我不知道如何做此事。）

第四句型：
主语 + 不完全及物动词 + 宾语 + 宾语补语

例: He made me happy.
不完全 vt. o. 形容词做宾语补语
（他使我快乐。）

We elected him chairman.
不完全 vt. o. 名词做宾语补语
（我们选他当主席。）

第五句型：
主语 + 授予动词 + 间接宾语（授予对象）+ 直接宾语（被授予的东西）

例: I gave him a book.
授予 vt. 间接宾语 直接宾语
= I gave a book to him.
（我给他一本书。）

I told him a lie.
授予 vt. 间接宾语 直接宾语
= I told a lie to him.
（我对他说了个谎。）

2. 祈使句、感叹句、疑问句：

以上所列五大句型的示范例句均为陈述句，亦是常见的句子。除了陈述句外，尚有祈使句、感叹句、疑问句三类。但不论形态如何改变，绝不超出此五大句型。兹将此三类句型介绍如下：

a. 祈使句

简单地说，祈使句就是把主语 You 及助动词 should 或 must 省略的句子。此类句型一开头即为原形动词，亦由上列五大句型演变而成。句尾可视语气强弱置感叹号或句号。

第一句型：

肯定型：You must run now.
（run：完全vi.）

→ Run!
（跑！）

否定型：Don't run!
（别跑！）

第二句型：

肯定型：You must be quiet now.
（be：不完全vi.；quiet now：表语）

→ Be quiet!
（安静！）

否定型：Don't be quiet!
（别不吭声！）

第三句型：

肯定型：You must open the door now.
（open：完全 vt.；the door：o.）

→ Open the door.
（开门。）

否定型：Don't open the door.
（别开门。）

第四句型：

肯定型：You must make him do it.
（make：不完全 vt.；him：o.；do it：o.c.）

→ Make him do it.
（叫他做这事。）

否定型：Don't make him do it.
（别叫他做这事。）

第五句型：

肯定型：You must send him a letter.

授予 vt. 间接宾语 直接宾语

→ Send him a letter.

（给他寄封信。）

否定型：Don't send him any letters.

（别给他寄任何信。）

注意

否定型的祈使句一共有两种：一为 Don't 起首，另一为 Never（绝不）起首。使用 Never 时，不必加 Do，即无 Do never 的用法。

例: Never try it. (√)

Do never try it. (×)

但: Don't ever try it. (√)

= Never try it.

（绝对不要去试。）

b. 感叹句

感叹句的形成，均由 How 或 What 引导。句型如下：

1) What + n. + 主语 + 动词……！

例: What a great man he is!

（他是个多伟大的人呀！）

由于此处 What 为形容词，译成“多么的”，之后一定要加名词，以供修饰。造句的方法如下：

第一步：先置 What 于句首，即成：

What...

第二步：再将含有名词做及物动词的宾语、表语或做补语的句子置于其后；

a) 名词做及物动词的宾语：

What he has a beautiful car.

vt. o.

b) 名词做表语：

(1) be 动词的表语

What he is a great man.

be 动词 表语

(2) 宾语补语

What you have made him a good boy.

不完全vt. o. 宾语补语

第三步：将此宾语、表语或补语置于 What 之后，句尾再置感叹号即成。

What he has a beautiful car. (×)

o.

→ What a beautiful car he has! (√)

（他的车多漂亮呀！）

What he is a great man. (×)

表语

→ What a great man he is! (√)

（他是个多么伟大的人呀！）

What you have made him a good boy. (×)

宾语补语

→ What a good boy you have made him! (√)

（你使他变成多么好的一个男孩呀！）

2) How + adj. 或 adv. + 主语 + 动词……！

由于此处 How 为副词，译成“多么地”，之后一定要加形容词或副词，以供修饰。造句的方法如下：

第一步：先置 how 于句首，改成大写；

How...

第二步：在 How 之后造一个含有形容词或副词的句子；

How he is great.

adj.

How he studied hard.

adv.

第三步：再将形容词或副词置于 How 之后，句尾添加感叹号即成。

How he is great. (×)

adj.

→ How great he is! (√)

（他真了不起呀！）

How he studied hard. (×)

adv.

→ How hard he studied! (√)

（他多用功啊！）

注意
How 之后亦可置带有形容词修饰的单数可数名词，但绝不可置复数名词或不可数名词。句型如下：
How + adj. + a(n) + 单数名词 + 主语 + 动词……！

例: How a great man he is! (×，great 应置于 How 之后)
How great a man he is! (√)
= What a great man he is! (√)
（他是个多么伟大的人呀！）

换言之，How 之后仅可与单数名词连用；而 What 则可与单数、复数或不可数名词连用。

例: How great men they are! (×，men 是复数名词)
→ What great men they are! (√)
（他们真是了不起的人啊！）
How good music it is! (×，music 是不可数名词)
→ What good music it is! (√)
（这音乐真棒！）

但 how 之后可接 many、much、little、few 之类的数量形容词，再接复数或不可数名词。

例: How many students there are in the classroom! (√)
（那个教室里的学生真多啊！）
How few friends he has! (√)
（他的朋友真少！）
What many students there are in the classroom! (×)
What few friends he has! (×)
How much money he has made! (√)
（他赚了那么多钱！）
How little time is left! (√)
（没剩下多少时间了！）
What much money he has made! (×)
What little time is left! (×)

c. 疑问句

疑问句一共有两类：一为一般疑问句，一为特殊疑问句。

1) 一般疑问句：

此类疑问句不以 What、When、Where、How 等疑问词为句首。皆可用 Yes / No 回答，是由陈述句变化而成。形成方式如下：

a) 句中有 be 动词时，将该 be 动词与主语倒置，句尾再加问号即成。

例:He is nice.

→ Is he nice?

（他为人好吗？）

（Yes, he is. 或 No, he isn't.）

They aren't happy about it.

→ Aren't they happy about it?

（难道他们对这事不感到高兴吗？）

（Yes, they are. 或 No, they aren't.）

b) 句中若有助动词，如 can（could）、may（might）、will（would）、shall（should）、must、have（has、had）等，则将该助动词与主语倒置，句尾再加问号即成。

例:Thcy can handle the problem.

→ Can they handle the problem?

（他们能处理这个问题吗？）

（Yes, they can. 或 No, they can't.）

He hasn't reported to the committee yet.

→ Hasn't he reported to the committee yet?

（他还没向委员会报到吗？）

（Yes, he has. 或 No, he hasn't.）

c) 句中若仅有一般动词，而无 be 动词或助动词时，先按动词时态及主语人称之不同，在句首添加 Do、Does 或 Did 等助动词，再将主语之后的动词一律改为原形动词，句尾再加问号即成。

例:He left early.

一般过去时

→ Did he leave early?

原形 vi.

（他很早就离开了吗？）

（Yes, he did. 或 No, he didn't.）

They enjoy dancing.

一般现在时

→ Do they enjoy dancing?
原形 vt.
（他们喜欢跳舞吗？）
（Yes, they do. 或 No, they don't.）

注意:

(1) 一般疑问句若以否定形式起首时，均译成“难道不……吗？”。

例: Isn't he happy?
（他难道不高兴吗？）

Doesn't he want it?
（他难道不要它吗？）

Won't he join us?
（他难道不愿加入我们吗？）

(2) 不论问句以否定或肯定形式起首，在回答句中，只要认为肯定，就用 Yes 回答；若认为否定，则用 No 回答。

例: Q: Is he happy?
（他快乐吗？）

A: Yes, he is.
（是的，他很快乐。）

或: No, he isn't.
（不，他不快乐。）

Q: Isn't he happy?
（他难道不快乐吗？）

A: Yes, he is.
（不，他很快乐。）

或: No, he isn't.
（是的，他不快乐。）

* 针对以否定形式起首的疑问句，按中文的习惯，Yes 最好译成“不”，No 则译成“是的”。

2) 特殊疑问句：

此类疑问句均以 When、Why、Where、How、What、Who、Whom、Which 等疑问词为句首。由于表示疑问，故不可用 Yes / No 回答。形成方式如下：

a) 先将疑问句按中文的结构译出，如：

你要到哪里去？
You will go where? (×)

他是谁？
He is who? (×)

你住在哪儿？
You live where? (×)

你当时见到了谁？
You saw whom then? (×)

他为何哭了？
He why cried? (×)

b) 再将句中的疑问词移至句首，改成大写：

例: Where you will go? (×)
Who he is? (×)
Where you live? (×)
Whom he saw then? (×)
Why he cried? (×)

c) 再将疑问词之后的结构按一般疑问句的倒装原则倒装，即告完成。

例: Where you will go? (×)
→ Where will you go? (✓)
Who he is? (×)
→ Who is he? (✓)
Where you live? (×)
→ Where do you live? (✓)
Whom he saw then? (×)
→ Whom did he see then? (✓)
Why he cried? (×)
→ Why did he cry? (✓)

注意

(1) 在 "Whom did he see then?" 的疑问句中，Whom 做 see 的宾语，故用宾格，但在美语中，多以 Who 取代 Whom，形成下列习惯的用法：

Who did he see then?

(2) what、who、which 这三个疑问词，因具名词性质，故在特殊疑问句中，可直接置于句首做主语，而无须采用倒装结构。

谁来了？

→ Who came? (√)
S

发生什么事了？

→ What has happened? (√)
S

哪一个被打破了？

→ Which was broken? (√)
S

3. 结语：

至此我们已为同学们介绍了五大句型，以及祈使句、感叹句和疑问句的造句法。同学们从现在起，就应具备单句分析能力。因此赖老师建议你马上开始大量阅读文章，练习结构分析。有分析的能力，一如我们在建造房子时架好了钢筋结构一样，剩下的工作就是搬砖头——记单词或短语。那就要看你用功的程度了。不过，同学们目前仅具有简单句的分析能力当然仍是不足的，因此我们将在下一章与同学们共同研究句子的连接方法，使我们更能以较长、较复杂的句子结构表现我们的意思。同学们可要耐心学习哦！

EXERCISE

I. 请指出下列句子中的动词属于五大类型中的哪一类：

A. 完全不及物动词

B. 不完全不及物动词

C. 完全及物动词

D. 不完全及物动词

E. 授予动词

1. Melvin sold his bicycle to his cousin.
2. I hung my coat on the rack.
3. The rain fell in torrents.
4. Show the guests the way to the garden.
5. The janitor took the key from the center.
6. His intervention made the matter complicated.
7. Harold proved eligible for the position.
8. The doctor felt my pulse.
9. The icy wind feels bitter.
10. How's John doing?

II. 请选出一个正确的答案：

11. The bread tastes ______.
    (A) with it　(B) of garlic　(C) sweetly　(D) to be hot
12. The boys are ______.
    (A) on upstairs　(B) in upstairs　(C) upstair　(D) upstairs
13. The room ______ fifteen feet across.
    (A) measures　(B) has measured　(C) measuring　(D) is measured

14. The baby slept ______.

(A) for sound sleep (B) to be sound

(C) a sound sleep (D) in a sound sleep

15. I always have my bedroom ______ tidy and clean.

(A) look (B) to look (C) looked (D) looks

16. ______ that the newcomers know computers very well.

(A) The fortune (B) To be fortunate

(C) Fortunately (D) It is fortunate

17. In the U.S. Senate, ______, regardless of population, is equally represented.

(A) each state (B) where each state

(C) each state that is (D) for each state

18. "What did you do with the door?"

"The door was painted ______."

(A) whitely (B) white

(C) with white (D) with white hands

19. While in college, he used to ______ long hair.

(A) had (B) wear (C) reserve (D) reserving

20. The people in general looked upon the situation ______.

(A) as critical (B) to be critical (C) being critical (D) critical

Ⅲ.请选出错误的画线部分：

21. I never feel badly (A) if I fail (B) to win a prize (C); the effort gives (D) me satisfaction.

22. Bats deterministic (A) their positions by means (B) of echolocation, a system (C) that (D) does not rely on sight.

23. My reaction (A), I suppose (B), could have been called (C) to be instinctive (D).

24. Everyone who (A) comes (B) must take (C) a ticket with him (D).

25. Judy found her difficult to make herself understood.
(A) (B) (C) (D)

26. Just as I finished eating, my brother explained me a question.
(A) (B) (C) (D)

27. The computer makes possibly a phenomenal leap in human proficiency.
(A) (B) (C) (D)

28. A person ought not to forget to use tact and courtesy in dealing with others, if
(A) (B) (C)
he expects them like him and be his friends.
(D)

29. The students in the dormitories were forbidden, unless they had
(A) (B)
special passes, from staying out after 11:30 p.m.
(C) (D)

30. Because he could not think clearer, his efforts in trying to solve the problem
(A) (B) (C)
failed.
(D)

标准答案

1. (E)	2. (C)	3. (A)	4. (E)	5. (C)	6. (D)	7. (B)	8. (C)	9. (B)	10. (A)
11. (B)	12. (D)	13. (A)	14. (C)	15. (A)	16. (D)	17. (A)	18. (B)	19. (B)	20. (A)
21. (A)	22. (A)	23. (D)	24. (C)	25. (A)	26. (C)	27. (B)	28. (D)	29. (D)	30. (A)

习题解说

1. sold（sell 的过去式）

可做授予动词，与介词 to 连用。

2. hung（挂）（hang 的过去式）
   为完全及物动词，此处的 on the rack 做副词用，修饰 hung。
3. fell（落下）（fall 的过去式）
   为完全不及物动词；in torrents 做副词用，修饰 fell。
4. show 可做授予动词，本句中的 the guests 及 the way 均为其宾语。
5. 与第 2 题同理。
6. make 为使役动词，此处以过去分词 complicated 做其宾语补语。
7. prove 可做不完全不及物动词，表“经证实为……”，此处的 eligible（合格的）为表语。
8. feel 做完全及物动词时，表“触摸”。
9. feel 做不完全不及物动词时，表“感觉起来……”。
10. 此处 do 为完全不及物动词，表“进展”。
11. a. taste 之后须接形容词做表语，表“尝起来……”。
    b. taste of...　　尝起来有……的味道
       taste of garlic　　有蒜味
       taste of fish　　有鱼味
12. upstairs（楼上）为地点副词可做表语，故之前无须再加介词。
13. measure 可做不完全不及物动词，其后接表距离的名词，意思是“量起来有……长”。
14. sleep 做及物动词时，其宾语必须为同系宾语 sleep。
15. have 为使役动词，其宾语之后须以原形动词做宾语补语。
16. that 从句是名词性从句，被句首的 It 代替。
17. each state 为本句的主语，is represented 则为被动语态的动词，regardless of population 是插入的形容词短语，修饰主语。
18. white 为形容词，此处作表语。
19. wear long hair　　留长发
    wear short hair　　留短发
20. look upon A as B　　将 A 视为 B
21. feel 为感官动词，故之后应置形容词 bad 作表语。
22. 本句的主语为 Bats，但缺少动词，故将 deterministic 改为 determine。
23. (D) 应删除 to be，保留形容词 instinctive。call 表“称作”，是不完全及物动词，应以形容词或名词做补语。

They call me stupid.（他们叫我呆子。）
adj.
They call me a liar. （他们叫我骗子。）
n.

24. take 表示“带走”，表“带来”要用 bring。
25. 本句中 found 的真正宾语为 to make herself understood，difficult 为宾语补语，故 (A) 中的 her 应改为形式宾语 it。
26. explain 做授予动词时，间接宾语无论位置如何，之前均须加介词 to，故 (C) 应改为 explained to me。
    explain to 人 + 事　　向某人解释某事
    = explain 事 + to 人
27. (B) 中的 possibly 应改为 possible。
    make...possible　　使……成为可能
    possible 为 make 的宾语补语，原本应置于宾语之后，但因宾语过长，故将 possible 移至宾语之前，以美化句子。
28. expect 表“期望”，用“expect sb to V”（期望某人……），故 (D) 应改为 them to like him and (to) be。
29. forbid sb to V　　禁止某人……
    forbid 的宾语补语必须为不定式，不可用 from V-ing，故 (D) 中的 from staying 应改为 to stay。
30. think 在此处为完全不及物动词，必须用副词修饰，故 clearer 须改为 clearly。

A Quick Note

第二章　两句的连接方法

概述

我们从事英语写作时，总希望能用更多的单词、短语或句子来表示我们心中的意思，而我们从事英语阅读时，往往亦因复杂的修饰语弄得头昏脑胀看不下去。因此，我们得先熟悉单句的造句法，然后再精通两句或两句以上的连接方法，以克服这些障碍。

我们在第一章既已详细讨论了单句的形成，故在本章中我们将研究两句的连接方法。赖老师建议同学们此时不妨洗把脸，深呼吸三次，以便有清醒的头脑与赖老师一起研究下去。（赖老师现在等你 5 分钟以便让你有时间去洗澡——哦，不，洗脸。）

注意

我们现在开始正式的讨论·

两句连接的方法不外乎下列六种方式：

第一种：破折号（—）

例: He is versatile—he speaks five different languages and plays the piano very well.
（他多才多艺——他会说五种语言且钢琴弹得很好。）

第二种：冒号（:）

例: He has finally made his goal known to us: he wants to be a scientist.
（他终于让我们知道他的目标：他要当科学家。）

第三种：分号（;）

例: He is nice; quite often he is seen helping others.
（他人很好；常有人看见他在帮助别人。）

第四种：并列连词

例: He enjoys taking pictures, and he has decided to pursue the art as his life career.
（他喜欢摄影，并且决定要追求此种艺术作为他的终身事业。）

第五种：副词性连词

例: He deserves our respect because he is honest.
（他值得我们尊敬，因为他诚实。）

第六种：关系词

例: He is a man who never tells lies.
（他是个从不说谎的人。）

由于这些连接符号或连词牵涉甚广，我们必须逐项讨论于后。

第一节　连接符号

通常用来连接两句的标点符号只有三个，即破折号（—）、冒号（:）、分号（;）。兹将此类连接符号介绍如下：

1. 破折号：

a. 此类符号有别于连字符（-）。前者用于连接句子或同位语，而后者则用以连接单词，形成复合词。

例：连字符：

Water-skiing is my hobby.
单词　单词
（滑水是我的爱好。）

The tiger is a man-eating animal.
单词　单词
（老虎是一种会吃人的动物。）

b. 破折号连接句子时，用来强调第一个句子，以补充意思的不足。此时破折号有“也就是说”，或“换句话说”的意思。

例：He is trash—he is good for nothing.
（他是废物——他什么都不行。）

= He is trash. That is to say, he is good for nothing.
（他是废物。换句话说，他什么都不行。）
＊trash 原意为“垃圾”，是集合名词，不可数，故其前不置冠词 a。

c. 破折号亦可用来连接同位语。

例：He finally made his purpose known to us—to chase Susan.
不定式短语，做同位语
（他终于让我们知道了他的目的——追求苏珊。）

His hobby—taking pictures—is far more interesting than mine.
动名词短语，做同位语
（他的爱好——摄影——比我的爱好有趣多了。）

2. 冒号：

此类符号亦可用以连接句子，来强调前面句中的名词。

例: He has made his goal known: he wants to be a scientist.

名词

（他已经让大家知道他的目标了：他要当科学家。）

3. 分号：

a. 此类符号在文章中较常出现，等于“逗号 + 连词（and、so、but...）”。

例: He is a man of principle; we all respect him.

= He is a man of principle, so we all respect him.

（他是有原则的人，因此我们都尊敬他。）

He is a photographer; quite often he travels abroad to take pictures.

= He is a photographer, and quite often he travels abroad to take pictures.

（他是个摄影师，常常出国摄影。）

He is nice; no one likes him, though.

= He is nice, but no one likes him.

（他人很好，然而没人喜欢他。）

b. 句中的对等语原本用逗号相隔，再以并列连词相连，但若某对等语中间有插入语时，会多出一些逗号。为了句意清楚起见，可用分号取代逗号。

同学们看了上面这一段话后，一定会说：“哇！赖老师语无伦次！”别急，我们且先看下面的例子：

例: He said that he had no money, that he had no friends to count on, and that he expected me to help him.

上列句中有三个 that 从句，以 and 连接，共作 said 的宾语，因此这三个句子称为对等语或对等句，用逗号相隔。

现在赖老师要在句中加入插入语，请注意标点符号的变化：

例: He said that he had no money; that, because of his ill temper, he had no friends to count on; and that he expected me to help him.

插入语

（他说他没钱，又说因脾气不好而没有朋友可投靠，所以希望我能帮助他。）

本句用分号置于对等 that 从句之前，使读者很容易看出三个从句的对等关系。

同理:

He enjoys dancing, swimming, and jogging.

置入插入语之后：

He enjoys dancing, <u>which is his hobby</u>; swimming,

插入语

<u>which he often does on Sundays</u>; and jogging.

插入语

（他喜欢跳舞，那是他的爱好；也喜欢去游泳，而且周日常去；还喜欢慢跑。）

第二节 并列连词

1. 单一连词：

基本的并列连词一共只有三个：and、or、but。此种连词可用以连接对等的单词、短语或句子，故称为并列连词。

a. 单词

例：He and I enjoy singing.

对等的主语

（他和我都喜欢唱歌。）

He is kind and handsome.

对等的形容词做表语

（他心地好，人又帅。）

Is he sad or happy?

对等的形容词做表语

（他是伤心还是高兴？）

He doesn't like her but hates her.

对等的动词

（他不是喜欢她，而是恨她。）

b. 短语

例：I came to see him and (to) tell him the truth.

对等的不定式短语

（我来是要见他并告诉他实情。）

Does he work in Taipei or in Shanghai?

对等的介词短语

（他是在台北还是在上海工作？）

He is not good at English but poor at it.

对等的形容词短语做表语

（他英语不是很好，而是很差。）

c. 句子

例：He works hard, and his father is proud of him.

对等的分句

（他很努力，而他父亲以他为荣。）

He doesn't study, but his teacher likes him.

对等的分句

（他不学习，但他老师却喜欢他。）

Did he fail because he was lazy or because he was careless?

对等的状语从句

（他失败是因他懒惰还是因他粗心呢？）

I like John, who is easy to get along with but whose brother is too

对等的定语从句（分别由 who 及 whose 引导）

arrogant to associate with.

（我喜欢约翰，他很容易相处，而他弟弟却很自大，难以相处。）

2. and、or、but 衍生的其他连词：

虽然基本的并列连词只有 and、or、but 三个，但亦可由此三个变化成下列数个连词：

and	→	both...and...	（一方面……同时也……）
or	→	either...or...	（要不就是……要不就是……）
		neither...nor...	（既非……亦非……）
but	→	not...but...	（并非……而是……）
		not only...but also...	（不仅……而且……）

这些连词亦可连接对等的单词、短语或句子。

a. 单词

例：Both Peter and Mary work hard.

对等的主语

（彼得与玛丽都努力工作。）

He is not kind but cruel.

对等的形容词作表语

（他非但不仁慈，反而很残忍。）

He will either stay or leave.

对等的动词

（他不是走就是留。）

b. 短语

例：He went to the United States not only to learn English but (also) to know more about American culture.

（他去美国不仅去学英语，也是去了解美国文化。）

（“not only...but also...”连接对等的不定式短语）

He succeeded both because of his intelligence and because of his hard work.

（他成功既因他的聪明，亦因他的努力。）

（“both...and...”连接对等的副词短语）

c. 句子

例: He succeeded both because he was intelligent and because he worked hard.

（他成功既因他聪明，亦因他努力。）

（“both...and...”连接对等的状语从句）

Not only can she sing, but she can (also) dance.

（她不仅会唱歌，她也会跳舞。）

（“Not only...but (also)...”连接对等的分句）

3. as well as 与 rather than 作并列连词:

下列连词亦视为并列连词，可连接对等的单词、短语或句子。

as well as...　　以及……

rather than...　　而非……

a. 单词

例: We as well as John like it.

对等的主语

（我们和约翰都喜欢它。）

He is happy rather than sad.

对等的形容词

（他很快乐，而不是伤心。）

b. 短语

例: He is interested in music rather than in painting.

（他对音乐有兴趣，而非对绘画有兴趣。）

（rather than 连接对等的介词短语）

He came here to learn English as well as to know more about life.

（他来此地学英语并多了解人生。）

（as well as 连接对等的不定式短语）

c. 句子

例: He failed because he was lazy rather than because he was not intelligent.
（他失败是因为懒惰，并非是因为他不聪明。）
（as well as 连接对等的状语从句）

I love her because she is intelligent as well as because she is considerate.
（我爱她是因为她聪明，也因为她体贴。）
（as well as 连接对等的状语从句）

> **注意**
> as well as 或 rather than 连接主语时，该句动词始终要随第一个主语做变化。

例: He as well as I is interested in music.
= He no less than I is interested in music.
= He together with me is interested in music.
= He along with me is interested in music.
（他和我都对音乐有兴趣。）

上列句中，由于 as well as（以及）与 no less than（以及）为并列连词，故之后接主格形式 I，以与 He 对等。而 together with（以及）或 along with（以及）则为介词，故之后接宾格形式 me，以做为 with 之宾语。

例: He rather than I is interested in music.
= He instead of me is interested in music.
= He, not I, is interested in music.
（他对音乐有兴趣，而我则不。）

上列句中，由于 rather than 为并列连词，故之后接主格形式 I，以与 He 对等。而 instead of 则为介词，故之后接宾格形式 me，以做为 of 之宾语。not 亦可视为并列连词，等于 rather than，唯使用时，not 之前恒加逗号。

例: I like this book, not that one.
= I like this book rather than that one.
（我喜欢这本书，而不喜欢那本。）

4. 使用 “both...and...” 等连词应注意事项：

使用 both...and.../either...or.../neither...nor.../not...but.../not only...but also...等连词时，要注意下列事项：

a. 连接主语时，“both...and...”之后始终接复数动词；其余连词连接主语时，动词则要随最近的主语做单复数变化。

例: Both he and I are happy about it.
（他与我对此事都高兴。）

Either he or I am wrong.
（不是他就是我错。）

Neither you nor he is to blame.
（既不是你也不是他该负责。）

*be to blame = should be responsible　　应负责

Not he but I am to be responsible for it.
（不是他而是我应对此事负责。）

Not only they but (also) John has passed the exam.
（不仅他们考试及格，连约翰也考及格了。）

b. both...and... / neither...nor... / not...but...等三组连词通常不用来连接句子，而"not only...but also..."则可用来连接句子，唯 not only 引导的句子要采用倒装结构。赖老师相信此刻同学们又不知所云了。没关系，请你耐心看下面的解说，就会明白了。

1) 句子是可以单独存在的，两个句子可以通过连词形成并列句，也可以与状语从句、定语从句并存形成主从复合句。

例: He is good.　　　　　　句子
主语
John seems to like it.　　　　句子
主语
Peter is a man who never lies. (句子)
主句　　定语从句
He said that he liked it.
主语 vt. 名词性从句做宾语
When he came, I was studying.
状语从句　　主句

2) Both he is good at English, and he is good at math. (×)
分句　　分句

→ He is good at both English and math. (√)
（他擅长英语和数学。）

Either you should listen to me, or you should get out of my sight. (可)
分句　　分句

= You should either listen to me or get out of my sight. (佳)
动词短语　　动词短语

（你要不就听我的话，要不就给我滚。）

Neither you can talk here, nor you can eat here. (×)
分句　分句

You can neither talk nor eat here. (√)
（你不能在这儿说话，也不能在这儿吃东西。）

Not he is wrong, but you are wrong. (可)
分句　分句

→ Not he but you are wrong. (佳)
（错不在他，而在你。）

但:Not only can she sing, but she can also dance. (√)
分句　分句

c. not only 由于是否定副词的关系，若置于第一个分句之前，该主句要采用倒装结构。而 but also 则为连词，所连接的第二个分句不须倒装。倒装原则依动词形式之不同，可分为下列三种情况：

1) be 动词与主语倒装：

例: Not only he is clever, but he is (also) polite. (×)
→ Not only is he clever, but he is polite. (√)
（他不仅聪明而且有礼貌。）

2) 助动词与主语倒装：

例: Not only she can sing, but she can (also) dance. (×)
→ Not only can she sing, but she can dance. (√)
（她不但会唱歌而且会跳舞。）

Not only he has learned a lot from his teacher, but he has (also) done quite well in his studies. (×)
→ Not only has he learned a lot from his teacher, but he has done quite well in his studies. (√)
（他不仅从老师那儿学到很多，而且他的学习很优异。）

3) 一般动词：
倒装时要按主语人称与动词时态另加 do、does 或 did 于主语前，原有的动词一律改为原形动词。

例: Not only she sings well, but she (also) dances beautifully. (×)
→ Not only does she sing well, but she dances beautifully. (√)
（她不仅歌唱得好，舞也跳得好。）

Not only I hate him, but I (also) feel like killing him. (×)
→ Not only do I hate him, but I feel like killing him. (√)
（我不仅恨他，也想杀了他。）

Not only he wrote good poems, but he could compose music. (×)
→ Not only did he write good poems, but he could compose music. (√)
（他不仅诗写得好，也能作曲。）

d. "not only...but also..." 之中的 also 通常可以省略。若不省略，则连接单词或短语时 but also 不可分开，但连接句子时，but also一定要分开，也就是将 also 置于句中：

1) 连接单词或短语：

例: She is not only beautiful but (also) kind.
（她不但美丽而且心地很好。）

She is interested not only in music but (also) in art.
（她不仅对音乐有兴趣，对艺术也有兴趣。）

He came here not only to learn English but (also) to know more about life.
（他来此不仅要学英语，也要多了解人生。）

2) 连接句子：

例: Not only can she dance, but also she can sing. (×)
→ Not only can she dance, but she can (also) sing. (√)

e. not only...but also...
= not only...but...as well

例: She is not only beautiful but (also) kind.
= She is not only beautiful but kind as well.

Not only can she sing, but she can (also) dance.
= Not only can she sing, but she can dance as well.

f. not only... but also...
= not merely...but also...
= not just...but also...

例: He enjoys not only dancing but (also) singing.

= He enjoys | not just / not merely | dancing but singing as well.

（他不仅喜欢跳舞，也喜欢唱歌。）

5. 单一连词的独立用法:

and、or、but 通常置于两个对等的句子之间，以发挥连词的功能。但有时，我们亦可见到 and、or、but 变成大写，置于单句句首，形成独立的用法。只是此类用法必须要有上下文才能成立。

无上下文:

And he took my advice. (×)

有上下文:

He was not sure how to handle the problem, but I told him not to worry about it until his father came. And he took my advice. (√)

（他不能确定如何处理这个问题，但是我告诉他在他父亲来以前不用担心，而他接受了我的建议。）

无上下文:

But he left just the same. (×)

有上下文:

Since it was raining hard, I asked him to stay lest he should catch a cold walking in the rain. But he left just the same. (√)

（因为雨下得很大，我要他留下来以免走在雨中着凉，但他还是走了。）

*just the same = still　　仍然

第三节 副词性连词

在主从复合句中，because、if 等连词引导的从句充当状语，类似副词的功能，所以我们把这类连词叫做副词性连词。

1. 副词性连词只能连接从句：

例: I like him because he is easy to get along with.
（我喜欢他是因为他很容易相处。）

When he came, I was writing a letter.
（当他来时，我正在写信。）

上列句中，because 及 when 就是副词性连词，用以连接主句和从句。

2. 常用的的副词性连词：

because（因为）、though（虽然）、if（如果）、unless（除非）、as soon as（一旦）、once（一旦）等。

3. 副词性连词引导状语从句：

副词性连词冠于任何一个从句前面，该从句就成为状语从句，而状语从句绝不可能单独存在，一定要与主句共存。整个状语从句可视为副词，用来修饰主句。

例: He is nice. 句子

because he is nice 状语从句

I like him. Because he is nice. (×)

理由

because he is nice 乃状语从句，不可单独存在。

兹改正如下：

I like him because he is nice. (✓)
主句 状语从句

或：

Because he is nice, I like him. (✓)
状语从句 主句

4. 状语从句的位置：

同学们应注意到，在上列改正过的结构中，because 引导的状语从句若置于主句之后，because 之前就不必加逗号。但 because 从句若置于主句之前，则两句之间就应置逗号。由此我们得知一个惯用的法则：任何一个副词性连词所引导的从句若置于主句之后，两句之间通常不置逗号。但若该状语从句置于主句之前，则两句之间通常置逗号。

例: Though he did poorly on the test, his father didn't scold him.
状语从句 主句

= His father didn't scold him though he did poorly on the test.
主句　　　　　　　　　　状语从句
（虽然他考试考得不好，他父亲并未责备他。）

If I am free, I'll write you.
状语从句　　主句
= I'll write you if I am free.
主句　　状语从句
（我有空的话，就会给你写信。）

As soon as he heard the news, he cried.
状语从句　　　　　　主句
= He cried as soon as he heard the news.
主句　　　　状语从句
（他一听到这个消息就哭了。）

以上只是一个通则，英美人士的写作中亦偶见有人将状语从句置于主句之后时，两句之间仍置逗号。

5. 避免双重连接：

此类情形尤其常发生在下列情况中：

a. Because...so...　　　(×)

b. Though...but...　　　(×)

例: Because she is nice, so I like her very much. (×)

理由

Because 与 so 均为连词，造成双重连接，这是错误的结构。

故: Because she is nice, I like her very much. (✓)

或: She is very nice, so I like her very much. (✓)

（因为她人很好，所以我很喜欢她。）

例: Though / Although / Even if / Even though she is nice, but I don't like her. (×)

理由

though（或 although、even if、even though）与 but 均为连词，故形成双重连接，这亦是错误的结构。

故：

Though Although Even if Even though	she is nice, I don't like her. (√)

或: She is nice, but I don't like her. (√)
（她人很好，但我不喜欢她。）

6. 条件句与主句的时态：

when（当）、if（如果）、once（一旦）、as soon as（一旦 = once）、unless（除非）等副词性连词所引导的从句，亦可表示一种条件，形成所谓的条件句。若用来表示将来的状况时，该条件句的时态要采用一般现在时（或现在完成时），而主句的时态则用一般将来时。即：

If Once As soon as Unless When	+ 一般现在时（或现在完成时）动词, 主语 + will + 原形动词

例: When I will be rich, I will buy a car. (×)
→ When I am rich, I will buy a car. (√)
（我有钱时，就会买辆车。）

If he will have time, he'll come here. (×)
→ If he has time, he'll come here. (√)
（他若有时间就会来。）

As soon as I will have done it, I'll let you know. (×)
→ As soon as I have done it, I'll let you know. (√)
（我一做完就会让你知道。）

Once I will be free, I will take a trip abroad. (×)
→ Once I am free, I will take a trip abroad. (√)
（我一旦有空就会出国旅行。）

Unless he will come back tomorrow, I will leave. (×)
→ Unless he comes back tomorrow, I will leave. (√)
（除非他明天回来，否则我就要走了。）

同理:
It will be another two years before he will graduate. (×)

→ It will be another two years before he graduates. (✓)

主句　　　　条件句

（他还要两年才毕业。）

How long is it before he will come? (×)

→ How long will it be before he comes? (✓)

主句形成的疑问句　　　　条件句

（他还要多久才来？）

7. 连接性副词：

有些副词有连接的意味，但却不能做连词用，此类副词就称为连接性副词。此类副词前面要有分号，用以连接两句。

a. however、nevertheless（然而）——有连词 but 的意味。

例：He is nice; however, / nevertheless, I don't like him.

= He is nice, but I don't like him.

= He is nice. However, / Nevertheless, I don't like him.

（他人很好，然而我却不喜欢他。）

> **注意**
>
> however 或 nevertheless 之后通常要加逗号。however 亦可插入在句中，两旁以逗号相隔。

例：He is nice; I, however, don't like him.

= He is nice. I, however, don't like him.

b. therefore、thus（因此）——有连词 so 的意味。

例：He is kind; therefore, / thus we all like him.

= He is kind, so we all like him.

= He is kind. Therefore, / Thus we all like him.

（他很仁慈，因此我们都喜欢他。）

注意

therefore 之后通常要加逗号，thus 则不加逗号。

therefore 亦可插入在句中，两旁以逗号相隔。

例: He is kind; we, therefore, like him.

= He is kind. We, therefore, like him.

c. moreover、furthermore、in addition（此外）——有连词 and 的意味。

例: She dances well; furthermore, / moreover, / in addition, she is good at singing.

= She dances well. Furthermore, / Moreover, / In addition, she is good at singing.

= She dances well, and she is good at singing.

（她舞跳得好，而且擅长唱歌。）

d. besides（此外）

besides 与 in addition 均表"此外"，不过前者多用于有否定或消极意味的句中，而 in addition 则用于肯定句或积极意味的句中（如上例）。

例: I don't think I will go to the movies with you, John. I'm too tired; besides, I have no money.

（我想我不会跟你去看电影了，约翰。我太累了；此外，我也没钱。）

注意

furthermore、moreover、besides、in addition 通常只置于主语前，而不插入句中。

8. while 做副词性连词及并列连词的用法：

a. 表"当……"时，while 视为副词性连词，引导状语从句。

例: While I was writing a letter, she was doing the dishes.

While I was writing a letter：状语从句；she was doing the dishes：主句

（当我写信时，她正在洗盘子。）

b. 表“而……”时，while 视为并列连词，连接并列句。

例: He is nice, | while / whereas | his brother is bad.
　　分句　　　　　　　　　　　　分句

= While he is nice, his brother is bad.
　　　　分句　　　　　　分句

（他很好，而他弟弟却很坏。）

9. 其他重要的副词性连词：

a. as（当；虽然；因为）

1) as 做“当”解时，相当于 when 之意。

例: As I was young, I was quite happy.

（我年轻时很快乐。）

2) as 做“虽然”解时，等于 though；though 引导的状语从句有下列句型变化：

例: Though he is rich, he isn't happy.
　　　　　　　　adj.

= Rich as he is, he isn't happy.

= As rich as he is, he isn't happy.

（虽然他有钱，却并不快乐。）

＊上句句首的 As 视作虚词，无意义，第二个 as 则视为连词，译成“虽然”。

3) as 做“因为”解时，相当于 because 之意。

例 As he has apologized to me, I'm going to forgive him.

= Because he has apologized to me, I'm going to forgive him.

（由于他已向我道歉，因此我会原谅他。）

b. where（= in the place where = in the place in which）（在……的地方）

例: Where I live, people are very nice.

= In the place where I live, people are very nice.

（在我住的地方，大家都很友善。）

Put the book where I can see it.

= Put the book in the place where I can see it.

（把书放在我可以看到的地方。）

Where there is a will, there is a way.
= In the place where there is a will, there is a way.
（在有意志力的地方，就有一条道路——有志者事竟成。——谚语）

c. once（一旦）

例: Once you hear any good news, let me know.
= As soon as you hear any good news, let me know.
（一旦听到什么好消息，立刻让我知道。）

d. or（否则）

例: You must work hard, or I'll fire you.
= You must work hard; otherwise I'll fire you.
（你要努力工作，否则我就炒你鱿鱼。）

＊or 是连词，用以连接两个否定的句子；otherwise 是连接性副词，并非连词，故之前置分号，以连接两句。

e. nor（也不）

nor 是连词，用以连接两个否定的句子；nor 之后的分句要采用类似疑问句结构的倒装句型。

例: She can't sing, nor can she dance.
（她不会唱歌，也不会跳舞。）

He isn't clever, nor is he diligent.
（他既不聪明，也不勤奋。）

He never lies, nor does he bully other kids.
（他从不说谎，也不欺负其他孩子。）

f. so that（这样的话；以便）

so that 引导的状语从句句中应有助动词 may、will、can 等。

例: I got up early so that I could get to school on time.
= I got up early in order that I could get to school on time.
（我早起，这样我就可以准时上学。）

注意

英美人士也有人习惯用 so 取代 so that，此时 so 不得译成“因此”，仍应译成“这样的话”或“以便”，故上句亦可改写成：

I got up early so I could get to school on time.

g. so...that...（如此……以至于……）

例: He is so nice that we all like him.

（他人这么好，因此我们都很喜欢他。）

> **注意**
> 英美人士也有人习惯将 that 省略，改以逗号取代，故上句亦可改写成：
> He is so nice, we all like him.

h. in that（因为）

in that 相当于 because，只是 in that 引导的状语从句多置于主句之后，而 because 引导的状语从句可置于主句之前或之后。

例: He is great in that he speaks five different languages.

主句

（他很了不起，因为他能说五种语言。）

i. except that（只可惜，只不过是）

例: He is nice except that he is a little shy.

（他人不错，只不过有点儿害羞。）

j. since（因为；自从）

since 表“因为”时，相当于 because 之意；表“自从”时，所引导的状语从句采用一般过去时，主句则为现在完成时或现在完成进行时。

例: Since you've finished the work, you may leave anytime.

（由于你工作做完了，可以随时离开。）

He has been studying quite hard (ever) since he went to college.

（他自从上大学后，就一直很用功。）

EXERCISE

I. 请选出一个正确的答案：

1. Strike _____ the iron is hot.
   (A) before (B) after (C) while (D) during
2. The chairman introduced the speaker _____ then he left the hall.
   (A) : (B) . (C) , (D) ;
3. We do not necessarily grow wiser _____ we grow older.
   (A) as (B) than (C) that (D) which
4. The lecturer will come, _____ he will send a substitute.
   (A) or (B) and (C) otherwise (D) but
5. I cannot afford a new car _____, I have an old Ford.
   (A) , besides (B) ; besides (C) , beside (D) ; beside
6. I will not accept the position, _____ do I want you to take it.
   (A) neither (B) either (C) nor (D) or
7. You will not be able to keep your appointment _____ you hurry.
   (A) for (B) because (C) unless (D) if
8. Put the manuscript _____ the editor can find it.
   (A) when (B) where (C) which (D) how
9. I do the work _____ he gets the credit!
   (A) then (B) ; (C) for (D) so
10. We were so late _____ we missed the concert.
    (A) that (B) and (C) because (D) before
11. You have broken the law; _____, you must be punished.
    (A) so (B) since (C) therefore (D) because

12. Although he is rich, _____ he is not happy.
(A) × (B) but (C) however (D) because

13. It will not be long _____ I come back.
(A) when (B) after (C) before (D) if

14. You must not waste time _____ life is short.
(A) so (B) though (C) in that (D) because of

15. _____ you insist, I will reconsider the matter.
(A) Since (B) But (C) When (D) For

16. _____ I know, he is very honest.
(A) As soon as (B) As well as (C) As far as (D) As long as

17. _____ to New York, her father has not heard from her.
(A) Because she went (B) After she went
(C) When she went (D) Since she went

18. She is going to buy a hat after she _____ a check.
(A) will cash (B) cashes (C) would cash (D) should cash

19. Go _____ me some ice cream.
(A) for get (B) and get
(C) to getting (D) as well as getting

20. It is _____ day that travel advisories have been issued for most of the major highways.
(A) such snowy (B) so snowy (C) such a snowy (D) such snowy a

21. The concert will _____ commence until the conductor arrives.
(A) soon (B) not (C) immediately (D) now

22. Either you or he _____ wrong.
(A) are (B) am (C) be (D) is

23. The sentence "In spite of his wealth, he is not happy." is equal to "_____"
(A) Rich as he is, he is not happy.
(B) Although he is wealth, he is not happy.
(C) Although he is rich, but he is not happy.
(D) Although he is not happy, but he is rich.

24. Smith wrote his first poem _____.
    (A) while he worked a porter in a saloon in New York
    (B) while he was working as a porter in a saloon in New York
    (C) while worked as a porter in a saloon in New York
    (D) while he was worked as a porter in a saloon in New York

25. It is not safe to get out a car _____.
    (A) unless it is in motion
    (B) until it has come to a stop
    (C) after you have opened the window
    (D) before the traffic light turns red

II. 请选出画线部分的错误：

26. Few of the gold seekers who (A) flocked to California were (B) experienced miners, neither (C) did they feel that they had (D) to be.

27. Even although (A) Juan is studying (B) physics now, he is planning to spend (C) next (D) year studying biology and paleontology.

28. John, a (A) versatile young man, is (B) skilled in either (C) drawing and singing (D).

29. Nothing (A) is such hard (B) that (C) it will not become easy by (D) practice.

30. I went (A) to see (B) the zoo during (C) I stayed in Bangkok (D).

标准答案

1. (C)	2. (D)	3. (A)	4. (A)	5. (B)	6. (C)	7. (C)	8. (B)	9. (B)	10.(A)
11. (C)	12. (A)	13. (C)	14. (C)	15. (A)	16. (C)	17. (D)	18. (B)	19. (B)	20. (C)
21. (B)	22. (D)	23. (A)	24. (B)	25. (B)	26. (C)	27. (A)	28. (C)	29. (B)	30. (C)

习题解说

1. 本句的中译为“趁热打铁。”，while 是副词性连词，指在某一段时间内，相当于 during the time 之意。
2. then 为副词，之前须加分号，以连接两个对等的句子。
3. 此处的副词性连词 as 表“当”。
4. or 和 otherwise 均表“否则”，但前者为连词，后者为副词，故此处须选 or。
5. besides 为连接性副词，连接两句时，前面须加分号。
6. nor 是连词，neither 是副词，故此处用 nor 连接两句。
7. unless 和 if 均可引导条件句，但前者表“除非”，后者表“如果”，语意相反。
8. where 可做副词性连词，等于 in the place where（在……的地方）引导状语从句，表示地点。

   There are many trees where I live.

   （我住的地方有许多树。）
9. 没有并列连词连接的两个句子之间可用分号或破折号连接。
10. so + 形容词/副词 + that 从句　　如此……以至于……
11. so 和 therefore 均表“因此”，但前者为连词，后者为副词，本题的空格前已有分号，故空格中应填入 therefore。
12. Although 和 but 均为连词，二者不可同时出现，以免造成双重连接。
13. it will not be long before...　　再过不久就……
14. in that　　由于
    = because
15. since　　既然
    = now that

16. as far as one knows　　就某人所知
= to one's knowledge
= to one's understanding
17. since 引导的状语从句用一般过去时，其所修饰的主句则用现在完成时。

She has	studied	since she came home.
	been studying	

（她从回家后就一直在学习。）
18. 表时间或条件的状语从句中，必须用一般现在时代替一般将来时。
19. Go and get me some ice cream.
= Go to get me some ice cream.
（去帮我弄点冰淇淋来。）
20. such a(n) + 形容词 + 单数名词 + that 从句

She is	such a charming girl	that every boy is pursuing her.
	so charming a girl	

（她是如此迷人的一位女孩，每个男孩都在追她。）
21. not...until...　　直到……才……
22. either...or... 连接两个主语时，动词的单复数须以靠近的主语做变化。
23. although + 主语 + be 动词 + 形容词
= 形容词 + as + 主语 + be 动词
Although he is fat, he runs fast.
= Fat as he is, he runs fast.
（他虽然胖，但跑得很快。）
24. ...while he worked as a porter...
= ...while working as a porter...
25. 与 21 题同理。
26. neither 为副词，不可做连词，故 (C) 应改为 nor。
27. Even although 应改为 Even though。
28. either 无法与 and 形成连词短语，必须改成 both。
both...and...　　两者都……
either...or...　　不是……就是……
29. such 是形容词，表“这样的”，之后只能接名词，如 such a man（这样的人）；so 是副词，表“如此地”，之后应接形容词，原句 hard（困难的）是形容词，故之前的 such 应改为 so。
30. during 为介词，无法连接从句，应改为 while。

第三章　关系词

概述

本章原属于上一章的最后一节，因为关系词也是起连接的作用，但关系词种类繁多，使用时又相当复杂，为让同学们清楚了解关系词的各种用法，赖老师决定另辟本章专讲关系词，以使同学们更加深入了解句子的连接方法。

关系词一共分为下列数种：

a. 关系代词

b. 关系代词所有格

c. 关系副词

d. 关系指示代词

e. 复合关系代词

f. 复合关系副词

g. 准关系代词

以上 a 至 e 项的关系词均引导定语从句，f、g 两项则具有副词的功能，兹分项说明。

第一节 关系代词

1. 关系代词引导定语从句：

关系代词（简称“关代”）有连词的功能，用以引导定语从句。

例: He is a man who always means what he says.

关代 who 引导的定语从句

（他是个说话算话的人。）

That's the book which I like.

关代 which 引导的定语从句

（那是我喜欢的书。）

He works hard, which is a fact that we all know.

关代 which 引导的定语从句　关代 that（= which）引导的定语从句

（他努力工作是我们都知道的事实。）

在上列三个例句中，赖老师用了关系代词 who、which、that 分别代替人、物或整个句子。

第一例中，who 代替 a man；

第二例中，which 代替 the book；

第三例中，which 代替 He works hard 整个句子，而 that 则等于 which，代替 a fact。

2. 关系代词的种类及其功能：

a. 代替人时，主格用 who（在所引导的定语从句中做主语），宾格用 whom（在所引导的定语从句中做宾语）；

b. 代替事物时，主格或宾格均用 which；

c. 代替整个句子时，主格或宾格均用 which。

请参看下列表格：

关系代词	主格	宾格
代替人	who	whom
代替事物	which	which
代替整个句子	which	which

3. 关系代词使用三原则：

a. 关系代词之前要有先行词（即表人或事物的名词）；

b. 关系代词在所引导的定语从句中要做主语、宾语或表语；

c. 否则关系代词之前一定要有介词。

我们先用代替人的关系代词 who、whom 加以解说。

例: He is a good student who studies hard. (√)
（他是个用功的好学生。）

> **注意**
> 在本例中，who 之前有先行词 a good student，who 在所引导的定语从句中做主语，其后有动词 studies，故属正确的用法。

例: He is a boy whom everyone loves. (√)
（他是个大家都喜欢的男孩。）

> **注意**
> 在本例中，whom 之前有先行词 a boy，whom 在所引导的定语从句中做及物动词 loves 的宾语，故属正确的用法。

例: He is a man whom I enjoy working. (×)
（他是个我喜欢工作的人。——无此中文说法）

> **注意**
> 在本例中，whom 之前有先行词 a man，但在所引导的定语从句中，已有主语 I，而 working（工作）乃不及物动词变成的动名词，之后不能接宾语。因此 whom 既无法做主语，又无法做宾语，使得该定语从句形成错误的结构。此时关系代词之前应置介词。

改正：

He is a man for whom I enjoy working.
（他是个我很乐意为他效力的人。）

或：

He is a man with whom I enjoy working.
（他是个我很喜欢与之共事的人。）

我们再以代替事物的关系代词 which 加以解说。

例: This is a problem which we should solve right away. (√)
（这是个我们应该马上解决的问题。）

> **注意**
> 在本例中，which 之前有先行词 a problem，在所引导的定语从句中，which 做及物动词 solve 的宾语，故结构正确。

例: He has a car which was made in Germany. (√)
（他有一辆德国生产的汽车。）

> **注意**
> 在本例中，which 之前有先行词 a car，在所引导的定语从句中，which 做主语，其后有及物动词 make 的被动语态 was made，故结构正确。

例: The house which we live is very large. (×)

> **注意**
> 在本例中，which 之前有先行词 a house，但在所引导的定语从句中，已有主语 we，且 live（住）为不及物动词（我们不能说："We live the house."，而要说"We live in the house."），故 which 无法做主语或宾语，而属于错误的结构。此时 which 之前就应置介词。

改正：

The house in which we live is very large. (√)

（我们住的房子很大。）

4. 介词与关系代词：

关系代词之前有介词时，介词可移至所引导的定语从句句尾，此时可省略关系代词。

例: He is a man with whom I enjoy working.

= He is a man whom I enjoy working with.

= He is a man I enjoy working with.

The house in which we live is very large.

= The house which we live in is very large.

= The house we live in is very large.

> **注意**
> 有些固定的短语动词（即两个或三个词形成的短语，视作一个完整的动词，如："动词 + 介词"、"动词 + 名词 + 介词"），在定语从句中出现时，不宜将介词置于关系代词之前，以保持该动词的完整性。

例: pay attention to... 注意……
call on... 拜访……
take over... 接管……
get rid of... 摆脱……

此类短语动词在英语中比比皆是，赖老师只是列举三四个短语供同学们参考。

例: This is a question to which you should pay attention. (劣)

→ This is a question (which) you should pay attention to. (佳)

（这是你应注意的问题。）

The man on whom I called yesterday is my teacher. (×)

→ The man (whom) I called on yesterday is my teacher. (√)

（我昨天拜访的人是我的老师。）

5. which 可代表之前的整个主句：

关系代词 which 若用以代替整个主句时，which 之前一定要有逗号。

例: John, who was lazy, scored quite high marks on the exam, which somewhat surprised me.

整个主句

（约翰很懒却考了相当高的分，这点使我有些惊讶。）

6. which 亦可代表前句中的部分概念：

例: He smokes three packs of cigarettes a day, which definitely does harm to his health.

（他每天抽三包烟，这对他的健康一定有害。）

注意

本例中，which 代替 smokes three packs of cigarettes a day 这件事。

7. 限制性定语从句与非限制性定语从句的区别：

a. 非限制性定语从句：

先行词为专有名词（如 Tom、John、Africa）及独一性名词，如 father（爸爸只有一个）、mother（妈妈只有一个），之后若接关系代词所引导的定语从句时，该关系代词之前一定要置逗号。此时该定语从句就称为非限制性定语从句。换言之，专有名词或独一性名词本身就具有特殊性，不必再用定语从句加以限定。翻译成中文时，按顺序译出来。

例: I met John, who is my classmate.

专有名词

（我遇到约翰，他是我的同班同学们。）

He has just come back from New York, which is a very big city in the United States.

专有名词

（他刚从纽约回来，那是美国的一座大城市。）

Here comes my father, who is an English teacher.

独一性名词

（我父亲来了，他是个英语老师。）

That's my only son, who is attending college now.

独一性名词

（那是我的独子，他正在上大学。）

I went to the train station this morning, which was crowded with passengers.

（我今早去火车站，车站里挤满了旅客。）

注意

此处的 the train station 指的是说者或听者都知道的那个火车站，故视为独一性名词，之后的从句采用非限制性定语从句。

b. 限制性定语从句：

先行词为一般名词且本身并未具特殊性，可用定语从句加以限制，以加强其特殊性。限制性定语从句，将之译成"……的"，其关系代词前不置逗号。翻译时，先译定语从句，再译先行词。

例: He is a boy who works hard.

（他是个很用功的男孩。）

本例中，who 之前无逗号，故为限制性定语从句，先译定语从句 who works hard（用功的），再译先行词 boy，而成：

他是个用功的男孩。

例: I like the book which he bought yesterday.

（我喜欢他昨天买的那本书。）

但若一般名词之前已有形容词加以修饰而具有特殊性，或该名词本身就具有特殊性（如 a good student 好学生、a gentleman 绅士），该名词之后的定语从句，可依作者的喜好用限制性从句或非限制性从句均可。

例: He is a good boy who studies hard.

限制性定语从句

（他是个用功的好孩子。）

或: He is a good boy, who studies hard.

非限制性定语从句

（他是个好孩子，很用功。）

I like that good book which he bought yesterday.

限制性定语从句

（我喜欢他昨天买的那本好书。）

或: I like that good book, which he bought yesterday.

非限制性定语从句

（我喜欢那本好书，那是他昨天买的。）

我们由上得知，限制性定语从句与非限制性定语从句之别，在口语中听不出来，但在书写时就有显著的差异，同学们使用时不可不谨慎，以免闹出笑话。

例: This is my mother who loves me very much. (×)

独一性名词

（这是我那位很爱我的妈妈。——本句暗示还有一位或数位妈妈不是那么爱我。）

→ This is my mother, who loves me very much. (✓)

（这是我妈妈，她很爱我。）

He is a man, who never breaks his word. (×)

（他是男人，他从不食言。——本句暗示读者是白痴，分辨不出他是个男人。）

→ He is a man who never breaks his word. (✓)

（他是个从不食言的人。）

或: He is a gentleman, who never breaks his word. (✓)

名词本身就具有特殊性

（他是个君子，从不食言。）

或: He is a gentleman who never breaks his word. (✓)

（他是个从不食言的君子。）

8. 关系代词的省略：

限制性（即关系代词之前无逗号）定语从句中，若关系代词为及物动词的宾语，则该关系代词可省略。若关系代词为介词的宾语，介词移至定语从句的句尾时，该关系代词亦可省略。

例: This is the boy whom I saw yesterday.

o.　　vt.

= This is the boy I saw yesterday.

（这是我昨天看见的男孩。）

I enjoy reading the book which I bought yesterday.

o.　　vt.

= I enjoy reading the book I bought yesterday.

（我喜欢看我昨天买的书。）

This is a question which you should pay attention to.
o. prep.

= This is a question you should pay attention to.
（这是一个你应该注意的问题。）

This is the house in which he lives.
prep. o.

= This is the house which he lives in.
o. prep.

= This is the house he lives in.
（这是他住的房子。）

9. that 亦可做关系代词:

that 亦可做关系代词，取代 who、whom 或 which，但使用时有两个条件:

a. that 之前不准有逗号，换言之，that 仅出现在限制性定语从句中。

b. that 之前亦不可有介词。

例: I like the girl | that / who | is sitting there. (✓)

（我喜欢坐在那里的女孩。）

I like the pretty girl, that comes here every Monday. (×)

→ I like the pretty girl, who comes here every Monday. (✓)

（我喜欢那个漂亮女孩，她每星期一来这里。）

He is a man | that / whom | we all respect. (✓)

（他是个我们都尊敬的人。）

This is the knife with that he killed Mary. (×)

→ This is the knife with which he killed Mary. (✓)
prep.

但: This is the knife | which / that | he killed Mary with. (✓)
prep.

（他就是用这把刀杀了玛丽。）

10. 只能使用 that 的情况:

在下列情况中，只能用 that 做关系代词，绝不可使用 which、who 或 whom。

a. 序数词后:

序数词： the	first		第一
	second		第二
	⋮		⋮
	⋮		⋮
	last		最后

例: Gambling is the last thing which I would do. (×)

→ Gambling is the last thing that I would do. (✓)

（赌博是我最不愿做的一件事。）

He was the first man who came up with such an idea.（劣)

→ He was the first man that came up with such an idea.（佳)

（他是第一个想出这个点子的人。）

b. 最高级之后：

例: He is the best student whom I've ever taught. (×)

→ He is the best student that I've ever taught. (✓)

（他是我教过最好的学生。）

The most beautiful scene which I've ever seen is Guilin. (×)

→ The most beautiful scene that I've ever seen is Guilin. (✓)

（我所见过最美的风景是桂林。）

c. "the very + 名词"中的 very 为形容词，是一种强调用法，之前一定置定冠词 the。翻译时 very 一词不必译出。

例: He is the very man that I met yesterday.

= He is just the man that I met yesterday.

（他正是我昨天遇见的人。）

d. all 之后

例: All the students that are studying here are hardworking. (勿使用 who 取代 that)

（所有在此学习的学生都很用功。）

All that he said is true. (勿使用 which 取代 that)

= Everything that he said is true. (勿使用 which 取代 that)

（他所说的都是实话。）

注意
all 之后的关系代词 that 在所引导的定语从句中做宾语时， that 通常均予省略。

故: All (that) he said is true.
All (that) you have to do is (to) wait.
（你所要做的就是等待。）

e. "the only + 名词" 之后：

例: He is the only friend that I have.
（他是我唯一的朋友。）

f. 句中若有两个相同关系代词引导的定语从句出现时，为避免重复，第二个关系代词通常改用 that 取代。

例: He works hard, which is a fact which is known to us.（劣）
→ He works hard, which is a fact that is known to us.（佳）
（他很用功，这是我们皆知的事实。）

g. 关系代词若在 be 动词后做表语，表示某人的身份时，要使用 that，不可使用 who 或 which。

例: He is not the man who he once was. (×)
→ He is not the man that he once was. (✓)
（他已不是当年的他了。）

h. 两个名词性质不一，但却共用一个关系代词时，该关系代词要用 that 取代。

例: Look at the boy and the dog that are coming this way.
（注意看正朝这边走来的男孩和狗。）

i. 在下列句中，宜用 that 取代 who 或 which，以避免与疑问词重复：

例: Who who lies can win our trust? (劣)
疑问词 关系代词
上列问句中第一个 Who 是疑问词，做主语，第二个 who 则为关系代词，但两词外形重复，故应改为：

Who that lies can win our trust? (佳)
（说谎的人有谁会赢得我们的信任呢？）

如此，使 Who 形成问句中的主语，can win our trust 则为其谓语部分；而 that lies 则为定语从句，修饰 who。

例: What is it which you want? (劣)

上列句中 what 是疑问词，which 为关系代词，外形均有疑问词的样子，故 which 宜用 that 取代，即：

What is it that you want? (佳)

（你要的是什么？）

如此，使 What is it（那是什么）做疑问句，而 that you want（你要的）则为定语从句，修饰 What。

11. 限制性定语从句可化简为分词短语：

限制性定语从句中，若关系代词为主语时，该定语从句可化简为分词短语。法则如下：

a. 删除该关系代词；

b. 之后的动词变成现在分词；

c. 若动词为 be 动词，变成现在分词 being 之后，可将 being 省略。

例: The girl who danced here yesterday is my sister.

限制性定语从句

→ The girl who danced here yesterday is my sister.

dancing (现在分词)

= The girl dancing here yesterday is my sister.

（昨天在这跳舞的女孩是我妹妹。）

Who is that boy that is standing over there?

限制性定语从句

→ Who is that boy that is standing over there?

(being)

= Who is that boy standing over there?

（站在那边的男孩是谁？）

I like the car which is parked in front of the post office.

限制性定语从句

→ I like the car which is parked in front of the post office.

(being)

= I like the car parked in front of the post office.

（我喜欢停在邮局前面的那辆车。）

12. 非限制性定语从句不能化简为分词短语：

例：I met John, who said that he loved Mary very much. (√)

非限制性定语从句

（我遇见约翰，他说他很爱玛丽。）

→ I met John, ~~who said~~ that he loved Mary very much. (×)

saying

* 本例若化简成分词短语会造成误导，而成为修饰主语 I 的分词短语，译成："我一方面见到约翰，一方面又说他很爱玛丽。"句意与原句不合，故非限制性的定语从句不可化简为分词短语。

13. 非限制性定语从句可化简为先行词的同位语：

| who / which | + be + n.

此时就可化简为先行词的同位语，即：

a. 删除 who 或 which；

b. 之后的 be 动词变成现在分词 being；

c. 再将 being 省略，形成同位语。

例：I met John, who is a good friend of mine.

→ I met John, ~~who~~ ~~is~~ a good friend of mine.

(being)

= I met John, a good friend of mine.

同位语

（我遇到约翰，他是我的好朋友。）

He works hard, which is a fact that is known to all of us.

→ He works hard, ~~which~~ ~~is~~ a fact ~~that~~ ~~is~~ known to all of us.

(being) (being)

= He works hard, a fact known to all of us.

同位语

（他很用功，这是我们都知道的事实。）

注意

主语同位语可置于主语前后位置。

例：John, a good friend of mine, came to see me yesterday.

主语 主语同位语

= A good friend of mine, John came to see me yesterday.
主语同位语 主语
（我的好友约翰昨天来看我。）

14. 注意定语从句与插入语的关系：

定语从句中的关系代词不受插入语的影响。

a. 插入语的形成方式：“主语 + 表认知的动词”，如：

I believe （我相信）
I think （我认为）
I feel （我觉得）
I know （我知道）
I consider （我认为）
I find （我发现）

b. 定语从句置入插入语的方法：

1) 先造一个含有限制性从句的定语从句。

例: He is a man who never breaks his word.
限制性从句
（他是个从不食言的人。）

He is the man whom I met yesterday.
限制性从句
（他就是我昨天遇见的人。）

2) 再将插入语置于关系代词之后。

例: He is a man who I think never breaks his word.
S 插入语
（我认为他是个从不食言的人。）

本例中，who 原本就做定语从句中的主语，并未因添加插入语 I think 而变成 whom。

例: He is the man whom I believe I met yesterday.
o. 插入语
（我相信他就是我昨天遇见的那个人。）

本例中，whom 原本就做定语从句中及物动词 met 的宾语。

例: He is a man whom I think never breaks his word. (×)

本例中，whom 之后有动词 breaks，且已有宾语 his word，故 whom 应改为主格 who，以做为定语从句中的主语。

c. 我们曾在第一章谈到 think、believe、feel、consider、find 等动词可做完全及物动词或不完全及物动词。赖老师再给同学们复习一下：

I | think | that he is nice.
  | find | 名词性从句
  | believe |
  | ⋮ |

上列句中的 think、find、believe 等为完全及物动词，分别译成“认为……”、“发现……”、“相信……”，之后 that 引导的名词性从句做其宾语。

= I | think | him to be nice.
  | find | 宾语 宾语补语
  | believe |
  | ⋮ |

上列句中的 think、find、believe 等为不完全及物动词，分别译成“认为……是……”、“发现……是……”、“相信……是……”，之后的 him 做其宾语，to be nice 则为宾语补语。

因此，此类动词在“ who + be + 表语 ”的定语从句中亦有两种句型变化。

1) 做完全及物动词时：此类动词属于插入语。

例：He is a man who | I think | is nice. (✓)
S | I find |
| I believe |

（他是个我认为/发现/相信很善良的人。）

2) 做不完全及物动词时：此类动词不再是插入语。

例：He is a man | I think | him to be nice. (×)
| I find |
| I believe |

* He is a man 是句子，I think him to be nice 也是句子，两句无连词连接，故属错误，应将 him 改为关系代词 whom，以引导定语从句。

→ He is a man | I think | whom to be nice. (×)
| I find |
| I believe |

* whom 虽已是关系代词，但应置于先行词 a man 之后。

→ He is a man whom | I think | to be nice. (✓)
宾语 | I find | 宾语补语
| I believe |

（我认为/发现/相信他是个很善良的人。）

换言之，以后见到这样的结构，表认知的动词之后有 is、are、was、were 等 be 动词时，要用关系代词的主格 who；表认知的动词之后有 to be 时，则用关系代词的宾格 whom。

15. 定语从句可化简为不定式短语：

关系代词所引导的定语从句中，若该关系代词之前有介词时，可将该从句变换成不定式短语。

例: He has no house in which he can live.

prep.

= He has no house in which to live.

= He has no house to live in.

He has no house which to live in. (×)

（他没有房子住。）

Lend me your pen with which I can write my address.

= Lend me your pen with which to write my address.

= Lend me your pen to write my address with.

Lend me your pen which to write my address with. (×)

（把你的笔借我，我好写我的住址。）

第二节　关系代词所有格

1. 关系代词所有格的功能：

关系代词所有格乃人称代词所有格（his、your、their、our、its 等）变化而成，和关系代词一样，引导定语从句，修饰前面的名词。请参阅下列例句，注意关系代词所有格的功能。

例: She has an uncle. His name is Peter.

= She has an uncle whose name is Peter.

（她有一个名叫彼得的叔叔。）

＊上句 whose name is Peter 是定语从句，修饰先行词 an uncle。

I like that house. Its location looks good to me.

= I like that house, whose location looks good to me.

（我喜欢那栋房子，它的地点看起来不错。）

＊上句 whose location looks good to me 是定语从句，修饰先行词 that house。

2. 关系代词所有格使用三原则：

由上例可以看出，whose 可以代替人或物，引导定语从句，修饰前面的名词。和关系代词一样，我们若想正确使用关系代词所有格，一定要遵循下列三原则：

a. 关系代词所有格之前要有先行词（即名词或代词）；

b. 该关系代词所有格之后的名词要做定语从句中的主语或宾语；

c. 否则该关系代词所有格之前一定要有介词，该介词亦可移至定语从句句尾。

例: I hate John, whose words are seldom true.
S

（我讨厌约翰，他的话很少是实话。）

本例中，whose words 之前有名词 John，whose words 本身亦做定语从句中的主语，其后有动词 are，故结构正确。

例: I hate John, whose words I don't believe.
o.　vt.

（我讨厌约翰，他的话我都不相信。）

本例中，whose words 之前有名词 John，whose words 本身亦做定语从句中及物动词 believe 的宾语，故结构正确。

例: I hate John, whose words I have no trust. (×)

本例中，whose words 之前虽有名词 John，但在其所引导的定语从句中已有主语 I，及物动词 have 之后亦有宾语 no trust，故 whose words 无法做主语或宾语，结构错误，因此 whose words 之前要置介词 in。即：

I hate John, in whose words I have no trust. (可)
= I hate John, whose words I have no trust in. (佳)

3. 取代 whose 的结构：

稍早赖老师提到 whose 除可代替人以外，亦可代替物。只是代替物时，“whose + n.”亦可被“the + n. + of which”或“of which + the + n.”所取代。即：

whose + n.
= the + n. + of which
= of which + the + n.

例: I like to study in this school, whose faculty and facilities are top-notch.
= I like to study in this school, the faculty and facilities of which are top-notch.
= I like to study in this school, of which the faculty and facilities are top-notch.
（我喜欢在这所学校念书，它的师资及设备均是一流的。）

本例的 the faculty and facilities of which 部分，其中 which 原为 it，代替 this school，即：the faculty and facilities of it（= this school）are top-notch。但 it 应改为关系代词 which，以便形成定语从句，达到连接的目的。

例: This is a fancy car, whose color I like very much.
o. vt.
= This is a fancy car, the color of which I like very much.
= This is a fancy car, of which the color I like very much.
（这是一辆漂亮的车，我非常喜欢它的颜色。）

4. 限制性定语从句与非限制性定语从句：

与关系代词一样，关系代词所有格之前若无逗号，即为限制性定语从句；若有逗号，即为非限制性定语从句。

例: This is Tom, whose father is an English teacher. ——非限制性定语从句
（这位是汤姆，他父亲是英语老师。）

I met a boy whose father is an English teacher. ——限制性定语从句
（我遇到一位父亲是英语老师的男孩。）

第三节 关系副词

1. 关系副词的种类:

关系副词一共有四种，均由“介词＋关系代词 which”变化而成:

where (= in which, on which, at which)
when (= in which, on which, at which)
why (= for which)
how (= in which)

例: This is the city where I met Mary.
（这就是我与玛丽相遇的城市。）
He came on Friday, when it was raining very hard.
（他星期五来这儿，那天雨下得很大。）
I don't know the reason why he cried.
（我不知道他哭的原因。）
That's | how / the way | he handled the thing.
（那就是他处理这件事情的方式。）

2. 关系副词的功能:

where 用以修饰表地点的名词；
when 用以修饰表时间的名词；
why 用以修饰 the reason；
但 how 和 the way 只能用其中之一。
为使同学们有清楚的概念，赖老师特别分项说明如下。

3. where 的用法:

where 引导的定语从句只用来修饰表地点的名词。我们在初中时已学到，表大地方（如城市、国家、区域）时，介词要用 in；表建筑物（如车站、商店、银行等）时，介词要用 at；表内部（在……之内）时，介词要用 in；表外在（在……上面）时，介词要用 on。因此，关系副词 where 可等于 in which、on which、at which。

例: This is the city in which I met Mary.
大地方
= This is the city where I met Mary.
I met him at the station, at which there were many passengers.
建筑物

= I met him at the station, where there were many passengers.
（我在车站遇见他，那里有许多旅客。）

I bought a cabinet in which I could store books.
在……之内

= I bought a cabinet where I could store books.
（我买了一个柜子，我可以把书放在里面。）

Do you see the desk on which there is a book?
在……上面

= Do you see the desk where there is a book?
（你看见那张上面有一本书的桌子了吗？）

4. when 的用法：

when 所引导的定语从句只用以修饰表时间的名词。我们已知，表日子时，介词要用 on（如 on Sunday，on Dec. 21）；表年、月或一段时间时，介词要用 in（如 in July、in 1981、in those days）；表几时几刻时，介词要用 at（如 at 8 o'clock）。

因此，关系副词 when 可等于 at which、on which、in which。

例: He came on Friday, on which it was raining hard.
日子

= He came on Friday, when it was raining hard.
（他星期五来这儿了，那天雨下得很大。）

That's the year in which he graduated.
年

= That's the year when he graduated.
（就在那年他毕业了。）

The sun rose at 5:30, at which most people were still in their dreams.
时刻

= The sun rose at 5:30, when most people were still in their dreams.
（太阳五点半升起，那时许多人还在睡梦中。）

5. why 的用法：

why 只用以修饰 the reason（理由），是由 for which 变化而成。

例: I don't know the reason for which he cried.

= I don't know the reason why he cried.
（我不知道他为什么哭。）

That's the reason for which he committed suicide.
= That's the reason why he committed suicide.
（那就是他自杀的原因。）

6. how 的用法：

how 只用以修饰 the way，是由 in which 变化而成。

例: That's the way in which he handled the problem. (可)
= That's how he handled the problem. (佳)
= That's the way he handled the problem. (佳)
（那就是他处理这个问题的方法。）

＊在前面第 2 要点曾提及，the way 与 how 不能并存，只能择其一。故下列说法是错误的：

That's the way how he handled the problem. (×)
I am sick of the way in which he looks at me. (可)
= I am sick of the way he looks at me. (佳)
（我讨厌他看我的样子。）

7. 关系副词使用要点：

a. 在限定修饰的定语从句中，除 where 以外，when 及 why 均可省略，而 how 则一定予以省略。

例: That's the place he was born. (×)
→ That's the place where he was born. (✓)
（那就是他出生的地方。）

I shall never forget the day when he came.
= I shall never forget the day he came. (✓)
（我永远也不会忘记他来的那天。）

That's the reason why he left. (✓)
= That's the reason he left.
（那就是他离开的原因。）

I am sick of the way how he looks at me. (×)
→ I am sick of the way he looks at me. (✓)

b. 不过 where、when、why、how 所修饰的名词若置于 be 动词之后做表语时，我们亦可省略该名词，而保留关系副词。

例: That is the place where he was born.
= That's where he was born.
（他就是在那儿出生的。）

That is the day when he'll come.

= That's when he'll come.

（那就是他要来的日子。）

That is the reason why he left.

= That's why he left.

（那就是他离开的原因。）

That is the way he did it.

= That's how he did it.

（那就是他处理的方式。）

c. where、when、why、how 亦可视为疑问代词，引导名词性从句，此时可做及物动词的宾语（见第一章）。

例: I know where he is.

vt.　名词性从句

（我知道他在哪里。）

I don't know when he'll come.

vt.　名词性从句

（我不知道他何时会来。）

I wonder why he left.

vt.　名词性从句

（我不知道他为何离去。）

I don't know how he'll do it.

vt.　名词性从句

（我不知道他将如何做此事。）

d. where 亦可做副词性连词，等于 in the place where。

例: Put it where you found it.

= Put it in the place where you found it.

= in which

（把它放在你发现它的地方。）

Where there is smoke, there is fire.

= In the place where there is smoke, there is fire.

= in which

（有烟的地方就有火——无风不起浪。——谚语）

Where he lives, life is busy.

= In the place where he lives, life is busy.

= in which

（在他住的地方，生活很忙碌。）

e. the moment (when)...　　一……就……

= the instant (when)...

= the minute (when)...

以上三个短语均视为副词性连词，之后的 when 均予省略，等于 as soon as 的意思，引导状语从句，修饰主句。

例: As soon as / The moment / The instant / The minute | he heard the sad news, he burst into tears.

（他一听到这悲伤的消息就哭起来了。）

其他类似的用法还有：

例: The time (when) he came, I was sleeping.

= When he came, I was sleeping.

（他来的时候，我正在睡觉。）

The day (when) he left，it was raining.

= When he left, it was raining.

（他离开的那一天，正下着雨。）

Every time (when) she cries, I lose my temper.

= Whenever she cries, I lose my temper.

（每次她哭，我就会发脾气。）

f. 偶尔在口语或文章中，我们会听到或见到有些人用 that 取代 when、why 当关系副词使用，只是这并非常态用法，仅列数例，供同学们参考。记住，严谨的写作不可用 that 做关系副词。

例: I remember the day that he came.

= when

（我记得他来的那天。）

Probably that's the reason that he left.

= why

（那很有可能就是他离开的原因。）

第四节 关系指示代词

1. 关系指示代词由指示代词变化而成：

which 也可做关系指示代词。顾名思义，关系指示代词就是由指示代词变化过来的关系词，亦引导定语从句修饰前面的名词。

指示代词： that （那个……）
this （这个……）
those （那些……）
these （这些……）

例: He speaks German, this language I don't understand. (×)

理由

本句无连词。

可将 this 改为关系指示代词，以连接两句。

→ He speaks German, which language I don't understand. (√，罕)
定语从句

2. 关系指示代词的功能：

和关系代词一样，“关系指示代词 + n.”可代表先行词或前面句中的部分内容，在所引导的定语从句中要做主语或宾语。

例: He is arrogant, this attitude I am sick of. (×)
→ He is arrogant, which attitude I am sick of. (√，罕)
（他很自大，那种态度我很讨厌。）

His car is blue, that color I like very much. (×)
→ His car is blue, which color I like very much. (√，罕)
（他的车是蓝色的，那种颜色我很喜欢。）

He stayed there for a week, during this time he did nothing. (×)
→ He stayed there for a week, during which time he did nothing. (√，罕)
（他在那里待了一个星期，在这段时间里他什么都没做。）

第五节 复合关系代词

1. 复合关系代词的种类：

代替人：

whoever （凡……的人）

= anybody who

whomever （凡……的人）

= anybody whom

代替人或物：

whichever （三者以上）

= any one | which / who | （同一类的任何一个……）

whichever （二者）

= either | which / who | （同一类的任何一个……）

代替物：

what = the thing(s) which （所……的东西）

whatever = anything which （……的任何东西）

由上得知，复合关系代词是由两个词类复合而成：一方面含有先行词（如 anybody、the thing、anything），一方面又含有关系代词（如 who、whom、which）。

2. whoever 的用法：

同学们在使用 whoever 做复合关系代词时，一定要注意下列步骤：

a. 先视 whoever 为两个词，即：anybody who。

b. anybody 是代词，可在主句中当做主语或宾语；who 为关系代词，引导定语从句，并在该从句中做主语。

1) 我们可先用 anybody 做主语造一个句子：

例: Anybody should be punished.

（Anybody：主语）

（任何人都应受处罚。）

再造一个以 who 为主语的定语从句：

例: who makes such a mistake

然后将 who makes such a mistake 置于 anybody 之后，即成：

Anybody who makes such a mistake should be punished.

主语 定语从句 及物动词的被动语态

= Whoever makes such a mistake should be punished.

（凡犯此错的人都应受罚。）

2) 我们再用 anybody 做宾语造一个主句：

例: I hate anybody.

宾语

（我讨厌任何人。）

再造一个以 who 为主语的定语从句：

例: who tells lies

然后将 who tells lies 置于 anybody 之后，即成：

I hate anybody who tells lies.

宾语 定语从句

= I hate whoever tells lies.

（我讨厌任何说谎的人。）

千万不可写成：

I hate whomever tells lies. (×)

> **理由**
>
> whomever 等于 anybody whom，而 whom 只能做宾语，不可能做主语，故 whom 之后不可能有动词 tells。

3. whomever 的用法：

我们已知 whomever 等于 anybody whom。因 whom 在定语从句中只能做宾语，而且此处的 anybody，也只能在主句中做宾语，因此 whomever 绝不可做主语。造句的方法如下：

a. 先造一个以 anybody 做宾语的主句：

例: Give it to anybody.

介词 宾语

（把它给任何人。）

b. 再造一个以 whom 为宾语的定语从句：

例: whom you like

c. 然后将 whom you like 置于 anybody 之后，即成：

Give it to anybody whom you like.

定语从句

= Give it to whomever you like.

（把它给任何你喜欢的人。）

4. whichever 的用法：

whichever 是指同一类的任何东西，如三本以上的书其中任何一本，或两本书的任何一本。其造句的方法则与 whoever 及 whomever 完全一样，故赖老师不再详述，只提供下例供同学们参考。

例: There are many books here. You may take | any book which / any one which | you like.

同类东西

= There are many books here. You may take whichever you like.

（这里有许多书，你可以拿任何一本你喜欢的。）

5. what 的用法：

what 是最常见的复合关系代词，也是最容易使用的一种。

a. 首先我们要了解，what 做复合关系代词时，可视为 the thing / things which，通常译成“所……的东西”。

例: What he said is true.

（他所说的话是真的。）

I am interested in what he is doing.

（我对他目前所做的事很有兴趣。）

b. 以 what 造句时，要注意下列原则：

1) 前面不可有先行词（名词）；

2) 将 what 视为 the thing / things which；

3) which 在所引导的定语从句中可做主语、宾语或在 be 动词后做表语。

例: What bothers me is that I have no time.

= The thing which bothers me is that I have no time.

主语 定语从句

（让我困扰的是我没有时间。）

本例中 what 之前无名词。what 变成 the thing which 之后，which 在所引导的定语从句中做主语，故结构正确。

例: I don't believe the words what he said. (×)

本例中，what 之前多了先行词 the words。

→ I don't believe what he said. (√)

= I don't believe the words (which) he said.

（我不相信他说的话。）

6. whatever 的用法:

a. whatever 与 whichever 很类似，不同之处为：whichever 指同一类的任何一项，而 whatever 指不同类的任何东西。例如：三辆汽车中的任何一辆要用 whichever 表示；他有汽车、房子，还收藏了许多名画，这些东西的任何一项则要用 whatever 表示。

b. what 等于 the thing / things which，译成“所……的东西”；whatever 等于 anything that（即 anything which），译成“所……的任何东西”，语气要比 what 更强。由于 whatever 的造句法与 what 完全相同，在此我们不再赘述。仅举下列数例，供同学们参考。

例: Whatever he said is true.

= Anything which he said is true.

　　主语　　定语从句

（他所说的任何话都是真的。）

I am interested in whatever he is doing.

= I am interested in anything that he is doing.

（我对他所做的任何事情都感兴趣。）

7. 加油站:

到目前为止，赖老师已为同学们介绍了所有复合关系代词的用法，法则略嫌繁多，希望同学们要耐心地阅读，你若是放弃的话，赖老师会难过的。记住，当年赖老师发愤学英语时，所吃的苦头非你所能想象。在学习英语的道路上，让我们一起互勉吧！

8. whatever 及 whoever 亦可做副词性连词:

whatever 及 whoever 亦可做副词性连词，此时就不等于 anything which 或 anybody who，而分别等于 no matter what（不论什么）或 no matter who（不论谁）。

例: Whatever he says, I don't believe him.

= No matter what he says, I don't believe him.

（不论他说什么，我都不相信他。）

Whoever does it, he should finish it by ten.

= No matter who does it, he should finish it by ten.
（不论谁去做，都应该在 10 点前完成。）

同学们要注意的是 whatever 或 whoever 做副词性连词时，所引导的状语从句与主句中间有逗号相隔。而做复合关系代词时，则无逗号相隔。
比较：

a. 复合关系代词

例：

Whatever Anything that	he says is a lie.

（他所说的任何话都是谎言。）

Whoever Anybody who	makes the mistake should be punished.

（任何犯下这样错误的人都应受处罚。）

b. 副词性连词

例：

Whatever No matter what	he says, it is a lie.

（不论他说什么，那都是谎话。）

Whoever No matter who	makes the mistake, he should be punished.

（不论谁犯这样的错，都应受处罚。）

9. however 有两种词性：
一为连接性副词，译成“然而”；一为副词性连词，译成“无论如何”，用法如下：

a. 连接性副词
由于在本书第二章中，我们已叙述其用法，因此在此仅举例让同学们复习一下。
例：He is nice; however, I don't like him.
= He is nice. However, I don't like him.
= He is nice. I, however, don't like him.
（他人很好，然而我却不喜欢他。）

b. 副词性连词
此时 however 等于 no matter how。
使用 however 造句时，注意下列步骤：
1) 先将 however 转换为 no matter how；

2) 由于 how 为副词，可修饰形容词或副词，故预先造一个含有形容词或副词的句子，以便稍后由 how 修饰：

例: He is nice.
adj.

He works hard.
adv.

3) 再将上例置于 no matter how 之后，即成：

No matter how he is nice...
adv. adj.

No matter how he works hard...
adv. adv.

4) 最后将句中的形容词或副词移位到 how 之后，形成状语从句，再接主句，即完成整个句子。

例: No matter how nice he is, I don't like him.
adv. adj.

= However nice he is, I don't like him.
（不论他有多好，我都不喜欢他。）

No matter how hard he works, I don't respect him.
adv. adv.

= However hard he works, I don't respect him.
（不论他工作有多努力，我都不会尊敬他。）

> **注意**
> however 或 no matter how 亦可修饰动词，此时 however 或 no matter how 之后直接接主语即可。

10. whether 的用法：

表“不论是否”时，只需 whether 即可，不可使用 no matter whether。whether 本身就可做副词性连词，引导状语从句，以逗号与主句相隔。

例: No matter whether he is rich... (×)

→ Whether he is rich (or not), Jane will marry him. (✓)
（不论他是否富有，简都将嫁给他。）

别忘了，whether 亦可用以引导名词性从句（参阅第一章）。

比较下列之不同：

a. 引导状语从句

例: Whether he is rich (or not) , it doesn't matter. (有逗号相隔)

状语从句 主句

（他是否富有，那都没关系。）

b. 引导名词性从句

例: Whether he is rich (or not) doesn't matter.（无逗号相隔）

名词性从句做主语 动词

= It doesn't matter whether he is rich (or not).

（他是否富有都没关系。）

11. however 的特殊句型：

however 做副词性连词所引导的状语从句中，主语之后若含有“be 动词 + 形容词”时，同学们要特别注意下列结构变化：

例: However poor he is, he doesn't want anyone to help him.

adj.

= However poor he may be, he doesn't want...

= Be he ever so poor, he doesn't want... (罕)

（不论多穷，他都不会要求别人的帮助。）

第六节　准关系代词

1. 准关系代词的种类:

准关系代词只有三个：than、as、but。

例: I have more money than you (do).
（我比你有钱。）

He has as much money as I (do).
（他的钱和我的一样多。）

There is nothing but he knows.
（没有他不知道的事情。）

同学们在看到上列三个例子之后，一定感到一头雾水，不知赖老师在说什么。别急，且听赖老师慢慢道来。

2. 准关系代词形成的条件:

than、as、but 做准关系代词时，前面必须有个先行词（名词）。在上例中，我们见到 than 之前有名词 money，as 之前亦有名词 money，而 but 之前则有代词 nothing。这就告诉我们一个重要的概念：than、 as、but 之前若有名词，就可形成准关系代词。

3. than 做准关系代词的用法:

than 之前若有名词时，than 就等于：“than + the + 前面的名词 + 关系代词（who、whom、which）”。换言之，我们可将 than 视为关系代词，在所引导的从句中要做主语、宾语或 be 动词后的表语。

a. 主语:

例: I have more money than is needed.
　　　　　　　　　n.　准关代
（我现有的钱比所需的要多。）

＊此处 than 等于 than the money which，which 做主语，之后有动词 is needed。

More guests than were invited came.
　　　　n.　准关代　　　　　动词
（来的客人比受邀请的多。）

＊此处 than 等于 than the guests who，who 做主语，之后有动词 were invited。整句中 More guests 是主语，came 是其动词，中间的 than were invited 可视作定语从句，修饰 More guests。

There are more books than are needed.
　　　　　　　复数名词　复数动词
（这里的书超过需求量。）

＊此处 than 等于 than the books which，which 做主语，之后有动词 are needed。

明白了这个道理之后，我们以后千万不要再造这样的句子：

I have more money than it is needed. (×)

本例中多了主语 it，使得 than 无法再做主语，故应将 it 删除，此句方正确。

b. 宾语：

than 做宾语的用法，是我们常见的一种句型。只是我们已习以为常，而未注意 than 是个准关系代词。

例: I have more money than he needs.

n.　准关代　vt.

（我现有的钱比他所需要的多。）

＊本句中的 than 即等于 than the money which，which 做 needs 的宾语。

I have more books than you have. (劣)

n.　准关代　vt.

（我的书比你的多。）

＊本句中的 than 即等于 than the books which，which 做 have 的宾语。但 than you have 中的 have 与前面的 I have 中的 have 动词相同，故为避免重复，第二个 have 就改成 do，并可省略，而成：

I have more books than you do. (佳)

或将 do 省略，改写如下：

I have more books than you.

c. be 动词后的表语：

例: He is a better student than you are.

n.　准关代　be 动词

（他是个好学生，比你还好。）

＊than 即等于 than the student that，that 实际是 be 动词 are 后之表语。此处的 that 原应为 who，但关系代词做 be 动词之后的表语时，均用 that 取代。

且上句中的 are 与句首主语 He 之后的 is 同属 be 动词，亦可省略，故上句亦可改写成：

He is a better student than you.

4. as 做准关系代词的用法：

如同 than 一样，as 之前若有名词时，as 就等于"as + the + 前面的名词 + 关系代词（who、whom、which）"。换言之，我们可将 as 视为关系代词，在所引导的从句中要做主语、宾语或 be 动词后的表语。只是 as 若做准关系代词时，只用于下列短语中：

such + n. + as...　　（像……那样的……）
the same + n. + as...　　（和……相同的……）
as + adj. + n. + as...　　（和……一样的……）

a. such + n. + as...

1) 主语：

例:I don't like such a man as tells lies.
n.　准关代

（我不喜欢那种会说谎的人。）

＊本句中的 as 即等于 as the man who，关系代词 who 在其后的定语从句中做主语，之后有动词 tells lies。

2) 宾语：

例:I respect such an honest man as you described.
n. 准关代　vt.

（我尊敬像你描述的这样诚实的人。）

＊此处的 as 即等于 as the man whom，关系代词 whom 做及物动词 described 之宾语。

3) be 动词后的表语（通常省略 be 动词）：

例:In our company there is not such a man as David (is).
n.　准关代

（我们公司里没有像大卫这样的人。）

＊本句中 as 即等于 as the man that，that 做 be 动词 (is) 后之表语。

Such a lazy student as John (is) will get nowhere.
n.　准关代

（像约翰这么懒的学生不会有什么成就的。）

＊本句中 as 即等于 as the student that，that 做 be 动词 (is) 后之表语。

b. the same + n. + as...

1) 主语：

例:I have the same book as is laid on the desk.
n.　准关代

（我有一本书，和放在桌上那本一样。）

＊此处 as 即等于 as the book which，关系代词 which 做主语。

2) 宾语：

例:I have the same dictionary as you bought yesterday.

n. 准关代

（我有一本词典，和你昨天买的一样。）

＊本句中 as 即等于 as the dictionary which，关系代词 which 做及物动词 bought 之宾语。

3) be 动词后的表语（通常省略 be 动词）：

例:I have the same dictionary as this one (is).

n. 准关代

（我有一本词典，和这本一样。）

＊本句中 as 即等于 as the dictionary that，关系代词 that 做（is）后之表语。

c. as + adj. + n. + as...

1) 主语：

例:He is as diligent a man as ever lived.

n. 准关代

（他是有史以来最勤勉的人。）

＊此处的 as 即等于 as any man that，关系代词 that 做主语，ever lived 为动词。

2) 宾语：

例:I have as good a dictionary as you (do).

n. 准关代

（我有一本和你的一样好的词典。）

＊此处的 as 即等于 as the dictionary which，关系代词做 (do) 之宾语；此处的 do 等于及物动词 have（有）。

3) be 动词后的表语（通常省略 be 动词）：

例:He is as good a man as John (is).

n. 准关代

（他是个和约翰一样好的人。）

＊as 即等于 as the man that，关系代词 that 做 (is) 后之表语。

5. "such + n." 之后绝不可用 like（像）加以修饰：

例:Such a man like him is bad. (×)

→ Such a man as he (is) is bad. (✓)

（像他这样的人不好。）

6. 比较 "the same...as..." 与 "the same...that..." 的不同：

the same...as... 和……相同的……（两个人或物）
准关代

the same...that... 就是同一个……（一个人或物）
关代

理由

I have the same book as he is reading. (两本书)
（我有一本书，与他正在看的那一本相同。）
I borrowed the same book which he did last week. (×)
→I borrowed the same book that he borrowed last week. (√) (同一本书)
（我借了一本书，就是他上周借的那一本。）

7. as 可代替主句：

单独使用 as 时，as 亦可做关系代词，等于 which，用以代替整个主句。

例: He is nice, which is known to us.

= He is nice, as is known to us.

（他人很好，我们都知道。）

He works hard, which we all know.

= He works hard, as we all know.

（他很努力，我们都知道。）

但使用 as 取代 which 时，要注意下列要点：

a. as 引导的从句可置于主句的前后，而 which 引导的从句则只能置于主句之后。

例: He is nice, which we all know.
主句
= He is nice, as we all know.
= As we all know, he is nice.
→ Which we all know, he is nice. (×)

b. as + be + p.p. 时，be 动词可以省略。

例: He is nice, which was mentioned before.

p.p.

= He is nice, as was mentioned before.

p.p.

= He is nice, as mentioned before.

（如前所述，他人很好。）

c. 注意下列特殊例子：

例: He was drunk, as usual.

（和往常一样，他又醉了。）

本句实由下列句子化简而成：

He was drunk, as is usual with him.（as 等于 which）

例: His conditions are as follows.

（他的条件如下。）

本句实由下列句子化简而成：

His conditions are as what follows.

第二例中，不管前面的名词是单数或复数、动词是何种时态，as 后的动词一定要用 follows。

例: He listed the names as follows.

（他列出的名单如下。）

8. 只能与单数可数名词使用的结构：

在第四项中，赖老师造了下列几个短语：
as good a student as...
as diligent a man as...

这两个短语告诉我们一个重要的讯息，即：

下列四组短语之中，若置名词时，只能置单数可数名词。

so...that...	（如此……以至……）
as...as...	（和……一样地……；第一个 as 为副词，译成“一样地”，第二个 as 为连词，译成“和”）
too...to...	（太……而不……）
how...	（多么地……）

例: He is so good a boy that I like him.
（他是个这么好的男孩，因此我喜欢他。）

He is as handsome a man as Peter (is).
（他是个英俊的人，和彼得一样。）

He is too old a man to do it.
（他太老了，不能做这事。）

How great a man he is!
（他这个人真伟大！）

a. 如果同学们不太容易记这四组短语的话，赖老师发明了一个口诀，帮你来记：
书呆子（so...that...）、阿西（as...as...）和土土（too...to...）一块儿说一声“好”（how...）。

b. 但同学们会问，为什么不可写成下列的句子呢？

例: He is a so good student that I like him. (×)
He is an as handsome man as Peter. (×)
He is a too old man to do it. (×)
How a great man he is! (×)

赖老师解答如下：

so（如此地）、as（一样地）、too（太）、how（多么地）均为副词，故之后应置形容词以供修饰，然后再置不定冠词（a 或 an）及单数名词。

c. 此类“书呆子”、“阿西”和“土土”一块儿说声“好”四种结构中，不可置复数名词或不可数名词：

1) so...that...

例: This is so good music that I love it. (×)
不可数名词
They are so good students that I like them. (×)
复数名词

> **注意**
> 但使用“such...that...”时则可置任何名词。

例: This is such good music that I love it. (√)
不可数名词
（这音乐那么动听，因此我很喜欢它。）
They are such good students that I like them. (√)
复数名词
（他们是那么好的学生，因此我很喜欢他们。）

He is such a good student that I like him. (√)

单数可数名词

（他是那么好的学生，因此我很喜欢他。）

2) as...as...

例: This is as good music as that. (×)

不可数名词

They are as good students as those. (×)

复数名词

改正：

This music is as good as that. (√)

（这音乐和那音乐同样动听。）

These students are as good as those. (√)

（这些学生和那些学生一样好。）

3) too...to...

例: This is too difficult work to do. (×)

不可数名词

They are too difficult problems to handle. (×)

复数名词

改正：

This work is too difficult to do. (√)

= This is too difficult a job to do. (√)

单数可数名词

（这工作太难而无法做。）

These problems are too difficult to handle. (√)

（这些问题困难得无法处理。）

4) how...

例: How good music it is! (×)

不可数名词

How good students they are! (×)

复数名词

注意

但 what 之后则可接任何名词。

例: What good music it is! (√)
不可数名词
（这音乐棒极了！）

What good students they are! (√)
复数名词
（他们真是好学生！）

What a good student he is! (√)
单数可数名词
（他真是好学生！）

9. 数量词不受限：

只有“so...that.../ as...as.../ too...to.../ how...”与下列表数量的形容词连用时，可不必与单数可数名词连用。

many（许多的） few（少量的）	+ 复数名词
much（许多的） little（少量的）	+ 不可数名词

例: He has so many things to do that he can't go picnicking with us.
（他有这么多事情要做，因此不能和我们一起去野餐。）

There is so much work to do that I don't think I can go to bed early.
（有这么多工作要做，我想我无法早睡。）

He has too little money left to buy a car.
（他剩下的钱太少，无法买车。）

I have as much money as he (does).
（我的钱和他的一样多。）

I don't know how much time you can give me for that job.
（我不知道你能给我多少时间做那项工作。）

10. 准关系代词 but 的用法：

but 做准关系代词时，只用于“no + 名词”之后；此时 but 等于 who（whom、which）...not。

句型如下：

There is no + 名词 + who / whom / which / (that) ...not

= There is no + 名词 + but...

a. 定语从句中有 be 动词时，保留该 be 动词。

例: There is no one who is not interested in it.

= There is no one but is interested in it.

（没有人不对它感兴趣。）

There is nothing which he is not fond of.

= There is nothing but he is fond of.

（没有什么东西是他不喜欢的。）

b. 定语从句中有一般时助动词（can、will、may、should...）时，保留该助动词。

例: There is nothing that he cannot do.

= There is nothing but he can do.

（没有什么事情是他做不来的。）

c. 定语从句中有 do、does、did 等助动词时，要先去掉 do、does、did，再依时态、人称将之后的动词还原。

例: There is no book which he doesn't like to read.

= There is no book but he likes to read.

（没有他不爱看的书。）

There was no one whom he didn't hate.

= There was no one but he hated.

（没有什么人是他不讨厌的。）

EXERCISE

I. 请选出一个正确的答案：

1. 1.The road _____ leads to the house is steep.
   (A) that　(B) who　(C) where　(D) whose
2. The artist _____ picture won the award is my uncle.
   (A) that　(B) who　(C) which　(D) whose
3. We visited the place _____ Lincoln was born.
   (A) which　(B) that　(C) where　(D) when
4. The house _____ is located on top of the hill belongs to me.
   (A) which　(B) when　(C) where　(D) whose
5. This is the year _____ our sales will reach the highest point.
   (A) which　(B) when　(C) how　(D) whose
6. Can you tell me the reason _____ you are always late?
   (A) which　(B) that　(C) why　(D) how
7. He is the man _____ factory I purchased.
   (A) that　(B) who　(C) where　(D) whose
8. This is _____ I recommend you to do.
   (A) what　(B) that　(C) which　(D) whatever
9. Where can I buy the same dictionary _____ you have?
   (A) that　(B) as　(C) which　(D) what
10. Give the book to _____ needs it.
    (A) who　(B) whom　(C) whoever　(D) whomever
11. The book _____ the cover is broken is mine.
    (A) whose　(B) that　(C) of which　(D) which
12. I like _____ you do for me.
    (A) who　(B) which　(C) that　(D) whatever

13. John is not such a man _____ would kill anyone.
(A) that (B) as (C) who (D) whom

14. There is nobody _____ has his faults.
(A) who (B) that doesn't (C) but (D) not

15. He has a larger vocabulary _____ I do.
(A) as (B) like (C) that (D) than

16. It is education that makes us _____ we are.
(A) who (B) whom (C) what (D) where

17. Was it you or the wind _____ shut the door?
(A) which (B) who (C) that (D) what

18. The retiring teacher made a speech _____ she thanked the class for the gift.
(A) which (B) what (C) that (D) in which

19. That is the most beautiful music _____ I have ever heard.
(A) that (B) which (C) what (D) as

20. On the bus I saw a student _____ I thought was your brother.
(A) whom (B) who (C) what (D) whomever

21. President Reagan greeted Carl Lewis _____ four gold medals at the Summer Olympics.
(A) who was the winner of (B) by winning
(C) , who was the winner of (D) though he was the winner of

22. Although he was listening, he didn't hear _____ because there was so much noise.
(A) what said (B) what did she say
(C) what she was saying (D) what said she

23. We are given just so much food _____ will keep us alive.
(A) as (B) that (C) what (D) but

24. The rich woman offered a reward to _____ find her lost car.
(A) who could (B) who would
(C) whoever could (D) whomever might

25. The boy ______ I believed to be honest deceived me.
(A) whom (B) what (C) who (D) which

II. 请选出错误的画线部分：

26. The electronics industry requires skills and technology that has been
(A) (B)
developing for decades in the industrially advanced countries.
(C) (D)

27. The detectives were finally able to arrest the man who his finger prints
(A) (B) (C)
had been found on the table.
(D)

28. Edgar Allan Poe is the classic example of a man of genius which never
(A) (B)
managed to adjust to the world.
(C) (D)

29. The biggest single hobby in America, the one that Americans spend most
(A) (B) (C)
time, energy and money, is gardening.
(D)

30. The show must win the approval of the critics and audience in New York,
(A) (B)
which it opens tonight at the Palace Theater.
(C) (D)

标准答案

1. (A)	2. (D)	3. (C)	4. (A)	5. (B)	6. (C)	7. (D)	8. (A)	9. (B)	10. (C)
11. (C)	12. (D)	13. (B)	14. (C)	15. (D)	16. (C)	17. (C)	18. (D)	19. (A)	20. (B)
21. (C)	22. (C)	23. (A)	24. (C)	25. (A)	26. (B)	27. (C)	28. (B)	29. (B)	30. (C)

习题解说

1. that 做关系代词，为定语从句中的主语。
2. whose 为关系代词的所有格，之后可接名词 picture。
3. where 为关系副词，引导定语从句，修饰 place。
4. which 为关系代词，表事物。
5. when 为关系副词，引导定语从句，修饰 the year。
6. why 为关系副词，引导定语从句，修饰 the reason。
7. whose 为关系代词的所有格，之后可接名词 factory。
8. what = the thing that，为复合关系代词。
9. 空格前有 the same，故空格内应置入准关系代词 as，as 同时做句尾及物动词 have 的宾语。
10. whoever 和 whomever 均为复合关系代词，但在本句中因为做 needs 的主语，故用主格 whoever，不可用 whomever; whoever = anyone who。
11. of which the cover = whose cover
12. whatever 为复合关系代词，相当于 anything that。
13. 空格前有 such，故空格内应置入准关系代词 as，此处 as 等于 as the man who。
14. There is nobody but has his faults.
 = There is nobody that does not have his faults.
15. 空格前有比较级形容词，故空格内应置入 than。
16. what = the thing that，为复合关系代词。
17. 当先行词包括人与物时，关系代词用 that。
18. 关系代词无法做该定语从句中的主语或宾语时，之前必须加介词。
19. 先行词之前有最高级形容词时，关系代词必须用 that。
20. 本题的关系代词为 was 的主语，I thought 只是插入语，故选 (B) who。
21. Carl Lewis 为专有名词，故不可用限制性定语从句修饰。
22. what she was saying 为名词性从句，做 hear 的宾语。
23. so much...as 中的 as 为准关系代词，做 keep 的主语，as 等于 as the food which。
24. whoever could 等于 anyone who could。
25. whom 在本题中为 believed 的宾语，之后的 to be honest 为宾语补语。
26. 本题中 that 的先行词为 skills and technology，故从句中的 has been 应改为 have been。

27. who his 应改为关系代词所有格 whose。
28. which 表示事物，应改为 who，才可代替 a man of genius。
29. 本题中的 that 无法在定语从句中做主语或宾语，故须改为 on which。

spend	时间 金钱 精力	+ on sth

30. which 应改为关系副词 where，引导定语从句，修饰 New York。

A Quick Note

第四章 非谓语动词

概 述

非谓语动词均由动词变化而成，有人称之为准动词。一共有三种：

1. 不定式：

原形不定式： study

置 to 的不定式： to study

例: You should help him study the lesson.

原形不定式（study）

（你应帮他学这一课。）

He refused to study the lesson.

（他拒绝学这一课。）

2. 分词：

现在分词： studying

过去分词： studied

例: He is studying.

现在分词（studying）

（他正在读书。）

The problem should be very carefully studied.

过去分词（studied）

（这个问题应仔细研究。）

3. 动名词：

例: He enjoys studying.

（他喜欢读书。）

这些词类在句中扮演多种角色，有的可做名词，有的可做形容词，有的可做副词。由于有这些非谓语动词的介入，使得英语生色不少。就语言学的观点而言，非谓语动词是个很值得研究的主题。而对同学们来说，非谓语动词扮演的角色太多、太复杂，学习起来稍嫌困难。但别担心，有赖老师在你身旁，一定会让你了解其中的奥妙，使你驾轻就熟。有人说，我们若清楚非谓语动词的用法，英语就懂了百分之九十，这样的说法一点儿也不为过。

第一节　不定式

1. 不定式的种类:

下例一为原形不定式（即原形动词），一为“to + 原形动词”。我们通常说的不定式是指第二种。

例: I will do it if I have time.

原形不定式（原形动词）

（我若有空就会做这件事。）

I want to do it if I have time.

to + 原形动词（俗称的不定式）

（我若有空就要做这件事。）

由于原形动词多置于助动词 will、can、may、should、ought to 等之后，用法比较简单，赖老师打算在本节后段再介绍。我们且先注意“to + 原形动词”的用法。

2. 不定式的功能:

“to + 原形动词”所形成的不定式有三种功能:

a. 不定式当名词用

例: To take a trip around the world has been my dream.

名词（做主语）

（环游世界一直是我的梦想。）

b. 不定式当形容词用

例: I have something to do.

形容词（修饰代词 something）

（我有事要做。）

c. 不定式当副词用

例: I came to see her.

副词（修饰动词 came）

（我来看她。）

3. 名词不定式的用法:

“to + 原形动词”所形成的名词不定式可当做名词看待。我们知道名词在句中可做主语、宾语及 be 动词后的表语，同理，名词不定式亦有完全相同的功能。

a. 名词不定式做主语:

用以表示一种意愿或未完成的事。

例: To marry her is my goal.
主语 动词
（娶她是我的目标。）

To win the championship is my ambition.
（赢得冠军是我的雄心。）

使用名词不定式做主语时，应注意下列事项：

1) 名词不定式做主语时，be 动词之后的表语若为名词，一定为表意愿、目的、企图等名词，以表某意愿或尚未完成的事。常用的此类名词为：
plan（计划）、purpose（目的）、attempt（企图）、goal（目标）、aim（目的）、ambition（雄心）、dream（梦想）、ideal（理想）、wish（希望）、hope（希望）、decision（决定）、determination（决定）、proposal（建议）。

例: To marry Jane is my dream.
（娶简是我的梦想。）

2) 名词不定式做主语时，可用形式主语 It 取代，而且是较常用的结构。句型为：
It is...to V

例: It is my goal to marry her.
（娶她是我的目标。）

It has long been my dream to travel around the world.
（长久以来环游世界一直是我的梦想。）

It is my ambition to win the championship.
（我的野心就是要赢得冠军。）

I know what to be in debt is. (可)
表语 主语 be 动词

→ I know what it is to be in debt. (佳)
名词性从句，作 know 的宾语
（我知道负债是怎么回事。）

It is difficult to learn English.
（学英语很难。）

b. 名词不定式做及物动词的宾语：

例: I want to see him.
vt. o.
（我要看他。）

He intends to try it.
vt. o.
（他有意要试一试。）

注意:

使用名词不定式做宾语时，应注意下列事项:

1) 名词不定式绝不可能做介词的宾语。

例: I am interested in to climb mountains. (×)
介

→ I am interested in climbing mountains. (√)
介 动名词

（我对爬山感兴趣。）

2) 名词不定式做及物动词的宾语时，该及物动词均为表意愿、企图的动词。常用的有下列几个:

want（要）、wish（希望）、hope（希望）、desire（欲望）、intend（意欲）、try（设法）、determine（决心）、decide（决定）、attempt（企图）、endeavor（努力）、like（喜欢）、love（爱）、expect（盼望）。

例: I want to take a trip abroad next year.
（明年我要出国旅游。）

He intended to visit John that morning.
（那天早上他想去探访约翰。）

3) 翻译下列中文时，注意表"想要"的动词:

译: 我想要买一辆车。

I think to buy a car. (×)

理由

think 只用以表示"想到某一件事"，而非表示意愿，通常用 that 引导的名词性从句做宾语。

例: I think that he is great. (√)
（我想他很了不起。）

"think of + 名词"，亦表"想到"。

例: I thought of Mary a while ago.
名词
（不久前我曾想到玛丽。）

I have been thinking of buying a car.
现在完成进行时　动名词
= I have been considering buying a car.
现在完成进行时　动名词
（我一直在考虑买辆车。）

故凡表“想要”时，均使用表“意愿”的动词，以名词不定式做其宾语。上列译句，应为：

例: I want / desire / intend / expect to buy a car. (✓)

另外，anticipate 及 expect 均表“期望”，只是 anticipate 之后接动名词做宾语，而 expect 之后则接名词不定式做宾语。

例: I anticipate seeing you agin.
= I expect to see you again.
（我期盼能再次与你见面。）

4) 名词不定式不可直接做不完全及物动词的宾语，一定要以形式宾语 it 代替，加了宾语补语之后，再接名词不定式。句型如下：

S + find（发现）/ think（认为）/ believe（相信）/ consider（认为）/ deem（认为）/ feel（觉得）/ make（使） + it + 名词/形容词（做补语）+ 名词不定式
it：形式宾语；名词不定式：真正宾语

例: I find to climb mountains interesting. (×)

理由
名词不定式不得直接做不完全及物动词的宾语，一定要用形式宾语 it 代替。

改正: I find it interesting to climb mountains. (✓)
（我发现爬山很有趣。）

同理: I think it necessary for him to do it.

（我认为他有必要做此事。）

I deem it an honor for me to give this speech.

（我认为能在这里演讲是我的荣幸。）

I thought it better not to go there alone.

（我认为最好不要单独去那里。）

I make it a rule to get up early.

（我习惯早起。）

> **注意**
>
> "make it a rule to V" 表"把……当做常例/习惯于……"，不可写成"make a rule to V"。
>
> I make a rule to get up early. (×)

c. 名词不定式在 be 动词后做表语:

此时主语均为表"意愿"、"企图"的名词。

例: My plan is to see him.

（我的计划是去看他。）

His only wish at present is to sleep.

（他此刻唯一的愿望就是去睡觉。）

His goal is simply to become a teacher.

（他的目标只是要当个老师。）

His resolution is to be a scientist.

（他的志愿是当一名科学家。）

注意:

使用名词不定式做表语时，应注意下列事项:

1) 名词不定式可做主语，亦可作 be 动词之后的表语，形成 A is B 的概念。

例: To see is to believe.

= Seeing is believing.

动名词　　动名词

（眼见为实。）

To love her this way is to worship her.

= Loving her this way is worshipping her.

动名词短语　　　　动名词短语

（这样爱她等于崇拜她。）

2) 下列句型中，be 动词之后的 to 可省略，改接原形动词做表语。

例: All you have to do is (to) take a good rest.

（你所要做的是好好休息。）

All I can do is (to) wait.

（我所能做的就是等待。）

What you should do is simply (to) apologize to him.

（你应做的事就是向他道歉。）

All I did yesterday was (to) eat and sleep.

（我昨天做的事就是吃和睡。）

4. 形容词不定式的用法:

此类不定式一定采用后位修饰，也就是置于名词的后面，做形容词用，修饰其前的名词。

例: I have some work to do.

名词

（我有些工作要做。）

There is one thing to be done.

名词

（有件事要做。）

I have no desire to get into an argument with him.

名词

（我无意与他起争执。）

注意:

使用形容词不定式时，应注意下列事项:

a. 形容词不定式可以等于关系代词做主语所引导的定语从句。

例: I have no friend to advise me.

= I have no friend who can advise me.

（我没有朋友可以给我忠告。）

There is one thing to be done.
= There is one thing which should be done.
（有件事要做。）

b. 形容词不定式也可等于关系代词做宾语所引导的定语从句。

例: I want something to eat.
= I want something which I can eat. (which 做 eat 的宾语)
（我要点吃的东西。）

I have something to do.
= I have something which I must do. (which 做 do 的宾语)
（我有事要做。）

There are many sights to see here.
= There are many sights which we can see here. (which 做 see 的宾语)
（这里有许多风景可看。）

I have no one to talk to.
= I have no one whom I can talk to. (whom 做介词 to 的宾语)
（我没有人可以交谈。）

注意:

1) 此类句型中，被修饰的名词一定要做不定式短语中动词的宾语，否则就要做介词的宾语。

例: He is a nice man to work. (×)

> 理由
>
> work 做“工作”解时为不及物动词，故本句应置介词 with 或 for，使 man 成为其宾语。

改正: He is a nice man to work for. (√)
（他人很好，可以替他工作。）
或: He is a nice man to work with. (√)
（他人不错，可以与他共事。）

我们亦可将上列句中介词 for 或 with 置于不定式前，与关系代词的宾格 whom 连用，但不及上两句通顺。即：

He is a nice man for whom to work. (劣)
或: He is a nice man with whom to work. (劣)

例: Give me a chair to sit. (×)

理由

sit 通常为不及物动词，故其后要置介词 in，使 a chair 做其宾语。

改正：Give me a chair to sit in.
或：　Give me a chair in which to sit.

2) 此类句型中，不定式短语多为主动语态，但有时亦可改为被动语态，以强调被动的概念。

例：There is something to do.
= There is something that we must do.
主动语态
（有一件事我们得去做。）

There is something to be done.
= There is something that should be done (by us).
被动语态
（有一件事得由我们做。）

以上两例的意思相同，所差的只是主动与被动语态的不同。不过有时，被动语态却比主动语态佳。

例：His article leaves nothing to be desired.
= His article leaves nothing that can be desired (by anyone).
（他的文章完美无缺——没有什么可以挑剔的。）

c. be 动词之后以"to + 原形动词"所形成的表语，可视为名词不定式，但有时亦可视为形容词不定式。

例：His plan is to build a house here.
名词不定式
（他的计划是在此建栋房子。）

He is to build a house here.
形容词不定式
（他将在此建一栋房子。）

第一例中，to build a house here 等于 his plan。两个词类可以相互调换，即：

例：To build a house here is his plan. (✓)
主语
（在这儿盖栋房子是他的计划。）

换言之，该不定式短语亦可用来当主语，故有名词的特性，因此视为名词不定式。第二例中，to build a house here 不等于 he，两个词类不能相互调换，即：
To build a house here is he. (×)
换言之，盖房子是动作，he 是人，两者不等，因此不能调换。to build a house here 只能作 be 动词之后的表语，视为形容词不定式，修饰主语 He。

d. be 动词之后加的形容词不定式有下列意义：

1) 主动形式：

a) 表将来（= will）

例：He is to come tomorrow.
= He is going to come tomorrow.
= He will come tomorrow.
（他明天会来。）

b) 表义务（= should）

例：You are to do it.
= You should do it.
（你应做它。）
What am I to do?
=What should I do?
（我该怎么办？）

2) 被动形式：

a) 表当然（= should）

例：Such a lazy man is to be fired.
= Such a lazy man should be fired.
（这么懒的人应被解雇。）

b) 表可能（= can）

例：My hat was nowhere to be found.
= My hat could not be found anywhere.
（我的帽子找不到了。）

5. 副词不定式的用法：

该不定式可用以修饰动词、形容词或副词，我们且分项讲解如下：

a. 修饰动词：

副词不定式修饰动词时，一定置于该动词之后。

例: He came to see me.
vi.
（他来看我。）

He has agreed to do it.
vi.
（他已同意做那件事。）

He sang a song to please her.
vt.
（他唱首歌以取悦她。）

He tends to lie.
vi.
（他爱说谎。）

You'll soon get to know him.
vi.
（你很快就会了解他。）

b. 修饰形容词:

副词不定式修饰形容词，一定置于该形容词之后。

例: He is able to handle the problem.
adj.
（他能处理这个问题。）

He is apt to lie.
adj.
= He tends to lie.
（他爱说谎。）

This book is good to read.
adj.
（这本书很好，值得一读。）

c. 修饰副词：

副词不定式修饰副词时，一定置于该副词之后。

例: He is old enough to go swimming alone.

adv.

（他长大了，足以单独去游泳了。）

He is too old to swim.

adv.

（他老得不能游泳了。）

注意:

使用副词不定式时，应注意下列事项:

a. 副词不定式修饰动词时，多半表示目的，此时该副词不定式亦同时修饰含该动词的整个句子。

例: He sang a song to please her.

vt.

→ He sang a song to please her.

整个句子

He came to see me.

vi.

→ He came to see me.

整个句子

He rushed all the way here to catch the train.

vi.

→ He rushed all the way here to catch the train.

整个句子

（他一路赶来以便赶上火车。）

＊上列句中，all the way（一路），以及 here 均为副词，亦修饰 rushed。

注意:

1) 表“目的”的副词不定式，通常置于动词之后，但亦可移位至主语之前，以逗号相隔。

例: He sang a song to please her.

= To please her, he sang a song.

（为了取悦她，他唱了一首歌。）

You should work very hard to win the award.

= To win the award, you should work very hard.

（为了赢得那个奖，你应该努力奋斗。）

2) 副词不定式移位至主语之前时，一方面保有其副词特性，仍修饰句中动词或整个句子；但亦兼有形容词的功能，修饰句中主语，该主语通常是表“人”的名词或代词。

例: To please her, he sang a song.

副词不定式　　整个句子

→ To please her, he sang a song.

形容词不定式　主语

因此，同学们要切记下面这个概念：

不定式若出现在主语之前，一定具有形容词的功能，以修饰该主语。但这种修饰必须是合理的修饰，换言之，该不定式所表的动作，必须是它所修饰的主语的动作，否则就造成“不连接修饰”（dangling modification）的错误。故此类主语通常是表“人”的名词或代词。

例: To please her, he sang a song. (✓)

人

理由:

he 是人，有 please her（使她高兴）的能力。

例: To please her, a song was sung. (×)

物

理由:

a song 是物，是个无思想的东西，故无 please her 的能力。

例: To win the award, hard work is needed by Ed. (×)

物

→ To win the award, Ed should work hard. (✓)

人

注意:

hard work 是名词，表“勤奋”，但是个无思想的抽象名词，故无 win the award 的能力。

b. 副词不定式置于动词之后，表“目的”时，绝不可以逗号相隔。

例: He sang a song, to please her. (×)

→ He sang a song to please her. (✓)

c. 表“目的”的副词不定式亦可被下列短语取代：

例: He sang a song to please her.

= He sang a song | in order to please her.
so as to please her.
with an eye to pleasing her.
with a view to pleasing her. |

（他唱了首歌以取悦她。）

注意:

in order 及 so as 之后的 to 为不定式，之后接原形动词；with an eye 及 with a view 之后的 to 为介词，之后接动名词。

6. 独立不定式：

有些不定式只用以修饰整个主句，而不修饰句中的主语或副词，此类不定式就称为独立不定式。使用时通常置于句首（偶有插入句中的独立不定式），不必考虑主语是人或是物。

例: To tell the truth, I don't like him.

独立不定式 整个主句

（老实说，我不喜欢他。）

To be frank with you, he is good-for-nothing.

独立不定式 整个主句

（老实对你说，他一无是处。）

To do him justice, he has done his best.
独立不定式　整个主句
(平心而论，他已尽力了。)

To make matters worse, it began to rain.
独立不定式　整个主句
(更糟的是，开始下雨了。)

He is nice, to be sure, but I don't like him.
整个主句　独立不定式
(他人很好，这是可以肯定的，但是我不喜欢他。)

He is, so to speak, a rascal.
独立不定式
(他可以说是个小混混。)

*so to speak 表"可以这么说"，使用时一定插入在 be 动词及名词之间。

He knows French, not to mention English.
独立不定式
(他懂法语，更别说是英语了。)

7. 疑问词 + 不定式 = 名词短语：

a. 形态：

where to go	去哪里
when to do it	何时做那件事
how to swim	如何游泳
what to do	做什么
which to buy	买哪一个
whom to see	去看谁

注意:

where、when、how 均为疑问副词，不能做其后不定式中原形动词或介词的宾语。而 what、which、whom 则为疑问代词，一定要做其后不定式中原形动词或介词的宾语。故：

how to do (×)
adv.　vt.

理由:

do 为及物动词，how 是副词，不能做 do 的宾语。

how to do it (√)

adv. vt. o.

what to do (√)

n. vt.

whom to do it (×)

n. vt. o.

理由:

do 为及物动词，已有宾语 it，而此处 do 又非授予动词，不可能有双宾语，故 whom 无法再做其宾语。

whom to do it with (√)

prep.

（和谁一起做此事）

理由:

whom 可做介词 with 的宾语。

b. 功能：

名词短语等于名词，故在句中可做主语、宾语或在 be 动词后做表语。

1) 主语：

例: What to do was the question.

主语

（问题是做什么。）

2) 宾语：

例: He is learning how to do it.

及物动词 宾语

（他正在学如何做这事。）

We have no idea as to who(m) to select.

介词 宾语

（我们不知道要选谁。）

注意:

下列句中的 as to（有关）通常予以省略:

例: I am at a loss (as to) how to do it.

介词 宾语

（有关如何做此事，我不知道。）

3) be 动词之后的表语：

例：The problem is where to start.

be 动词 表语

（问题是从哪里开始。）

8. that 从句可化简为不定式：

凡句中主语为形式主语 It，之后接单一的动词，或及物动词的被动语态，再接 that 引导的名词性从句时，结构可加以改变，而将 that 从句变成不定式。

a. 形态：

1) 单一动词

例：It | seems / appears | that he works hard.

形式主语 | 单一动词 | 名词性从句

= He | seems / appears | to work hard.

不定式

（他似乎很努力。）

It | happened / chanced (罕) | that I was there.

形式主语 | 单一动词 | 名词性从句

= I | happened / chanced | to be there.

不定式

（我刚巧在那里。）

2) be + 过去分词

例：

It is said	（据说）	that he is good.
It is reported	（据报道）	
It is rumored	（谣传）	
It is known	（据了解）	
It is thought	（一般认为）	
It is believed	（一般相信）	

= He | is said / is reported / is rumored | to be good.

b. 如何变化：

1) 时态相同时，to 之后加原形动词。

例: It seems that he works hard.

时态相同

= He seems to work hard.

单数动词

（他似乎很努力。）

It appears that they are nice.

时态相同

= They appear to be nice.

复数动词

（他们似乎人很好。）

It was said that he loved music very much.

时态相同

= He was said to love music very much.

单数动词

（据说以前他很喜欢音乐。）

It is said they love music very much.

时态相同

= They are said to love music very much.

复数动词

（据说他们很喜欢音乐。）

2) 时态不同时，to 之后加“have（曾经、已经）+ 过去分词”。

例: It seems that he worked hard.

时态不同

= He seems to have worked hard.

（他似乎曾经努力过。）

It is said that he was a thug in the past.

时态不同

= He is said to have been a thug in the past.

（据说他以前是流氓。）

3) 此类句型分析如下：

He	seems	to work hard.
主语	不完全 vi.	不定式短语，做表语
They	were said	to be nice.
主语	不完全 vt. 的被动语态	不定式短语，做主语补语

9. to be 的省略：

seem 或 appear 之后若有 to be 时，to be 可予以省略。

例: He seems / appears to be nice.

= He seems / appears nice.

（他人似乎很好。）

10. prove + to be：

prove 一词可做及物动词，表“证明”，之后用名词或名词性从句做宾语。但亦可做不完全不及物动词，表“显示”、“竟然是”，之后采用“to be + n. / adj.”结构。

a. prove 做及物动词，表“证明”：

例: The investigation proved his guilt.

proved：完全 vt.　his guilt：名词做宾语

（调查证明他有罪。）

The investigation proved that he was guilty.

proved：完全 vt.　that he was guilty：名词性从句做宾语

（调查证明他有罪。）

b. prove 做不完全不及物动词，表“显示”、“结果是”：

例: What he said proved to be true.

proved：不完全 vi.　to be true：不定式做表语

（他的话竟然是真的。）

The report proved to be false.

proved：不完全 vi.　to be false：不定式做表语

= The report turned out to be false.

不完全 vi. 不定式做表语

（这份报告结果是错的。）

注意:

prove 或 turn out 之后的 to be 亦可省略，故上列例句亦可改写为：

The report | proved false. / turned out false.

11. 不定式短语做宾语补语：

具有使役动词意味的不完全及物动词，加了宾语之后，要用不定式短语做宾语补语。此类常用的动词有:

cause、get	促使……
lead	引导……
allow、permit	允许……
advise	劝告……
persuade	说服……
enable	使能够……
tell	告诉……
beg、ask	请求……
order	命令……
want、wish、expect、intend	期望……

例: The sad story caused him to cry.
（这个悲惨的故事使他哭了。）

His speech led me to understand the importance of learning English.
（他的演说引导我了解学英语的重要性。）

He advised me not to smoke again.
（他劝我别再吸烟。）

His timely help enabled me to finish it early.
（他适时的帮助使我能提早完成那件事。）

I'll get someone to help you.
（我会找人帮助你。）

I expect him to do it.
（我希望他去做此事。）

注意:

a. wish 与 hope 两者皆可做完全及物动词，以不定式做宾语。

例: I wish to do it. (✓)

vt. 宾语

= I hope to do it. (✓)
完全 vt.　宾语
（我希望做此事。）

然而，wish 及 hope 亦可做不及物动词，之后接介词 for，再接名词。

例：All we can do now is | wish for / hope for | a miracle.
（我们现在能做的也只有期待奇迹了。）

b. lead 加了宾语之后，可接 to 引导的不定式短语，但此 to 亦可视为介词，接名词或动名词为其宾语。

例：His speech led me to understand the importance of learning English.
不定式 (to + V)
= His speech led me to the understanding that it is important to learn English.
介词　动名词
（他的演讲引导我了解学英语的重要性。）

c. allow、permit 可做完全及物动词，直接用动名词做宾语。

例：They don't | allow / permit | smoking in the room.
动名词
（他们不允许在房间里吸烟。）

d. allow 及 permit 亦可做不完全及物动词，接了宾语之后，再接不定式短语做宾语补语，句型如下：

allow / permit sb to V　允许某人……

例：They don't | allow / permit | anyone to smoke in the room.
宾语　宾语补语
（他们不允许任何人在房间里吸烟。）

12. 意愿动词与虚拟语气的关系：

表意愿的动词 expect、intend、want、hope 如用一般过去时，再接"to have + 过去分词"时，则等于"would have + 过去分词"，形成表与过去事实相反的虚拟语气。即：

would have + 过去分词　本来想……
= | expected to / wanted to / intended to / hoped to | have + 过去分词

例: I would have done it, but I was busy.

= I | expected to / intended to | have done it, but I was busy.

（我本打算做这件事，但当时我很忙。）

不过，我们亦可将这些表意愿的动词改为过去完成时，之后接“to + 原形动词”，亦形成表与过去事实相反的虚拟语气。即：

would have + 过去分词

= | expected to / intended to / ⋮ | have + 过去分词

= | had expected / had intended / ⋮ | to + 原形动词

例: I would have done it, but I was busy.

= I expected to have done it, but I was busy.

= I had expected to do it, but I was busy.

13. was / were to have + 过去分词 = should have + 过去分词

本应该……（但却未……）

本结构亦可表与过去事实相反的虚拟语气。

例: I was to have done it, but I didn't have time then.

= I should have done it, but I didn't have time then.

（我本应该把它做完了，但我没时间。）

They were to have started out early, but it was raining heavily.

= They should have started out early, but it was raining heavily.

（他们本应提早出发，但当时正在下大雨。）

14. 不定式做主语的结构变化：

不定式短语做主语时，若短语中最后一个词为宾语，该宾语可移置句首做主语，其余部分则移至句尾。

例: To please my father is hard. (可)

（短语中有宾语 my father）

= My father is hard to please. (佳)

（我老爸很难取悦。）

To get along with him is easy. (可)
（短语中有宾语 him）

= He is easy to get along with. (佳)
（和他相处很容易。）

了解此种关系后，就不可写出下列的句子：

My father is hard to please him. (×)

He is easy to get along with others. (×)

15. 不定式的省略：

不定式短语中的动词如果在前面的句中已出现过，为避免重复，可予以省略，但 to 则保留。

例: You may go if you want to (go).
（如果你想去，你就去吧。）

A: Would you like to go dancing with me?

B: Yes, I would like to (go dancing with you). / I'd be glad to (go dancing with you).

（A：你愿意和我去跳舞吗？）
（B：好呀！我很愿/乐意 (和你去跳舞)。）

16. 不定式有时亦可形成感叹句：

例: To think that such a lazy boy should have passed the exam!
（想想看这样一个懒小子居然会考试及格！）

17. 原形不定式：

就是原形动词，通常出现在助动词之后。

can / could / shall / should / will / would / may / might / ought to / must + 原形动词

例: I can do it.
（我能做那件事。）

He should finish it.
（他应该完成那件事。）

He must obey the law.
（他必须遵守法律。）

18. 知觉动词与原形不定式的关系：

表“看”、“听”、“感觉”的知觉动词之后，可接原形不定式，做宾语补语，表已发生的事实。

看：see、watch、observe、look at
听：hear、listen to
感觉：feel

例: I saw him enter the room.
（我看见他进入了房间。）

I never heard him speak English.
（我从未听过他说英语。）

I felt the house shake.
（我感觉房子摇动了。）

I was watching the swallows fly to and fro.
（我当时正在看燕子飞来飞去。）

注意:

改为被动语态时，原形不定式就要变成“to + 原形动词”。

例: I saw him enter the house. (佳)
= He was seen to enter the house (by me). (罕)
I never heard him speak English. (佳)
= He was never heard to speak English (by me). (罕)

19. 使役动词与原形不定式的关系：

let（让）、make（使）、bid（叫）、have（叫）等使役动词之后亦必须以原形不定式做宾语补语。

例: Let me try it.
= Allow me to try it.
（让我试试它。）

I made him wash the car.
（我叫他洗车。）

Bid him (to) come. (罕)
= Tell him to come.
（叫他来。）

I had him wash the car.
= I got him to wash the car.
（我叫他洗车。）

注意:
除 have 外，let、bid、make 均可使用于被动语态中。此时做宾语补语的原形不定式要改为“to + 原形动词”。

例: They bade him (to) do it.
= He was bidden to do it.
（他们叫他做这件事。）

They made John clean the window.
= John was made to clean the window.
（他们叫约翰打扫窗户。）

I let him leave.
= He was let to leave. (罕)
= He was allowed to leave. (佳)
（我让他离开。）

但:They had him do it. (√)
He was had to do it. (×)

20. help（帮助）的用法:

a. help + 宾语 + (to) + 原形动词

例: He helped me (to) do the work.
（他帮助我做这个工作。）

b. help + 宾语 + with + 名词

例: He helped me with the work.
（他帮我做这个工作。）

c. help (to) + 原形动词

例: He helped (to) do the work.
（他帮忙做这个工作。）

d. help with + 名词

例: He helped with the work.
（他帮忙做这个工作。）

21. 原形不定式的特殊结构：

下列为与原形不定式连用的特殊结构。这些结构经常出现在各种英语试题中，同学们应牢记。

a. do nothing but + 原形不定式

例: He did nothing but eat all day.
（他整天什么都不做，只是吃。）

解说:

第一步：句中 but 可视为并列连词，连接对等且形态相同的词类 did，即：
He did nothing but did...

第二步：我们知道 do、does、did 在肯定句中，可视为强调性的助动词，之后要接原形不定式。

例: 未强调前: He works hard.
（他用功。）
强调后: He does work hard.
（他的确用功。）
未强调前: He worked hard.
强调后: He did work hard.

第三步：因此，在 He did nothing but did...中，did 之后要接原形不定式，即成：
He did nothing but did eat all day.

第四步：并列连词 but 之后相同的词类可以省略。本句中第一个 did 为及物动词的一般过去时，而第二个 did 则为强调性的助动词，虽性质不一，但外形相同，故第二个 did 可予以省略，即成：
He did nothing but eat all day. (✓)

b. choose / expect / want / desire nothing but + to + 原形动词

例: He wanted nothing but to sleep.
（他什么都不要，只想睡觉。）

解说:

第一步：句中 but 可视为并列连词，连接对等的动词 wanted，即：
He wanted nothing but wanted...

第二步：由于 want、desire、choose、expect 均为表意愿的及物动词，通常要用“to + 原形动词”做宾语。

例: He | wanted | to sleep.
　　| desired |
　　| expected |
　　| chose |

（他要睡觉。）

第三步：因此，在 He wanted nothing but wanted...中，wanted 之后要接“to + 原形动词”，即成：

He wanted nothing but wanted to sleep.

第四步：由于本句 wanted 为相同词类，故第二个 wanted 予以省略，即成：

He wanted nothing but to sleep. (✓)

c. be interested in nothing but + 动名词/名词

例: He is interested in nothing but singing.

动名词

= He is interested in nothing but (is interested in) singing.

（他除了唱歌外，对什么都不感兴趣。）

d. enjoy nothing but + 动名词/名词

例: I enjoy nothing but dancing.

动名词

= I enjoy nothing but (enjoy) dancing.

动名词

（我除了跳舞外什么都不喜欢。）

e. cannot but + 原形不定式

= cannot help + 动名词

*此处的 help 等于 stop 或 resist，表“抗拒”。

= cannot help but + 原形不定式

不得不/忍不住……

例: When I heard the story, I couldn't but laugh.

= When I heard the story, I couldn't help laughing.

= When I heard the story, I couldn't help but laugh.

（我听到这个故事，忍不住笑了出来。）

第二节　分词

概述

分词一共只有两种：现在分词和过去分词。现在分词原则上由原形动词加 -ing 形成，而过去分词多半为原形动词加 -d 或 -ed 形成，但也有数百个不规则动词，它们由原形变过去分词是不规则的，因此，同学们在使用分词时应多查词典，以完全了解动词的三态变化(原形、过去式、过去分词）。兹以原形动词 do 为大家解说分词的形态。

现在分词
- 单纯式：doing
- 完成时：having done
- 被动式：being done
- 完成进行时：having been doing
- 完成被动式：having been done

过去分词：done

分词在句中可用以表示进行、完成或被动语态的概念。

a. 进行：be + 现在分词

例: He is doing the work.
（他正在做这个工作。）

b. 完成：have + 过去分词

例: He has done the work.
（他已经做完这个工作。）

c. 被动：be + 过去分词

例: The job was done.
（这工作做完了。）

上述各例中的分词所涉及的进行时、完成时、被动语态的用法，我们将另辟有关时态或语态的章节讲解。在本节中，我们着重以分词当修饰语的用法，这也是分词最重要的功能。让赖老师一步步带着你了解以分词做修饰语的各种用法。

1. 分词可做形容词用：

例: The student raised a confusing question.
（confusing: adj.; question: n.）
（这个学生提出一个令人困惑的问题。）

The teacher was <u>confused</u>.
adj.
（这位老师感到迷糊了。）

注意
上列第一例中 confusing 为现在分词做形容词，修饰其后的名词，译成“令人困惑的”。
第二例中 confused 为过去分词做形容词用，置于 be 动词 was 之后，做表语，修饰主语 the teacher，译成“感到困惑的”。
上述两例告诉我们一个重要的概念：
分词做形容词用时，可置于名词之前，修饰该名词；亦可置于 be 动词之后，纯做表语。

＊分词做形容词用时，如何判断应使用现在分词或过去分词？
这是个很重要的问题，如果不弄清楚的话，我们很可能写出下面的错误句子而不自觉：

例: When he heard the story, he was very <u>exciting</u>. (×)
→ When he heard the story, he was very <u>excited</u>. (✓)
（他听到这个故事时很兴奋。）

注意:
exciting　　令人兴奋的
excited　　感到兴奋的
因此，同学们要正确使用分词做形容词用时，一定要牢记下面赖老师所列的法则（别怕，很简单）：
分词做形容词时，可以表示下列概念：

a. 表主动/被动的概念：
令人……的 → 现在分词
感到……的 → 过去分词
受到……的 → 过去分词

b. 表进行/完成的概念：
正在……的 → 现在分词
即将……的 → 现在分词
已经……的 → 过去分词

兹分项说明如下：

a. 表主动/被动的概念：
凡表“令人……的”意思时，我们就使用现在分词；凡表“感到……的”或“受到……的”时，我们就使用过去分词。

例: The competition is quite exciting.
现在分词
（这场比赛很刺激。——令人兴奋的）

He was excited when he heard the news.
过去分词
（他听到这个消息时很兴奋。——感到兴奋的）

The charming lady happens to be John's sister.
现在分词
（这位迷人的女子刚巧是约翰的妹妹。——令人着迷的）

The boy was charmed with the girl's elegance.
过去分词
（这个男孩着迷于这女孩的优雅气质。——感到着迷的）

The wounded soldier was rushed to hospital.
（受伤的士兵被急忙送到医院。——受伤的）

What an interesting story it is!
（多有趣的故事呀！——令人感兴趣的）

He was interested in the question.
（他对这问题感兴趣。——感到有兴趣的）

b. 表进行/完成的概念：

凡表“正在……的”或“即将……的”意思时，我们就使用现在分词；凡表“已经……的”时，我们就使用过去分词。

例: The retiring teacher walked into the classroom.
（这位即将退休的老师步入教室。——即将退休的）

The retired soldier died last month.
（那位退役军人上个月去世了。——已经退休的）

Do you see that speeding car?
（你看见那辆开得飞快的车吗？——正在快速行驶的）

The aging father found it hard to do the work.
（那位日渐年迈的父亲发现很难做这工作。——年华正在老去的）

He is aged, but he stays young at heart.
（他已上了年纪，但他的内心保持年轻。——已经上年纪的）

*aged [ˋedʒɪd] *a.* 上了年纪的，年事已高的

He is gone.
= He has gone.
（他已离开。——已经离开的）

We're closed.
= We've closed.
（我们已经打烊。——已经打烊了）

He is retired.
= He has retired.
（他已退休。——已经退休的）

We are finished with the work.
= We have finished the work.
（我们工作已做完了。——已经做完的）

We are sold out of this book.
= We have sold out of this book.
（我们这本书已卖完了。——已经卖完的）

I am | prepared / ready / all set | for the exam.
（我已准备好应试。——已经准备好的）

赖老师举了那么多的例子，无非想证明，只要理解上面所列的原则，那么分词做形容词的用法并不难。

我们且练习一下下列填空题：

Get me some ______ (boiled、boiling) water to drink.

正确的答案应为 boiled（已经煮开过的）。

→Get me some boiled water to drink.
（给我弄点开水喝。）

我们若选 boiling（正在滚开的），那我们喝下 boiling water（正在滚开的水）之后，我们的食道必然被烫熟了，这还了得？！

我们再练习一下下列的填空题：

He is sweeping _______ (falling、fallen) leaves in the _______ (falling、fallen) rain.
（他在雨中扫落叶。）

正确答案应为：
第一个空格：fallen（已经掉下来的）
第二个空格：falling（正在落下的）

如果我们的答案是这样：
He is sweeping falling leaves in the fallen rain.（×）
就成了：他在已经落下来的雨中扫正在落下的树叶。

那么这个人一定是扁平如纸的人，可以躺在地上（已经落下的）雨水中，同时又可以挥着扫帚扫一片一片正在掉下来的树叶，如果有一天我们真见到这样的人，我们就得赶紧逃跑，因为那不是人，那是妖怪！

2. 分词可做表语用：

a. be 动词（或 remain、become、appear、seem 等系动词）之后的表语：

做表语的分词均为形容词，可以译成“……的”。此类分词之前均可用 very 修饰。常用的此类分词如下：

interested （感到有兴趣的）
interesting （令人感兴趣的）
tired （感到累的）
tiring （令人累的，累人的）
thrilled （感到刺激的）
thrilling （令人刺激的）

此类分词实在太多，故不一一举例，这些可做形容词用的分词均可置于系动词（如 become、feel、seem 等）之后做表语。

例: He is interested in it.
形容词，做表语
（他对它有兴趣。）

The baby is tiring.
形容词，做表语
（这个婴儿真累人。）

He seems tired.
（他似乎累了。）

The experience is thrilling.
（这个经历真够刺激。）

He became more and more interested in learning English.
（他对学英语越来越有兴趣。）

但并非所有的分词均可当形容词用。有些分词无法译成“……的”。

killed　　不能译成“感到杀的”
killing　　不能译成“令人杀的”
written　　不能译成“感到写的”
writing　　不能译成“令人写的”

此类分词，只能置于 be 动词之后（不可置于系动词如 become、remain、appear、feel、seem 等之后），不视为形容词，而视为动词的进行时或被动语态。

例: He was killed.
vt. 的一般过去时被动语态
（他被杀了。）

He was killing the termites.
vt. 的过去进行时
（他正在杀白蚁。）

He was writing a letter.
vt. 的过去进行时
（他正在写一封信。）

The letter was being written.
vt. 的过去进行时被动语态
（这封信还正在写。）

He was leaving.
vi. 的过去进行时
（他正要离去。）

He became killed. (×)
He appeared writing a letter. (×)

b. 及物动词之后的宾语补语：

例: I found him killed.
vt. 宾语 宾语补语
（我发现他被杀了。）

I want it done right away.
vt. 宾语 宾语补语
（我要这件事立即完成。）

They found him tired.
vt. 宾语 宾语补语
（他们发现他累了。）

可做形容词用的分词当然可做宾语补语，如上述第三例句中的 tired（感到累的）。但不可做形容词用的分词又如何做补语呢？到底要使用现在分词还是过去分词做补语呢？我们且先做下面这道练习题：

As he talked to me, I found him ______ (trembling、trembled).

（他跟我谈话时，我发现他在发抖。）

这个题目的正确选择应为 trembling。理由是什么？且看赖老师解说如下：

使用不可当形容词的分词做宾语补语时，

第一步：先检查该分词原来动词的性质为及物或不及物动词。

方法：我 ______ 他。

他被我 ______。

将任何一个动词置入上列两空格中，再将整句译成中文，意思合乎逻辑时，该动词就是及物动词，否则就是不及物动词。

例 将 kill（杀）填入空格中，得到的翻译为：
我杀了他。
他被我杀了。
本句合逻辑，故 kill 为及物动词。

例 将 tremble（发抖）填入空格中，得到的翻译为：
我发抖他。
他被我发抖。
本句意思不合逻辑，故 tremble 为不及物动词。

第二步：

1) 动词若为及物动词，做宾语补语时，有两种分词形态：

a) 现在分词 + 宾语

b) 过去分词

已知 kill 为及物动词，

故：I found him killing cockroaches.
现在分词 宾语
（我发现他正在杀蟑螂。）

或：I found the cockroaches killed.
过去分词
（我发现那些蟑螂被杀死了。）

2) 动词若为不及物动词，做宾语补语时，一律变成现在分词。

已知 tremble 为不及物动词，

故：I found him trembling.
现在分词

熟悉这个概念之后，我们就可大胆地造出下列句子：

例: I want the car painted.
过去分词
（我要这辆车漆好。）

理由:
paint（漆）是及物动词，做宾语补语时，因之后无宾语，故变成过去分词。

I kept John waiting.
（我让约翰等我。）

理由:
wait 是不及物动词，故做补语时，变成现在分词。

As I came in, I saw John singing.
（我进来时，看见约翰正在唱歌。）

理由:
此处 sing 做“唱歌”解，是不及物动词，故做补语时，变成现在分词。

I found him writing a letter.
（我发现他正在写信。）

理由:
write 之后有了宾语 letter 为及物动词，故应改为现在分词做补语。

c. with 复合结构中的宾语补语：

with 复合结构就是一种由介词 with 引导的短语，置于句尾，用以修饰句中的主语，以表示主语所处的状态。

例: He talked to me with his legs shaking.
主语　　with 复合结构
（他和我说话时两腿发抖。）

本例中 with 之后有宾语 his legs，而 shaking 为其宾语补语。shaking 由不及物动词 shake（发抖）转变而成。

此类分词转变而成的宾语补语，形成的方式与及物动词之后的宾语补语完全相同，故在此我们省略不提，仅提供例句供同学们参考。

例: He stood with his arms folded.
宾语补语（由 vt. 变成）
（他站着两手交叉在胸前。）

He sat there with his eyes closed.

宾语补语（由 vt. 变成）

（他闭着双眼坐在那儿。）

He talked to me with his legs trembling.

宾语补语（由 vi. 变成）

（他和我说话时双腿发抖。）

注意

with 复合结构中的宾语补语（即分词）亦可用介词短语取代。

例: He came here with a gun in one hand.

介词短语做宾语补语

（他来这里时一手握着枪。）

He talked to me with a pipe in his mouth.

介词短语做宾语补语

（他和我说话时嘴里叼着烟斗。）

有些以介词短语做宾语补语的 with 复合结构亦可有下列化简的用法：

He came here gun in hand.

He talked to me pipe in mouth.

在这些化简的短语中，我们可明显地注意到 with 已省略，原有的冠词或所有格亦均予以省略。

3. 分词可作名词用：

凡可做形容词用的分词（也就是可以译成“……的”之分词），前面若有定冠词 the，可当做单数或复数的名词使用。

例: The wounded were rushed to the hospital.

= Wounded people were rushed to the hospital.

（伤者被急送医院。）

The unexpected has happened.

= Something (which) we didn't expect has happened.

（意外的事情发生了。）

The young should learn to cherish life.

= Young people should learn to cherish life.

（年轻人应懂得珍惜生命。）

4. 分词可作副词用：

少数的现在分词有副词 very 的意味，可修饰其后的形容词。

例：It's freezing / biting cold today.
　　adv. adj.

（今天天气非常冷/冰冻般的冷/如皮肤被咬般的冷。）

The tea is boiling hot.
　　adv. adj.

（茶非常热/滚烫般的热。）

He was hopping mad on hearing his dismissal.
　　adv. adj.

（当听到自己被解雇时，他简直气疯了/气得要跳脚。）

We're having a ripping good time.
　　adv. = very adj.

（我们此刻玩得愉快极了。）

但也有过去分词做副词用的例子。

例：An estimated 54 people were killed in the air crash.
　　adv. adj.

= It is estimated that 54 people were killed in the air crash.

（据估计有 54 个人在空难中丧生。）

A great many students are more and more interested in learning English.
　　adv. adj.

（许多学生对学英语越来越感兴趣。）

> **注意**
>
> 少数形容词亦有副词的功能，修饰之后的形容词。

例：He is dead wrong. (dead 为副词，等于 completely，表“完全地”)
　　adv. adj.

（他大错特错。）

It's awful hot today. (awful 为副词，等于 very，表“非常地”)
　　adv. adj.

（今天热得要命。）

＊awful 亦做形容词，表“差劲的”，等于 terrible。

That movie is awful.
（那部影片烂透了。）

The answer is	doubtless doubtlessly without doubt undoubtedly adv.	correct. adj.

（这个答案毫无疑问是正确的。）

5. 分词结构——动词变化：

一句中有两个动词同时存在，彼此一定要有连词相连。

例: He worked very hard and won the honor.
（他很努力而赢得该项荣誉。）

He studied very hard but failed the exam.
（他很用功，但考试未能及格。）

但若两个动词无连词相连时，就要注意下列的变化原则：

a. 若两个动词所代表的动作同时发生时，第二个动词一定要变成现在分词，若该动词是 be 动词，变成现在分词 being 之后要省略。

例: He came home cried.
crying.

（他哭着回来了。）

理由:
他一面回来，一面哭。came 与 cried 同时发生，因此 cried 应变成现在分词。

例: He sat in the corner read a newspaper.
reading

（他坐在角落里看报纸。）

理由:
他一面坐在角落，一面看报纸。sat 与 read 同时发生，因此 read 应变成现在分词。

理由:

He sat in the corner	playing with his keys. listening to the teacher's lecture. looking silently at Mary.

（他坐在角落里玩着他的钥匙/听老师讲课/默视着玛丽。）

例: He came home ~~was~~ tired.
being

→ He came home tired.

理由:

他一面回家，一面感到累。故 came 与 was tired 同时发生。由于 was 是 be 动词，变成 being 之后应予以省略。

例: He left ~~was~~ young and came back ~~was~~ old.
being　　　　　　　　being

→ He left young and came back old.

（他少小离家老大回。）

理由:

本句由 and 连接两个主要动词 left 及 came。他一面离去，一面是年轻的状态，故 left 与 was young 同时发生，left 之后的 was 变成现在分词 being，再予以省略。他一面回来，一面是老的状态，故 came 之后的 was 变成现在分词 being，再予以省略。

例: He died ~~was~~ a nobody.
being

→ He died a nobody.

（他默默无闻地死去。）

理由:

他死去的同时是个无名小卒，故 die 与 was 同时发生，was 变成现在分词 being 之后，再予以省略。

例: We are born ~~are~~ equal.
being

→ We are born equal.

（我们生而平等。）

Everyone is born ~~is~~ free.
being

→ Everyone is born free.

（人人生而自由。）

比较：

Everyone is born freely. (×)
adv.（修饰 is born）

（每个人都是自由地生下来。）

理由:

freely 是副词，如此一来就修饰了句中动词 is born，岂不表示每个人都可以自由自在地到处乱诞生？

b. 若两个动词所代表的动作并非同时发生，而是有先后次序时，第二个动词就要变成“to + 原形动词”形成的不定式短语。

例: He came here ~~saw~~ me.
to see

→ He came here to see me.

（他来这儿看我。）

理由:

他先来，再看我。故 came 与 saw 并非同时发生，第二个动词就变成不定式。

如果我们写成这样的句子：

He came here seeing me. (×)

那就变成：

他一面来，一面看我。

这样的话，他还没走到目的地，恐怕因为边走边伸长脖子看我的关系，脖子一定会扭到，甚至脑袋都掉下来了。

例: He stood up ~~smoked~~ a cigarette.
to smoke

→ He stood up to smoke a cigarette.

（他站起来抽烟。）

理由:

他先站起来，再抽烟。故 stood up 与 smoked 并非同时发生，第二个动词 smoked 就应变成不定式 to smoke。

若写成这样的句子：

He stood up smoking a cigarette. (×)

便可能有两种解释：

1) 他一面站起，一面抽烟。——小心给呛着了
2) 他一面站起来，一面身上冒烟。——这可不好玩了

比较：

He stood there smoking a cigarette. (√)

（他站在那儿抽烟。）

了解这个道理之后，我们就明白下列各句为何要使用不定式。

例: He rushed here to tell me the story.
（他赶到这里来告诉我这件事。）

He sang a song to please her.
（他唱首歌来取悦她。）

He drew a map to show me the way.
（他画了张地图来告诉我路的走法。）

现在我们可以将两种句型的结构分析如下：

第一型：	He	stood	there	smoking a cigarette.
	主语	不完全vi.	副词	现在分词做伴随状语
第二型：	He	stood	up	to smoke a cigarette.
	主语	完全vi.	副词	不定式短语做副词用，修饰前面的动词

c. 若两动词有逗号相隔，而无连接时，就不必考虑动词所代表的动作先后发生的次序，第二个动词一定要变成现在分词。

例: He left home at six in the morning, ~~arrived~~ here about four in the afternoon.
arriving
（他早上 6 点离开家，约下午 4 点抵达此地。）

He ran away quickly, ~~looked~~ as if something terrible had happened.
looking
（他很快地跑开了，看起来好像发生了什么可怕的事。）

6. 分词结构——单句化简法：

两句在一起，若无连词相连时，往往第一个句子要化简，变成分词短语。规则如下：

a. 两句的主语相同时，被化简句子的主语要删除，若主语不同时则要保留；

b. 之后的动词要变成现在分词；

c. 若该动词为 be 动词时，变成现在分词 being 之后，可予以省略，但亦可不省略，以强调“因为……”的意思。

例: He has nothing to do, he feels bored. (×)

理由

两句无法连接。

改　正：化简第一个句子。

第一步：删除相同的主语 He；

第二步：其后动词 has 变成现在分词 Having，即：

He has nothing to do, he feels bored.

Having

→Having nothing to do, he feels bored. (√)

（他没事可做，所以觉得无聊。）

例: He was sick of studying, he ran away from home. (×)

理由

两句无法连接。

改　正：化简第一个句子。

第一步：删除相同的主语 He；

第二步：其后动词 was 变成现在分词 being；

第三步：being 可予以省略，即：

He was sick of studying, he ran away from home.

Being

→Being sick of studying, he ran away from home. (√)

或：Sick of studying, he ran away from home. (√)

（他厌倦念书，所以离家出走了。）

例: The sun set, the cowboys rode back to the ranch. (×)

理由

两句无法连接。

改　正：化简第一个句子。

第一步：由于第一句的主语 The sun 与第二句的主语 the cowboys 不相同，故应予以保留；

第二步：其后动词 set 变成现在分词 setting，即成：

The sun set, the cowboys rode back to the ranch.

setting

→The sun setting, the cowboys rode back to the ranch. (√)

（夕阳西下，牛仔们策马回到牧场。）

使用单句化简法时应注意事项：

a. 变成否定分词结构时，not 要置于分词前。

例：He was not satisfied with the result, he decided to try again.
Being
→ Being not satisfied with the result, he decided to try again. (×)
→ Not (being) satisfied with the result, he decided to try again. (√)
（他不满意此结果，决定再试一次。）

b. 句中有助动词 do、does、did 时，可直接删除。

例：He didn't intend to see her, he left early.
Not intending
→ Not intending to see her, he left early.
（他不打算见她，便提早走了。）

c. 句中有完成时助动词 have、has、had，要视为动词而变成现在分词 having。

例：He had done the work, he felt happy.
Having
→ Having done the work, he felt happy.
（他做完了这项工作，觉得很高兴。）

I have not seen her for ages, I miss her.
Having
→ Having not seen her for ages, I miss her. (×)
→ Not having seen her for ages, I miss her. (√)
（好久没看见她了，我很想她。）

d. 主语不同时，所形成的分词结构，称为分词的独立主格结构。所谓分词的独立主格结构，就是独立修饰不同主语的分词结构。

例：This being the case, you'd better be careful.
↑
分词的独立主格结构
（这样的话，你最好小心点。）

* This being the case 原为 This is the case，但如此一来，本句与 You'd better be careful 无连词连接。故将第一个句子化简为分词短语。由于主语 This 与第二个句子的主语 you 不同，故予以保留，之后的动词 is 变成现在分词 being，being the case 独立修饰不同的主语 This，故称分词的独立主格结构。

All things considered, I decided to major in business administration.

（全盘考虑后，我决定主修企业管理。）

*All things considered 原为 All things were considered，但如此一来，本句与 I decided to major in business administration 无连词连接，故将第一个句子化简为分词短语。由于主语 All things 与第二个句子的主语 I 不同，故予以保留，之后的动词 were 变成现在分词 being，再予以省略，considered 独立修饰不同的主语 All things，故称分词的独立主格结构。

e. 有时，我们亦可消灭第二个句子，变成分词结构。

例: He was reading a book, his wife knitting beside him.

= He was reading a book, and his wife was knitting beside him.

（他在看一本书，而他太太在旁边编织。）

We will go picnicking tomorrow, weather permitting.

= We will go picnicking tomorrow if weather permits.

（如果天气好，我们明天就去野餐。）

7. 分词短语——定语从句化简法：

在限制性定语从句（即关系代词之前无逗号）中，若关系代词做主语时，可化简成分词短语，法则如下：

a. 删除关系代词；

b. 其后动词变成现在分词；

c. 若该动词为 be 动词，变成现在分词 being 之后，可予以省略。

例: The man who is talking to Mary over there is my father. (✓)

（那边那位正在对玛丽说话的男士是我爸爸。）

第一步：将 who 删除；

第二步：将 who 之后的 is 变成现在分词 being；

第三步：再将 being 省略，上句即化简成：

The man talking to Mary over there is my father. (✓)

Who is the boy that is locked behind the door? (✓)

限制性定语从句

→ Who is the boy ~~that is~~ locked behind the door?

(being)

= Who is the boy locked behind the door? (✓)

（被锁在门后的男孩是谁？）

注意:

使用定语从句化简法应注意的事项:

a. 非限制性定语从句（即关系代词之前有逗号）通常不得化简为分词短语。

例: I like Tom, who is talking to Mary. (✓)

但: I like Tom, ~~who~~ ~~is~~ talking to Mary.
(being)

→ I like Tom, talking to Mary. (×)

b. 不过非限制性定语从句结构若为“关系代词 + be + 名词”时，则仍可化简，而形成同位语。

例: John, who is a good friend of mine, studies hard. (✓)

→ John, who ~~is~~ a good friend of mine, studies hard.
(being)

= John, a good friend of mine, studies hard. (✓)
主语 主语同位语

（约翰，我的一个好友，很用功。）

> **注意**
>
> 形成同位语时，可置于主语之前或之后。故本句亦可改为：
>
> A good friend of mine, John studies hard.
> 主语同位语 主语

例: He studies hard, which is a fact that is known to all of us.

→ He studies hard, ~~which~~ ~~is~~ a fact ~~that~~ ~~is~~ known to all of us.
(being) (being)

= He studies hard, a fact known to all of us. (✓)

（他用功是众人皆知的事实。）

8. 测验站:

由于我们在第 5、6、7 项为同学们介绍的分词结构实在很重要，因此赖老师特别出了下列几道翻译题，请同学们用分词结构翻译出来，以测验自己的理解程度。

试译下列各句:

a. 我不知道如何处理（deal with）这个问题，就向他请教（consult）。

译：____________________

b. 我进门时，发现书被散得满地都是（scatter around）。

译：____________________

c. 他光着脚（barefooted）走进屋子里。

译：______________________________

d. 他挥手向她道别。

译：______________________________

示范译句：

a. Not knowing how to deal with the problem, I consulted him.
b. As I entered the room, I found books scattered around.
c. He came into the room (being) barefooted.
d. He said goodbye to her, waving his hand.

9. 分词结构——状语从句化简法：

once、when、while、if、unless、though 等连词所引导的状语从句中，若主语与主句中的主语相同时，亦可化简为分词结构，规则与单句化简法完全相同。

例: If ~~I am~~ free, I'll go with you.
(being)

= If free, I'll go with you.
（如果有空，我将和你一起去。）

In those days, when ~~he didn't know~~ how to proceed in an emergency, he
not knowing
would consult his father.

= In those days, when not knowing how to proceed in an emergency, he would consult his father.
（在那段日子里，当他不知道如何处理紧急状况时，就会请教他父亲。）

He will do it if ~~he is~~ properly encouraged.
(being)

= He will do it if properly encouraged.
（如果适当地鼓励他，他会去做。）

Unless ~~you are~~ otherwise instructed, you should do as I said.
(being)

= Unless otherwise instructed, you should do as I said.
（除非另有指示，你应照我的话去做。）

While ~~I was~~ here, I had a good time.
(being)

= While here, I had a good time.
（在这里时，我很愉快。）

Though ~~he was~~ seriously injured, he was not at all daunted.
(being)

= Though seriously injured, he was not at all daunted.
（虽然受伤很严重，但他一点都不畏惧。）

Once ~~I am~~ available, I'll let you know.
(being)

= Once available, I'll let you know.
（一旦我有空，我会让你知道。）

注意

上列六个连词中，once、if、unless 所引导的状语从句若化简为分词短语，多限于“主语 + be + 分词/形容词”的结构；而 when、while、though 则不受此限制。

例: Once I have money, I'll buy a car. (✓)
（我一旦有钱，就会买车。）

→ Once having money, I'll buy a car. (×)

但 Once I'm rich, I'll buy a car. (✓)
be adj.

= Once rich, I'll buy a car. (✓)
（我一旦有钱，就会买车。）

Though I have money, I won't buy a car. (✓)
（我虽然有钱，却不会买车。）

= Though having money, I won't buy a car. (✓)

Though I am rich, I won't buy a car. (✓)
be adj.

= Though rich, I won't buy a car. (✓)
（我虽然有钱，却不会买车。）

10. 表身体组织的名词可变成过去分词当形容词用:

例: The girl has big eyes.

→ I love the big-eyed girl.
（我喜欢这个大眼睛的女孩。）

She has red hair.

→ Do you see the red-haired girl there?
（你看见那边的红发女孩吗？）

The soldier has only one leg.

→ The one-legged soldier was a hero.
（那个独腿士兵是个英雄。）

类例用法：

a broken-hearted man	一个心碎的人
a bare-footed boy	一个赤脚的男孩
a black-skinned guy	一个黑皮肤的人
a two-headed snake	一条双头蛇

11. 少数现在分词可当介词使用：

including	（包括）
excluding	（除外）
considering	（考虑）
regarding	（关于）
concerning	（关于）

a. including / excluding

例: Everyone likes the movie, | excluding / including | John. (√)

→ Everyone likes the movie, John ~~is~~ (being) | excluded. / included. |

→ Everyone likes the movie, John | excluded. / included. |

= Everyone likes the movie, | exclusive of / inclusive of | John. (√)

（每一个人都喜欢这部电影，除了/包括约翰。）

b. considering

例: <u>Considering</u> his performance, he can be a good teacher. (√)
介词

→ His performance ~~is~~ (being) considered, he can be a good teacher.

= His performance <u>considered</u>, he can be a good teacher. (√)

（从他的表现看来，他可以当个好老师。）

c. regarding / concerning

例: He wrote an article | regarding / concerning / about / on (介词) | environmental pollution.

（他写了篇有关环境污染的文章。）

12. 独立分词短语：

某些独立分词短语有副词的功能，通常置于句首，修饰整个句子。

例: Generally speaking, men are physically stronger than women.
（一般而言，男人比女人强壮。）

Strictly speaking, he is not good enough.
（严格说来，他不够好。）

Frankly speaking, he is not the man I want.
（老实说，他不是我想要的人。）

Judging from his appearance, he seems to be rich.
（从他的外表看，他似乎很有钱。）

Talking of novels, have you read his works?
（谈到小说，你是否看过他的作品？）

According to John, the fire broke out at ten in the morning.
（根据约翰的说法，火灾是在早上 10 点发生的。）

Seeing that you have no time, I'll have Peter replace you.
（既然你没时间，我会叫彼得代替你。）

13. 与使役动词有关的重要分词短语：

下列为与使役动词有关的分词短语，由于经常出现，故同学们应熟记。

例: I started the ball rolling.
（我给那件事开了个头。）

The news set my heart throbbing.
（这个消息使我心悸不已。）

I am sorry to have kept you waiting.
（我很抱歉让你等候。）

I couldn't make myself understood.
（我无法让别人听懂我的话。）

I had my shoes repaired.
（我把我的鞋拿去修好了。）

He got a new suit made.
（他订做了一套新西装。）

You should leave it unsaid.
（你应该别提这事。）

I like my eggs half boiled.
（我喜欢煮得半熟的蛋。）

I had my watch stolen.
（我的表被偷了。）

第三节　动名词

概述

动名词的形态与现在分词完全一样。

例: He is dancing.
现在分词
（他正在跳舞。）

His hobby is dancing.
动名词
（他的爱好是跳舞。）

Not knowing what to do, he felt embarrassed.
现在分词
（不知道该做什么，他觉得很尴尬。）

Not knowing what to do was an embarrassment for him.
动名词
（不知道该做什么，对他来说是件尴尬之事。）

由于动名词与现在分词的形态完全相同，因此同学们往往将之混为一谈，以至在从事英语翻译时，造成意思的偏差，同学们不可不谨慎。破解这一难题的秘诀，就是要牢记一个概念：动名词具有名词的性质，名词在句中可做主语、宾语及表语；同样地，动名词在句中亦可做主语、宾语及表语。我们分项讲解如下：

1. 动名词的第一功能——主语：

例: Working with him is fun.
主语　动词
（和他一起工作很有趣。）

Seeing is believing.
主语　动词
（眼见为实。）

Losing his fortune drove him mad.
主语　动词
（失去财富使他发疯了。）

Not knowing what to do was an embarrassment for him.

主语 动词

（不知道该做什么，对他是件尴尬之事。）

注意:

a. 上述各例中，Working、Seeing、Losing 以及 Not knowing 均做主语，故为动名词。

b. 动名词做主语时，仍有动词的意味，若该动名词原为及物动词，之后仍须加宾语。宾语即使为复数，所形成的动名词短语仍视为单数，之后接单数动词。

例: Helping others give me great pleasure. (×)

动名词短语 复数动词

→ Helping others gives me great pleasure. (√)

单数动词

（帮助别人使我很愉快。）

理由:

本句并非 others 做主语，而是整个帮助别人的动作做主语，故之后动词用单数。

c. 动名词短语做主语时，亦可被形式主语 it 代替，而将该动名词短语移至句尾，改变成不定式短语。

故上列例句可改写为：

It gives me great pleasure to help others.

注意:

只有在 It is no use 的结构中，真正主语仍应为动名词。

例: It is no use crying over spilt milk. (√)

形式主语 真正主语

（覆水难收。）

It is no use to cry over spilt milk. (×)

这是习惯用法，同学们应牢记。

例: It is no use reasoning with such a stubborn man.

= It is of no use / useless to reason with such a stubborn man.

= There is no use / no sense / no point in reasoning with such a stubborn man.

（和这样固执的人讲理是没有用的。）

2. 动名词的第二功能—— be 动词后的表语：

例: Seeing is <u>believing</u>.
　　　　　　表语
（眼见为实。）

His hobby is <u>collecting stamps</u>.
　　　　　　　　表语
（他的爱好是集邮。）

注意:

a. be 动词之后可用不定式或动名词做表语。但赖老师之前提过，用不定式做表语时，通常表示一种意愿、目的、计划或未完成的事；用动名词做表语时，则表示一种经历或已知的事。

例: His ambition is <u>winning the championship</u>. (劣)
→ His ambition is <u>to win the championship</u>. (佳)
（他的野心是要赢得冠军。）

理由:
ambition 表“野心、企图”，为尚未完成的事，故用不定式短语做表语为佳。
同理:

My	hope	（希望）	is <u>to fulfill the mission</u>.
	goal	（目标）	（完成任务）
	desire	（欲望）	
	wish	（愿望）	
	intention	（意图）	
	plan	（计划）	
	purpose	（目的）	

例: My favorite sport is skating.
（我最喜爱的运动是滑冰。）

注意:
我最喜爱的运动是已知的事，故使用动名词 skating 作表语。

例: Seeing is believing.
（眼见为实。）

理由:
眼见为实，表示一种经历，故用动名词 believing 做表语。但若主语改用不定式 To see，则为求对称的美观，表语亦改用 to believe，即：
To see is to believe.
（眼见为实。）

b. 有时 be 动词之后的 V-ing 可能为动名词，亦可能为现在分词。

例: She is dancing.
现在分词
（她在跳舞。）

Her hobby is dancing.
动名词
（她的爱好是跳舞。）

分辨的方法:

由于动名词与主语均具有名词的性质，故有“A is B = B is A”的逻辑特性。

因此我们只需将 V-ing 与主语换位，如果语意顺畅，即可断定该 V-ing 是动名词，否则必为分词。

例: Her hobby is dancing.
主语
（她的爱好是跳舞。）
换位：

Dancing is her hobby.
（跳舞是她的爱好。）
判断：语意顺畅，得知 dancing 为动名词。

She is dancing.
主语
（她在跳舞。）
换位：

Dancing is she. (×)
（跳舞就是她。）
判断：跳舞是动作而非人，故 dancing 不可能等于 she，因此，得知 dancing 为现在分词。

注意:

be 动词之后的现在分词有两种特性。一种为纯做形容词用的分词，可译成“……的”；另一种则为动词的进行时，分析结构时，要将之前的 be 动词视为一体，译成“正在……”。

例: She is charming.
主语 be 动词 形容词（译成“令人着迷的”，作表语）
（她很迷人。）

She is dancing.
主语 不及物动词 dance 的现在进行时（译成“正在跳舞”）
（她正在跳舞。）

That question is interesting.
主语 be 动词 形容词（译成“令人感兴趣的”，作表语）
（那问题很有趣。）

John was writing a letter.
主语 及物动词 write 的过去进行时（译成“正在写”）
（约翰正在写信。）

3. 动名词的第三功能——动词的宾语：

例: He detests gambling.
vt. o.
（他憎恨赌博。）

Some people do not enjoy smoking.
vt. o.
（有些人不喜欢吸烟。）

I remember seeing him.
vt. o.
（我记得见过他。）

＊下列及物动词习惯上均用动名词做宾语：
consider（考虑）、contemplate（意图）、imagine（想象）、fancy（想）、avoid（避免）、risk（冒险）、escape（逃掉）、deny（否认）、admit（承认）、stop（停止）、quit（停止、戒）、suggest（建议）、recommend（建议）、mind（介意）、remember（记得曾）、finish（完成）、practice（练习）、anticipate（预期）。

例: I've considered traveling abroad next year.
（我已考虑明年出国旅游。）

He recommended doing it soon.
（他建议快点做此事。）

You must quit smoking right away.
（你必须立即戒烟。）

He denied stealing the money.
（他否认曾偷了这笔钱。）

He practiced playing the piano every day.

（他每天练习弹钢琴。）

注意:

a. anticipate V-ing　　期望……

= expect to V

例: I anticipate cooperating with him.

= I expect to cooperate with him.

（我期望与他合作。）

b. stop V-ing　　停止……

= quit V-ing

= cease V-ing

= cease to V

例: He | stopped / quit / ceased | writing when he saw me.

= He ceased to write when he saw me.

（当他看见我时，他就停止写字。）

stop to V　　停下原来的工作而去做……

例: He stopped to talk to me when he saw me.

（当他看见我时就停下来和我说话。）

c. allow（允许）、permit（准许）、forbid（禁止）的用法：

例: He | allowed / permitted | me to smoke.

me: o.　to smoke: 不定式短语（做宾语补语）

（他允许我吸烟。）

He | allowed / permitted | smoking.

smoking: o.

（他准许吸烟。）

He forbade me to smoke.

me: o.　to smoke: 不定式短语（做宾语补语）

（他禁止我吸烟。）

He forbade smoking.

smoking: o.

（他禁止吸烟。）

d. remember、forget、regret 的用法：

1) 表追述过去已发生的事物时：

remember（记得曾） forget（忘记曾） regret（后悔曾）	+ 动名词

例：I remember | seeing her before. / having seen her before. |

（我记得曾见过她。）

I forgot | mailing that letter. / having mailed that letter. |

（我忘记我已寄了那封信。）

I regret | doing it. / having done it. |

（我后悔做了此事。）

2) 表以后要做或未完成的事物时：

remember（记得要） forget（忘记要） regret（遗憾要）	+ to V

例：I'll remember to see him tomorrow.

（我会记得明天去看他。）

I forgot to mail this letter.

（我忘了寄这封信。）

I regret to tell you the bad news.

= I'm sorry to tell you the bad news.

（我很遗憾要告诉你这个坏消息。）

e. 下列动词可用不定式或动名词做宾语，意思不变。

I	like（喜欢） dislike（不喜欢） love（爱） hate（恨）	to do it. doing it.
I	continued（继续） began（开始） started（开始）	to do it. doing it.

4. 动名词的第四功能——介词的宾语：

例: He is fond of taking a walk.

prep. o.

（他喜欢散步。）

His illness prevented us from starting our own business.

prep. o.

（他的病使得我们无法开展我们的事业。）

None would have dreamed of there being such a place.

prep. o.

（做梦也没人想到会有这样一个地方。）

The book is worth reading.

prep. o.

（这本书值得看。）

注意

比较 worth、worthy、worthwhile 的用法。

a. worth *prep.* 值得

worth 视为介词，置于 be 动词之后，可接动名词或名词做其宾语。

例: The issue is worth paying attention to.

（这个问题值得注意。）

The car is worth a fortune.

（这辆车值不少钱。）

b. worthy *adj.* 值得的（与 of 连用）

be worthy of + 名词　　值得……

例: The issue is worthy of everyone's attention.

（这个问题值得每个人注意。）

c. worthwhile *adj.* 值得的（置于名词前，亦可置于 It is 之后，形成下列结构）

例: That's a worthwhile book to read.

（那是一本值得看的书。）

It is worthwhile to read that book.

= It pays to read that book.

（那本书值得看。）

5. 所有格与动名词的关系：

a. 本书第一章中，我们曾提到 that 引导的名词性从句可做主语。

例: That he teaches well is something that pleases me. (√)
主语
（他教得很好是件让我高兴的事。）

此时亦可将 that 从句化简成动名词短语，仍做句中的主语。
第一步：去除 that；
第二步：将 that 从句中的主语变成所有格；
第三步：将 that 从句中的动词变成动名词。
故：~~That~~ ~~he~~ teaches well is something that pleases me.
(His teaching)
→ His teaching well is something that pleases me.
主语

例: That John refused to do his homework made his father angry.
主语
= John's refusing to do his homework made his father angry.
（约翰不肯做作业使得父亲生气。）

That he didn't finish the work on time disappointed me.
主语
= His not finishing the work on time disappointed me.
（他未能准时做完工作使我失望。）

That they had helped John with the work won our great admiration. (√)
主语
= Their having helped John with the work won our great admiration. (√)
（他们帮约翰做这项工作赢得了我们的赞许。）

b. 之前我们也谈过，that 引导的名词性从句可做表认知的及物动词（think、feel、find、believe 等）以及表意愿的及物动词（hope、wish、expect、desire 等）的宾语。

例: I believe that he works hard.
vt.　　o.
（我相信他工作努力。）

I hope that he may join us.
vt. o.
（我希望他能加入我们。）

但并非所有的及物动词均可用 that 从句做宾语。表示喜欢、厌恶、在乎之意的及物动词，如 like、dislike（不喜欢）、enjoy、mind 等就不可接 that 从句做宾语。

例: I don't like that he smokes here. (×)
vt. o.

I don't enjoy that John joins us. (×)
vt. o.

补救的方法就是将 that 从句改为“所有格 + 动名词”的短语。

例: I don't like that he smokes here. (×)
(his smoking)
→ I don't like his smoking here. (√)
（我不喜欢他在此抽烟。）

I don't enjoy that John joins us. (×)
(John's joining)
→ I don't enjoy John's joining us. (√)
（我不喜欢约翰加入我们。）

Would you mind that I open the window? (×)
my opening
→ Would you mind my opening the window? (√)
= Would you mind if I opened the window? (√)
（如果我开窗你介意吗？）

比较:
Would you mind opening the window?
（请你打开窗户，你介意吗？）

注意
that 从句亦不可直接做介词的宾语。

例: I am curious about that he stays up late every night. (×)
prep. o.

此时，亦须将 that 从句变成“所有格 + 动名词”的短语。

例: I am curious about that he stays up late every night. (×)

prep. his staying

→ I am curious about his staying up late every night. (√)

prep.

（我对他每晚熬夜很好奇。）

In spite of that I helped him, he failed. (×)

prep. my helping

→ In spite of my helping him, he failed. (√)

prep.

（尽管我帮助了他，他还是失败了。）

但若 that 从句中的主语是物而非人时，就不用所有格，而直接将主语做宾语，之后接现在分词。

例: In spite of that the sun shone, the air was very cold. (×)

→ In spite of the sun shining, the air was very cold. (√)

o. 现在分词

（尽管阳光普照，空气还是很冷。）

口语中，that 从句中的主语即使是人，亦可采用本结构。

例: I insisted on | his going there. (正式)

所有格 动名词

| him going there. (非正式)

宾语 现在分词

（我坚持他去那里。）

What is the use of | his helping us? (正式)

所有格 动名词

| him helping us? (非正式)

宾语 现在分词

（他帮我们有什么用？）

但考试时，仍应以正式的用法为标准。

6. 动名词亦可与名词连用，形成复合名词：

例: a sleeping car （火车的）卧铺车厢

a dining room 饭厅

a walking stick 手杖

a laughing stock 笑柄

a writing pad　　便条纸
a starting point　　起点
a sewing machine　　缝纫机
a visiting card　　名片
drinking water　　饮用水

注意:

动名词与做形容词用的现在分词均可置于名词前。分辨的方法如下：

a. 若为“动名词 + 名词”，则后者有前者的功能，即动名词有“用来……”之意。

例: a walking stick
动名词
（手杖——用来走路的棍子）

a sleeping car
动名词
（卧铺车厢——用来睡觉的车厢）

a dining room
动名词
（饭厅——用来吃饭的房间）

b. 若为“现在分词 + 名词”，则后者有前者的性质，即现在分词有“正在……”或“会……”之意。

例: a walking dictionary
现在分词
（活字典或识字很多的人——会走路的字典/非用来走路的字典。）

a sleeping baby
现在分词
（睡觉中的婴儿——正在睡觉的婴儿/非用来睡觉的婴儿。）

a barking dog
现在分词
（正在叫的狗/非用来叫的狗。）

7. “动名词 + 宾语”做主语的变化：

例: Writing letters is a trying job for me. (佳)
= The writing of letters is a trying job for me. (可)
（对我而言，写信是件苦差事。）

Shooting birds is forbidden here. (佳)

= The shooting of birds is forbidden here. (可)

（在此射鸟是被禁止的/此处禁止射鸟。）

8. 有些动名词亦可做可数的普通名词用：

例: As an old saying goes, "Honesty is the best policy."

（俗语有云：“诚实为上策。”）

A knocking at the door was heard.

（敲门声被听见。）

He has a good understanding of the problem.

（他对此问题很了解。）

Don't forget to take your belongings (恒用复数) with you.

（别忘了带你的东西。）

9. 常用的动名词惯用语：

a. There is no V-ing　　不可能……

= It is impossible to V

例: There is no reasoning with such a stubborn man.

= It is impossible to reason with such a stubborn man.

（和这么固执的人理论是不可能的。）

b. It is no use V-ing　　……是无用的

= It is of no use to V

例: It is no use trying to escape.

= It is of no use to try to escape.

（想逃走是没有用的。）

c. cannot { help / resist / refrain from / stop } + V-ing　　忍不住……

= cannot but V

= cannot help but V

例: He couldn't help crying when he saw her.

= He couldn't but cry when he saw her.

（当他看见她时，忍不住哭了。）

d. on V-ing　一……就……

例: | On / Upon | hearing it, he cried.

例:	On Upon	hearing it, he cried.
=	As soon as Once The moment The instant	he heard it, he cried.
= He had	no sooner heard it than hardly heard it when scarcely heard it when	he cried.
=	No sooner had he heard it than Hardly had he heard it when Scarcely had he heard it when	he cried.

（一听到那件事他就哭了。）

EXERCISE

Ⅰ. 请选出一个正确的非谓语动词：

1. They don't allow people _____ here.
   (A) smoke　(B) to smoke　(C) smoking　(D) to smoking
2. _____ on the sofa, my father was reading the newspaper.
   (A) Sat　(B) Seat　(C) To sit　(D) Sitting
3. Peter is, _____, a walking dictionary.
   (A) so to tell　(B) to say so　(C) so to speak　(D) so to talk
4. I won't consider _____ my job at this time.
   (A) quit　(B) to quit　(C) quitting　(D) to quitting
5. You'd better have that bad tooth _____ out.
   (A) pull　(B) to pull　(C) to be pulled　(D) pulled
6. It is necessary _____ that work today.
   (A) to him to do　(B) of him to do　(C) for him to do　(D) of him doing
7. It is very kind _____ so.
   (A) for you to do　(B) of you to do
   (C) to you to do　(D) for you doing
8. Strictly _____, your writing is poor.
   (A) speak　(B) to speak　(C) speaking　(D) spoken
9. _____ with his sister's grades, his grades are not so good.
   (A) Compare　(B) Compared
   (C) Comparing　(D) By comparing
10. I meant _____ you, but I forgot.
    (A) to say　(B) saying　(C) to tell　(D) telling
11. Your idea, although quite good, needs _____ out.
    (A) try　(B) to try　(C) trying　(D) being tried

12. The boy stood _____ at the sight of blood.
(A) horrified (B) horrible (C) to horrify (D) horrifying

13. Does anyone _____ Mark live here?
(A) call (B) called (C) to call (D) calling

14. She knelt down before him, with tears _____ down her face.
(A) streaming (B) to streaming (C) stream (D) streamed

15. Do you understand the language _____ on that island?
(A) to speak (B) speaking (C) is spoken (D) spoken

II. 请选出一个正确的答案：

16. John was never heard _____ the Taiwan dialect.
(A) to speak (B) speak
(C) to have been spoken (D) spoke

17. You were opposed to _____ to go with us to the library, weren't you?
(A) our inviting her (B) us invite her
(C) that we invite her (D) we inviting her

18. Walking along the river, _____.
(A) I met several groups of hikers
(B) the river met several groups of hikers
(C) it was several groups of hikers
(D) we met by several groups of hikers

19. He asked me if John had the ability _____.
(A) to do that (B) to doing (C) of doing that (D) do that

20. Asked if he could come to the party that night, _____.
(A) nothing was said from anyone
(B) they did not get an answer from him
(C) nothing was said by him
(D) John nodded his head and left the room

21. It is sometimes difficult _____ you have just met.
(A) to make pleasant conversation at people
(B) making pleasant conversation on people
(C) making pleasant conversation for people
(D) to make pleasant conversation with people

22. The same thing, _____, would have been disastrous.
(A) had it happened in crowded places
(B) if happened in crowded places
(C) if had happened in crowded places
(D) if has happened in crowded places

23. Because of greatly reduced air pollution, this city is still _____.
(A) a good place where to live　　(B) lived as a good place
(C) a good place to live in　　(D) living in as a good place

24. The meeting is to be adjourned, everything _____ undecided.
(A) left　(B) to leave　(C) leaving　(D) leaves

25. I never know _____ when I go on a trip.
(A) what clothes should take　　(B) what clothes to take
(C) what clothes will I take　　(D) I take what clothes

III. 请选出错误的画线部分：

26. Medical researchers have not yet (A) been able to have developed (B) an effective (C) vaccine against (D) influenza.

27. Last week I boarded (A) the ordinary train, which, as I expected (B), was crowded (C) and there was no seat left, so I had to keep stood for (D) more than two hours.

28. I didn't know how (A) to get (B) to your house, so (C) I stopped asking (D) the way.

29. Strange to say, she takes to play baseball.
(A) (B) (C) (D)

30. Her mother did not approve of her to go to the party without dressing formally.
(A) (B) (C) (D)

标准答案

1. (B)	2. (D)	3. (C)	4. (C)	5. (D)	6. (C)	7. (B)	8. (C)	9. (B)	10. (C)
11. (C)	12. (A)	13. (B)	14. (A)	15. (D)	16. (A)	17. (A)	18. (A)	19. (A)	20. (D)
21. (D)	22. (A)	23. (C)	24. (A)	25. (B)	26. (B)	27. (D)	28. (D)	29. (D)	30. (B)

习题解说

1. allow sb to V　　允许某人从事……
2. 本句原为 My father sat on the sofa, my father was reading...，因两句无连词连接，而将前句化为分词结构，即：删除相同的主语 My father，之后的动词 sat 变成现在分词 Sitting，故 (D) 应为正选。
3. so to speak　　可以说是
   此为独立短语，可置于句首或句中修饰全句。
4. consider + V-ing　　考虑要……
5. 使役动词 have 可用原形动词或过去分词做宾语补语，但拔牙是让人拔，因此用表被动语态的过去分词 pulled。
6. necessary 修饰整个不定式短语，故用 for him to do。
7. kind 是修饰不定式短语中的 you，故用 of you to do。
8. strictly speaking　　严格说来
   此为独立的分词短语，常置于句首，做副词，修饰全句。
9. Compared with his sister, he is...
   = If he is compared with his sister, he is...
10. mean to V　　有意要……

11. need V-ing　　需要被……
= need to be p.p.
That car needs repairing.
= That car needs to be repaired.
（那辆车需要修理了。）
12. stand、lie、sit 等动词之后可接分词做补语，此处的 horrified 表“感到恐惧的”，为过去分词做形容词。
13. Does any one called Mark live here?
= Does any one who is called Mark live here?
14. “with + 宾语 + 分词”结构，此处因表主动语态，故用现在分词 streaming 做宾语补语。
15. 本题的 spoken 为过去分词，由 which is spoken 化简而来。
16. 在被动语态中，知觉动词（hear、see、feel 等）之后的不定式短语不可将 to 省略。
17. a. be opposed to V-ing　　反对……
b. our inviting her 是从 we invite her 变化而成。
18. 空格前有分词短语“Walking along the river”（沿着河走），故主语必须是人，人才有走路的能力，(A) 应为正选；(D) 应删除 by。
19. ability 之后必须用 to V 来修饰，不可用 of V-ing。
20. (Being) asked if...
= When John was asked if...
21. a. 以 it 做形式主语时，真正主语必须为不定式短语，不可用动名词。
b. make conversation with　　和……谈话
22. had it happened in crowded places
= if it had happened in crowded places
23. to live in 为不定式做形容词用，修饰 place。
24. ...everything left undecided.
= ...and everything is left undecided.
25. “what + 名词 + to V”形成名词短语。
what clothes to take
= what clothes I will take
26. be able to 之后不可用不定式的完成时，故 to have developed 应改为 to develop。

27. “keep + V-ing” 表 “持续做某事”，keep stood 应改为 keep standing（表持续站着）。

28. stop V-ing　停止做某事

stop to V　停下来去做某事

按照语意，(D) 中的 asking 应改为 to ask。

29. | take to | V-ing　喜欢……

| enjoy |

30. her to go 应改为 her going，做 approve of（赞同）的宾语。

第五章　助动词及易用错的动词

第一节　助动词

概　述

1. 助动词的定义：

助动词顾名思义就是一种帮助动词的词类，英语称作 helping verb 或 auxiliary。使用时置于动词前，使动词能表现出时态、语态、否定句、疑问句等变化。

例：I must go at once.
（我必须立刻走。）

He used to live in Taiwan.
（他以前住在台湾。）

May I go home now?
（我现在可以回家了吗？）

You need not do it.
（你不必做这件事。）

2. 助动词的种类：

be (am、is、are、was、were、have / has / had been)、have (has、had)、do (does、did)、shall (should)、will (would)、can (could)、may (might)、must、 ought to、need、dare、used to。

为方便同学们透彻了解它们的功能及用法，赖老师特别分项讲解如下：

第一种　be 动词

1. be 动词原为不完全不及物动词，译成“是”此时要用名词或形容词做表语。

例：He　is　handsome.
主语　不完全 vi.　adj. 做表语
（他很英俊。）

They　are　good students.
主语　不完全 vi.　n. 做表语
（他们是好学生。）

2. 但 be 动词之后亦可接现在分词或过去分词表进行时或被动语态，此时 be 动词就称为助动词。

a. be + 现在分词 = 进行时

例: He is（助动词） reading（现在分词） a book.

（他正在看书。）

b. be + 及物动词的过去分词 = 被动语态

例: He was（助动词） elected（过去分词） chairman.

（他当选为主席。）

有关进行时被动语态的用法，我们在时态和语态一章再详加讨论。

第二种 have

have、has、had + 过去分词 已经……

以上结构构成动词的完成时，have 为助动词，译成“已经”。

例: He has written the letter. (现在完成时)

（他已把信写好了。）

I had finished the task before he came. (过去完成时)

（在他来之前我已完成此工作。）

有关完成时的用法，我们在时态一章再详加讨论。

第三种 do

do、does、did 等助动词可用以形成下列结构：

1. do / does / did + not + 原形动词

例: I didn't know what to do.

（我不知要怎么做。）

He did not see me.

（他没看见我。）

注意:

a. 任何动词与 not 连用，形成否定时，一定要靠 do、does、did 再加上 not 协助，不可造这样的句子：

例: I not love him. (×)
→ I don't love him. (√)
（我不爱他。）

He not lives here. (×)
→ He doesn't live here. (√)
（他不住在这儿。）

b. 动词前若置 not 以外的否定副词，如：

never（从未）、seldom（不常）、rarely（很少）、hardly（几乎不）、scarcely（几乎不/非常少）等，则不须与 do、does、did 连用。

例: He did never live here. (×)
→ He never lived here. (√)
（他从未住过这儿。）

He does seldom sing. (×)
→ He seldom sings. (√)
（他很少唱歌。）

2. 疑问句：

例: Did you understand it?
（你懂吗？）

Where does he live?
（他住哪儿？）

3. 强势语气：

即在肯定句的动词前，按时态、人称置入 do、does 或 did，再将动词改为原形，此时 do、does、did 均译成“的确”。

例: He worked hard.
一般过去时
（他很用功。）

→ He did work hard.
（他真的很用功。）

He loves to do it.
一般现在时
（他喜欢做这事。）

→ He does love to do it.
（他的确喜欢做这事。）

注意

有时祈使句（即一开头就是原形动词的句子），前面亦可加 Do，造成强势语气，Do 译成“务必”。

例: Be quiet.
（安静。）

→ Do be quiet.

= Be sure to be quiet.
（务必要安静。）

Study hard.
（用功。）

→ Do study hard.

= Be sure to study hard.
（务必要用功。）

4. 否定倒装句：

例: Never did I know that he was so stupid.
（我从不知道他这么笨。）

＊容赖老师在倒装结构一章中，再为诸位慢慢道来。

5. 代动词（pro-verb）：

此种助动词用以代替句中已出现过的动词及其后的其他词类。

例: Did you read this book?

Yes, I did (= read this book).
（你看过这本书吗？）
（是的，我看过这本书。）

I work as hard as he does (= works).
（我工作和他一样辛苦。）

第四种 shall、will

1. shall、will 表“将要”，之后接原形动词。

2. 传统的语法常在 shall 及 will 二词上做文章，所谓第一人称 I 之后须用 shall，we 之后可用 shall 或 will，you 之后须用 shall 等。现在的英语可没有如此的用法。而且英美人士多已用 will 取代 shall 表单纯的一般将来时。因此赖老师建议你只须使用 will 就好，既口语化，又是常态用法。

例: I will tell you the truth tomorrow.
（我明天会告诉你事实真相。）

He will be twenty the day after tomorrow.
（后天他就 20 岁了。）

Will you be here tomorrow?
（你明天会在这儿吗？）

＊上列结构中，不论主语为第几人称均可用 will。

3. 但在下列结构中，则仍习惯用 shall 代替 will:

a. 征求对方意见时:

Shall I...?　　要不要我……？

例: Shall I open the door?
= Would you like me to open the door?
（要不要我开门呢？）

b. 请求对方合作时:

Shall we...?　　我们……好吗？

例: Shall we go for a walk?
= Let's go for a walk, shall we?
（我们散个步，好吗？）

c. 命令对方时:

You shall...　　你必须……
= You must...

例: You shall obey the law.
（你必须遵守法律。）

注意:

条约中尤其出现此类用法:

例: Article One: You (或 One) shall wash your (或 one's) hands after using the toilet.
（第一条：如厕后要洗手。）

d. 向对方保证某种承诺时：

You shall...　　你一定会……

例: You shall have the present.

= I promise that you will have the present.

（我保证你会得到礼物的。）

第五种　should

1. should 之后接原形动词。

2. should 的主要功能就是表示一种义务，译为“应当”，此时等于 ought to。

例: We (You / One / A man) should be kind to others.

（吾人应善待他人。）

3. 但在下列结构时，习惯上亦用 should，有其不同的意思：

a. It is natural / proper / right / advisable / desirable / no wonder that...should　　……会……

乃自然的、适当的、正当的、恰当的、较好的、无疑的。

例: It is natural that he should get angry.

（他会生气是很自然的事。）

It is proper that one who works hard should be successful.

（努力的人会成功，这是合理的。）

It is no wonder that such a naughty boy should be punished. (罕)

= No wonder such a naughty boy should be punished. (常用)

（这样顽皮的孩子受到处罚，也就不足为奇了。）

b. It is necessary / imperative / essential / important / urgent that...should (应当)...　　……应当……是有必要的。

例: It is necessary that he (should) finish the work before leaving.

（他必须在走之前完成工作。）

注意
在本结构中的 should 通常予以省略，而保留其后的原形动词。

例: It is important that he finish the job before leaving.
（重要的是，他必须在走之前完成工作。）
It is imperative that he do the work now.
（他现在应该赶紧做这项工作。）

c. It is | surprising / amazing | that...should (居然)...　令人惊异的是……居然……

例: It is surprising that he should be so kind.
（令人惊讶的是，他竟然这么仁慈。）

d. It is | a pity / a regret / regrettable | that...should (居然)...　令人遗憾的是……居然……

例: It is a pity that he should be so rude.
（他这么粗鲁，真令人遗憾。）
* 见虚拟语气一章。

4. 意志动词如表“建议”（propose、recommend、suggest）、“要求”（ask、demand、desire、require、insist、request）、“命令”（order、command）、“规定”（rule、regulate）等，之后若有 that 从句做宾语时，that 从句中亦使用 should，而 should 往往亦予以省略。

例: He suggested that we (should) leave at once.
（他建议我们立刻离去。）
They demanded that he (should) be quiet.
（他们要求他安静。）

5. lest 表“以免”，为副词性连词，所引导的从句亦使用 should，而 should 亦可予以省略。

例: He came early lest he (should) be late.
= He came early for fear that he might be late. (might 不可省略)
（他怕迟到而来得很早。）
* 见虚拟语气一章。

6. If 从句若表示与将来状况相反时，应使用 should，表“万一”之意。

例: If you should be late again, you will spoil the plan.
（你万一再迟到，就会破坏这个计划。）

＊见虚拟语气一章。

7. 在一般过去时中，要用 should 代替 shall。

例: I said to him, "I shall be at home this evening."
（我告诉他：“今晚我会在家。”）

I told him that I should be at home that evening.
（我告诉他那天晚上我会在家。）

8. should have + 过去分词

a. 表示与过去事实相反的虚拟语气，译成“早应……”。

例: If you had not helped me, I should have died.
（你当时要是没救我，我就死了。）

You should have done it earlier.
（你应该早点儿做好的。）

It was such a fine sight. You should have seen it.
（这么好的景色，你当时真该看看的。）

b. 表示“居然已经”，往往出现在下列结构中：

例: It is surprising that he should have passed the examination.
（令人惊讶的是他居然已通过了考试。）

It is a pity that he should have done such a stupid thing.
（真遗憾他竟然做了这么愚蠢的事。）

第六种 would

1. would 是 will（将要）的过去式，用以表示过去将来时。

例: He said, "I will try again."
（他说：“我会再试试。”）

He said that he would try again.
（他说他会再试试。）

Did you know when he would come?
（你当时知道他何时会来吗？）

> **注意**:
> 新闻英语中，常出现 will 与一般过去时动词连用的现象。

例: He said that he will visit the country sometime in July.
一般过去时 vt. 一般将来时 vt.
（他说7月份要找个时间造访该国。）

> **注意**:
> 本句暗示 He said 虽为过去状态，但 he will visit...in July 则表示作者写本句时是七月前写的，七月尚未到来，故用 will。换言之，will 用于尚未到来的时间，而 would 则用于过去的时间。为了方便了解，赖老师特编下列两段对话：

对话一：

A: I saw John a few days ago.
B: What did he say?
A: He said that he would call on you yesterday.
B: But he didn't show up yesterday.

A：几天前我看到约翰。
B：他说了些什么？
A：他说昨天要拜访你。
B：但他昨天并没有出现。

对话二：

A: I saw John a few days ago.
B: What did he say?
A: He said that he will call on you tomorrow.
B: I'll be expecting him then.

A：几天前我看到约翰。
B：他说了些什么？
A：他说明天要去拜访你。
B：到时候我会等他的。

2. would + 原形动词 （如果……）就会……
would have + 过去分词

本句型属虚拟语气，分别表与现在和过去事实相反。

a. 与现在事实相反：

例: If I had money now, I would buy a car. (But I don't have money now.)
（如果我现在有钱，我会买辆车——但我现在没钱。）

b. 与过去事实相反：

例: If I had had money then, I would have bought a car. (But I didn't have money then.)

（当时我要是有钱，早就买车了——但我当时没钱。）

＊见虚拟语气一章。

3. would rather + 原形动词　　宁愿……

例: I would rather go than stay here.

= I would sooner go than stay here.

= I would as soon go as stay here.

（我宁愿走也不要留在这儿。）

4. I would rather + (that) 从句　　我多么希望……

= I wish + (that) 从句

本句型属虚拟语气，若与现在事实相反，that 从句用一般过去时；若与过去事实相反，则用过去完成时。

a. 与现在事实相反：

例: I would rather (that) he were here.

= I wish (that) he were here.

（我多么希望他现在在这里。）

b. 与过去事实相反：

例: I would rather (that) he had been here yesterday.

= I wish (that) he had been here yesterday. (But he wasn't here.)

（我多么希望他昨天就在这里。）

5. Would you mind + | V-ing / if 从句 | ?　　您介不介意……？

= Do you mind + | V-ing / if 从句 | ?

例: Would you mind | doing it for me? / if you did it for me? |

= Do you mind | doing it for me? / if you do it for me? |

（请您帮我做这事好吗？）

注意:

a. Would you mind 的口气要比 Do you mind 客气。

同理:

"Would you please do it for me?" 要比

"Will you please do it for me?" 语气客气得多。

（请您帮我做这事好吗？）

b. Would you mind 之后 if 从句中，动词使用一般过去时，以便与一般过去时的助动词 Would 配合。Do you mind 之后的 if 从句中，动词要使用一般现在时，以便与一般现在时的助动词 Do 配合。

第七种　can、could

助动词 can 有下列意思及用法：

1. 表"能力"（= be able to），译成"能够"。

例: He can cope with the problem.

= He is able to cope with the problem.

（他能够处理这个问题。）

2. 表"可能性"，译成"有可能"。

例: He can be wrong | to say so. / if he says so. |

（他要是这么说就可能错了。）

3. 表"许可"（= may），译成"可以"。

例: You can go home now.

（你现在可以回家了。）

You can't smoke here.

（你不可以在这儿抽烟。）

4. 在疑问句或否定句中，表"可能性"，译成"有可能"或"不可能"。

例: Can it be true? No, it can't be true.

（这可能是真的吗？不，这不可能是真的。）

5. 表对过去事物的否定推论：

can't have + 过去分词　　不可能曾……

例: He is so honest that he can't have stolen your money yesterday.
（他这么老实不可能昨天偷你的钱。）

注意:

a. can 仅用以表对过去事物的否定推论，无法做肯定推论。换言之，无下列用法：

例: He can have stolen your money. (×)
（他可能偷了你的钱。）

b. 表对过去事物的肯定推论，有两种句型：

1) must have + 过去分词　　一定曾经……

例: He looks nervous; he must have stolen your money.
（他看起来紧张兮兮的，一定是偷了你的钱。）

2) may have + 过去分词　　可能曾经……

例: He looks nervous; he may have stolen your moeny.
（他看起来紧张兮兮的，很可能偷了你的钱。）

c. 疑问句中表对过去事物的推论，则用“Can + S + have + 过去分词？”，译成“有可能……吗？”。

例: Can he have stolen your money?
（他有可能偷了你的钱吗？）

6. could 为 can 的过去式，通常与另一一般过去时动词连用，用以表示过去的状况。

例: She could speak English well when she was ten.
（她 10 岁时英语就说得很好了。）

When she entered the house, she could smell something burning.
（她走进屋子时，闻到有东西烧焦了。）

7. 一如 would，could 亦可使用在疑问句中，以表示客气的语气。

例: Could / Would you please do it for me?
（请你帮我做这事好吗？）

8. could = was / were able to

使用于一般过去时中，表示过去的能力。

例: When young, he could eat eight bowls of rice at a time.
= When young, he was able to eat eight bowls of rice at a time.
（他年轻时可以一次吃 8 碗饭。）

9. can 与 not 连用时，不要写成 can not，而要写成 cannot 或 can't。

例: He can not write letters. (非习惯用法)
→ He cannot (或 can't) write letters. (√)
（他不会写信。）

> **注意**
> could 与 not 连用时，则应写成 could not 或 couldn't，不要写成 couldnot。

10. 有关 can 的惯用语:

a. I | can but / can only | do so.
（我只能这么做。）

b. I cannot but laugh.
= I cannot help but laugh.
= I cannot help laughing.
（我忍不住大笑。）

* 上列三句中，cannot but 之后接原形动词，cannot help but 之后亦接原形动词，而 cannot help 之后则接动名词，此时等于 resist（抗拒）或 stop（停止）之意。

c. We cannot be too careful in choosing friends.
（我们在择友时要越小心越好/我们择友时再小心也不为过。）

d. I couldn't care less.
（我一点儿都不在乎。——我已经不在乎到了极点，因此我不能低于比现在不在乎的程度了。）

e. I couldn't agree more.
（我同意极了。——我已经同意到了极点，因此我不能比现在更加同意了。）

第八种　may、might

助动词 may 之后接原形动词，有下列意思及用法：

1. 表“许可”，译成“可以”。

例: You may take whatever you like.
（你喜欢什么就可以拿什么。）

May I go home?
（我可以回家吗？）

Might I make a suggestion?
（我可以提出一个建议吗？）

> **注意**
> might 与 would、could 一样，在疑问句中使用一般过去时，有客气的语气。

2. 表“推测”，译成“可能”，此时等于 can。

例: It may be true.
（这或许是对的。）

He may come, or he may not (come).
= Perhaps he will come; perhaps he will not (come).
（他也许会来，也许不会。）

3. may not 有两种意思：

a. 可能不会

例: It's getting late; he may not come.
（越来越晚了，他可能不会来了。）

b. 不可以（= must not）

例: You may not / must not cheat during exams.
（你不可以在考试中作弊。）

4. might 亦可与另一一般过去时动词连用，以表示过去的状况。

例: He said, "You may go."
（他说：“你可以走了。”）

He said that I might go.
（他说我可以走了。）

I thought that it might rain.
（我当时认为可能会下雨。）

5. might + 原形动词　　也许会……
might have + 过去分词　　当时也许会……

可用于虚拟语气中，分别表示与现在事实及过去事实相反。

a. 与现在事实相反：

if 从句中的动词使用一般过去时。

例: If he tried hard, he might succeed. (But he doesn't try hard.)
（假如他努力，也许会成功——但他并不努力。）

b. 与过去事实相反：
if 从句中的动词使用过去完成时。

例: If he had tried hard, he might have succeeded. (But he didn't try hard.)
（假如当时他努力，早就成功了——但他当时并未努力。）

6. 有关 may 的惯用语：

a. may well + 原形动词　　大可/足可以……

例: He knows so many things that he may well be called a genius.
（他懂那么多东西，因此大可被称为天才。）

b. may as well + 原形动词　　不妨……（语气缓和）
比较:
had better + 原形动词　　最好……（语气较强）

例: You may as well stay home.
（你不妨留在家中。）

You had better stay home.
（你最好留在家中。）

c. may as well + 原形动词 + as + 原形动词　　与其……倒不如……
= had better + 原形动词 + than + 原形动词

例: You may as well stay home as go out with them.
（你与其和他们出去，倒不如留在家里。）

注意
"may as well...as..."（与其……倒不如……）表较大的可能性，might as well ...as...（与其……倒不如……）则表较小的可能性。

例: You might as well die as make friends with Mary.
（你与其和玛丽交朋友，倒不如死了算了——但我相信你不太可能去死。）

第九种　must

1. must 之后接原形动词。

2. 表“义务”，译成“必须”。

例: You must finish the work before leaving.
（你一定要在离开前完成工作。）

3. must（必须）与 have to（必须；不得不）的比较：

a. must 表示一种义务上强制的必须，而 have to 有勉强的意味，译成“有必要”。

例: You must love your country. (佳)
（你必须爱国。）

You have to love your country.
（你得爱国——暗示你若不爱国，别人也拿你没办法。）

b. must 只用于表示现在或将来的状况；而 have to 则可用于表过去、现在及将来的状况。

1) must

例: 现在: You must come now. (✓)
（你现在必须来。）

将来: You must come tomorrow. (✓)
（你明天必须来。）

过去: You must come yesterday. (×)
（你昨天必须来。）

2) have to

例: 过去: He had to come yesterday.
（他昨天非来不可。）

现在: He has to come now.
（他现在非来不可。）

将来: He will have to come tomorrow.
（他明天非来不可。）

c. 否定时：

1) must not　不可以
= may not

例: You must not do it.
（你绝不可做这事。）

2) don't have to　不必
= need not

例: You don't have to do it.
（你不必做这事。）

d. 在口语中，have to 经常被 have got to 或 gotta 取代。

例: I have to tell you the truth.
= I've got to tell you the truth.
= I gotta tell you the truth.
（我得告诉你事实真相。）

4. must 表示对现在状况或过去状况的推论。

a. 对现在状况的推论：
must + 原形动词　　一定……

例: It must be true.
（这一定是真的。）

b. 对过去状况的推论：
must have + 过去分词　　一定曾经……

例: It must have rained last night.
（昨晚一定下过雨。）

第十种　ought to

ought to 之后接原形动词，有下列意思及用语：

1. ought to 可表“义务”，译成“应当”，等于 should。

例: You ought to / should be kind to others.
（你应该要和善待人。）

You ought not to / shouldn't talk like that.
（你不该那样说话。）

2. ought to 亦可表“推论”，译成“应当会”。

例: Since he works hard, he ought to / should succeed.
（由于他很努力，应该会成功。）

3. ought to / should | have + 过去分词　　本应会……（却不如此）

形成与过去事实相反的虚拟语气。此时 if 从句中的动词要用过去完成时。

例: If he had worked hard, he ought to / should have been successful.

（如果他当时努力，应该早就成功了。）

4. ought to / should | have + 过去分词　　应当已经……（可能如此）

亦可表示"推论至目前为止已完成的动作"，常与 by now（到现在为止）连用。

例: He ought to / should have arrived in New York by now.

（他现在应该已到达纽约了。）

第十一种　need

1. 在肯定句中，need 为一般动词，同样具有人称及时态的变化，译成"必须"或"需要"，之后接不定式短语或名词做宾语。

例: He needs to go.
　　　　　　不定式

（他需要走。）

He needs my help.
　　　　　　名词

（他需要我的帮助。）

> **注意**
> 某物需要某种方法处理时，need 之后可接不定式短语，但一定为被动语态；也接动名词，但一定为主动语态。

例: The car needs to be cleaned. (√)
　　　　　　不定式（被动语态）

= The car needs cleaning.
　　　　　　动名词

（这辆车需要清洗。）

理由:

本句实等于：

The car needs the process of cleaning.

（这辆车需要清洗的过程。）

The car needs being cleaned. (×)

同理：

→The window needs to be fixed. (√)

= The window needs fixing. (√)

（这窗户需要修理。）

The window needs being fixed. (×)

2. 否定句中，need 与 not 连用，此时 need 为助动词，句型如下：

need not + 原形动词

例: He need not go. (√)

（他不必去。）

He need not to go. (×)

He needs not go. (×)

但:He need not go. (need 是助动词)

= He doesn't need to go. (need 是动词)

3. 表过去状况时：

a. didn't need to + 原形动词　　当时不必……（而且亦未如此做）

例: He didn't need to attend the party, so he stayed home.

（当时他不必参加派对，所以就留在家里。）

b. need not have + 过去分词　　当时不必……（但却如此做）

例: He needn't have attended the party, but he went there just the same.

（当时他可以不必参加派对，但他还是去了。）

4. 在疑问句中，need 做一般动词或助动词皆可。

例: Does he need to go? (need 为一般动词)

= Need he go? (Need 为助动词)

（他需要去吗？）

5. 注意 need 在反意疑问句中的变化：

a. 一般动词

例: He needs to go, doesn't he? (needs 为动词)

（他需要去，不是吗？）

He doesn't need to go, does he?

（他不必去，对吧？）

b. 助动词

例: He need not go, need he? (need 与 not 连用，是助动词)
（他不必去，对吗？）

第十二种 dare

1. dare 可做助动词，用于否定句或疑问句中。

dare not + 原形动词　　不敢……
Dare one + 原形动词？　　某人敢……吗？

例: He dares not go. (×)
→ He dare not go. (√)
（他不敢去。）

Dare he go?
（他敢去吗？）

2. How dare + 一般陈述句？　　……怎敢……？

例: How dare you say such a thing to me?
（你怎敢在我面前说这种话？）

3. 在 whether 从句中，dare 亦可做助动词。

例: I wonder whether he dare do it.
（我怀疑他敢不敢做这事。）

4. 在肯定句中，dare 为一般动词，有时态和人称的变化，之后接不定式。

例: He dares to go. (现在)
（他敢去。）

He dared to go. (过去)
（当时他敢去。）

5. dare not + 原形动词　　不敢……

= do not dare (to) + 原形动词

例: He dare not answer the phone.
= He doesn't dare (to) answer the phone.
（他不敢接电话。）

I have never dared (to) speak to him.
（我从来不敢与他说话。）

6. dare 亦可做及物动词，表“向某人挑战”之意，句型如下：

dare sb to + 原形动词

= challenge sb to + 原形动词

例: He dared me to jump the stream.
（他向我挑战跳过这条小溪。）

7. I daresay +（that）从句　　我敢说……

例: I daresay he will be late again.
（我敢说他又会迟到。）

* daresay 是一个词，亦可做 dare say。

第十三种　used to

1. used to 视为助动词，之后接原形动词，句型如下：

used to + 原形动词　　过去曾经……

例: He used to live here.
（他以前住过这儿。）

I used to call on him every Sunday.
（我以前每个星期天都去拜访他。）

There used to be a big tree here.
（这儿以前有一棵大树。）

2. 由于 used to 可视为助动词，故我们要注意其在问句及否定句中的用法。

例: There used to be a pond in this garden.
（这座花园里以前有个池塘。）

→ Did there use to be a pond in this garden?
（这座花园里以前有池塘吗？）

I didn't use to like coffee, but I'm quite fond of it now. (罕)
（我以前不喜欢咖啡，但现在很喜欢了。）

> **注意**
>
> used to 的主语若为人时，问句中有两种变化：
>
> 例: He used to work hard.
> 人
> （他以前很用功。）

→ Used he to work hard? (罕)
或 Did he use to work hard? (常用)
（他以前很用功吗？）

3. 在下列结构中，used 非助动词，而是 use 的过去分词：

a. 人 + be used to + 名词 / 动名词　　某人习惯于……
（used: adj.；to: 介）

本结构的 used 是形容词，译成“习惯的”，等于 accustomed，之后的 to 为介词，译成“针对”。

例: He is used to working alone.
（He: 人；working: 动名词）
（他习惯单独工作。）

He hasn't been / got used to city life yet.
（He: 人；city life: n.）
（他还不习惯都市生活。）

He is used to speaking aloud. (佳)
（He: 人）
= He is accustomed to speaking aloud. (佳)
= He has accustomed himself to speaking aloud. (罕)
（他习惯大声说话。）

b. 物 + be used to + 原形动词　　被用来……
本结构中的 used 是过去分词，置于 be 动词之后，形成被动语态，译成“被用来”，之后的 to 为不定式，其后接原形动词。

例: The book can be used to teach us English writing.
（这本书可用来教我们英语写作。）

A lot of energy was used to deal with the problem.
（许多精力都用来解决这个问题。）

c. 物 + be used as + 名词　　被用做……

例: The knife was used as a weapon. (✓)
（weapon: n.）
（这把刀被用来当武器。）

不可写成：
The knife was used to be a weapon. (×)

第二节　易用错的动词

1. lie、lay：

lie　*vi.*　躺（其后不加宾语）
动词变化为 lie、lay、lain、lying。
lie　*vi.*　说谎 (其后不加宾语)
动词变化为 lie、lied、lied、lying。
lay　*vt.*　放置；生产 (其后加宾语)
动词变化为 lay、laid、laid、laying。

> **注意**
> lay 为及物动词，可用被动语态即“be laid”，而 lie 是不及物动词，无被动用法，即无“be lied”或“be lain”的用法。

a. lie（躺）

例: He will lie on the bed for a while.
（他将在床上躺片刻。）
He lay on the bed a while ago.
（他刚才躺在床上。）
He has lain on the bed for two hours.
（他在床上躺了两个钟头了。）
He has been lying there all day.
（他一整天都躺在那儿。）

b. lie（说谎）

例: Don't lie to me.
（别对我撒谎。）
He lied to me.
（他对我撒谎。）

c. lay（放置；生产）

例: He will lay a book on the desk.
宾语
（他将会把一本书放在桌上。）
He laid a book on the desk a while ago.
（他刚才把一本书放在桌上。）

He has laid a book on the desk.
（他已把一本书放在桌上。）

A book has been laid on the desk.
（一本书已经被放在桌上。）

A book has been lain on the desk. (×)

2. sit、set、seat：

sit *vi.* 坐（其后不加宾语）
动词变化为 sit、sat、sat、sitting。
set *vt.* 安置
动词变化为 set、set、set、setting。
seat *vt.* 使就座
动词变化为 seat、seated、seated、seating。

注意:

a. seat 为及物动词，其后须加上宾语。sit 虽亦可做及物动词，但仅限于 sit oneself 之口语用法，且并不常用。

例: He came in and sat down. (✓)
（他进来，并坐了下来。）
He came in and seated down. (×，seated 之后应加宾语，且不能与 down 连用)
（他进来，并坐了下来。）

b. seat 之后若无宾语，则应采用被动语态（即"be seated"），此时 seated 可视为形容词，表"坐着的"。

例: John sat by the window, looking out at passersby.
= John was seated by the window, looking out at passersby.
（约翰坐在窗边，看着窗外路过的行人。）
May I seat you here? (此处 seat 表"使就座")
（我可以安排你坐在这里吗？）

c. set 亦为及物动词，表"摆设"。

例: He sat the table for dinner. (×)
→ He set the table for dinner. (✓)
（他摆桌子准备吃晚饭。）

3. rise、raise、arise、arouse：

rise *vi.* 起床；升起（其后不加宾语）
动词变化为 rise、rose、risen、rising。
raise *vt.* 举起；饲养

动词变化为 raise、raised、raised、raising。

arise　*vi.*　起因于（与 from 连用）

动词变化为 arise、arose、arisen、arising。

arouse　*vt.*　激起

动词变化为 arouse、aroused、aroused、arousing。

注意

raise 和 arouse 为及物动词，其后须接宾语，亦可用被动语态。

例: He rose at 7 every morning.

= He got up at 7 every morning.

（他每天早上 7 点起床。）

The sun raises in the east. (×)

→ The sun rises in the east. (✓)

（太阳从东方升起。）

Accidents	arise from	carelessness.
	result from	

（意外源于粗心。）

Raise your hand if you have any questions.

（有任何问题请举手。）

Many cattle are raised on this farm.

（这座农场饲养了许多牛。）

His bitter words aroused my anger.

（他尖锐的话语引起了我的愤怒。）

4. hang:

hang　*vt. & vi.*　挂

动词变化为 hang、hung、hung、hanging。

hang　*vt.*　吊死

动词变化为 hang、hanged、hanged、hanging。

例: The picture hangs on the wall.

= The picture is hung on the wall.

（图片挂在墙上。）

Tom Dooley was hanged.

（汤姆·杜利被吊死了。）

The picture is hanged on the wall. (×)

The robber was hung. (×)

They hanged the murderer yesterday.

（昨天他们把凶手吊死了。）

5. fly、flow：

fly *vi.* 飞

动词变化为 fly、flew、flown、flying。

flow *vi.* 流

动词变化为 flow、flowed、flowed、flowing。

例：The airplane flew high in the sky.
（飞机在高空中飞行。）

This is the place from which the river flows.
（这就是这条河流出的地方——发源地。）

The bird flowed all the way here from Canada. (×，应改为 flew)
（鸟儿从加拿大一路飞到这儿。）

6. take、bring：

take （从此处）拿走

bring （从别处）拿来

例：Take the book to the library, please.
（请把这本书拿去图书馆。）

Bring them back here.
（把他们带回这里来。）

Take him in my office. (×，Take 应改为 Bring)
（带他到我的办公室来。）

Take it with you when you go there.
（你去那里时，把它带着。）

Bring it with you when you come here.
（你来这里时，把它带着。）

7. refuse：

refuse 拒绝

a. refuse + 名词

例：He refused my suggestion.
（他拒绝我的建议。）

b. refuse to + 原形动词

例：He refused going with me. (×)
→ He refused to go with me. (√)
（他拒绝和我走。）

> **注意**
> reject（排斥）意思与 refuse 相近，但却应接动名词做宾语。
> **例**: He rejected to work with Mary because he thought she was too selfish. (×)
> → He rejected working with Mary because he thought she was too selfish. (√)
> （他拒绝与玛丽共事，因为他认为她太自私了。）

c. refuse 之后不可接 that 从句。

例: He refused that he had done something wrong. (×)
→ He denied that he had done something wrong. (√)
= He refused to admit that he had done something wrong. (√)
（他拒绝承认做错事。）

8. spend:

人 + spend + 时间（或金钱）+ | 动名词 / on + 名词 |

例: I spent two hours to to write this letter. (×)
→ I spent two hours writing this letter. (√)
（我花了两小时写这封信。）

I spent all my income buying books.
= I spent all my income on books.
（我将所有的收入花在买书上。）

9. take、cost:

It takes +（人）+ 时间 + to V
It costs +（人）+ 金钱 + to V

例: It takes (one) about two hours to go from here to Paris.
（从这里到巴黎花了我两个小时。）

It cost (me) five dollars to buy that book.
（买那本书花了我 5 块钱。）

I cost five dollars to buy that book. (×)

理由:
"I cost five dollars..."表示"买我这个人只要花 5 元就可以了"，即"我这个人只值 5 元"，不合逻辑。

10. answer、reply to:

answer + 名词　　回答……
= reply to + 名词
　　　介

例: He failed to reply her question. (×)
→ He failed to answer her question. (√)
= He failed to reply to her question.
（他未能回答她的问题。）

注意

answer 也可接 that 从句做宾语，而 reply to 不可接 that 从句做宾语，须删除介词 to 方可接 that 从句。

例: When asked if he would buy a car, John answered that he had no money.
= When asked if he would buy a car, John replied that he had no money.
（约翰被问到是否要买车时，他回答他没钱。）
When asked if he would buy a car, John replied to that he had no money. (×)

11. reach、get to、arrive in / at:

reach + 宾语　　到达……
= arrive + in（大地方） / at（小地方）
= get to + 宾语

例: I reached / arrived in / got to Chicago at 12.
（我 12 点到达芝加哥。）

注意:

a. 大地方乃指城市、国家、地区等，小地方乃指建筑物如车站、邮局等。

例: By the time I arrived at the station, the train had gone.
（等我到车站时，火车已经驶离了。）

b. 与副词 home、there、here 等连用时，一律不加介词。

例: I arrived at / got to there at 12. (×)
→ I reached / got there at 12. (√)
（我 12 点到达那里。）

12. 动词 + 介副词 + 宾语:

= 动词 + 宾语（普通名词、专有名词、代词）+ 介副词例: We have to carry out that mission.
= We have to carry that mission out.
（我们必须执行那项任务。）

注意
代词一定要置于介副词之前。故：
例: We have to carry out it. (×)
We have to carry it out. (✓)
（我们必须执行这件事。）

类似此类结构的动词短语如下：

bring up	抚养	figure out	想出
call down	斥责	give up	放弃
call off	取消	put out	熄灭
cross out	删去	take off	脱掉（衣服等）
do over	重做	take over	接管
talk over	商讨	pick up	拾起
think over	考虑	put off	延期
think up	设计	put on	穿
try on	试穿（衣服等）	try out	试验（机器、想法等）
hand in	交出	turn down	拒绝
look over	检查	turn in	交出
look up	查（生词、电话号码等）	turn off	关上
make out	了解	turn on	打开（开关等）
pick out	挑选		

注意
由上得知，我们不可说：
This shirt looks good. Can I try on it? (×)
应说：
This shirt looks good. Can I try it on? (✓)
（这件衬衫很好看。我可以试穿吗？）

13. 动词 + 介词 + 宾语：

动词 + 介词 + 宾语（普通名词、专有名词、代词）
例: I called him on yesterday. (×)
→ I called on him yesterday. (✓)
（我昨天拜访了他。）

类似此结构的短语动词如下：

	call for	要求；需要	go over	复习
	come across	偶然遇见	go through	检查
=	run into		keep on	继续
=	meet...by chance		look after	照顾
	get over	复原	look for	找寻
=	recover from		look into	调查
	get through	做完	take after	像

14. “动词 + 介词 + 名词（代词）”的重要短语：

a. agree on... 就（条约、定义）达成协议

例: We finally agreed on the contract.

= We finally reached an agreement on the contract.

（我们终于就条约达成了协议。）

b. agree to + 事物 同意某事

例: I agree to his coming here.

（我同意他来。）

c. agree with + 人 同意某人

例: I agree with him on this point.

（关于这点，我同意他的看法。）

d. consist of... 包括……

例: This class consists of 10 students.

= This class is composed of 10 students.

= This class is made up of 10 students.

（这个班共有 10 名学生。）

e. argue with + 人 与某人争论
argue over + 事物 争论某事
approve of + 事物 赞同某事物
care for 喜欢
complain about / of 抱怨
consent to 同意
comment on 评论
count on 依赖
= depend on
= rely on

laugh at	取笑
hear from	听到某人的音讯；接到某人的来信

15. "动词 + 宾语 + 介词 + 宾语"的重要短语：

例: Add this number to that number.
（将这个数与那个数相加。）

He blamed me for the fault.
（他把错归咎于我。）

I congratulated him on his success.
（我恭贺他的成功。）

He explained it to me.
（他向我解释此事。）

He won't excuse me for being rude.
（他不会原谅我的粗鲁行为。）

16. 重要的三词（三词以上）短语动词：

例: He fell in love with Mary.
（他爱上了玛丽。）

He will get in touch with her when he goes to New York.
联络
（他到纽约时会和她联络。）

He has | made up his mind / = decided | to study hard.
（他已下决心要努力学习。）

Who takes charge of this class?
掌理
= Who is in charge of this class?
（这个班由谁负责？）

He'll | take care of / look after | my children when I go on a trip.
（我去旅行时，他会照顾我的小孩。）

Students have complete access to books in the library.
有完全使用权
（学生可以任意使用图书馆内的书。）

I look forward to seeing you soon.
（我期盼能很快见到你。）

17. prefer 的用法：

a. prefer + | 名词
动名词 | + to（介） + | 名词
动名词 |

例：I prefer coffee to tea.

（我比较喜欢喝咖啡胜过喝茶。）

I prefer going to the movies to watching TV.

（我比较喜欢看电影胜过看电视。）

b. prefer to + 原形动词 + | instead of + 动名词
rather than（连词） + 原形动词 |

例：I prefer to go to the movies instead of watching TV.

= I prefer to go to the movies rather than watch TV.

= I prefer going to the movies to watching TV.

I prefer to go to the movies rather than watching TV. (×)

18. mind 的用法：

mind + if 从句

= mind + 动名词

例：Would you mind if I opened the door? (语气客气)

(Would 为一般过去时，if 从句之动词亦用一般过去时)

= Do you mind if I open the door? (语气无上句客气)

(Do 为一般现在时，故 if 从句之动词亦用一般现在时)

（你介不介意我把门打开？）

Would you mind if you came over here?

= Do you mind if you come over here?

（你介不介意到这里来？）

注意：

上列四句皆可化简为“mind + 动名词”，法则如下：

a. 同主语可省略，若为不同主语，则 if 从句之主语变为所有格；

b. if 从句之动词变为动名词。

例：Would you mind ~~if I~~ open~~ed~~ the door?

(my opening)

(不同主语)

（你介不介意我把门打开？）

Would you mind ~~if you~~ ~~opened~~ the door?
(同主语) opening
（你介不介意去把门打开？）

19. “动词 + 动名词”的结构：

下列动词只能接动名词，不能接不定式。

admit	承认	mention	提到
avoid	避免	pardon	原谅
appreciate	感激；体会	miss	想念
consider	考虑	practise	练习
delay	延期	= practice	
mind	介意	quit	停止
deny	否认	risk	冒险
detest	憎恨	postpone	延迟
enjoy	喜欢	resent	愤恨
escape	逃避	regret	后悔
excuse	原谅	keep	保持
finish	结束	finish	结束
forgive	原谅	imagine	想象

例: I really appreciate your helping me.
（我实在感谢你的帮助。）

He considered studying another language.
（他考虑学习另一种语言。）

He has finished writing this book.
（他已经写完这本书。）

I enjoy talking with you.
（我喜欢和你谈话。）

He practiced to speak English every day. (×)
→ He practiced speaking English every day. (✓)
（他每天练习说英语。）

20. prevent sb from V-ing 阻止某人……

例: The heavy rain prevented me to get to work on time. (×)
→ The heavry rain prevented me from getting to work on time. (✓)
（大雨使我不能准时上班。）

注意

以下动词结构与 prevent 相同：

ban sb from V-ing　　禁止某人……
= bar sb from V-ing
= prohibit sb from V-ing
stop sb from V-ing　　阻止某人/使某人不能……
= keep sb from V-ing
save sb from V-ing　　拯救某人免于……
restrain sb from V-ing　　限制某人/使某人不能……

注意

以上短语中，ban、bar、prohibit 均表“禁止”，均与介词 from 连用；forbid 亦表“禁止”，但常与不定式连用，形成下列结构：

forbid sb to V　　禁止某人……

例：I forbid him to smoke here.
= I prohibit him from smoking here.
（我禁止他在此处抽烟。）

不过，亦有人将 forbid 与 from 连用，故上句亦可改写如下：

I forbid him from smoking here.

只是此用法较为罕见，应试时仍以“forbid sb to V”为最佳选择。

21. encourage sb to V　　鼓励某人……
discourage sb from V-ing　　阻止某人/使某人不敢……

例：I encouraged him to do it.
（我鼓励他做此事。）

I discouraged him to come here. (×)
→ I discouraged him from coming here. (√)
（我阻止他来这里。）

22. persuade sb to V　　劝某人去……
dissuade sb from V-ing　　劝阻某人……

例：I persuaded him to come with me.
= I prevailed on him to come with me.
= I talked him into coming with me.
（我劝他和我一起来。）

I dissuaded him to come with me. (×)
→ I dissuaded him from coming with me. (√)
（我劝他别跟我来。）

23. resemble sb / sth 像……

例: You resemble your brother.
= You bear a close resemblance to your brother.
= You look like your brother.
（你很像你哥哥。）

24. decide、determine:

a. decide 表“决定”可做及物或不及物动词。做及物动词时，可接不定式或名词性从句做其宾语，句型如下：

decide to V 决定要……

decide + that 从句 / whether 从句 / 疑问词形成的名词性从句 决定……

例: I've decided to take a trip to Tokyo this summer.
= I've decided that I will take a trip to Tokyo this summer.
（今年夏天我已决定要到东京玩儿一趟。）

We haven't decided when we will set out yet.
（我们尚未决定要何时出发。）

You need to decide whether we will cancel the trip.
（你必须决定我们是否要取消这个行程。）

decide on sb / sth 选定某人/某物

例: We have decided on John as representative of our company.
（我们已选定约翰担任本公司的代表。）

decide against sb / sth 不选定某人/某物

例: We decided against John's idea, thinking that it was not feasible.
（我们决定不采用约翰的点子，因为我们认为那不可行。）

b. determine 表“判定”（= judge）或“决定”（= decide），可用名词或名词性从句做宾语。

例: The court will determine whether he is guilty.
（法院会判定他是否有罪。）

The market determines our prices.
（市场决定我们的产品价格。）

c. determine 可变成过去分词 determined，做形容词用，表“已经下定决心的”、“心意已决的”，句型如下：

be determined to V 一心一意要……；决心要……

例: I'm determined to go on with the project even if I may run into many setbacks.

（即使我可能会遭遇许多挫折，我心意已决非要继续执行该计划不可。）

25. afford:

afford 表“有能力买”、“有能力做”，使用本动词时须与助动词 can 或 cannot 连用。afford 之后可接名词或不定式短语做宾语，结构如下：

can / cannot afford + 名词　　有/无能力买/做……

can / cannot afford to V　　有/无能力做……

例: I can afford that car. (佳)

= I can afford to buy that car.

（我买得起那辆车。）

Since he has lots of money, he can afford a new house.

= Since he has lots of money, he can afford to buy a new house.

（由于他钱多，因此可以买得起新房子。）

The poor boy didn't afford to go to school. (×)

→ The poor boy couldn't afford to go to school. (✓)

（这个穷孩子读不起书。）

26. wait、await:

a. wait 表“等候”，为不及物动词，须与介词 for 连用，方可接宾语，即：

wait for sb/sth　　等候某人/某事物

例: I'll wait for you at the station.

（我会在车站等你。）

We are still waiting for the weather to improve.

（我们仍在等候天气转好。）

但 wait 亦可做及物动词，专门用在下列短语中：

wait one's turn　　（耐心）等候某人的机会

例: I'm waiting my turn to take revenge.

（我正在等候报复的机会。）

b. await 亦表“等候”，为及物动词，之后多接表“事物”的名词做宾语。

await sth　　等候某事物

= wait for sth

例: We're still awaiting your reply.
= We're still waiting for your reply.
（我们仍在等候你的回答。）

27. succeed、fail:

a. succeed 可做不及物动词，表“成功”，须与介词 in 连用，方可接名词或动名词做宾语，形成下列短语：

succeed in + 名词/动名词　　在……获得成功/成功地……

例: John succeeded in business after years of hard work.
（经过多年的努力，约翰经商成功了。）
How many of you have succeeded in passing the test?
（你们之中有几个人考试及格了？）

b. succeed 亦可做及物动词，表“继承”，以人做宾语，形成下列短语：

succeed + 人 + as...　　继承某人担任……的职位

例: John succeeded his father as president of this company.
（约翰继承父亲担任本公司的总裁。）

c. fail 可做不及物动词，表“失败”，之后不可接“in + 动名词”，而接不定式短语，做副词用，修饰 fail。

例: He failed in passing the test. (×)
→ He failed to pass the test. (✓)
（他这次考试没考及格。）

d. fail 亦可做及物动词，表“未通过（考试）”、“使（某人）不及格”或“辜负（某人）”。

例: He failed the test.
= He failed to pass the test.
（他这次考试没考及格。）
The teacher failed one-third of his students.
= The teacher flunked one-third of his students.
（老师让三分之一的学生不及格。）
You are the only person I trust. Don't fail me.
（你是我唯一信赖的人。别令我失望/辜负我。）

28. depend、depend on：

depend 不加宾语表“依情形而定”。

depend on 加宾语表“依赖”。

例：I depend on him to give me advice.
　　　　　　　　宾语

（我靠他给我建议。）

He is trustworthy, so you can depend on / rely on / count on him for help.

（他值得信赖，因此你可以指望他给你帮助。）

A: Can you come tomorrow?

B: That all depends.

（A：你明天能来吗？）

（B：那要看情形而定了。）

29. 感官动词：

look（看起来）、feel（感觉起来/摸起来）、sound（听起来）、taste（尝起来）、smell（闻起来）其后只能加形容词，若要加名词，要与 like 连用。

例：He looks happily. (×)

→ He looks happy. (√)

He looks a happy man. (×)

→ He looks like a happy man. (√)

（他看起来很快乐。）

It tastes good.

（这尝起来很好吃。）

It tastes like an apple.

（这尝起来像苹果。）

30. 表“设法、企图”的动词用法：

try	+ to + 原形动词	设法……
attempt		企图……
manage		设法……
endeavor		努力……

例：I'll try to study harder.

= I'll attempt to study harder.

= I'll manage to study harder.

（我要设法用功一点儿。）

We'll endeavor to save our company from going bankrupt.
（我们会努力拯救公司免于破产。）

31. anger、angry：

anger 是及物动词，表“使（某人）生气”。

angry 则为形容词，表“生气的”，有下列重要用法：

be angry with + 人　　生某人的气

be angry at + 事物　　气某事物

例：He angered me.

= I was angered by him.

（他使我生气。）

I'm angry with him. (对人用 with)

= I'm mad at him.

（我很生他气。）

I'm angry at her attitude. (对事用 at)

（我很气她的态度。）

32. 授予动词：

授予动词有两个宾语，句型有下列三种，所表达的意思则完全相同：

a. 主语 + 授予动词 + 间接宾语（人）+ 直接宾语（物）

例：I gave him a book.

（我给他一本书。）

He bought me a pencil.

（他给我买一支铅笔。）

He wrote me a letter.

（他写封信给我。）

I asked him a question.

（我问他一个问题。）

b. 主语 + 授予动词 + 直接宾语（物）+ to / for / of + 间接宾语（人）

例：I gave a book to him.

He bought a pencil for me.

He wrote a letter to me.

I asked a question of him.

注意:

1) 直接宾语（物）+ to + 间接宾语（人）

下列动词均与介词 to 连用：

give（给予）、send（寄送）、lend（借给）、write（写给）、bring（带给）、deliver（传递给）、show（显示给）、teach（教给）、tell（向……告诉/讲述）、sell（卖给）、pay（付给）。

例: I taught English to him.

（我教他英语。）

I paid thirty dollars to him.

（我付他 30 元。）

2) 直接宾语（物）+ for + 间接宾语（人）

下列动词均与介词 for 连用：

make（为……制作）、leave（为……留下）、do（为……做）、buy（为……买）。

例: He made a chair for me.

= He made me a chair.

（他为我做了把椅子。）

He bought a book for me.

= He bought me a book.

（他为我买了一本书。）

Could you do a favor for me? (少用)

= Could you do me a favor? (常用)

（可否请您帮我一个忙？）

* 为何上列句型要使用介词 for?

因为 buy、do、make 等动词都有代劳的意味（为某人买东西、为某人做事、为某人制造东西），故采用 for。

3) 直接宾语（物）+ of + 间接宾语（人）

ask（问）、expect（期望）、require（要求）、demand（要求）。

例: I asked a question of him.

（我问他一个问题。）

I expected nothing of him.

（我对他不抱期望。）

但无下列说法：

I expected him nothing. (×)

I required / demanded nothing of him.

（我对他无所求。）

但无下列说法：

I required / demanded him nothing. (×)

→ I required / demanded nothing of him. (✓)

＊为何上列句型要使用介词 of?

此乃因为此处的 of 等于 from（从……），凡表“要求”、“期望”的动词（如 ask、require、demand）均属此用法。

4) 直接宾语（物）+ on + 间接宾语（人）

例: I played a joke on him.

（我开了他一个玩笑。）

c. 授予动词在下列结构中，属被动语态，仍可接宾语：

主语（人）+ be + 授予动词 + 宾语

例: He was given a book (by me).

I was bought a pencil (by him).

I was written a letter (by him).

I was taught English (by him).

33. 知觉动词

此类动词分三大类，分别为“看”、“听”、“感觉”。知觉动词加了宾语后，再接原形动词或现在分词做宾语。用原形动词表示强调“已发生的事实”，用现在分词则强调“正在……”。

a. 看：see、watch、notice、behold、look at

例: I saw him cry.

（我看到他哭了。）

I saw him crying.

（我看到他正在哭泣。）

b. 听：listen to（聆听）、hear（听到）

例: I heard him talk.

（我听到他说话了。）

I heard him talking.

（我听到他正在说话。）

c. 感觉：feel

例: I felt him leave.

（我感觉他离开了。）

I felt him leaving.
（我感觉他正要离开。）

34. remember、forget、regret:

remember to V	记得要……
remember + V-ing	记得曾……
forget to V	忘了要……
forget + V-ing	忘了曾……
regret to V	抱歉/遗憾要……
regret + V-ing	后悔曾……

例: I'll remember to see him.
（我会记得要去看他。）

I remembered to see him.
（我记得要去看他的。）

I remember seeing him before.
（我记得曾经看过他。）

I forgot to see him.
（我忘了要去看他。）

I forgot seeing him before.
（我忘了曾经见过他。）

I regret to tell you the truth.
（我很遗憾要告诉你真相。）

I regret telling you the truth.
（我后悔曾告诉你真相。）

EXERCISE

I. 请选出一个正确的答案：

1. Rose went to the party, although she ______.
   (A) was knowing she would not like it
   (B) knew she was not liking it
   (C) knew she would not like it
   (D) was knowing she did not like it

2. Novelist Edna Ferber ______ her youth in Appleton, Wisconsin.
   (A) spending (B) was spent (C) spent (D) who spent

3. Of the two houses, the family preferred ______.
   (A) the one in a more isolation (B) the more isolated one
   (C) one being in more isolation (D) one that is more isolated

4. I came to lunch so early because I thought the bell had already ______.
   (A) rang (B) ring (C) been rang (D) rung

5. You ______ your visa extended before it expires.
   (A) had better to get (B) had to get better
   (C) had better get (D) had better got

6. The health program outlined in the article seems very sound to me, but it has ______ considerable public outcry.
   (A) met with (B) met up with (C) run up with (D) run against

7. My typist has not returned my paper yet, but she promised ______ by tomorrow.
   (A) for me to have it ready (B) it was ready for me
   (C) me it was ready (D) to have it ready for me

8. Al said that he wouldn't mind ______.
   (A) to wait for us (B) wait for us
   (C) waiting for us (D) waiting us

9. She said that she would rather not ______ it right now.
(A) discussing (B) to discuss (C) discuss (D) discussion

10. Anna said in her letter that she'd appreciate ______ from you sometime.
(A) to hear (B) having heard (C) hearing (D) to hearing

11. I have a letter from your uncle. Do you object ______ it?
(A) to my reading (B) that I read
(C) from my reading (D) to I read

12. Our city has changed a great deal. It doesn't even resemble ______.
(A) the one of three years ago (B) one three years ago
(C) the one since three years (D) one from three years

13. Uncle Dick has already arrived. Do you expect ______ to see him?
(A) going (B) go (C) to go (D) that you go

14. Scientists continue to speculate ______ causes sunspots.
(A) for what (B) what about (C) whatever (D) about what

15. Ann doesn't like milk. She says that she never ______ it at home.
(A) use to drinking (B) used to drinking
(C) used to drink (D) use to drink

16. Edward likes classical music, and I think that he prefers it ______ any other kind.
(A) than (B) over (C) to (D) against

17. Would you please ______ the listening comprehension script until after you have listened to the tape?
(A) not to read (B) not read (C) don't read (D) don't to read

18. Greater efforts to increase wheat production must be made if bread shortages ______ avoided.
(A) will be (B) can be (C) are to be (D) were to be

19. It's not too cloudy to take a picture. I think it ______.
(A) is quite enough light (B) has enough much light
(C) is light enough (D) has very light enough

20. The future price of gold ______ by a number of inter-related factors.
(A) is going to determine (B) will determine
(C) will be determine (D) will be determined

21. Mr. Bundy is so strange today. And your manners ______, too.
(A) like this is (B) are like his (C) like he is (D) like him are

22. I want to go to the dental clinic, but you ______ with me.
(A) need not to go (B) do not need go
(C) need not go (D) need go not

23. Dr. Samuels became a politician because he wanted to ______.
(A) make his society changed
(B) bring about changes in his society
(C) bring about a changed society
(D) result in new changes for his society

24. I bite my nails. I must break ______.
(A) the habit to me (B) the habit with myself
(C) myself of the habit (D) of the habit myself

25. You don't object ______ you by your first name, do you?
(A) that I call (B) to my calling (C) for calling (D) that I am call

26. I'm not going to ask the teacher why he gave me that grade; I intend ______.
(A) to let rest the matter (B) the matter to be let resting
(C) letting the matter to rest (D) to let the matter rest

27. Tanbark was spread on the streets to ______ of traffic when Mrs. Campbell was appearing on the stage.
(A) lessen the sound (B) deaden the noise
(C) decrease the voices (D) take away the noise

28. What did he say in the letter? I really can't ______ it out.
(A) make (B) put (C) run (D) come

29. I am sorry I lost the race, but I really wasn't fast enough to catch ______ the other runners.
(A) up (B) up with (C) to (D) with

30. How will it turn out? Well, it all ______.
(A) depends on (B) is depending (C) depends (D) depend

II. 请选出错误的画线部分：

31. One of the workers has(A) hung(B) the curtains that had(C) been laying(D) on the floor.

32. Although his lawyer felt very(A) badly(B) about the verdict, he advised(C) him not to give up(D).

33. The landlady suspicioned(A) that someone must(B) have broken into(C) the house while she was watching(D) the TV show.

34. Because of(A) the accident, Grandmother will forbid my brother and me(B) from swimming(C) in the river unless someone agrees(D) to watch us.

35. Ellen would prefer(A) going(B) to the theater more frequently, but her schedule prevents(C) her to attend at(D) more than one play a month.

标准答案

1. (C)	2. (C)	3. (B)	4. (D)	5. (C)	6. (A)	7. (D)	8. (C)	9. (C)	10. (C)
11. (A)	12. (A)	13. (C)	14. (D)	15. (C)	16. (C)	17. (B)	18. (C)	19. (C)	20. (D)
21. (B)	22. (C)	23. (B)	24. (C)	25. (B)	26. (D)	27. (B)	28. (A)	29. (B)	30. (C)
31. (D)	32. (B)	33. (A)	34. (C)	35. (D)					

习题解说

1. know、like（喜欢）等词为瞬间即知的动词 (即顷刻间即可了解自己是否喜欢、讨厌、知道、明白等动词)，不可能用进行时。
2. 主语 Novelist Edna Ferber 之后应接一般过去时及物动词 spent。
3. (B) 是最好的答案，因名词避免重复，故用 one 代替 house，同时前有定冠词限定两个房子之一。
4. had 之后用过去分词 rung（原形 ring、过去式 rang）。
5. had better 为助动词，故其后用原形动词 get。
6. meet with = encounter　　遭遇到
7. promise（答应，允诺）之用法：

   promise to V

   promise sb to V

   promise + (sb) + that 从句

   He promised to come with me.

   （他答应跟我来。）

   He promised me to come here by 6.

   （他答应我 6 点钟之前要来。）

   He promised (me) that he would come here by 6.

   （他答应 6 点钟之前要来。）
8. mind + V-ing　　在意……

   wait for...　　等待……
9. would rather not + 原形动词　　宁愿不……
10. appreciate + V-ing　　感激……

    (B) 虽为动名词，但 she'd appreciate...= she would appreciate...，时态上是表示“将来”，故不能用表完成之 having heard。
11. 表“反对”的动词如下：

    I object to going to the movies with him.
    （to：介）

    = I oppose going to the movies with him.

    = I am opposed to going to the movies with him.
    （to：介）

    （我反对和他去看电影。）
12. the one = the city，是限定用法，故 one 之前应加 the。

13. expect 的用法：

I expect to go on a trip this summer.

（我盼望今夏去旅行。）

I expect you to go on a trip this summer.

（我指望你今年夏天去旅行。）

I don't expect much of you.

（我对你不抱很大的期望。）

I expect some changes in the plan.

（我预期该项计划将有所改变。）

14. speculate about... 深思……/思虑……

= speculate on...

15. used to V 过去曾经……

be used to V-ing 习惯于……

16. prefer A to B 喜欢 A 胜于 B

17. please 若表“请”，视为副词，其后接原形动词：

肯定句：Please come here at 8.

Please to come here at 8. (×)

（请你 8 点来。）

否定句：Please don't make noise.

Please not make noise. (×)

（请不要发出噪音。）

惯用语：Would you please + 原形动词？ 请你……好吗？

Would you please open the door?

Would you please not open the door?

Would you please not to open the door? (×)

18. be to 可表“预定、义务、可能”。

a. 预定 (= be expected to)

He is to be here by nine this evening.

（预定他今晚 9 点来此地。）

b. 义务 (= must)

He is to finish all the work before he leaves.

(= must)

（他必须在走之前完成所有的工作。）

c. 可能 (= is likely to)

It is to rain today.

（很可能今天会下雨。）

本题之 is to = must。

19. 此处的 light 为形容词，表“明亮的”，故 enough 做副词，应置于 light 之后。

20. determine 为及物动词，其后应有宾语，否则须用被动语态。

He determined the policy.

= The policy was determined by him.

21. And your manners are like his (manners), too.

（你的态度也像他的态度。）

22. need not 为助动词，之后要加原形动词。

(B) 应改为 do not need to go。

23. change 可做不及物动词和及物动词, 但意义不同。

He has changed a lot since he came here.

不及物动词

（自从他来这儿之后，人变了许多。——他还是人，只是气质变了。）

He has been changed a lot since he came here.

及物动词

（自从他来这儿之后，他被改变了许多。——很可能他被改变成另一种东西，而非人。）

如用 (A) 的话，则 make his society changed 暗示 make his society changed（into something else），因此是错的，应改为 make his society change（不及物动词），即社会还是社会，只是有些地方有所改变。

(B) 为正选。...bring about 在此处等于 promote（促成）。

(C) bring about a changed society（促成一个改变的社会）暗示在已存在的社会中，再带来一个已改变的社会，语意错误。

(D) result in（导致）之主语不能是“人”，而是“原因”。

His carelessness resulted in this accident.

原因 = caused

= brought about

= led to

= culminated in

但 bring about 的主语可为“人”亦可为“原因”。

He brought about this accident.

（他造成此次车祸。）

His carelessness brought about this accident.

（他的粗心导致了此次车祸。）

24. | break | oneself of... 戒除……
| rid |

25. 请见第 11 题解答。

26. a. intend to V 打算……

b. let the matter rest 让事情平息下来

27. deaden 使（声音）渐消

lessen 减少（数量）

decrease 减少（产量）

take away 拿走（实物）

28. make out 理解（= understand）

put out (the fire) 灭（火）

come out (of) （从……）走出来

run out 用光（与 of 连用）

He ran out of money.

（他花光了钱。）

29. catch up with 赶上

Run faster, or he will catch up with you.

（跑快一点儿，否则他会赶上你。）

30. depends 之后若有宾语，应加 on，此处无宾语，故不加 on。

31. (D) laying 应改为 lying，因其后无宾语，故用不及物动词 lie（躺）之现在分词形式，表进行的动作。

32. badly 应改为 bad，因感官动词 felt 之后只能加形容词。

33. (A) 应改为动词 suspected，因 suspicion 做名词用。

34. (C) 应改为 to swim。

forbid sb to V 禁止某人……

35. (D) 应改为 from attending at。

prevent sb from V-ing 阻止某人……

第六章　时态及语态

概 述

记得以前上初中的时候，每次上英语课就提不起兴趣，主要是因为乡下的孩子比较保守，不敢跟着老师大声念，尤其有些英语单词念起来颇像闽南语中的脏话。每每在亲朋好友面前“秀”一两个英语单词，就会被回骂一声“夭寿”，害得我一直不敢开口说英语。及至老师教到时态时，就被那些复杂（当时觉得）的规则吓坏了，从此再也不学英语了。18 岁之后，发誓要把英语学好时，我就强迫自己每天一定看 16 小时的英语。我的方法无它，就是勤背诵、勤查词典。不知不觉中，文章越来越看得懂。但练习写作时，就发现自己最大的毛病乃时态运用不当，频频出错。于是，我就买了一本虹桥书局出版的英语版 *Mastering American English*。这本语法书用浅显的例句，把时态变化交待得很清楚。从此，我如鱼得水。阅读文章时，就特别注意时态的用法，久而久之，便习惯其中用法，而且我也不必再看任何语法参考书了。

说了那么多话，无非希望同学们明白，学英语，一如学其他外语，急不得也。有道是“慢工出细活。”希望同学们一方面细看这本英语语法书，一方面多看英语文章，以印证赖老师在书中所说的重点。从此以后，你的英语一定和我的一样好，甚至超越我。耐心地努力下去吧！

第一节　时态

1. 时态的种类:

a. 一般时:

1) 一般现在时: He writes a letter every day.
（他每天写信。）

2) 一般过去时: He wrote a letter yesterday.
（他昨天写了一封信。）

3) 一般将来时: He will write a letter tomorrow.
（他明天要写一封信。）

b. 完成时:

1) 现在完成时: He has written the letter.
（他已经写好这封信。）

2) 过去完成时: He had written the letter when I came.
（我回来时他早就把信写好了。）

3) 将来完成时: He will have written the letter before I come.
（我回来之前，他就会把信写好。）

c. 进行时:

1) 现在进行时: He is writing a letter now.
（他现在正在写信。）

2) 过去进行时: He was writing a letter when I came.
（我来时，他正在写信。）

3) 将来进行时: He will be writing a letter when I come.
（我来时，他将正在写信。）

d. 完成进行时:

1) 现在完成进行时: He has been writing a letter for two hours.
（他已经写信写了两个小时。）

2) 过去完成进行时: When I called, he had been writing a letter for two hours.
（我打来电话时，他信已持续写了两个小时了。）

2. 使用一般现在时的时机：

主语 + 一般现在时动词

a. 表知觉、状态、所有：

例: I smell something burning.
（我闻到东西烧焦的味道。）

You look worried.
（你看起来愁眉苦脸的。）

This medicine tastes bitter to me.
（对我而言，这个药很苦。）

He has a book.
（他有一本书。）

Your hands feel cold.
（你的手摸起来很冰冷。）

He is a student.
（他是学生。）

I see a man standing there.
（我看到一个人站在那里。）

b. 表习惯性的动作：

例: He goes to school every day.
（他每天上学。）

He writes a letter every day.
（他每天写信。）

He always takes a bus home.
（他总是乘公交车回家。）

注意

表习惯性的动作常以时间副词修饰。

例: It rains a lot in summer.
（夏天雨量大。）

They seldom take a trip.
（他们很少去旅行。）

千万不可造这种句子：

He writes a letter. (劣)
（他写信。）

He comes back. (劣)
（他回来。）

因这两个例子无时间副词修饰，故不是习惯性的动作，因此无意义。

c. 表真理、事实、格言：

例: The sun rises in the east.
（太阳从东方升起。）

He who is lazy is doomed to failure. (to 是介词)
= He who is lazy is doomed to fail. (to fail 是不定式)
（凡是懒惰的人注定要失败。）

Honesty is the best policy.
（诚实是上策。）

d. 表将来：

begin、start、arrive、leave、come、go 等动词可用一般现在时表将来。

例: They arrive tomorrow.
（他们明天到。）

The meeting begins at 7.
（会议 7 点开始。）

They start the day after tomorrow.
（他们后天出发。）

Does he come tomorrow?
（他明天要来吗？）

3. 使用一般过去时的时机：

主语 + 一般过去时动词

a. 表过去的动作、习惯、状态：

例: I saw him yesterday.
（我昨天看到他。）

He always rose early in the morning.
（他以前都很早起床。）

He was born in 1970.
（他于 1970 年出生。）

b. 表过去的经历（亦可用现在完成时表示）:

Did you ever see her before?

= Have you ever seen her before?

（你以前见过她吗？）

c. 句中若有 after、until、before 等连词引导的从句，由于时间先后很清楚，可用一般过去时代替过去完成时。

例: After I had finished the work, I went home.

= After I finished the work, I went home.

（我做完工作之后就回家了。）

I had not studied English until I was 10.

= I didn't study English until I was 10.

（我 10 岁开始学英语。）

Before I moved here, I had lived in Japan for a long time.

= Before I moved here, I lived in Japan for a long time.

（我搬来这里之前曾在日本住过很长一段时间。）

4. 使用一般将来时的时机:

主语 + will + 原形动词（will 译成“将要”）

表将来发生的动作或状态:

例: It will rain tomorrow.

（明天会下雨。）

He will be a student soon.

（他很快就当学生了。）

Will you be able to come?

（你能来吗？）

注意

a. 由连词 when、unless、if、once（一旦）等所引导的状语从句表示某条件时，一定要用一般现在时，而主句用一般将来时。

例: When I have money, I will buy a car.

一般现在时　一般将来时

（我有钱的时候就会买车。）

I won't buy a car unless I have money.

一般将来时　一般现在时

（除非我有钱，否则我不买车。）

If I see him, I will tell him the truth.

一般现在时　一般将来时

（我若见到他，就会把真相告诉他。）

Once I receive the letter, I will let you know.

一般现在时　　一般将来时

（我一旦收到信，就会让你知道。）

千万不要造下列的句子：

When I will have money, I will buy a car. (×)

I won't buy a car unless I will have money. (×)

b. is / am / are going to + 原形动词 = will + 原形动词　　将要……

例: He is going to come.

= He will come.

（他将要来。）

5. 使用现在完成时的时机：

主语 + have + 过去分词（have 译成“已经”或“曾经”）

a. 用以表示到现在为止完成的动作:

例: I have just finished my homework.

（我刚做完功课。）

She has already come.

（她已经来了。）

He has gone to New York.

（他已到纽约去了。——人在纽约）

He hasn't gone to work yet.

（他还没去工作。）

b. 用以表示到现在为止的经历：

例: I have met him several times.

（我见过他几次。）

I have never met such a man as he.

（我从未见过像他这样的人。）

c. 用以表示到现在为止仍在继续的动作或状态：

例: She has lived here for 10 years. (And she still lives here.)
（她已经在这里住了 10 年。——她仍然住在这里。）

She has studied English since 2000. (And she still studies English.)
（她从 2000 年就开始学英语。——她现在还在学。）

注意

表“曾去过”的经历时，用“have been”，而非“have gone”。

例: He has gone to Hong Kong.
（他已经到香港去了。）

(And he is now in Hong Kong.)
（他现在在香港。）

He has been to Hong Kong.
= He has gone to Hong Kong and come back again.
（他曾去过香港。）

6. 使用过去完成时的时机：
主语 + had + 过去分词（had 译成“已经”或“曾经”）
用以表示截至过去某时为止所完成的动作或经历：

例: He had studied English for 10 years before he left for the States.
（他赴美之前已学过 10 年英语。）

He had already left when I came.
（我来时他已离开了。）

He was angry because he hadn't seen Mary.
（他没看到玛丽，因此生气了。）

He told me that he had seen the movie once.
（他告诉我，这部电影他已看过一次。）

注意

过去完成时不能单独存在，要与另一个一般过去时从句或表过去之副词短语连用，即在过去不同时间发生的两个动作：

先发生的动作 ⟶ 用过去完成时表示

后发生的动作 ⟶ 用一般过去时表示

例: I lost the book which my father had given me.
（我弄丢了父亲给我的书——我父亲先给我书，我后来弄丢了。）

7. 使用将来完成时的时机：

主语 + will have + 过去分词（will have 译成"将已经"）

用以表示到将来某时为止所完成或仍在继续的动作或经历等：

例: He will have arrived in Chicago by this time tomorrow.
（明天这个时候，他将已抵达芝加哥。）

When you come (或 By the time you come), everything will have been finished.
（你来的时候，每一件事将已全部完成。）

He will have lived here for 10 years by the end of this month.
（到月底，他就在此地住满 10 年了。）

8. 使用现在进行时的时机：

主语 + is / am / are + 现在分词（is / am / are 译成"正在"）

a. 用以表示现在正在做的动作：

例: He is writing a letter.
（他正在写一封信。）

What are you doing?
（你正在做什么？）

He is taking a trip now.
（他现在正在旅游。）

I am doing the laundry.
（我正在洗衣服。）

b. 用以表示即将发生的动作，常与表将来的副词连用，此时 is / am / are 译成"即将"：

例: He is coming today.
= He will be coming today.
（他即将于今天来。）

They are leaving soon.
= They will be leaving soon.
（他们很快就要离开。）

9. 使用过去进行时的时机：

主语 + was / were + 现在分词（was / were 译成"正在"）

a. 用以表示过去某时正在做的动作：

例: He was studying English then.
（那时他正在学英语。）

He was taking a bath when you called.
（你打电话来的时候，他正在洗澡。）

b. 表一般过去时中即将发生的事：

例: He was dying.
= He was going to die.
= He was about to die.
（那时他快死了。）

10. 使用将来进行时的时机：
主语 + will be + 现在分词（will be 译成"将在"）
用以表示于将来某时将进行的动作：

例: He will be studying English (at) this time tomorrow.
（明天此时，他将在学英语。）

11. 使用现在完成进行时的时机：
主语 + have / has been + 现在分词（have / has been 译成"一直都在"）
用以表示一直继续到现在且仍将继续下去的动作：

例: She has been working with this company for 5 years.
（她在这家公司工作已有 5 年的时间。——她仍将工作下去。）

They have been standing here since 7 this morning.
（他们从早上 7 点就一直站在这儿。——现在还在站着。）

He has been teaching at this school since 2001.
（他从 2001 年就一直在这个学校任教。——他仍将继续教。）

12. 使用过去完成进行时的时机：
主语 + had been + 现在分词（had been 译成"一直都在"）
用以表示一直继续到过去某时，而当时仍在继续进行的动作。与过去完成时一样，过去完成进行时不能单独存在，须与一般过去时连用：

例: I had been sleeping when he came.
（他来的时候，我仍在睡觉。）

He told us that he had been studying German since 2001.
（他告诉我们他从 2001 年起就一直在学德语。）

13. 使用将来完成进行时的时机：

主语 + will have been + 现在分词（will have been 译成“将一直在”）

表一直继续到将来某时，而仍将继续进行的动作：

例: I will have been teaching English for ten years by the end of this year.
（到今年年底，我教英语将已有 10 年了。）

14. 时态的前后一致：

a. 主句若为一般现在时，从句除过去完成时、过去完成进行时不能用以外，其他时态皆可用。

例: I think
- he has come.
- he is coming.
- he already came.
- he will have done it by the end of this month.
- he was singing a song when I came yesterday.
- he had come. (×)
- he had been sleeping. (×)
- he had been sleeping when I came.
(✓，因有一般过去时状语从句“when I came”)

b. 主句若为一般过去时，则从句不得用表现在或将来的时态，但可使用一般过去时、过去完成时、过去进行时、过去完成进行时。

例: I thought
- he was nice.
- he had come back.
- he would come back.
- he was working hard.
- he had been working hard.
- he will come back. (×)
- he has been working hard. (×)

c. 从句表示真理时，无论主句是过去、现在或将来时，该从句都用一般现在时。

例: They knew that the sun rises in the east.
（他们知道太阳从东边升起。）

We know that the sun rises in the east.
（我们知道太阳从东边升起。）

She will know that the sun rises in the east.
（她将会知道太阳从东方升起。）

15. "for + 一段时间" 与完成时的关系：

for during in through down through over	the	past last	five years	过去 5 年来

= since five years ago 自从 5 年前起

这些短语与现在完成时或现在完成进行时连用。

例: I have been studying English for the past two weeks.
（过去两个星期来，我都一直在学英语。）

16. since 与完成时的关系：

a. since 表 "自从" 时，可做介词，之后接名词或动名词；since 亦可做副词性连词，之后接主语及动词，引导一般过去时的状语从句。不论 since 做介词或副词性连词，所修饰的主句应用现在完成时或现在完成进行时，句型如下：

主语 + have / has + 过去分词 + since... 自从……以来就一直……

或：主语 + have / has been + 现在分词 + since...

例: I have lived here since 2000.
（自 2000 年起我就一直住在这里。）

I have been studying English since I went to college.
（自我上大学后，我就一直在学英语。）

b. since 之后须接明确的某时间做宾语，不可接一段时间做宾语。

例: Peter has lived here since two years. (×，two years 是一段时间)

→ Peter has lived here since 2002. (√，2002 是明确的某时间)
（彼得自 2002 年就一直住在这里。）

c. since 之后若有一段时间，则须在一段时间之后接 ago。

例: Peter has lived here since two years ago. (√)
（彼得自两年前起就一直住在这里。）

= Peter has lived here for two years.
（彼得在这里已住了两年了。）

d. 现在完成时或现在完成进行时的动词与 "for + 一段时间" 连用时，该动词所表示的动作必须可接续进行，否则就不可与 "for + 一段时间" 连用。

例: I have lived here for five years. (√)
（我在这里连续住了 5 年。）

理由:
我每天住在这里，持续住了 5 年，故 live（住）表示的动作可持续进行。

例: He has been teaching English for two months. (√)
（他教英语已有两个月了。）

理由:
他每天都教英语，持续教了两个月，故 teach（教）表示的动作可持续进行。

例: He has died for two months. (×)
（他死了 3 年了。）

理由:
他每天都死一次，持续死了 3 年——不合逻辑，故 die（死）表示的动作无法持续进行，不可与 for three years 连用。应改为：

例: He has died. (√)
（他已过世了。）
He has married Jane for twenty years. (×)
（他跟简结婚已有 20 年了。）

理由:
他每天都娶简一次，持续娶了 20 年——不合逻辑，故 marry（与……结婚）表示的动作无法持续进行，不可与 for twenty years 连用，应改为：

例: He has married Jane. (√)
（他已娶了简。）

e. 上列动作无法持续的动词，若采用下列结构时，则可与 since 连用：
It is + 一段时间 + since...
例: It is three years since he died. (√)
= Three years have passed since he died.
（他过世已 3 年了。）
It is twenty years since he married Jane. (√)
= Twenty years have passed since he married Jane.
（他与简结婚已有 20 年了。）

17. 常用的不规则动词变化：

a. A－A－A 型　（三态同形）

原形	过去式	过去分词	
burst	burst	burst	爆发
cost	cost	cost	值，花费
cast	cast	cast	丢，掷
cut	cut	cut	切
hit	hit	hit	击
hurt	hurt	hurt	伤害
let	let	let	让
read	read	read	读
set	set	set	置，放
shut	shut	shut	关
upset	upset	upset	使……难过

b. A－B－B 型　（过去式与过去分词同形）

say	said	said	说
lay	laid	laid	置；下蛋
pay	paid	paid	付款
sell	sold	sold	卖
tell	told	told	告诉
catch	caught	caught	抓住；捕捉
teach	taught	taught	教
buy	bought	bought	买
bring	brought	brought	带来
think	thought	thought	想
have has	had	had	有；使； 吃喝；经历
hear	heard	heard	听
make	made	made	做
build	built	built	建造
lend	lent	lent	借给
send	sent	sent	寄，送
spend	spent	spent	花费
sit	sat	sat	坐
get	got	got	得到

lose	lost	lost	失去；输
win	won	won	赢得
smell	smelt	smelt	闻，嗅
hold	held	held	握
meet	met	met	遇见
feed	fed	fed	饲，喂
feel	felt	felt	感觉
keep	kept	kept	保持
sleep	slept	slept	睡
lead	led	led	领导
leave	left	left	离开
mean	meant	meant	意指
stand	stood	stood	站立；忍受
understand	understood	understood	了解
find	found	found	发现
hang	hung	hung	挂；吊
strike	struck	struck	打击

c. A－B－A 型　（原形与过去分词同形）

run	ran	run	跑；经营
come	came	come	来
become	became	become	成为

d. A－B－C 型　（三态不同形）

begin	began	begun	开始
drink	drank	drunk	喝
ring	rang	rung	摇铃；鸣响
sing	sang	sung	唱
sink	sank	sunk	沉
swim	swam	swum	游泳
break	broke	broken	打破
speak	spoke	spoken	说话
steal	stole	stolen	偷
freeze	froze	frozen	冰冻
choose	chose	chosen	选择
hide	hid	hidden	藏

bite	bit	bitten	咬
tear	tore	torn	撕
wear	wore	worn	穿，戴；磨损
drive	drove	driven	驾驶
ride	rode	ridden	骑
rise	rose	risen	上升
write	wrote	written	写
take	took	taken	拿取
mistake	mistook	mistaken	误会
shake	shook	shaken	摇动
know	knew	known	知道，认识
grow	grew	grown	生长
throw	threw	thrown	投
draw	drew	drawn	画；拉
fly	flew	flown	飞
blow	blew	blown	吹
do	did	done	做
eat	ate	eaten	吃
fall	fell	fallen	落
give	gave	given	给
go	went	gone	去
lie	lay	lain	躺，卧
see	saw	seen	看
show	showed	shown	显示
forget	forgot	forgotten	忘记
be, am, is are	was were	been	是；在

e. 有两种变化的动词

burn	burned burnt	burned burnt	燃烧
dream	dreamed dreamt	dreamed dreamt	梦见
learn	learned learnt	learned learnt	学习

spell	spelled spelt	spelled spelt	拼写

f. A－B 型　（变化不完全的助动词）

原形	过去式	过去分词
shall	should	
will	would	
can	could	
may	might	

第二节　语态

1. 语态的种类：

语态有两类，即主动语态及被动语态，形成被动语态时动词一定是及物动词。

主动语态：I did the work.

vt.

（我做了这工作。）

被动语态：The work was done by me.

（这工作被我做了。）

注意

不及物动词只有主动语态，而无被动语态。

例: On the bed was lain by me. (×)

→ I lay on the bed. (✓，lay 为不及物动词 lie 的过去式，表“躺”)

（我躺在床上。）

I laid a book on the desk. (✓，laid 为及物动词 lay 的过去式，表“放”)

（我把一本书放在桌上。）

→ A book was laid on the desk. (✓)

（一本书被我放在桌上。）

2. 主动语态变成被动语态的方式：

原句的宾语做主语，之后置 be 动词，再接过去分词。

例: Everyone　loves　him.

主语　及物动词　宾语

→ He is loved by everyone.

（他受大家爱戴。）

The class stared at him.

主语　短语动词　宾语

→ He was stared at by the class.

（他被全班同学盯着看。）

I will take care of him.

主语　短语动词　宾语

→ He will be taken care of by me.

（他会受我照顾。）

请参看下列表格：

时态＼语态		主动语态	被动语态
一般时	现在	He does it.	It is done by him.
	过去	He did it.	It was done by him.
	将来	He will do it.	It will be done by him.
完成时	现在	He has done it.	It has been done by him.
	过去	He had done it.	It had been done by him.
	将来	He will have done it.	It will have been done by him.
进行时	现在	He is doing it.	It is being done by him.
	过去	He was doing it.	It was being done by him.
	将来	He will be doing it.	(缺)

3. 主动语态和被动语态时态要一致：

例: Everyone loves him.

一般现在时

→ He is loved by everyone.

一般现在时

（他现在受到大家爱戴。）

Everyone loved him.

一般过去时

→ He was loved by everyone.

一般过去时

（他当时受到大家爱戴。）

Everyone will love him.

一般将来时

→ He will be loved by everyone.

一般将来时

（他将会受到大家爱戴。）

He is doing that work.
现在进行时
→ That work is being done by him.
现在进行时
（那件工作正被他做。）

4. 授予动词有两种被动语态：

例: I gave him a book. (主动)
= He was given a book by me. (被动)
= A book was given to him by me. (被动)
（我给他一本书。）

The law firm offered him a job.
= He was offered a job by the law firm.
= A job was offered to him by the law firm.
（这家律师事务所给了他一份工作。）

5. "动词 + 介词"亦可变成被动语态：

有些动词之后须与介词连用，形成短语动词，再置宾语时，要把"动词 + 介词"形成的短语动词视为及物动词，可变被动语态。

例: I was laughed by them. (×)
→ They laughed at me. (√)
= I was laughed at by them.
（他们笑我。）

The case was looked by police. (×)
→ Police looked into the case. (√)
= The case was looked into by police.
（警方调查了那件案子。）

6. 否定句的语态变化：

例: They do not love him.
= He is not loved by them.
（他们不爱他。）

EXERCISE

I. 请选出一个正确的答案：

1. The government ______ employ wide surveillance, but the Department of Justice objected to it.
   (A) is about to　(B) was about to　(C) in order to　(D) ought to
2. The United States ______ to build a supersonic aircraft, but there was no support for it in the Congress.
   (A) has intended　(B) is intended
   (C) had intended　(D) is intending
3. There's a police car in front of our neighbor's house. What do you suppose ______ ?
   (A) is happened　(B) has happened
   (C) would happen　(D) did happen
4. I came so early for lunch today because I thought the bell ______ .
   (A) had already rang　(B) has already rung
   (C) already had rung　(D) had already rung
5. James has just arrived, but I didn't know he ______ until yesterday.
   (A) will come　(B) was coming
   (C) had been coming　(D) comes
6. The streets are all wet. It ______ during the night.
   (A) must be raining　(B) must have been rain
   (C) had to rain　(D) must have rained
7. I will go home for vacation as soon as I ______ my exams.
   (A) will finish　(B) finish　(C) am finishing　(D) finished
8. Martin visited his aunt two days before he ______ town.
   (A) left　(B) will leave
   (C) had left　(D) is going to leave

9. As yet we ______ nothing from my brother.
(A) did not hear (B) had not heard (C) has heard (D) have heard

10. I ______ to Taipei before I entered this school.
(A) once gone (B) have once gone
(C) had once gone (D) had once been

11. The commander-in-chief ______ the Pacific Ocean when the telegram reaches him.
(A) will cross (B) will be crossing
(C) has crossed (D) had crossed

12. The whole area was flooded because it ______ for weeks.
(A) rains (B) has rained
(C) had been raining (D) was raining

13. Our sales ______ for months, so we are now in great financial difficulty.
(A) have been dropping (B) had been dropping
(C) have been dropped (D) are dropping

14. I will lend you the book when I ______ reading it.
(A) will have (B) finish (C) am finishing (D) will finish

15. The moment I ______ the news, I turned pale.
(A) have heard (B) hear (C) heard (D) was hearing

16. While I ______ with my wife last night, an old friend of mine showed up.
(A) was talking (B) had talked (C) talked (D) would talk

17. We will wait right here until David ______ back.
(A) has got (B) will have got (C) gets (D) get

18. We have been told the final outcome of the negotiations, but we shall never know what ______ on behind the scenes.
(A) goes (B) went
(C) had gone (D) will have been going

19. The clock has been working well since he ______ it for me.
(A) has fixed (B) had fixed (C) fixed (D) would fix

20. Joseph ______ Hong Kong by the end of this month.
(A) will have reached　　(B) has reached
(C) reaches　　(D) is reaching

II. 选出错误的画线部分：

21. She thought that she will (A) have to wait (B) in line because there were (C) many people (D) in the office.

22. It is possible that Indians originally have migrated (A) to the Western Hemisphere over (B) a bridge of land that once existed (C) between (D) Siberia and Alaska.

23. When (A) Harry Truman has become (B) the President of the United States, he was (C) not familiar with either (D) the foreign policy or the atomic bomb.

24. He has been sitting (A) at the table for several hours and drank (B) considerably (C) more wine than is (D) good for his health.

25. Before (A) he died, the old man who lives (B) next door to the drugstore used to feed (C) the pigeons three times (D) a day.

26. Medical researchers have not yet (A) been able to have developed (B) an effective (C) vaccine against (D) influenza.

27. Learning a foreign (A) language is especially difficult for those who (B) had never learned (C) one (D) before.

28. Unfortunately, two of the boys has been bit by snakes the last time the family camped in the valley.
(A) two of the (B) has been bit (C) last time (D) in

29. To Mrs. Foster and Miss Rosen the advice sounded wrong, but everyone else at the meeting consider it perfect.
(A) wrong (B) else (C) consider (D) perfect

30. In all the years that Paul and I have been friends, I never knew him friendly to anyone else.
(A) In all (B) have been (C) never knew (D) anyone else

标准答案

1. (B) 2. (C) 3. (B) 4. (D) 5. (B) 6. (D) 7. (B) 8. (A) 9. (D) 10. (D)
11. (B) 12. (C) 13. (A) 14. (B) 15. (C) 16. (A) 17. (C) 18. (B) 19. (C) 20. (A)
21. (A) 22. (A) 23. (B) 24. (B) 25. (B) 26. (B) 27. (C) 28. (B) 29. (C) 30. (C)

习题解说

1. a. but 之后的从句中动词 objected to 是一般过去时，因此不可能选 (A)。
   b. was about to = was going to 正要
   c. (C) 非动词
   d. (D) ought to 不能用在一般过去时，只用在现在或将来时中。
   He ought to go now.
   （他现在该走了。）
   He ought to go tomorrow.
   （他明天该走了。）
   ought to 若表过去时，应加 have 形成虚拟语气，表与过去相反的事实。
   He ought to have gone yesterday. (But he didn't go.)

（他昨天就该走了。—— 但他当时并没走。）

2. but 之后从句中动词为一般过去时“there was...”，故前面的从句可用过去完成时。

   I had intended to go, but I had no money.

= I intended to have gone, but I had no money.

= I would have gone, but I had no money.

（我本来想走了，但却没钱。）

3. a. happen 为不及物动词，故不可用被动语态。

   b. (C) 助动词是过去时，可是事情现在已发生，故时态不对。

   c. (D) 本句为疑问句，故不必用“did + 原形动词”来强调。

4. a. (B) 主句 I thought 为一般过去时，故从句不可能用一般将来时。

   b. already 应置于完成时助动词 had 之后。

   c. (A) rang 应改为过去分词 rung。

5. a. (A) 时态错误，因 but 之后的主句是一般过去时，故从句不可能用一般将来时。

   b. (B) was coming = would come

   c. (C) coming 不可能用在完成进行时中。

      He has come. (✓)

   （他已来了。）

      He has been coming. (×)

   （他一直都在来。）

6. “must have + p.p.”表示对过去事实之推测，表“一定已经/曾经……”。

7. 若主句为一般将来时，条件句一定是一般现在时。

8. before 从句的动作一定是最后发生，故用一般过去时。

9. as yet　　至目前为止（= so far）

   本短语常用于否定意味的现在完成时句子中。

10. before 引导的从句若为一般过去时，为了表示更早之前的行为，主句常用过去完成时。

11. 表将来某时正在进行的动作，用将来进行时。

12. 表示比一般过去时中的动作更早发生并且一直持续的事情，用过去完成进行时。

13. 表示从过去至今仍在持续的状态或行为，用现在完成进行时。

14. 主句为一般将来时，故 when 引导的条件句应为一般现在时。

15. The moment 视作连词，等于 As soon as，表“一……就……”，所引导的状语从句是一般过去时，主句亦应为一般过去时。

16. while（当……时），引导的状语从句表示持续的状态或行为，故常用进行时。

17. 表时间的状语从句中，必须用一般现在时代替一般将来时。
18. 本句中 but 之后的主句虽为一般将来时，但名词性从句中的事件为过去发生，故用一般过去时。
19. since 引导时间状语从句时，该从句用一般过去时，主句用现在完成（进行）时。
20. "by + 时间名词"表"等到……时"，所引导的从句或短语在句中出现时，主句常用将来完成时或过去完成时。
21. (A) will 应改为 would。
22. (A) 应改为 may have migrated（当时很可能移至）或 must have migrated（当时一定移至），表对过去事实的推测。originally 表示"原先"，是叙述过去概念，故不可用现在完成时。
23. (B) has become 应改为 became，叙述过去的事实用一般过去时。
24. (B) drank 应改为 drinking。
    He has been sitting...and drinking...
25. (B) live 应改为 lived。
    before he died 暗示 He has already died and is no longer in the world. 故 who lives 应改为一般过去时 who lived。
26. (B) 应改为 to develop。
    不定式之前若有完成时，不得再用完成时。
27. (C) 应改为 have never learned，过去完成时不得与一般现在时连用，要与一般过去时连用。
    I think he had gone. (×)
    → I think he has gone. (√)
    （我想他走了。）
    I wish he had gone. (√，wish 之后的从句表与过去事实相反的虚拟语气时，可采用过去完成时。)
    （真希望他走了。）
28. (B) 应改为 had been bitten。
    last time 引导的从句为一般过去时，故主句应为过去完成时。
29. (C) 应改为 considered。
    两句发生在过去的同时，故应用一般过去时。
30. (C) never knew 应改为 have never known。
    (B) 为现在完成时，故时间包括到现在，因此 (C) 不能用一般过去时。

A Quick Note

第七章　虚拟语气

概　述

虚拟语气（the subjunctive mood）是一种表示假设状态的句型，由 if 引导的状语从句与主句构成。依时态的不同而形成下列四种基本句型：

a. 纯条件的虚拟语气
b. 与现在事实相反的虚拟语气
c. 与过去事实相反的虚拟语气
d. 与将来状况相反的虚拟语气

兹列举四种代表性的例句如下：

a. 纯条件的虚拟语气——用现在时

例: If he is here, I will beat him.
（如果他在这儿，我会揍他。）

b. 与现在事实相反的虚拟语气——用过去时

例: If he were here, I would beat him. (But he is not here.)
（如果他现在在这儿，我会揍他。—— 但他现在不在这儿。）

c. 与过去事实相反的虚拟语气——用过去完成时

例: If he had been here, I would have beaten him. (But he was not here.)
（如果他当时在这儿，我会揍他。—— 但他当时不在这儿。）

d. 与将来状况相反的虚拟语气—— if 从句要用助动词 should，译成“万一”，主句则用过去时或现在时助动词。

例: If he should be here, I would (或 will) beat him.
（万一他在这儿，我会揍他。）

第一节 纯条件虚拟语气

1. 基本句型：

使用纯条件虚拟语气时，if 从句的动词用现在时，主句则是现在时助动词加上动词原形。

句型如下：

If + 主语 + 一般现在时动词, 主语 + will / may / can / should / shall / must / ought to + 原形动词

例: If he is here, I will beat him.
（如果他在这儿，我会揍他。）

If anyone makes such a mistake, he must be punished.
（谁要犯了这样的错误，就要受处罚。）

If he comes, you should (ought to) tell him the truth.
（如果他来了，你就该告诉他事情的真相。）

2. 使用时机及要点：

a. 纯条件虚拟语气的 if 从句中，时态为一般现在时，表示若 if 的条件存在，就会有预期的结果。在上列的第一个例句中，“If he is here，I will beat him.”即告诉我们，“他要是在这儿，我就会揍他。”至于他现在是否在这儿，我们不知道。我们只知,“他要是在这儿”这个条件存在的话，就会有“我就会揍他”的预期结果。

b. 表纯条件结构的副词性连词不只 if 一种。once（一旦）、when（当）、before（在……之前）、as soon as（一旦）、unless（除非）等副词性连词亦可构成条件句，其用法与 if 相同。

例: Once I have money, I will buy a car.
have：现在时动词　will：现在时助动词
（一旦我有钱，我会买辆车。）

When he finishes it, he may come.
finishes：现在时动词　may：现在时助动词
（他做完事，就可以来了。）

As soon as he arrives, I will let you know.
arrives：现在时动词　will：现在时助动词
（他一到，我就会让你知道。）

I will not do anything before he arrives.
现在时助动词　现在时动词
（他来之前，我什么都不会做。）

I won't do it unless you help me.
现在时助动词　现在时动词
（除非你帮助我，否则我不会去做这件事。）

c. 通常助动词不置于 if 从句中，只置于主句中。

例: If the news will be true, he may be safe. (×)
助动词　助动词
→ If the news is true, he may be safe. (√)
动词　助动词
（如果消息属实，他可能仍安然无恙。）

但 if 从句的主语为人时，可用 can（能够）、will（愿意）或 must（非要……不可）等助动词。

例: If he can come, I will be happy.
（如果他能来的话，我会很高兴。）

If he will do it, I will be happy.
= If he is willing to do it, I will be happy.
（如果他愿意做的话，我会很高兴。）

If he must do it, he should do it with care.
= If he has to do it, he should do it with care.
（如果他非做这事不可的话，他得小心做。）

注意
"If he will..."的用法比较少见，最好避免。

d. 我们已知纯条件虚拟语气的主句中，助动词均用一般现在时，但 should 为唯一例外。因为 should 表示"应当"之意，等于 ought to，故不受限制。

例: If I have time, I | should / ought to | do it.
（如果我有时间，我应当去办这件事。）

第二节 与现在事实相反的虚拟语气

1. 基本句型：

使用本虚拟语气时，if 从句的动词用过去时，主句则用过去时助动词。句型如下：

If＋主语＋一般过去时动词, 主语＋ would / could / might / should / ought to ＋原形动词

例: If I were rich, I would help you.
（如果我有钱，我就会帮助你。）

If he lived in my town, I could see him every day.
（如果他住在我住的镇上，我就能每天见到他了。）

2. 使用时机及要点：

a. 本虚拟语气旨在表示与现在事实相反的情况。换言之，一见到此类一般过去时句型出现时，我们就可确知事实并非如此。

例: If I were rich, I would help you.
（如果我有钱，我就会帮助你。）

= As I am not rich, I can't help you.
（因为我不是很有钱，所以无法帮助你。）

b. 不论主语为第几人称，if 从句中的 be 动词，均使用 were。

例: If you were in my shoes, what would you do?
（如果你站在我的立场，你会怎么做？）

If I was you, I wouldn't do it. (×)

→ If I were you, I wouldn't do it. (✓)
（如果我是你，我不会做这事。）

c. 主句中的助动词一定为过去时助动词。

如：

will → would、may → might、can → could、shall → should 或 ought to。

但 must（必须）只能表示现在或将来的状况，故只用于纯条件的虚拟语气，而绝不可用于与现在事实或过去事实相反的虚拟语气中。

例: If you did it for me, I would be very happy.
（如果你为了我这样做，我会很高兴。）

If I could fly, I would fly to you.
（如果我能飞，我会飞向你。）

If you had money, you must help the poor. (×)
→ If you had money, you ought to help the poor. (√)
→ If you had money, you should help the poor. (√)
（如果你有钱，就应该帮助穷人。）

或: If you have money, you	must should ought to	help the poor. (√)

第三节　与过去事实相反的虚拟语气

1. 基本句型：

本虚拟语气中，if 从句的动词要用过去完成时，主句则是助动词的过去时再加上"have + 过去分词"，句型如下：

If + 主语 + had + p.p., 主语 + would / could / might / should / ought to + have + p.p.

例: If I had arrived earlier, I could have met him.
（要是当时我早点到，就可以见到他了。）

If he had taken your advice, he might have avoided the mistake.
（要是他当时听了你的劝告，可能会避免这个错误。）

2. 使用时机及要点：

a. 本虚拟语气旨在表示与过去事实相反的情况。换言之，一见到此类过去完成时的句型出现时，我们就确知当时的事实并非如此。

例: If I had arrived earlier, I could have met him.
（要是当时我早点到，就可以见到他了。）

→ As I didn't arrive earlier, I didn't meet him.
（因为当时我没有早点到，所以没见到他。）

If he had taken your advice, he would have avoided making the mistake.
（要是他当时听了你的劝告，就会避免犯这个错了。）

→ As he didn't take your advice, he made the mistake.
（因他当时没听从你的劝告，所以他犯了这个错。）

If you had been in my shoes, you might have done it.
（如果当时你是站在我的立场，你可能会做这件事。）

→ As you were not in my shoes, you didn't do it.
（因为当时你不是站在我的立场，所以你没有做这件事。）

b. 注意 if 从句中 had 与 had had 的区别：

1) 在"if + 主语 + had + 名词"的结构中，had 为一般过去时动词，译成"有"，此为表示与现在事实相反的虚拟语气。主句中置一般过去时的助动词即可。

例: If he had money, he would buy a car.
vt. n.
（如果他现在有钱，就会买车了。）

2) 在“if + 主语 + had + 过去分词”的结构中，had 为过去完成时助动词，译成“曾经”或“已经”，之后置过去分词，此时为表示与过去事实相反的虚拟语气。主句使用“过去时助动词 + have + 过去分词”。

例: If he had had money, he would have bought a car.
助 p.p.
（如果他当时有钱的话，就会买车了。）

故: If he had money, he would have bought a car. (×)

第四节　与将来状况相反的虚拟语气

基本句型及要点：

使用本虚拟语气时，if 从句一定要加助动词 should，“if...should”译成“万一”。若假设的可能性很低，则主句要置过去时助动词（和与现在事实相反的虚拟语气相同），但若假设的可能性很高，则主句要用现在时助动词（与纯条件虚拟语气相同）。

句型如下：

a. 低可能性：

If + 主语 + should + 原形 V, 主语	would could might should ought to	+ 原形 V

例：If you should fall ill, the meeting would be put off.

（万一你生病，会议将延期。—— 你不太可能生病，会议不太可能延期。）

If it should rain, I would stay home.

（万一下雨，我就会留在家里。—— 不太可能下雨，而我也不太可能留在家里。）

b. 高可能性：

If + 主语 + should + 原形 V, 主语 +	will can may should ought to	+ 原形 V

例：If you should fall ill, the meeting will be put off.

（万一你生病，会议将延期。—— 你可能会生病，而会议亦可能延期。）

If it should rain, I will stay home.

（万一下雨，我就会待在家里。—— 可能会下雨，果真如此，我会待在家里。）

注意

表示与将来状况相反的虚拟语气，亦可与祈使句形成的主句连用。

例：If I should be late, be sure to wait for me.

（万一我迟到，务必要等我。—— 我可能会迟到，你务必要等我。）

第五节　使用虚拟语气应注意事项

1. 表示强烈与真理相反的虚拟语气句型：

If + 主语 + were to + 原形 V, 主语 + would / could / might / should / ought to + 原形 V

例: 真理: The cat can't smile.
（猫不会笑。）

假设: If the cat were to smile, I would pass out.
（假如猫会笑，我会昏倒。）

真理: The sun doesn't rise in the west.
（太阳不会从西边升起。）

假设: If the sun were to rise in the west, how surprised these sunflowers would be.
（要是太阳从西边升起，这些向日葵会多么吃惊啊！）

2. if 的省略：

虚拟语气的 if 从句中，若有过去完成时助动词 had，或表“万一”的助动词 should 或是 were 出现时，可将这些词类置于主语前，而将 if 省略。

a. had

例: If he had done it, he would have felt sorry.
= Had he done it, he would have felt sorry.
（如果他当时做了这件事，他会后悔的。）

b. should

例: If he should tell lies, I would punish him.
= Should he tell lies, I would punish him.
（万一他说谎，我会处罚他。）

c. were

例: If he were lazy, he might fail.
= Were he lazy, he might fail.
（如果他懒惰，就可能会失败。）

> **注意**
> 为方便记忆起见，我们可以把 had、should、were 记成“何秀华”。换言之，if 从句中若有 had（何）、should（秀）、were（华），就可省略 if，形成上列的倒装句。

3. 时态不一致的假设：

也就是 if 从句与过去事实相反，用过去完成时；主句与现在事实相反，则置助动词过去时。句型如下：

If + 主语 + had + p.p., 主语 + | would / could / might / should / ought to | + 原形 V + | now / today |

例：If I had started saving then, I would have been able to buy a car now. (×)

→ If I had started saving then, I would be able to buy a car now. (✓)
（如果当时我开始存钱，我现在就能买辆车了。）

If I had met her five years ago, she might be my wife today. (✓)
（如果 5 年前我遇见了她，今天她可能就是我的妻子。）

4. 可取代 if 的其他连词：

if = in case (that)、on condition that、provided / providing (that)、so long as（只要）、as long as（只要），此类连词通常只用在表纯条件的虚拟语气中。换言之，其引导的从句时态均为一般现在时。

例：If it is fine, we will start to do it.
（如果天气好，我们就开始着手做这件事。）

In case he comes, let me know.
= In case he should come, let me know.
（如果他来了，让我知道一下。）

I will take the trip with you on condition that you bear the expenses.
（如果你出钱的话，我就和你同行。）

I will pardon him provided / providing (that) he acknowledges his mistake.
（如果他认错，我会原谅他。）

Any book will do as long as it is interesting.
（只要书有趣，哪本书都可以。）

注意

in case + (that) 从句　　万一……

in case of + 名词　　万一……

例: In case an accident happens, don't panic.

= In case of an accident, don't panic.

（万一有意外发生，不要惊慌。）

5. but for...　　若非/要不是……

此类句型仅限于与现在事实及过去事实相反的虚拟语气。

a. 与现在事实相反: 若非……就……

If it were not +	that 从句（一般现在时）， for + 名词,	+ 主语 +	could would might should ought to	+ 原形 V
= But for + 名词,				

例: If it were not that he works hard, I wouldn't like him.
（works：一般现在时动词）

= If it were not for his hard work, I...
（hard work：名词）

= Were it not for his hard work, I...
（hard work：名词）

= But for his hard work, I...
（hard work：名词）

（要不是他努力工作，我才不会喜欢他。）

b. 与过去事实相反: 若非当时……就……

If it had not been	that 从句（一般过去时）， for + 名词,	+ 主语 +	would could might should ought to	+ have + p.p.
= But for + 名词,				

例: If it had not been that he lent me the money, I could not have bought that book.
（lent：一般过去时动词）

= If it had not been for the money (which) he lent me, I...
名词

= Had it not been for the money (which) he lent me, I...
名词

= But for the money (which) he lent me, I...
名词

（要不是当时他借钱给我，我是无法买到那本书的。）

注意

but for 亦可用介词 without 代替，之后仍接名词。

例: But for his help, I couldn't have done it.

= Without his help, I couldn't have done it.

（若非他的帮忙，我无法办这事。）

But for his timely warning, I might have been killed.

= Without his timely warning, I might have been killed.

（若非他及时警告，我可能已经丧命了。）

6. lest...(should)... 以免……

lest 为副词性连词，引导状语从句。在该从句中，助动词一律用 should。而 should 往往予以省略，故该从句中的动词必定是原形动词。

例: I got up early lest I (should) miss the train.

（我早起以免错过火车。）

I arrived on time lest he (should) be angry.

（我准时到达，免得他生气。）

注意

lest...should...

= for fear that + 主语 + | may + 原形 V（表现在或将来的状况）
might + 原形 V（表过去的状况）|

= for fear of + 动名词

例: You must study hard lest you should fail the exam.

= You must study hard for fear that you may fail the exam.

= You must study hard for fear of failing the exam.

（你必须努力学习，以免考试不及格。）

He did it carefully lest he should make the same mistake again.

= He did it carefully for fear that he might make the same mistake again.

= He did it carefully for fear of making the same mistake again.
（他很谨慎地做这件事，唯恐再次犯同样的错。）

7. as if... = as though... 仿佛……

as if 或 as though 均为副词性连词，引导状语从句，使用时有三种时态：

a. 表极大的可能 → 动词使用一般时态

例: It looks as if (as though) it is going to rain.
（看起来好像要下雨了。）

b. 表与现在事实相反 → 动词使用一般过去时

例: Mr. Wang loves me as if (as though) I were his own child.
（王先生爱我就像我是他的孩子一样。）

c. 表与过去事实相反 → 动词使用过去完成时

例: He looked as if (as though) nothing had happened.
（他看起来就像什么事都没发生过一样。）

注意

as if 或 as though 之后亦可接不定式短语，表示即将发生的状况。

例: She opened her lips as if (she was going) to speak.
（她张开双唇好像有话要说。）

8. What if...should...? 要是……的话会怎样/要怎么办?

本句型乃表示对将来状况存疑的虚拟语气。if 从句多置助动词 should。

例: What if he should come?

= What might happen / could I (we) do if he should come?

（要是他来了，会怎样/怎么办？）

What if it should rain?

= What might happen / could I (we) do if it should rain?

（要是下雨了，怎么办？）

*what if 之后亦可用一般现在时，故上列例句亦可改写如下:

What if he comes?

= What shall we do if he comes?

What if it rains?
= What may happen if it rains?

9. It is time + that 从句的一般过去时：

It is	time about time high time	+ that 从句的一般过去时	该是……的时候了

注意

使用本句型时，that 从句的动词要用一般过去时。

例: It is time (that) he went to bed.
（该是他上床睡觉的时间了。）

本句暗示现在该是他睡觉的时候了，但他却没有睡觉。其动作与现在事实相反，故用一般过去时。

例: It is time we did it.
（该是我们行动的时候了。）

It is high time our children learned some manners.
（该是我们的孩子学点规矩的时候了。）

注意

上列结构亦可改为不定式形式：

例: It is time he went to bed.
= It is time for him to go to bed.

It is high time our children learned some manners.
= It is high time for our children to learn some manners.

10. If only...　要是……就好了

本句型只用于与现在事实或过去事实相反的虚拟语气中。换言之，本句型的时态只能用一般过去时或过去完成时。

例: If only he were here.
= I wish he were here.
（要是他现在在这里就好了。）

If only I had known it earlier.
= I wish I had known it earlier.
（要是我早点知道这件事就好了。）

11. wish 的用法

a. wish 之后接 that 从句时，一定要使用虚拟语气。若与现在事实相反，要用一般过去时；若与过去事实相反，则要用过去完成时。换言之，that 从句中的时态绝无一般现在时。

例: I wish (that) he is here. (×)
→ I wish he were here. (√)
= It's too bad that he is not here.
（我真希望他现在就在这里。——但遗憾的是，他并不在这里。）
I wish he had been here. (√)
= It's too bad that he was not here.
（我真希望他当时就在这里。——但遗憾的是，他当时并不在这里。）

b. I wish (that)...　真希望……就好了
= I would rather (that)...
= Would that... (罕)

例: I wish I had studied harder when young.
= I would rather I had studied harder when young.
= Would that I had studied harder when young. (罕)
（真希望我当时能更用功就好了。）

12. hope 的用法：

hope 之后接 that 从句时，使用一般时态，表示极大的可能性。即表示现在的状况时用现在时，表示将来的状况时用将来时，表示完成的状况时用完成时，表示进行的状况时用进行时。

a. 表示现在的状况：
I hope (that) he is safe.
（我希望他安然无恙。）

b. 表示将来的状况：
I hope he will be back.
（我希望他会回来。）

c. 表示进行的状况：
I hope they are having a good time.
（我希望他们正玩得很愉快。）

d. 表示完成的状况：
I hope they have finished the work.
（我希望他们已经把工作做完了。）

13. I hope 与祈使句的关系：

I hope 接 that 从句时，从句中可使用助动词 may，形成祈使句。此时将 I hope that 删除，将 may 置于原 that 从句的主语之前，动词仍用原形动词，原句号改为感叹号。

例：I hope (that) he may live long.
= May he live long!
（愿他长命百岁！）

I hope you may pass the exam.
= May you pass the exam!
（祝你通过考试！）

注意

a. 以 God 为主语时，可省略 may。

例：I hope God may bless you. (外国人实际并不使用本句)
= May God bless you! (外国人常用本句)
= God bless you! (外国人最常用本句)
（上帝保佑你！）

b. 表“国家/君主万岁”时，可采用倒装结构。

例：I hope the king may live long. (外国人实际并不使用本句)
= May the king live long! (外国人常用本句)
= Long live the king! (外国人最常用本句)
（国王万岁！）

14. wish 和 hope 的异同：

a. 相同部分：

1) 均可用不定式做宾语

例：I wish to travel abroad.
= I hope to travel abroad.
（我希望能出国旅游。）

2) 亦可做不及物动词，与介词 for 连用，表“期望获得”之意，以名词做其宾语。

例：I wish for a chance to try it. (常用)
= I hope for a chance to try it. (罕)
（我希望能有机会尝试一下。）

I | wish / hope | a chance to try it. (×)

b. 不同部分：

表“祝福”时，只能使用 wish，之后接两个名词或代词做其宾语。

例: I wish you a good time.

（祝你们玩得愉快。）

I wish my parents longevity.

（祝我父母亲长命百岁。）

I hope you a good time. (×)

但: I hope (that) you (may) have a good time. (√)

（我希望你们能玩得愉快。）

I hope my parents longevity. (×)

但: I hope (that) my parents can live long. (√)

（我希望父母能长命百岁。）

15. 对过去事物的猜测的三种句型：

a. must have + 过去分词 一定曾经……

例: He is learned; he must have received a good education.

（他博学多闻，一定受过良好的教育。）

b. may have + 过去分词 可能曾经……

例: He looks tired; he may have stayed up late last night.

（他看起来很疲倦，可能昨晚熬夜到很晚。）

c. cannot have + 过去分词 不可能曾经……

例: He is honest; he cannot have stolen Mary's money.

（他是老实人，不可能偷了玛丽的钱。）

注意

若表猜测的结构为疑问句时，要用“Can...have...?”句型。

例: May he have done it? (×)

→ Can he have done it? (√)

（他可能做了这样的事吗？）

16. “didn't need to + 原形 V ” 与 “need not have + p.p.” 的区别：

“didn't need to + 原形 V ” 乃表示过去的事实，即 “不必……同时亦没有如此做”；而 “need not have + p.p.” 乃表示与过去事实相反的虚拟语气，即 “不必……但却这么做了”。

例: As I had enough money, I didn't need to borrow any from him.
（由于钱够，我当时不必向他借钱。—— 而且我也没借。）

Since you had enough money, you needn't have borrowed money from me, but why did you still borrow some?
（既然你的钱够用，你原本不必向我借，但为什么你还是借了些钱呢？）

17. 意志动词：

意志动词计有 “建议”、“要求”、“命令”、“规定”、“主张” 五大类。之后用 that 从句做宾语时，that 从句中要使用助动词 should，而 should 往往予以省略。

a. 建议：suggest、recommend、advise、urge（呼吁）、propose、move（提议）

b. 要求：ask、desire、demand、require、request、insist （坚持要求）

c. 命令：order、command

d. 规定：rule、regulate、stipulate

e. 主张：advocate、maintain

例: They suggested that he (should) come home on time.
（他们建议他准时回家。）

Mary desired that Peter (should) treat her nicely.
（玛丽请求彼得好好待她。）

The mayor ordered that the police officer (should) be investigated.
（市长下令要调查那名警官。）

The principal ruled that no student (should) play truant.
（校长规定学生不准逃学。）

18. suggest、insist、maintain 的另类用法：

suggest 若表示 “暗示”、insist 若表示 “坚信”、maintain 若表示 “坚决认为” 时，则之后的 that 从句用一般时态。

例:

His words	suggested implied hinted	that he wasn't telling a lie.

（他的话中暗示他绝不是在说谎。）

He	insists is convinced is sure	that the job isn't so difficult as one may think.

（他深信这份工作没有一般人想象的那么困难。）

John | maintained / believed | that he had met the girl before.

（约翰确信他曾经见过那女孩。）

19. insist on + 动名词　　坚持要……

例: He insisted on doing it that way.
（他坚持要那样做。）

注意

“insist on...”与“persist in...”均以动名词做宾语，但意思有别：

insist on...　　坚持要……（有固执的含义）

persist in...　　从事……很执着（有很努力且不轻易放弃的含义）

例: John insisted on going fishing even though a typhoon was coming.
（虽然台风就要来了，约翰却坚持要去钓鱼。）

Peter persisted in handling the problem all by himself.
（彼得执着于自己来解决这个问题。）

20. 表示“有必要的”形容词与 that 从句的关系：

表示“有必要的”形容词，修饰 that 从句时，该从句亦须使用助动词 should，而 should 往往予以省略。

注意

此类形容词通常有八个:

necessary（有必要的）、important（很重要的）、essential（不可或缺的）、imperative（有绝对必要的）、urgent（紧急的）、desirable（合意的）、recommendable（值得推荐的）、advisable（明智的）。

例: It is necessary that he (should) work hard.
（他必须努力工作。）

I think it essential that he (should) finish it before leaving.
（我认为他必须做完这件事再离开。）

It is desirable that he (should) not do that again.
（他不要再那样做才好。）

21. that 从句做同位语：

that 从句若是置于意志动词变成的名词之后，而与该名词形成同位语时，that 从句中也要使用助动词 should，而 should 往往予以省略。

例: It is my suggestion that he (should) study abroad.
（我建议他出国留学。）

They raised a proposal that the meeting (should) be postponed.
（他们提议延期开会。）

It is John's desire that someone (should) help him write the letter.
（约翰期望有人能帮他写信。）

EXERCISE

I. 请选出一个正确的答案：

1. What would you do if you ______ a million dollars?
   (A) have　(B) have had　(C) had　(D) shall have

2. Even if I ______, I wouldn't.
   (A) can　(B) shall　(C) could　(D) will

3. If he were alive, he ______ twenty years old now.
   (A) will be　(B) would be
   (C) would have been　(D) is

4. I don't think you ______ me even if I told you the truth.
   (A) will believe　(B) would have believed
   (C) would believe　(D) believed

5. If I had not called for a doctor, your friend _____.
   (A) had died　(B) will have died
   (C) will die　(D) would have died

6. I would have married her if she ______ such an extravagant girl.
   (A) were not　(B) wouldn't be
   (C) would not have been　(D) hadn't been

7. If it ______ convenient, let's meet at nine o'clock.
   (A) is　(B) being　(C) was　(D) were

8. If he ______ in a day or two, I would wait for him.
   (A) will return　(B) returns　(C) were to return　(D) had returned

9. If he ______ late, give him the message.
   (A) were coming　(B) would come
   (C) should come　(D) were come

10. ______ the doctor come a little sooner, the patient would have been saved.
(A) Had (B) Should (C) Were (D) If

11. ______ his aid, I could not have succeeded.
(A) But (B) Without (C) Not (D) Unless

12. I ______ abroad last year but for my illness.
(A) would go (B) would have gone
(C) had gone (D) went

13. I ______ had it not been that he grasped me.
(A) should have fallen (B) should fall
(C) had fallen (D) fell

14. I wish I ______ as tall as she.
(A) is (B) am (C) were (D) be

15. Oh, if only I ______ your advice then.
(A) take (B) took (C) should take (D) had taken

16. She talked and acted as if she ______ abroad for a long time.
(A) would have lived (B) might live
(C) lived (D) had lived

17. Mr. Smith is, ______, a walking dictionary.
(A) as it is (B) as though (C) as it were (D) as if

18. He would rather people ______ about his family.
(A) not talked (B) haven't talked
(C) didn't talk (D) wouldn't have talked

19. What if I ______?
(A) failed (B) should fail (C) would fail (D) had failed

20. If he ______ in Germany, what language would he probably speak now?
(A) had born (B) have been born
(C) had been born (D) would have been born

II. 请选出错误的画线部分：

21. They are the ones (A) who assert (B) that a better bridge could (C) have been built have (D) we had their assistance.

22. Had (A) anyone asked him (B), Barlow could told (C) the investigators some useful details about the robbery (D).

23. If the cook had been more careful (A) in measuring (B) the ingredients, the dinner will (C) have been much (D) better.

24. If you have (A) listened, you too (B) would have concluded that Peter is more capable (C) than any (D) other boy in his class.

25. Helen will graduate (A) with her class if (B) she had been able to meet (C) all of the requirements in time (D).

26. Had (A) they had enough cash on (B) hand, they will buy (C) this fancy furniture (D).

27. If the volume of British investment is to be (A) increased, other (B) demands on national resources would have to (C) be reduced or eliminated (D).

28. Sometimes I get (A) the idea that a student is expected (B) to think about getting educated for the sake of society as if he is (C) not a part of it (D).

29. I sometimes wish that my university is (A) as large as (B) the State University because our facilities are more (C) limited than (D) theirs.

30. You have confessed (A) that you are (B) sorry for your rebellion. So I will (C) recommend that you will not be punished (D).

标准答案

1. (C)	2. (C)	3. (B)	4. (C)	5. (D)	6. (D)	7. (A)	8. (C)	9. (C)	10. (A)
11. (B)	12. (B)	13. (A)	14. (C)	15. (D)	16. (D)	17. (C)	18. (C)	19. (B)	20. (C)
21. (D)	22. (C)	23. (C)	24. (A)	25. (A)	26. (C)	27. (C)	28. (C)	29. (A)	30. (D)

习题解说

1. What 之后有助动词 would，故空格内应置入一般过去时动词 had，形成与现在事实相反的虚拟语气。
2. 主句为过去时助动词 wouldn't，空格内亦应置入过去时助动词 could，形成与现在事实相反的虚拟语气。
3. If 从句有过去时动词 were，故空格内应置入 had，形成与现在事实相反的虚拟语气。
4. even if 引导的状语从句有过去时动词，故空格内应置入 would believe，形成与现在事实相反的虚拟语气。
5. If 从句为过去完成时，为与过去事实相反的虚拟语气，故应选 (D)。
6. 主句有"would have + p.p."，故 if 从句应为过去完成时。
7. 此为纯条件句，并不表示与事实相反，故用一般现在时。
8. if + 主语 + were to V, 主语 + were to + V
   本结构表示将来不太可能发生的假设。
9. should 用于虚拟语气的 if 从句中表"万一"。

10. if 从句中若有 had，可移至句首代替 if。

11. | without | N + 虚拟语气从句　　若非……
    | but for |

本句表与过去事实相反。

12. 同上。

13. Had it not been that...　　当时要不是……

= If it had not been that...

14. I wish + 虚拟语气从句　　但愿……

本句表与现在事实相反。

15. if only 用法有二：

a. 假设法：表“但愿”。

| If only | I had seen you then.
| I wish |

（我要是当时见到你就好了。）

b. 条件句: 表“只要”。

| If only | I have money, I'll buy a car.
| As long as |

（只要我有钱，我就要买车。）

16. as if + | 一般过去时（与现在相反） | 仿佛……
            | 过去完成时（与过去相反） |

17. as it were　可以说是（多作插入语）

= so to speak

He is, | as it were | , a hero.
       | so to speak |

（他可说是个英雄。）

18. | would rather | + that 引导的一般过去时从句　　宁愿……
    | would sooner |

19. What if + 主语 + should + V?　　万一……怎么办?

20. 本句的前半句表示与过去事实相反，后半句表示与现在事实相反。

21. 本句乃与过去事实相反的假设，故 have 应改为 had。

...had we had their assistance.

= ...if we had had their assistance.

22. could 要改为 could have，表与过去事实相反。
23. will 应改为 would。
24. have 应改为过去完成时助动词 had。
25. if 从句中表与过去相反，故主句中的 will graduate 应改为 would have graduated。
26. would buy 应改为 would have bought。
27. 本句为纯条件句，并非与事实相反的假设，故主句中的 would have to 应改为 will have to。

注意:

If...is to be increased

= If...has to be increased

28. was 应改为 were。
29. is 应改为 were。
30. recommend 为意志动词，其后的 that 从句中须用“should + V”，而 should 通常省略，故 will not be punished 应改为 (should) not be punished。

第八章　副词

概述

1. -ly 形成的副词：

如：

形容词		副词
slow（慢的）	⟶	slowly（慢慢地）
quick（快的）	⟶	quickly（很快地）
easy（容易的）	⟶	easily（容易地）
main（主要的）	⟶	mainly（主要地）

但亦有些副词却自成一格。

如：

very（非常地）　　ago（以前）

hard（努力地）　　enough（充分地）

never（从不）　　somewhat（有点儿）

somehow（不知怎地）

有的甚至用现在分词做副词用，专门修饰形容词。

例：It's biting cold today.

adv.　adj.

（今天天气冷死了——冷得会咬人一样。）

= It's freezing cold today.

adv.　adj.

（今天天气冷死了——冷得要把人冻僵一样。）

It's boiling hot today.

adv.　adj.

（今天天气热死了——热得要把水都煮沸了。）

2. 有些形容词本身亦可当副词用：

例：awful:

His writing is awful.

adj.

（他的文章糟透了。）

＊此处 awful 是形容词，表“差劲的”。

He is awful mad.

adv. adj.

（他气坏了。）

＊此处 awful 是副词，表“非常地”，相当于 very 或 awfully。

fine:

The dress is fine.

adj.

（这件连衣裙挺不错的。）

＊此处 fine 是形容词，表“不错的”。

The dress suits me fine.

vt. adv.

（这件连衣裙挺适合我的。）

＊此处 fine 是副词，表“令人满意地”或“很棒地”，相当于 well。

3. good and 可做副词：

更绝的是，good 与 and 合在一起，竟然也成了副词，译成“非常”（等于 very）或“完全”（等于 completely），只置于 be 动词之后，修饰形容词。

例：It's good and hot today.

adv. adj.

（今天热死了。）

同学们看到这里，不禁会叫道：“惨了，副词有那么多奇怪的形态，叫我不知如何是好？”赖老师认为，你无需害怕，也不必一一死记所有的副词形态及其用法。只要你多看文章，多查词典，每天读上三四个小时英语（我有 10 年时间几乎每天花 16 个小时学英语），自然就会熟悉副词的形态及其用法。

第一节 副词的功能

1. 修饰动词:

修饰动词（包括动词转化的不定式、动名词、分词），此时副词通常置于动词之后:

例: He studies hard. (动词)

vt. adv.

（他很用功。）

I love you very much. (动词)

vt. adv.

（我非常爱你。）

You have to study diligently. (不定式)

adv.

（你必须努力学习。）

Rising early is good for your health. (动名词)

adv.

（早起有益你的健康。）

比较:

He speaks English good. (×，形容词不可用以修饰动词)

vt. adj.

→ He speaks English well. (✓)

vt. adv.

（他英语说得很好。）

2. 修饰形容词:

此时副词通常置于该形容词之前:

例: He is very kind.

adv. adj.

（他心地善良。）

It is extremely dangerous to swim alone.

adv. → adj.

（单独游泳极为危险。）

比较:

This is probable true. (×，形容词不得修饰形容词)

adj. → adj.

→ This is probably true. (✓)

adv. → adj.

（这很可能是真的。）

3. 修饰副词:

此时副词通常置于该副词之前：

例: He studies very diligently.

adv. → adv.

（他非常努力地学习。）

He does things too carefully.

adv. → adv.

（他做事过于谨慎。）

4. 修饰全句:

此时副词通常置于句首：

例: Fortunately, he did not die.

adv. → 全句

（所幸他没死。）

Evidently, this answer is right.

adv.　　全句

（这答案显然是对的。）

注意

修饰全句的副词一定是置于句首，若置于句尾，则会修饰句中的动词，而造成语意的偏差。

例: Happily, he did not die.

adv.　　全句

（令人高兴地是，他没死。）

He did not die happily.

vi.　adv.

（他没有快乐地过世。—— 他死时不快乐。）

第二节 副词的位置

1. 一般规则：

在含有 be 动词（如 are、is、am、were、was）、助动词（如 can、shall、may、should、ought to、must）、完成时助动词（have、has、had）及一般动词的结构中，副词的位置有下列惯例：

a. 遇有 be 动词时，副词置于该 be 动词之后。

例: He is always kind.

（他为人一直都很好。）

They are really able to do it.

（他们确实有能力做这件事。）

b. 遇有助动词时，副词置于该助动词之后。

例: He can hardly walk.

（他几乎走不动了。）

He has never been to the United States before.

（他以前从未去过美国。）

c. 遇有一般动词时，副词置于该动词之前。

例: They often go fishing.

adv. vi.

（他们常去钓鱼。）

He really cares about you.

adv. vi.

（他真的很在乎你。）

同学们看到这里，一定会问：“在本章第一节中，赖老师曾说修饰动词时，副词应置于动词之后，为何此时又说副词应置于动词之前？”答案很简单：

1) 如果修饰动词的副词表示某种状态，则副词要置于动词之后。

例: She dances beautifully.

vi. adv.

（她舞跳得真美。）

beautifully 乃表示跳舞的样子很美（表示状态），故 beautifully 应置于 dances 之后。

同理：He drove (his car) fast.
vi. & vt.　　　　adv.
（他车开得很快。）

fast 乃表示开车的速度很快，故 fast 应置于 drove（his car）之后。

2) 如果修饰动词的副词表示肯定、否定或频率的意味，则此类副词多置于动词之前。

有肯定意味的副词：
surely（确定地）、certainly（确定地）、absolutely（绝对地）、probably（可能）、really（真正地）。

有否定意味的副词或频率副词：
never（从不）、seldom（很少）、hardly ever（几乎不曾）、always（总是）、often（常常）。

例：They certainly hope to win the game.
adv.　vt.
（他们当然希望赢得比赛。）

I really like him.
adv.　vt.
（我真的喜欢他。）

They always cheat on exams.
adv.　vi.
（他们考试总是作弊。）

He is trustworthy because he never lies.
adv.　vi.
（他值得信赖，因为他从不说谎。）

同学们看到上面的解释大概仍然不能完全理解赖老师想要表达的意思。没关系，赖老师换下列方式来讲解。我们可用中英文句型作比较：

中文：他跑得快。
英语：He ran fast. (√，fast 为状态副词)
vi. adv.
He fast ran. (×)

中文：他真的爱你。
英语：He really loves you. (√，really 为肯定意味的副词)
adv.　vt.
He loves you really. (×)

中文：他常常上学迟到。
英语：He often comes to school late.
adv. vi. adv.
(√，often 为频率副词，late 则为状态副词)

由此可知，中英文有很多结构是互通的。但这种通过中英文比较来了解英语中副词的位置，并不一定很准，同学们唯有通过博览文章才能学得习惯的用法，切记，切记！

2. 简化结构中副词位置的变化：

a. be 动词

简化前：He is really nice.
（他人真好。）
简化后：He is really. (×)
He really is. (√)

简化前：They are always eager to learn English.
（他们总是迫切想学英语。）
简化后：They are always. (×)
They always are. (√)

b. 助动词

简化前：He can hardly do it.
（他几乎做不了此事。）
简化后：He can hardly. (×)
He hardly can. (√)

简化前：He has never done it before.
（他从未做过此事。）
简化后：He has never. (×)
He never has. (√)

3. 状态副词在被动语态中的位置：

表示状态的副词在被动语态中，要置于过去分词前。
主动语态：He did the job well.
vt. adv.
（他把工作做得很好。）

被动语态：The job was well done. (√)
adv. p.p.
The job was done well. (劣)

主动语态：They decorated the room beautifully.
vt.　　　　　adv.
（他们把房间装饰得很漂亮。beautifully 修饰 decorated。）

被动语态：The room was beautifully decorated. (✓)
adv.　　　p.p.
The room was decorated beautifully. (劣)

4. 否定副词的位置：

否定副词 never（从不）、seldom（很少）、hardly ever（几乎不曾 = scarcely ever）、rarely（很少）修饰动词时，可直接置于该动词之前，无须另加助动词 do、does 或 did。但 not 不可直接置于动词之前，须另加 do、does 或 did，且之后的动词一律改为原形。

例: He never cheats. (✓)
vi.
（他从不骗人。）

They seldom do what the teacher has told them to do.
vt.
（他们很少去做老师要他们做的事。）

He hardly ever remained quiet.
vi.
（他几乎从未安静过。）

但:He not cheats. (×)
vi.
→ He does not cheat. (✓)
原形 vi.
（他不会骗人。）

They not enjoy singing. (×)
vt.
→ They do not enjoy singing. (✓)
原形 vt.
（他们不喜欢唱歌。）

5. can 与 not 连用习惯上写成 cannot：

例: He can not meet the requirements. (劣)
→ He cannot meet the requirements. (✓)
（他达不到要求。）

6. 时间副词的位置：

时间副词，如 yesterday、today、tomorrow、this year、at five（5 点钟）、in 2000，可置于句首或句尾。习惯的用法为：句子短时，时间副词置于句尾，句子长时，则置于句首。

长句：Yesterday I saw him chatting very pleasantly with a blonde girl in the park.

（昨天我在公园里看到他和一位金发女郎聊得很开心。）

短句：I saw him in the park yesterday.

（昨天我在公园里看到他。）

长句：In 1914, war broke out in the small town close to the border.

（1914 年，战争在这座邻近边境的小镇爆发。）

短句：War broke out in 1914.

（战争爆发于 1914 年。）

7. 地点副词的位置：

地点副词，如 here、there、home、downtown、upstairs、downstairs，以及表场所的介副词，如 in、out、up、down 等，均置于动词之后。

例：He came | here. / home. / in. / up. |

（他来这里/回家/进来/上来。）

注意

介副词与介词的区别如下：

a. in、out、up、down 之后有宾语时，就称为介词。

例：He sat in the corner.

介 o.

（他坐在角落里。）

He looked out (of) the window.

介 o.

（他望向窗外。）

b. in、out、up、down 之后若无宾语，则为介词变成的副词，简称介副词，视为地点副词。

例：He came in.

介副词

（他进来。）

He rushed out crying.
　　　　介副词
（他哭着冲了出去。）

He stepped down after the power struggle.
　　　　介副词
（他在权力斗争之后下台。）

8. 副词对等语及其在句中的位置：

副词对等语即指由两个以上的单词构成的短语或从句，具有副词的功能，用以修饰句中的动词或整个主句。

a. 副词短语：

包括介词短语及不定式短语两类。

1) 介词短语当副词用：

通常置于句尾，修饰句中的动词。

例：He loves her with all his heart.
　　vt.（loves）　介词短语（with all his heart）→ 修饰 vt.
（他全心全意地爱她。）

He achieved the goal by working hard.
　　vt.（achieved）　介词短语（by working hard）→ 修饰 vt.
（他经过努力达到了目标。）

He came by bus.
　　vi.（came）　介词短语（by bus）→ 修饰 vi.
（他坐公交车来的。）

注意

有时介词短语亦出现在句首，此时该短语仍被视为副词，修饰整个主句。但亦有形容词的功能，修饰主语。此类介词短语多半由 in、by 或 on 加动名词形成。

例：In doing the work, you must be careful.
　　介词短语做副词（In doing the work）→ 整个主句（you must be careful）

= When you do the work, you must be careful.

或:In doing the work, you must be careful.

介词短语做形容词 → 主语

（做这项工作时，你必须要谨慎。）

By working hard, he achieved the goal.

介词短语做副词 → 整个主句

= Because he worked hard, he achieved the goal.

或:By working hard, he achieved the goal.

介词短语做形容词 → 主语

（他努力工作达到目标。）

On / Upon seeing her, he ran away.

介词短语做副词 → 整个主句

= As soon as he saw her, he ran away.

或:On / Upon seeing her, he ran away.

介词短语做形容词 → 主语

（一看到她，他就跑开了。）

> **注意**
>
> in、by 或 on 加动名词所形成的介词短语，置于句首时，要合理地修饰主语，也就是被修饰的主语要有行使动名词所表示的动作能力。通常此类主语一定是人或动物，否则易形成不连接修饰（dangling modification）的错误结构。

例: On seeing her, he ran away. (✓)

On seeing her → he（人）

（一见到她，他就跑开了。）

理由:

he 为人，故可以做出 seeing her 所表示的动作。

例: On seeing her, tears came into his eyes. (×)
物

理由:
tears 为眼泪，不能做出 seeing her 的动作。本句译成：
眼泪看见她后，就涌入他的眼眶中。
（他的眼泪怎会看见人？可见此句不合逻辑。）

例: In doing the work, he must be careful. (√)
人

（做这工作时，他必须小心谨慎。）

理由:
he 为人，故可做出 doing the work 所表示的动作。

例: In doing the work, care must be taken. (×)
抽象名词

理由:
care 为抽象名词，表“谨慎”，显然“谨慎”不能自己去做工作，故本句犯了不连接修饰的错误。

2) 不定式短语当副词用:
不定式短语当副词用，除可修饰动词外，亦可置于形容词或副词之后，修饰该形容词或副词。

例: You will soon come to realize that you are mistaken.
vi.

（你很快会认识到自己错了。）

She went to Italy | in order / so as | to study music.
vi.

（她去意大利学音乐。）

I am sorry to have kept you waiting.
adj.

（我很抱歉让你久等了。）

He is rich enough to buy a car.
adj. adv.

（他有足够的钱可以买车。）

注意

表示“目的”的不定式短语置于句首时，亦同时有副词及形容词的功能。做副词用时，不定式短语修饰整个主句；做形容词用时，则修饰主句中的主语，而该主语亦要有行使不定式短语中动词所表动作的能力，故该主语亦通常为人或动物，否则易造成不连接修饰的错误结构。

例: To achieve the goal, you must work hard.
副词短语 → 主句

To achieve the goal, you must work hard.
形容词短语 → 人

（要达到目标，你就必须努力。）

To achieve the goal, hard work is necessary. (×)
抽象名词

理由:

hard work（努力）为抽象名词，不可能自行 achieve the goal，故形成错误的不连接修饰。

但有些不定式短语已成了固定的独立副词短语，称为独立不定式短语，置于句首时，只做副词用，修饰整个主句。此时就不必顾虑主句的主语。

例: To do him justice, he is qualified for the position.
副词短语 → 主句

（替他说句公道话，他有资格担任此职。）

To be frank with you, the trip wasn't interesting.
副词短语 → 主句

（老实跟你说，这次旅行并不好玩。）

To sum up, one can't do without friends.
副词短语　　　　主句

（总而言之，一个人不能没有朋友。）

b. 状语从句：

状语从句多用来修饰整个主句，可置于主句前后。但置于主句之前时，状语从句之后要加逗号。

例: Because he is nice, I like him.
状语从句　　　主句

= I like him because he is nice.
主句　　　状语从句

（我喜欢他，因为他人很好。）

If you have time, will you do it?
状语从句　　　主句 (疑问句型)

= Will you do it if you have time?
主句　　　状语从句

（如果有空的话，你会不会做这件事？）

> **注意**
>
> 这种原则亦适用于副词短语。
>
> 例: To achieve the goal, you must work hard.
> 副词短语　　　　主句
>
> = You must work hard to achieve the goal.
> 主句　　　　副词短语
>
> （要达到目标，你就必须努力。）
>
> By working hard, he achieved the goal.
> 副词短语　　　　主句
>
> = He achieved the goal by working hard.
> 主句　　　　副词短语
>
> （他经过努力达到了目标。）

9. 副词应尽量靠近被修饰的动词：

句中若含有两组以上的动词（包括由动词变成的分词及动名词），副词应尽量靠近被修饰的动词，以免造成句意的混淆。

例: Yesterday he mentioned seeing her.

adv. vt.

（他昨天提到曾经见到她。）

He mentioned seeing her yesterday.

动名词 adv.

（他提到昨天曾经见到她。）

理由:

yesterday 所放的位置不同，造成不同的句意。

例: You should handle the question with care that he raised yesterday. (劣)

vt.

（你应用那个昨天他提出来的谨慎来处理这个问题。）

理由:

本来 with care（以谨慎的态度）是副词，明确修饰动词 handle。而定语从句 that he raised yesterday 本应修饰 the question，但却因置于名词 care 之后，造成句意的偏差。

改正：

You should handle with care the question that he raised yesterday.

vt. adv. o. 定语从句，修饰 the question

（你应该小心处理他昨天提出的问题。）

10. 名词性从句修饰形容词:

名词性从句（由 that、whether 以及疑问词 where、when、how 等构成）具有名词的功能，在句中要做主语、宾语或在 be 动词之后做表语。但名词性从句亦可置于形容词之后，修饰该形容词。

例: I am sorry that I cannot attend your party.

adj.

（我很抱歉无法参加你的派对。）

I am not sure whether he'll come.

adj.

（我不确定他是否会来。）

第三节　重要的副词用法

1. very、much　　很、非常

a. very 不可单独修饰动词，而 very much 则可以，多用于肯定句中，其位置应在句尾。

例: I very like you. (×)

vt.

→ I like you very much. (√)

vt.　　adv.

（我很喜欢你。）

b. much 亦可修饰动词，但多限于疑问句或否定句中。若在疑问句中，much 应置于句尾；若在否定句中，much 可置于动词前或句尾。

例: Do you go to Sydney much? (罕)

vt.

= Do you go to Sydney often? (常用)

（你常去悉尼吗？）

I don't much like living in the country.

vt.

= I don't like living in the country much.

vt.

（我很不喜欢住在乡下。）

c. very 可修饰一般形容词或副词，但形容词或副词变成比较级时，则只能用 much 修饰。

例: He walked very slowly. (√)

adv.

（他走得很慢。）

I'm very happy to be of service. (√)

adj.

（我很高兴能帮得上忙。）

He walked very more slowly than I. (×)
→ He walked much more slowly than I. (✓)
（他走得比我慢多了。）

He is very happier than Peter. (×)
→ He is much happier than Peter. (✓)
（他比彼得快乐多了。）

d. 修饰 too 时只能用 much，不能用 very。

例: He is very too young. (×)
→ He is much too young. (✓)
（他太年轻了。）

注意

修饰比较级或 too 的副词通常有六个：

much、far、a lot、a great deal、still、even。

例: He is	much	more prudent than John.
	far	less diligent than John.
	a lot	better than John.
	a great deal	too young to work.
	still	
	even	

（他比约翰小心多了。）
（他没有约翰那么勤奋。）
（他比约翰好多了。）
（他太年轻因此还不能工作。）

e. 凡现在分词若可做形容词用，且可译成“令人……的”时，均使用 very 修饰。常用的此类现在分词如下：

interesting（令人觉得有趣的）　　boring（令人无聊的）
confusing（令人迷惑的）　　charming（令人着迷的）
tiring（令人累的）　　annoying（令人懊恼的）

例: She is indeed a very charming girl.
（她实在是个非常迷人的女孩。）

He raised a very interesting question.
（他提出一个非常有趣的问题。）

f. 凡过去分词若可做形容词用，且可译成“感到……的”时，此类过去分词均与情绪或心境有关，亦可用 very 或 very much 修饰。常用的此类过去分词如下：

interested（感到有兴趣的）　　bored（感到无聊的）
confused（感到迷惑的）　　charmed（感到着迷的）
tired（感到累的）　　annoyed（感到懊恼的）

例: I was | very / very much | annoyed with her son.
（我对她儿子感到很烦。）

He was | very / very much | interested in that book.
（他对那本书很有兴趣。）

g. very 亦可当形容词以修饰名词，表“正是那个”，放在定冠词 the 之后。此时名词之后若有定语从句修饰，其关系代词必须用 that 取代 who、whom 或 which。

例: He is | the very man / just the man / the same man | that came here yesterday.
（他就是昨天来的那位老兄。）

2. little、a little：

a. little 做副词时，视为否定副词，译成“一点儿都不”，等于 no（一点儿都不）之意。

例: The patient's condition is little better than (it was) yesterday.
adj.
（病人的情况并没比昨天好到哪去。）

b. a little 做副词时，译成“有点儿”。

例: The patient's condition is getting / becoming a little better.
adj.
（病人的情况好转了些。）

c. little 做否定副词时，通常修饰动词 think、dream、expect（期待）。

例: I little thought (或 dreamed, expected) that you would do it.
（我根本没料到你会做那件事。）

注意

然而，实际使用时，little 应置于句首，其后采用倒装结构，即：

Little did I	think dream expect	that you would do it.

3. no longer　　不再

= no more

= not...any longer

= not...anymore

例: He is no longer here.

= He is here no more. (少用)

= No longer is he here.

= No more is he here. (少用)

= He is not here any longer.

= He is not here anymore.

（他不再在这儿了。）

注意

no more 虽等于 no longer，但仅见于诗歌中，使用时，多置于句尾，或置于句首采用倒装结构，不可置于句中。

例: You can no longer see him.

No longer can you see him.

（你再也见不到他了。）

He loves the girl no more. (少用)

No more does he love the girl. (少用)

（他不再爱这女孩子了。）

He no more loves the girl. (×，no more 不可置于句中)

→ He no longer loves the girl. (√)

（他不再爱这女孩子了。）

4. sometimes、sometime、some time、some times：

a. sometimes　　有时候

此为频率副词（如 often、never、seldom 等），使用时通常置于句首，亦可置于句尾。

例: Sometimes he comes here for a visit.

= He comes here for a visit | sometimes / every now and then. | once in a while. |

（他有时候会来这儿看一看。）

b. sometime　某时（不知何时）

可用于一般过去时或一般将来时，使用时通常与另一明确的时间副词或副词短语连用。

例: 一般过去时：

I saw him sometime yesterday morning.

明确的时间副词

（我昨天早上某个时间见过他。）

一般将来时：

I'll be here sometime tomorrow.

明确的时刻

（我明天某个时间会在这儿。）

c. some time　一段时间

例: I'll stay here (for) some time.

（我会在这儿待一阵子。）

He was here sometime ago. (×)

→ He was here some time ago. (√)

（不久前他还在这儿。）

理由:

ago 非明确的时间副词，故无 sometime ago 的用法。

d. some times　有几次

= a few times

= several times

例: I have been to Thailand some times. (劣)

→ I have been to Thailand | a few / several | times. (佳)

（我曾去过几次泰国。）

注意

表有几次时，理论上可使用 some times，但实际使用时仍以 a few times 和 several times 为佳。

5. ago、before、since、after:

a. ago 表“距现在若干时间以前”，时态用一般过去时。

例: He came here a few days ago.

（他几天之前来过这儿。）

How long ago did he come?

（他多久之前来的？）

比较:

He had finished the work two hours ago. (×)

过去完成时

→ He finished the work two hours ago. (✓)

一般过去时

（他两小时前做完工作。）

b. before 表“距过去某时若干时间以前”，时态用过去完成时。

例: When I met Jim last Monday, he told me he had just gotten back from a trip to Lake Placid two days before. (✓)

（上周一我遇到吉姆时，他告诉我他两天前刚从宁静湖那儿旅游回来。）

比较:

When I met Jim last Monday, he told me he had just gotten back from a trip to Lake Placid two days ago. (×)

理由:

ago 只能用在一般过去时的结构。

注意

ago 不能单独使用，而 before 却可以。即 before 可单独做副词，修饰句中的动词，通常与现在完成时、过去完成时以及一般过去时连用。

例: I met him ago. (×)

→ I met him two hours ago. (✓)

一般过去时

（我两个钟头前遇见他。）

I met him before. (✓)

一般过去时

（我以前遇见过他。）

I have met him before. (✓)

现在完成时

（我以前曾遇见过他。）

I told him that I had met him before. (✓)
过去完成时
（我告诉他我以前曾遇见过他。）

c. since　　自从……

1) since 可做副词性连词，引导一般过去时的状语从句，修饰时态为现在完成（进行）时或过去完成（进行）时之主句。

例: I have studied English since I moved here in 2001.
现在完成时　　　　一般过去时
（自从 2001 年搬来这里后，我便一直学习英语。）

He told me that he had written two books since he moved here in 2001.
过去完成时　　　　一般过去时
（他告诉我自从 2001 年搬来这里后，他已经写了两本书。）

2) since 可做副词用，修饰现在完成（进行）时或过去完成（进行）时之主句。since 译成"之后"，可置于句尾或句中完成时助动词 have、has、had 之后。

例: I moved here in 2001 and have studied English since.
一般过去时　　　　现在完成时
= I moved here in 2001 and have since studied English.
（我于 2001 年迁到此处，之后就一直学习英语。）

> **注意**
> since 做副词时，句型结构一定为：
> 主语 + 一般过去时动词 + 明确的时间副词短语 + and + 主语 +
> have（has、had）+ | since + 过去分词 / 过去分词 + since |
>
> 例: He left town in 2002 and I haven't seen him since.
> 主语　一般过去时　明确时间副词　　现在完成时
> （2002 年他离城后，我便再没看见过他了。）

3) 做介词用，之后加明确的时间名词做宾语，亦可用动名词做宾语。

例: I have been studying English since | 2002. / Friday. |
介　　明确的时间名词
（自从 2002 年/星期五以后，我便一直学习英语。）

比较:

I have been studying English since ten years. (×，ten years 不是确定的时间名词)

改正:

I have been studying English <u>for</u> ten years. (✓)

（我已学了 10 年英语了。）

= I have been studying English <u>since ten years ago</u>.

（我自 10 年前起就一直在学习英语。）

I <u>have been studying</u> English <u>since</u> <u>moving</u> here in 2002.

现在完成进行时　　介　　动名词

（2002 年搬到这里后，我便一直在学习英语。）

> **注意**
>
> since 之前亦可用副词 ever 修饰。
>
> 例: <u>Ever since</u> he came here, he has been arguing with Mary.
>
> （自从他来到这，便一直和玛丽争吵。）
>
> He has been learning English <u>ever since</u> he was five years old.
>
> （自 5 岁时起，他就一直在学习英语。）
>
> He failed the exam two weeks ago and has felt discouraged <u>ever since</u>.
>
> （他两周前考试没通过，此后便很沮丧。）

d. after　之后

after 做副词时亦译成“之后”，但与 since 做副词不同的是: since 修饰完成时，而 after 则修饰过去时，此时等于 later 或 afterwards。

例: He fell ill on Monday and died three days <u>after</u>.

（他星期一生病，3 天后就死了。）

Soon <u>after</u>, he moved to the United States.

（不久之后，他便搬去美国。）

The war ended in 1945, and they lived happily <u>ever after</u>.

（战争于 1945 年结束，从此他们便过着快乐的日子。）

6. quite、rather

quite　十分地

rather　相当地

这两个词可修饰原级之副词或形容词。

例: He is quite old.
（他相当老了。—— quite 修饰形容词 old）

He is rather old.
（他蛮老了。—— rather 修饰形容词 old）

He studies quite hard.
（他相当用功。—— quite 修饰副词 hard）

注意

但 quite 修饰“形容词 + 单数名词”时，应在 a 或 an 之前：

例: He is a quite good student. (×)
→ He is quite a good student. (✓)
（他是个相当不错的学生。）

They are quite good students. (✓)
（他们是相当好的学生。）

7. someday、one day、the other day、some other day：

a. someday　将来有一天（用于将来时）

例: Keep on working hard, and someday you'll be successful.
（要不断努力，那么将来总有一天你会成功。）

b. one day　某日（表前几天时，可等于 the other day，也可指几年前的某一天，两者均用过去时）；将来总有一天（等于 someday，用于将来时）

例: I saw him downtown one day.
一般过去时
= I saw him downtown the other day.
（有一天我在城里看到他。）

One day you'll be sorry.
一般将来时
= Someday you'll be sorry.
（总有一天你会后悔的。）

c. the other day　前些时候（用于一般过去时）

例: I went to the National Park for a visit the other day.
一般过去时
（前几天我到国家公园玩了一趟。）

d. some other day　　改天（用于一般将来时）

例: I'm busy now. I will visit you some other day.

一般将来时

（我现在很忙，改天再去拜访你。）

8. so much so that...　　如此……以至……

谈这个结构之前，赖老师先请同学们看这个句子：

He is angry—so angry that he wants to kill the rival that has stolen his girlfriend's heart.

（他很生气—— 生气得要杀掉抢走他女友的情敌。）

这个句子语法是对的，但美中不足的是 angry 用了两次，就修辞的角度来看，本句犯了重复使用的毛病，为补救这个问题，我们可用 much so 代替 angry，而形成下列的标准结构：

He is angry—so much so that he wants to kill the rival that has stolen his girlfriend's heart.

于是，我们得到这样的概念：

much so 可在“so...that”结构中代替前面已提及的副词或形容词，以避免重复。

例: 代替副词：

He studies hard—so much so (原为 hard) that he is sure to pass the exam.

adv.

（他很用功—— 用功得一定会通过考试。）

代替形容词：

She is beautiful—so much so (原为 beautiful) that I'm crazy about her.

adv.

（她很美—— 美得令我为她发狂。）

9. somewhat、somehow、anyhow：

a. somewhat　　有一点儿

该词为一般副词，使用时通常置于形容词或副词之前，以修饰该形容词或副词。

例: It's somewhat cold today.

adv.　adj.

= It's a little / a bit cold today.

（今天有点儿冷。）

He did the job somewhat carelessly.

adv. → adv.

= He did the job | a little / a bit | carelessly.

（他这件事做得有些粗心。）

b. somehow 不知怎的（= for some unknown reason）；设法（= by some means）

1) 表示“不知怎的”时，做独立副词，通常置于句首，修饰全句。

例: He is nice; but somehow I don't like him.

adv. → I don't like him

（他人不错，但不知怎的，我就是不喜欢他。）

2) 表示“设法”时，做一般副词，修饰句中动词，通常置于句尾。

例: We must find the money somehow.

adv.（somehow → find）

（我们必须设法找到那笔钱。）

c. anyhow 况且，而且（= besides / in addition）；不管怎样（= anyway / at any rate）

例: I don't have time to go to the movies; they're too expensive anyhow.

（我没有时间去看电影，况且电影也太贵了。）

注意

表“不管怎样”时，anyhow 为独立副词，通常置于句首，之后有逗号，修饰逗号之后整个主句。

例: | Anyhow, / Anyway, / At any rate, | we can try.

（不管怎样，我们可以试试看。）

10. enough：

enough 可做形容词，表示“足够/充分的”、“足以”。enough 不论做形容词或副词，其后通常接不定式短语（即“to + 原形动词”）或“for + 名词”。

a. 形容词：

此时 enough 表“足够/充分的”，修饰名词，通常置于该名词前，亦可置于其后。

例：He has enough money (adj. n.) | to buy / for | a fancy car. (常用)

= He has money enough | to buy / for | a fancy car. (罕)

（他有足够的钱买一辆拉风的车。）

b. 副词：

此时 enough 表“足以”，修饰形容词或副词，应置于该副词或形容词之后，不可置于其前。

例：He is enough good for the position. (×)

→ He is good enough (adj. adv.) | for / to fill | the position. (√)

（他条件好，足以担任此职位。）

He ran fast enough (adv. adv.) to catch the train.

（他跑得够快而赶上了火车。）

11. likely、probably、possibly　可能地

以可能性之高低而言，likely 和 probably 表示“很可能”，而 possibly 则表示“有可能但不确定”。

例：He will (very / most) likely come.

（他很有可能会来。）

＊likely 做副词时，之前可用 very 或 most 加以修饰。

She will probably leave.

（她很可能将要离开。）

They will possibly help him.

（他们说不定会帮他。）

但 likely 亦可做形容词，其用法如下：

He is likely to come.

= It is likely that he will come.

（他很可能会来。）

但:

He is probable to come. (×，probable 不能修饰人)

He is possible to come. (×，理由同上)

改正:

It is probable that he will come. (✓)
（他很可能会来。）

It is possible that he will come. (✓)
（他说不定会来。）

12. Short Response（简应句）:

你是……，我也是/你不是……，我也不是。

a. 肯定句用 so（使用时，采用倒装结构）或 too。此处 so 是副词，表示“同样地”，并非连词，故之前应有连词 and 连接两句。

1) be 动词:

主语与 be 动词倒装。

例: He is nice, | and so is she. / and she is, too. |
（他人很好，她也很好。）

He was going home, | and so was she. / and she was, too. |
（他即将回家，她也是。）

2) 助动词:

主语与助动词倒装。

例: He will come, | and so will she. / and she will, too. |
（他要来，她也要来。）

He has gone, | and so has she. / and she has, too. |
（他走了，她也走了。）

3) 一般动词:

主语与 do、does、did 倒装。

例: He came, | and so did she. / and she did, too. |
（他来了，她也来了。）

He has a book, | and so does she. / and she does, too.

（他有一本书，她也有。）

注意

在对话中，两句指的是同一人时，不论句子是肯定句或否定句，均用 so 引导，且句子不倒装。此时 so 亦为副词，相当于 indeed（的确）。

例: A: He is stupid.
B: So he is. (= Indeed he is.)
（A：他很蠢。）
（B：他的确很蠢。）
A: You can't do it.
B: So I can't. (= Indeed I can't.)
（A：你不会做这事。）
（B：我的确不会。）

b. 否定句用 neither（或 nor，使用 neither 或 nor 时须采用倒装结构）或 either。neither 为副词，故 and 不可省略，但 nor 为连词，前面不必置 and。

1) be 动词:

主语与 be 动词倒装。

例: He isn't nice, | and neither is she. / nor is she. / and she isn't, either.

（他不好，她也不好。）

He wasn't going home, | and neither was she. / nor was she. / and she wasn't, either.

（他没回家，她也没回家。）

2) 助动词:

主语与助动词倒装。

例: He won't come, | and neither will she. / nor will she. / and she won't, either.

（他不来，她也不来。）

He hasn't gone, | and neither has she. / nor has she. / and she hasn't, either.

（他没去，她也没去。）

3) 一般动词：

主语与 do、does、did 倒装。

例：He never tells a lie, | and neither does she. / nor does she. / and she doesn't, either.

（他绝不说谎，她也绝不说谎。）

He has no book, | and neither does she. / nor does she. / and she doesn't, either.

（他没有书，她也没有。）

注意

also 只能用在肯定句中，置于 be 动词之后，或一般动词之前。

例：He is kind, and she is also kind.

（他很亲切，她也是。）

He has a pen, and she also has one.

（他有一支笔，她也有一支。）

13. 常见的“名词 + 介词 + 名词”副词短语：

hand in hand	手拉着手
side by side	肩并肩地
shoulder to shoulder	肩并肩地
arm in arm	臂挽着臂
word for word	逐字地
day by day	一天天
night after night	每夜
little by little	渐渐地
one by one	一个一个地
one after another	陆续地
face to face	面对面地

例: They walked hand in hand down the road.
（他们手牵手沿着那条路走下去。）

They came in one after another.
（他们陆续地走进来。）

14. not 要置于不定式短语、分词、动名词之前:

例: Since I have a lot of work to do, I decided not to go on a trip. (√)
（由于有很多事要办，我决定不去旅行。）

He pretended to not know me. (×)
→ He pretended not to know me. (√)
（他假装不认识我。）

Having not finished the work, I decided to stay. (×)
→ Not having finished the work, I decided to stay. (√)
（工作没完成，我决定留下来。）

He was disappointed at not having finished the work. (√)
（他很失望没把工作完成。）

15. 助动词 + 副词 + 本动词:

例: I can always count on you for advice.
（我总是可以指望你给我忠告。）

I never have seen him before. (劣)
→ I have never seen him before. (√)
（我以前从没见过他。）

16. 副词修饰被动语态时，通常置于过去分词之前:

例: His speech was well presented.
（他演说得很好。）

That case was finally settled.
（那件事终于解决了。）

That project had been checked very carefully before it was presented to the boss. (可)
= That project had been very carefully checked before it was presented to the boss. (佳)
（那份策划书在交给老板之前已很仔细地检查过。）

17. more than 与倍数的关系:

more than 应置于倍数之前。造句法则如下：

a. 先造一个含有“倍数词 + as...as...”的句子：

例: He has three times as much money as you do.
（他的钱是你的三倍。）

b. 再于“倍数词 + as...as...”的结构前置入 more than，即告完成。

例: He has three times more than as much money as you do. (×)
→ He has more than three times as much money as you do. (√)
（他的钱超过你的三倍。）

c. more than 亦可置于动词 double（增加一倍）之前。

例: Our income has more than doubled in one year.
（一年之内我们的收入增加了一倍多。）

18. more than 与 over 的关系：

over 做介词表“超过”时，可用 more than 代替。

例: He has stayed here over a year.
= He has stayed here more than a year.
（他已待在此地一年多。）

He has stayed here more than over a year. (×)
He has stayed here much over a year. (×，much 应删除)
Over five students are here.
= More than five students are here.
（这里的学生超过 5 人。）

19. 避免双重比较：

即 more richer、more better 等等。

例: She is more beautiful than Mary. (√)
（她比玛丽还美。）

She is better than Mary. (√)
（她比玛丽好。）

She is more better than Mary. (×，因 better 已经是比较级，不可再被比较级副词 more 修饰)
→ She is much better than Mary. (√)
（她比玛丽好很多。）

People in Japan lead a more richer life than those in many other countries. (×)
→ People in Japan lead a much richer life than those in many other countries. (√)
（日本的百姓比很多其他国家人民的生活富裕得多。）

20. 避免双重否定：

例: He hasn't never been to Japan before. (×)
→ He has never been to Japan before. (√)
= He hasn't ever been to Japan before.
（他从来没去过日本。）

* not ever = never

You'll have to hurry up; we have hardly no time left. (×)
→ You'll have to hurry up; we have hardly any time left. (√)
（你必须快点，我们快没时间了。）

注意

scarcely = hardly = almost not，为否定副词，不可再与 no 或 not 连用，但可与 any 连用；scarely any = hardly any = almost not any。

例: He cannot scarcely do this work. (×)
→ He can scarcely do this work. (√)
（他几乎不会做这工作。）

He has hardly no money. (×)
→ He has hardly any money. (√)
（他几乎没有钱。）

21. 关系副词 when、why、how、where：

例: This is the time when we should set out.
(= at which)
（这就是我们该出发的时候。）

This is the reason why he was late.
(= for which)
（这就是他为何迟到的理由。）

This is | the way / how | he succeeded.

（这就是他成功的方法。）

＊how 虽是 the way 的关系副词，却不能同时使用，换言之，无 the way how 的用法。

That is the place where I was born.
(= in which)

（那是我出生的地方。）

This is the reason because he was late. (×)

I came yesterday, where it was raining heavily. (×，yesterday 为时间，故 where 应改为 when)

That is the city how he lives. (×，city 为地方，故 how 应改为 where)

> **注意**
>
> 关系副词亦可做复合关系副词，代替前面的名词（先行词），故上述例句亦可改为：
>
> This is when we should set out.
> (= the time when)
>
> This is why he succeeded.
> (= the reason why)
>
> This is how he'll do it.
> (= the way)
>
> This is where I was born.
> (= the place in which)

22. 指示代词 that 及 this 可做副词用：

分别译成"那样"、"这样"。

例: The destination is too far away; I can't walk | that far. / so far. |

（目的地太远了；我走不了那么远。）

A: How big is the bear?

B: It is about this big.

（A：那只熊有多大？）

（B：大概有这么大。）

23. "I think so.":

think、hope、believe、be afraid、imagine 等动词之后加 so，可代替肯定句，加 not 则代替否定句。

例: A: Is he nice?

B: Yes, I think so. (so = that he is nice)

No, I think not. (not = that he is not nice)

（A：他人好吗？）

（B：我想他是好人。

我看他不是好人。）

A: Will he come?

B: I'm afraid not. (not = that he will not come)

I'm afraid so. (so = that he will come)

（A：他会来吗？）

（B：恐怕他不会来。

恐怕他会来吧。）

24. 副词 + 独立分词:

独立分词 speaking 应用副词修饰，如 strictly speaking（严格地说）、frankly speaking（坦白地说）、generally speaking（概括地说）。

例: Strict speaking, he is wrong. (×)

→ Strictly speaking, he is wrong. (√)

（严格地说，他是不对的。）

25. all（三人以上一起）、both（两人一起）:

例: John, Paul, and Peter will all come here tomorrow to celebrate Jack's birthday.

（约翰、保罗和彼得明天都要来这里庆祝杰克的生日。）

These five students are all good.

（这五位都是好学生。）

The two candidates are both qualified for this job.

（这两位人选都有资格做此工作。）

He and I will all go to America tomorrow. (×，all 应改为 both)

→ He and I will both go to America tomorrow. (√)

（他和我明天都要去美国。）

26. 容易混淆的副词:

a. close（近）、closely（仔细地，严密地）

例: I live close to his house.
= I live near his house.
（我住在他家附近。）
Watch him closely.
（好好盯着他。）

b. most（最）、mostly（大部分，大都）

例: Of all the books here, this one is the most interesting.
（在这些书中，这本最有趣。）
These books are mostly out of date.
（这些书大部分都过时了。）

c. near（近）、nearly（= almost，几乎）

例: He lives near, not far.
（他住附近，不在远处。）
He was nearly drowned.
（他差点淹死了。）

注意

near 虽可做介词，但在下列短语中，near 之后仍应置入 to，形成固定短语：
come near to + V-ing　　差一点儿就……
例: He came near to being drowned.
= He came close to being drowned.
= He was nearly drowned.
（他差点儿淹死了。）

d.

high deep wide	表实际空间（可以用尺量）的	高 深 宽
highly deeply widely	表程度而不指空间的	高 深 宽

例: The plane flew highly in the sky. (×)
→ The plane flew high in the sky. (√)
（飞机高高地在天上飞着。）

He was high praised. (×)

→ He was highly praised. (√)

（他大大地受到赞扬。）

We spoke high of him. (×)

→ We spoke highly of him. (√)

（我们赞扬他。）

We think high of him. (×)

→ We think highly of him. (√)

（我们很看重他。）

He dove deeply into the river. (×)

→ He dove deep into the river. (√)

（他潜入河中深处。）

He was deep hurt. (×)

→ He was deeply hurt. (√)

（他伤得很重。）

27. greatly 与 highly 之区别：

a. greatly 表“大量地，大大地”。

例: He was greatly surprised.

（他大大地吃了一惊。）

The number of traffic accidents has increased greatly.

（车祸次数大幅增加。）

b. highly 表“高高地”，通常与“表扬”、“奖励”、“推荐”等动词（如praise、recommend）连用。

例: We think highly of him.

（我们很看重他。）

EXERCISE

Ⅰ. 请选出一个正确的答案：

1. Anna didn't like our new roommate, and ______.
   (A) I don't too　(B) neither I did　(C) neither did I　(D) I didn't also

2. The population of many Alaskan towns has ______ doubled during the past three years.
   (A) much than　(B) as more as than
   (C) as more than　(D) more than

3. ______ he began working in the chemical plant, he experienced pain when he breathed.
   (A) Shortly before　(B) Not long after
   (C) No sooner than　(D) No longer

4. How many brand-new cars there are! Automobile production in the last ten years has increased ______.
   (A) highly　(B) infinitely
   (C) in the large scale　(D) greatly

5. Bill wasn't happy about the delay, and ______.
   (A) I was neither　(B) I wasn't, either
   (C) neither I was　(D) either was I

6. The second hurricane struck the coastal states ______ three days after the first one.
   (A) during　(B) just
   (C) not as much as　(D) not as little as

7. Who's that good-looking girl Frank is dancing with? I ______ her before.
   (A) never had seen　(B) had never seen
   (C) saw never　(D) have never seen

8. When Arthur applied for a job, Professor Adams was able to recommend him ______.

(A) very highly (B) with superb notices
(C) greatly (D) with high regard

9. Children learn very quickly. When they learn about a new subject, they often ______.

(A) become too interested in it (B) very much are interested in it
(C) become very interested in it (D) are interested very much in it

10. The price of unleaded gasoline is ______ a dollar a gallon.

(A) larger than (B) over
(C) as great as (D) as many as

11. John is very diligent. But his pay is not ______ for his work.

(A) enough good (B) good enough
(C) as good enough (D) good as enough

12. You didn't hear us come in last night. That's good. We tried ______ noisy.

(A) to be not (B) not to be
(C) not be (D) be not

13. This old desk isn't ______ to sell, but maybe we could give it to someone.

(A) goodly enough (B) good enough
(C) good as enough (D) enough good

14. She overslept and was ______ late that she missed the bus.

(A) so (B) too (C) much (D) very

15. Eric nearly always wins the science award. That's because his projects are ______.

(A) extremely presented well (B) well presented extremely
(C) presented well extremely (D) extremely well presented

16. Betty got married last week. ______ that she would get married so young.

(A) I never dream (B) Never do I have dreamed
(C) Do I never dream (D) I never dreamed

17. My brother never does his homework in the morning. ______.
(A) So does John
(B) John is too
(C) John doesn't too
(D) Nor does John

18. Take an umbrella when you go to Seattle, for it rains ______ there.
(A) frequently
(B) as frequent
(C) most of times
(D) much time

19. I walked 8 miles today. I never guessed that I could walk ______ far.
(A) that (B) this (C) such (D) as

20. Prices for bikes at that store can run ______ $250.
(A) as high as
(B) so high to
(C) as high to
(D) so high as

II. 请选出错误的画线部分：

21. Many of the observations made by (A) Leonardo a little greater (B) than 400 years ago about the (C) movement of birds' wings have been verified (D) by modern photos.

22. The state legislature has approved (A) the construction of a completely (B) self-contained paper-recycling plant that will produce (C) hardly no (D) harmful waste materials.

23. Of all the Christmas toys the boy saw (A) in (B) the window, the thing he wanted (C) more (D) was a new bicycle.

24. Rain clouds and smoke caused by pollution look so much (A) alike that one cannot (B) hardly tell the difference (C) between the two of them (D).

25. The large ship sailed very good in any weather, never requiring more than
(A) (B) (C) (D)
one man at the wheel.

26. A carefully trained observer can discover details very easy although others
(A) (B) (C)
never see them.
(D)

27. She spoke so indistinct that we did not know whether we were to precede or
(A) (B) (C) (D)
follow the procession.

28. A Cezanne painting was recently sold at an auction for much over the
(A)(B) (C)
initially announced price.
(D)

29. Interest in automatic data processing has grown rapid since the first large
(A) (B) (C) (D)
calculators were introduced in 1950.

30. Today divorce is not longer regarded as a disgrace nor a tragedy, not even a
(A) (B) (C) (D)
failure.

标准答案

1. (C)	2. (D)	3. (B)	4. (D)	5. (B)	6. (B)	7. (D)	8. (A)	9. (C)	10. (B)
11. (B)	12. (B)	13. (B)	14. (A)	15. (D)	16. (D)	17. (D)	18. (A)	19. (A)	20. (A)
21. (B)	22. (D)	23. (D)	24. (B)	25. (B)	26. (C)	27. (A)	28. (C)	29. (C)	30. (A)

习题解说

1. and neither did I.
= nor did I.
= and I didn't, either.
2. more than 在此做副词用，修饰动词 doubled。
3. shortly before...　就在……之前
not long after...　在……之后没有多久
4. greatly　大幅地
in the large scale 应改为 on a large scale。
5. 与第 1 题同理。
6. (A) during 要接限定的时间，例如 during those three days、during that period。
(B) just three days after the first one　就在第一个台风之后三天
(C) (D) not as much as 及 not as little as 只能修饰不可数名词，但 three days 是可数名词，不能被 much 或 little 修饰。
7. 过去完成时不能单独存在，一定要配合另一一般过去时从句。
I had finished my job. (×)
I had finished my job before you came. (√)
（你来以前我工作就做好了。）
8. (B) 无此短语
(C) recommend（推荐）并非表“量”的概念，故不能用 greatly。
(D) with high regard 为副词短语，表“尊敬地”，此处与语意不合。
9. (A) become too interested　（变得太有趣而不能……）
(B) very much 应置于 interested 之前。
(C) very 可修饰做形容词用的过去分词，如 tired（感到累的）、interested（感到有趣的）。
(D) very much 应置于 interested 之前。
10. over + 数词 = more than + 数词（超过……）
11. enough 做副词时，一定要置于其所修饰的形容词或副词之后。
12. 不定式短语与 not 合用时，not 一定要置于不定式之前。
13. 与第 11 题同理。
14. so...that...　如此……以至……
15. 副词修饰被动语态时，一定要置于过去分词之前。

16. 本句应用一般过去时 I never dreamed...表现在已知，但当时未想到。
如使用现在完成时时应为 I have never dreamed...或 Never have I dreamed...
17. 与第 1 题同理。
18. 动词应用副词修饰。
(B) 为形容词。
(C) 若改为 most of the time（大部分时间）就对了。
(D) much time “不少时间”通常做 spend、have 的宾语，用于否定句中。
I don't spend much time practicing English every day.
（我每天没有花很多时间练习英语。）
We don't have much time left.
（我们没剩多少时间了。）
19. that far　　那么远
= so far
20. as high as　　高达……
本短语中的 as 不可用 so 来替换，因为“so...as”只用于否定句中，而“as...as”则可用于肯定句或否定句中。
21. (B) greater 应改为 more，表时间。
22. (D) hardly no 应改为 hardly any = almost not any = almost no
23. (D) more 应为 most，三者以上的比较。
24. (B) cannot hardly 应改为 can hardly。
25. (B) very good 应改为 very well，以修饰动词 sailed。
26. (C) easy 应改为 easily，以修饰动词 discover。
27. (A) indistinct 应改为 indistinctly（不清楚地），以修饰动词 spoke。
28. (C) much over 应改为 over 或 more than。
29. (C) rapid 应改为 rapidly，以修饰 grown。
30. (A) not longer 应改为 no longer。

第九章　倒装结构

概述

倒装句是英语特有的句型。其目的是通过句中某些词类的倒置，可用以强调整个句子的语气。偶尔在一篇文章出现倒装的结构，可以使平淡的句子变得生动活泼。一般常出现的倒装结构有下列五种：

1. 否定倒装句：

例: I have never seen such a pretty girl as she (is).

→ Never have I seen such a pretty girl as she.

（我从没见过像她这么美的女孩。）

2. so / such 倒装句：

例: She is so kind that she deserves all my respect.

→ So kind is she that she deserves all my respect.

（她人很好，值得我尊敬。）

3. 地点副词倒装句：

例: A boy stood there.

→ There stood a boy.

（那儿站着一个男孩。）

4. 完全倒装句：

例: Those who help others are praiseworthy.

→ Praiseworthy are those who help others.

（助人的人值得称赞。）

5. as 取代 though 的倒装句：

例: Though he is nice, I dislike him.

→ Nice as he is, I dislike him.

= As nice as he is, I dislike him.

（他人虽然好，我却不喜欢他。）

以上所列的倒装句结构变化并不复杂，但很多同学在学习英语的过程中，不曾尝试整理这些句型，以至在写作的时候，不会运用或运用不当而犯错。对参加各类英语考试的同学们而言，本章甚为重要，因为倒装句是出题老师们极易列入的一个项目。同学们在阅读本章时，一定要有无比的耐心，细嚼慢咽。赖老师保证你一定能完全吸收，使自己的英语程度又往前迈进一大步！

第一节　否定倒装句

否定倒装句就是将否定副词、否定副词短语和否定状语从句移至句首的倒装句。使用此类倒装句要注意两个重点：

a. 何谓否定副词、否定副词短语和否定状语从句？
b. 如何倒装？

我们且一一分项说明：

1. 否定副词、否定副词短语和否定状语从句：

a. 常用的否定副词：

never（从不）、hardly（= scarcely，几乎不）、rarely（很少）、seldom（很少）、little（一点儿也不）。

b. 常用的否定副词短语：

by no means（绝对不）、in no way（绝对不）、on no account（绝对不）、under no circumstances（绝对不）、in no situation（绝对不）。

c. 常用的否定状语从句（一共只有三种句型，很好背）：

not until + S + V　（直到……）
only when + S + V（只有到……的时候）
only after + S + V　（只有到……之后）

2. 如何倒装：

先将否定副词、否定副词短语或否定状语从句移至句首，再检查原结构主语之后的动词，采用疑问句型倒装。

a. be 动词：

主语之后有 be 动词时，be 动词与主语要倒装。

例: He is never happy.
　　　　否定副词
→ Never is he happy.
（他从不快乐。）

He is hardly ever quiet.
　　　　否定副词
→ Hardly is he ever quiet.
（他几乎从未安静过。）

You are by no means the person we need.
否定副词短语
→ By no means are you the person we need.
（你绝非我们需要的人。）
I was not aware of it until he came.
状语从句
→ Not until he came was I aware of it.
否定状语从句
（直到他来，我才发觉这件事。）
He is happy only when Mary is with him.
否定状语从句
→ Only when Mary is with him is he happy.
（只有玛丽和他在一起时，他才快乐。）

b. 助动词：
主语之后有助动词时，助动词与主语要倒装。
例: He can hardly move.
否定副词
→ Hardly can he move.
（他几乎不能动。）
He has never done it before.
否定副词
→ Never has he done it before.
（他从来没做过这件事。）
He can do it under no circumstances. (实际不如此使用)
否定副词短语
→ Under no circumstances can he do it. (实际如此使用)
（他绝不可能做此事。）
He will not leave until Mary comes back.
状语从句
→ Not until Mary comes back will he leave.
否定状语从句
（直到玛丽回来，他才会离开。）

c. 一般动词：

主语之后有一般动词时，先在主语之前按动词时态及主语人称之不同，分别置助动词 do、does 或 did，再将动词变成原形动词。

例: He（第三人称单数） seldom（否定副词） sings.（一般现在时）

→ Seldom does he sing.（sing：原形 V）

（他很少唱歌。）

He little（否定副词） knew（一般过去时） that Mary's English could be so good.

→ Little did he know that Mary's English could be so good.（know：原形 V）

（他一点儿也没想到玛丽的英语会那么好。）

> **注意**
> 实际并无"He little knew..."的说法，只有"Little did he know..."的说法，换言之，little 只能置于句首采用倒装结构。

We（第一人称复数） by no means（否定副词短语） understand（一般现在时） what he says.

→ By no means do we understand what he says.

（我们无法理解他说的话。）

They didn't know the truth until Mary came.（until Mary came：状语从句）

→ Not until Mary came（否定状语从句） did they know（原形 V） the truth.

（直到玛丽来了，他们才了解实情。）

3. "only + 介词短语"及"only + then"：

"only + 介词短语"或"only + then"（唯有在那时）均可视为否定副词短语，置于句首时，亦采用倒装句。

例: Only by doing so（否定副词短语） you can succeed. (×)

→ Only by doing so can you succeed. (✓)

（只有这么做你才会成功。）

Only with his help（否定副词短语） I will be able to weather the difficulties. (×)

→ Only with his help will I be able to weather the difficulties. (✓)
（有了他的帮助，我才能克服困难。）

| Only at that time / Only then | I left. (×)

→ | Only at that time / Only then | did I leave. (✓)

（到那时我才离开。）

4. not only...but (also)...　不仅……而且……
= not merely...but (also)...
= not only...but...as well
= not merely...but...as well

注意

a. 本短语可用以连接对等的单词、短语和从句。

对等的单词：

例: Not only I but (also) he is wrong.
主语　主语
（不仅是我，连他也错了。）

She is not only kind but graceful as well.
形容词　形容词
（她人不仅亲切，而且优雅。）

对等的短语：

例: I came not only to see you but (also) to say goodbye to you.
不定式短语　不定式短语
（我来不仅是为了见你，也是来跟你道别的。）

He was fired not only because of his laziness but (also) because of his failure to meet my requirements.
副词短语　副词短语
（他被开除不仅是因为懒惰，还因为无法达到我的要求。）

对等的从句：

例: He was fired not merely because he was lazy but because he failed to meet my requirements.
状语从句　状语从句
（他被开除不仅是因为懒惰，还因为无法达到我的要求。）

b. 本短语亦可连接对等的句子，但由于 not only 置于句首，视为否定副词，第一个句子要倒装。but also 仅为连词，故其后的第二个句子不需倒装，但 also 则一定要省略，或移至句中。亦可将 also 省略后在句尾处加 as well。

例：Not only she can sing, but also she can dance. (×)
　　　　　　句子　　　　　　　　句子

→ Not only can she sing, but she can (also) dance. (√)

或：Not only can she sing, but she can dance as well. (√)

（她不仅会唱歌，而且还会跳舞。）

Before I left, not only I had closed the door, but also I had cleaned the room. (×)

→ Before I left, not only had I closed the door, but I had (also) cleaned the room. (√)

或：Before I left, not only had I closed the door, but I had cleaned the room as well. (√)

（我离开之前，不但关了门，还打扫了房间。）

5. not + a + 单数可数名词　　连一个……都没有

本短语若做及物动词的宾语时，亦可移至句首，采用倒装结构。

例：I did not see a soul (= a person) over there.

→ Not a soul did I see over there.

（我在那儿一个人也没看到。）

I was not able to discover a clue to the murder.

→ Not a clue to the murder was I able to discover.

（这起谋杀案我连一点蛛丝马迹也没法找到。）

6. hardly、scarcely：

这两个副词因为是否定副词，故置于句首时，句子要倒装。两词意思相同，均译成“几乎不”，用法亦相同。

例：Hardly he can do it. (×)

→ Hardly can he do it. (√)

（他几乎无法做这件事。）

Scarcely he was able to finish the job on schedule. (×)

→ Scarcely was he able to finish the job on schedule. (√)

（他几乎无法按照进度完成这项工作。）

注意

| scarcely / hardly | + any + 名词 | 几乎没有…… |

= almost not + any + 名词

= almost no + 名词

此时若做主语，置于句首，不可采用倒装结构。

例: Scarcely did any student pass the exam. (×)

→ Scarcely any student passed the exam. (√)

= Almost no student passed the exam. (√)

（几乎没有一个学生考试及格。）

Hardly did any student know the answer. (×)

→ Hardly any student knew the answer. (√)

= Almost no student knew the answer. (√)

（几乎没有一个学生知道这个答案。）

但句中有"scarcely / hardly + a + 单数名词"作及物动词的宾语时，可将"scarcely / hardly + a + 单数名词"置于句首，仍采用倒装句。

例: He hardly spoke a word.

→ Hardly a word did he speak. (√)

（他几乎一句话也没说。）

7. nowhere（= in no place） 在任何地方都不

此亦为否定副词，置于句首要采用倒装句。

例: Nowhere I could find such a man. (×)

→ Nowhere could I find such a man. (√)

（这种人我在任何地方都找不到。）

8. 表示"一……就……"的句型：

试译下列句子：

她一见到我就昏倒了。

本句有下列三种译法：

a. 同时态的状语从句：

例: As soon as she saw me, she passed out.

= Once she saw me, she passed out.

= | The instant / The moment | she saw me, she passed out.

有的词典也列出下列的用法：

| Immediately / Instantly / Directly | she saw me, she passed out.

此时 immediately、instantly、directly 视为副词性连词，等于 as soon as。但这种用法已不常见于报章杂志中，故同学们写作时，不宜使用。

b. On / Upon + N / V-ing, S + V

| Upon / On | seeing me, she passed out.

注意

upon 或 on 之后加名词或动名词时，亦表示“一……就……”之意，是由 as soon as 引导的状语从句变化而成。使用时要注意的是： as soon as 引导的状语从句中，主语若与主句的主语相同时，upon 或 on 之后加动名词；主语不同时，则状语从句中的主语要变成所有格，置于 upon 或 on 之后，再接动名词或名词。

同主语：

例: As soon as I finished the job, I went home.

→ | Upon / On | finishing the job, I went home.

（我一做完工作就回家。）

不同主语：

例: As soon as he arrived, I left.

→ | Upon / On | his arriving, I left.

或: | Upon / On | his arrival, I left.

（他一到我就走了。）

c. 否定倒装的状语从句：

1) 此类句型一共有三种：

a) no sooner...than...

（没有比……早多少）

b) hardly / scarcely...when...

（当……时，几乎没……）

c) hardly / scarcely...before...

（在……之前，几乎没……）

以上实际均译为“一……就……”。

2) 造句法：

中　　文：她一见到我就昏倒了。

第 一 步：先造一个过去完成时的句子表示先发生的动作：
She had seen me.

第 二 步：再造一个一般过去时的句子，表示后发生的动作：
She passed out.

第 三 步：两句放在一起：
She had seen me, she passed out.

第 四 步：加入 no sooner...than... 等连词：
She had no sooner seen me than she passed out.

字面翻译：她先见到我，没有比她后来昏倒早多少。

实际翻译：她一见到我就昏倒了。

She had hardly seen me when she passed out.

字面翻译：当她昏倒时，几乎没看到我。

实际翻译：她一见到我就昏倒了。

She had scarcely seen me before she passed out.

字面翻译：在她昏倒之前，几乎没看到我。

实际翻译：她一见到我就昏倒了。

注意

hardly 与 scarcely 均等于 almost not，故之后的 when 与 before 可以互换。只是现在的英语多采用“hardly / scarcely...when”，而很少有人采用“hardly / scarcely...before”。

3) 由于 no sooner、hardly、scarcely 均为否定副词，故置于句首时，过去完成时助动词 had 应与主语倒装。

No sooner had she seen me than she passed out.

Hardly had she seen me when she passed out.

Scarcely had she seen me when she passed out.

至此，我们应当对“一……就……”的句型完全了解。赖老师希望同学们能多加使用，练就更好的写作能力。

第二节　so / such 倒装句

在“so...that...”或“such...that...”的结构中，若将 so 或 such 及其所引导的词类置于句首时，亦采用倒装结构。句法与否定倒装句完全相同。

1. 句中有 be 动词时，该 be 动词与主语倒装：

例: He is so helpful that we all like him.

→ So helpful is he that we all like him.

（他这么乐于助人，因此我们都喜欢他。）

They are such lazy students that they have no hope of passing the exam.

→ Such lazy students are they that they have no hope of passing the exam.

（他们是这样懒惰的学生，因此想考试及格全都无望了。）

2. 句中有助动词时，该助动词与主语倒装：

例: He has done so well that he deserves our respect.

→ So well has he done that he deserves our respect.

（他做得这么好，所以值得我们尊敬。）

He will play such an important part in the movie that he will get a large percentage of the profits.

→ Such an important part in the movie will he play that he will get a large percentage of the profits.

（他在那部电影中所担任的角色如此重要，因此他将可分得相当大的利润。）

3. 句中若为一般动词时，不可直接倒装：

须在主语之前先按该动词时态及人称变化，分置 do、does 或 did，再将该动词变成原形动词。

例: He came so late that he missed the train.

→ So late did he come that he missed the train.

（他到得太晚，而没赶上火车。）

He did such a wonderful job that he won our respect.

→ Such a wonderful job did he do that he won our respect.

（他表现得如此棒，因而赢得我们的尊敬。）

She sings so well that she can make a good singer.

→ So well does she sing that she can make a good singer.

（她歌唱得这么好，所以一定可以当个好歌手。）

第三节　地点副词倒装句

1. 三种倒装句型：

地点副词（there、here）或地点副词短语（in the room、at the station、by the window 等）置于句首时，亦可形成倒装句，只是倒装的句法与前两种倒装句完全不同。此类倒装句全按动词的性质做变化，句型有三种：

第一种：

主语 + 不及物动词 + | 地点副词 / 地点副词短语 |

→ | 地点副词 / 地点副词短语 | + 不及物动词 + 主语

例：A girl (S) sat (vi.) | there. (地点副词) / by the door. (地点副词短语) |

→ | There / By the door | sat (vi.) a girl (S).

（那儿/门边坐着一个女孩。）

A book (S) is (vi.) on the desk (地点副词短语).

→ On the desk is (vi.) a book (S).

（桌上有本书。）

Mary (S) stood (vi.) in the doorway (地点副词短语).

→ In the doorway stood (vi.) Mary (S).

（玛丽站在门口。）

第二种：

主语 + be 动词 + 过去分词 + | 地点副词 / 地点副词短语 |

→ | 地点副词 / 地点副词短语 | + be 动词 + 过去分词 + 主语

例：A man was (be) locked (p.p.) behind the door (地点副词短语).

→ Behind the door was locked a man.
（门后锁着一个人。）

A school is located there.
be p.p. 地点副词

→ There is located a school.
（那里坐落着一所学校。）

第三种：

主语 + be 动词 + 现在分词 + | 地点副词 / 地点副词短语 |

→现在分词 + | 地点副词 / 地点副词短语 | + be 动词 + 主语

例: A girl is singing over there.
be 现在分词 地点副词短语

→ Singing over there is a girl, who is my girlfriend.
（那儿有个女孩在唱歌，她是我女友。）

Mary and David were sitting in front of the gate.
be 现在分词 地点副词短语

→ Sitting in front of the gate were Mary and David.
或:In front of the gate were sitting Mary and David.
（玛丽和大卫坐在大门前。）

2. 主语必为普通名词或专有名词：

此类倒装句中的主语一定是普通名词（如 a book、a man、the children 等），或专有名词（如 Mary、Peter、John 等）。若主语为代词（如 it、she、they 等）则不可采用倒装句；也就是说地点副词仍可放在句首，但句子不倒装。至于地点副词短语则不宜放在句首。

例: He stood there.
代词 地点副词

→ There stood he. (×)
→ There he stood. (√)
（他站在那儿。）

He stood in front of the house.
地点副词短语

→ In front of the house stood he. (×)
→ In front of the house he stood. (劣)
地点副词短语

→ He stood in front of the house. (佳)
（他站在房子前面。）

He was locked in there.
代词 地点副词

→ There was locked in he. (×)
→ There he was locked in. (劣)
（他被锁在那里面。）

He was locked behind the door.
地点副词短语

→ Behind the door was locked he. (×)
→ Behind the door he was locked. (劣)
地点副词短语

→ He was locked behind the door. (佳)
（他被锁在门后。）

He was singing there.
代词 地点副词

→ Singing there was he. (×)
→ There he was singing. (√)
（他在那里唱歌。）

He was singing in the backyard.
地点副词短语

→ Singing in the backyard was he. (×)
→ He was singing in the backyard. (√)
（他在后院唱歌。）

3. 介副词的倒装：

介副词亦视为地点副词，置于句首时，亦采用完全相同的倒装句。所谓介副词，就是由表示场所的介词（如 in、out、down、up、off 等）变成的副词。这些词之后有宾语时就称介词，若无宾语时就是介副词（由介词变成的副词）。

a. 介词

例: John walked in (或 into) the room.
介 宾语

（约翰走进房间。）

The boy looked out the window.
介 宾语

（这男孩向窗外看去。）

He came down the stairs.

介　　宾语

（他走下楼。）

He climbed up the mountain.

介　　宾语

（他爬上山。）

He fell off the roof.

介　宾语

（他从屋顶上摔下来。）

b. 介副词

例: He walked in.

介副词

（他走进去。）

He looked out.

介副词

（他往外看。）

He came down.

介副词

（他走下来。）

He climbed up.

介副词

（他爬上去。）

c. 倒装方式

例: A boy walked in.

vi.

→ In walked a boy.

（一个男孩走了进来。）

The car dashed off.

vi.

→ Off dashed the car.

（这辆车飞驰而去。）

John came down.

vi.

→ Down came John.

（约翰走了下来。）

注意

a. 主语为代词时，不得采用倒装结构。

例: In walked he. (×)

→ In he walked. (√)

代词

（他走进来。）

Off went they. (×)

→ Off they went. (√)

代词

（他们走了。）

b. away 视为地点副词，用法相同。

例: John went away.

→ Away went John.

（约翰走了。）

Away went he. (×)

→ Away he went. (√)

代词

（他走了。）

c. here 亦为地点副词，用法亦相同。

例: Mary comes here.

→ Here comes Mary.

（玛丽来了。）

Here comes she. (×)

→ Here she comes. (√)

代词

（她来了。）

4. there 与地点副词短语：

地点副词短语在句首时，前面可置 there 或其他相关副词，用以强调该地点副词短语。there 可置于地点副词短语之前或之后。但其他相关副词只能置于地点副词短语之前。

a. there:

例: On top of the hill lies a beautiful villa.
地点副词短语
= There on top of the hill lies a beautiful villa.
地点副词短语
= On top of the hill there lies a beautiful villa.
地点副词短语
（山顶上有栋漂亮的别墅。）

On the desk is a book.
地点副词短语
= There on the desk is a book.
= On the desk there is a book.
= There is a book on the desk.
（桌上有本书。）

b. 相关副词:

例: Deep in the mountains lies a small village.
相关副词 地点副词短语
（深山里有个小村落。）

Not far (away) from here is a post office.
相关副词 地点副词短语
（离这儿不远有家邮局。）

5. 倒装句的好处:

倒装句的主语在句尾，之后可接定语从句、分词短语或介词短语，用以修饰主语，因此可以扩大主语的内容，并可避免主语在句首时，主语与动词间修饰语过多的毛病。

例: 未倒装时:

A man who held a knife in one hand,
主语 定语从句

looking as if he wanted to kill somebody, stood there. (劣)
分词短语 vi. 地点副词

倒装之后:

→ There stood a man who held a knife in one hand, looking as if he wanted to
vi 主语

kill somebody. (佳)

（有个持刀的人站在那儿，看起来像要杀人的样子。）

A boy with a dog (which) he found the other day sat in the corner. (劣)

主语　介词短语　定语从句　vi. 地点副词短语

→ In the corner sat a boy with a dog (which) he found the other day. (佳)

vi. 主语

（角落里坐着个男孩和他前些天捡到的狗。）

6. here 与 there 的习惯用语：

注意下列用 here 或 there 置于句首的句子，主语为代词，因此不倒装。

a. Here we are.　（到了。）

解说：

某甲要去见某女生，但胆小如鼠，于是便请某乙陪他一块去。两人乘了一辆出租车，到了该女生家门口时，某甲、某乙以及出租车司机都可说这句话："Here we are."

b. Here you are.（或 Here you go.）　（拿去吧。）

解说：

某甲到麦当劳买汉堡，服务员叫他稍候片刻。不久，服务员就把汉堡递给某甲，同时说了一句：

"Here you go."

给任何人所要的东西时，均可使用这句话。

c. There you go again.　（你又来这一套。）

解说：

某甲见到女生会流口水。某乙对某甲的行为很了解。某日，某甲与某乙一块儿出游。一位漂亮的女生擦肩而过，某甲就口水直流，某乙边用脸盆接某甲的口水，边骂道："There you go again."。

看完这一段赖老师瞎编的故事，你一定知道如何使用此用语了吧！

d. There you are.（或 There it is.）　（在那里。）

解说：

某甲要到叔叔家去，由于是第一次拜访，在社区里找了老半天，仍然不得其门而入，幸好赖老师刚好路过，见状即带路。指着不远处一扇门说道："There you are."或"There it is."，某甲连声道谢后，就飞奔而去。

第四节　完全倒装句

1. 基本句型：

此类倒装句是由下列句型演变而成：

主语 + be 动词 + 形容词（含可做形容词的过去分词或现在分词）

→ 形容词 + be 动词 + 主语

例：He / One（主语） who is content is（be） happy（adj.）.

→ Happy is he / one who is content.

（知足者常乐。——凡是满足的人都是快乐的。）

= The humble / Humble people（主语） are（be） blessed（adj.）.

→ Blessed are the humble. / humble people.

（谦虚的人有福。——凡是谦虚的人都会受到保佑。）

2. 使用时机：

此类完全倒装句的主语，通常泛指所有的人或物。故主语有“凡是……的人或物”之意时，均可使用本倒装句。

例：A man（主语） who often helps others is（be） praiseworthy（adj.）.

→ Praiseworthy is a man who often helps others.

（常助人的人值得赞扬。）

但有过多修饰语的主语亦可采用本倒装句。

例：Noteworthy（adj.） is（be） the fact（主语） that he has talent for music（名词性从句，做 the fact 的同位语）.

（值得一提的是他有音乐天赋。）

第五节 as 取代 though 的倒装法

1. as 取代 though 的句型：

a. though + 主语 + be 动词 + 形容词

形容词可移至句首，再以 as 取代 though。

例：Though / Although | he is nice, I dislike him.
S be adj.

→ Nice as he is, I dislike him.

= As nice as he is, I dislike him.

= Nice though he is, I dislike him.

（虽然他很好，我还是不喜欢他。）

但不可写成：

Nice although he is, I dislike him. (×)

＊上列第四个例句句首的“As nice as he is”中，第一个 As 是副词，不具意义，第二个 as 是连词，译成“虽然”。

b. though + 主语 + be 动词 + 名词

名词可移至句首，再以 as 取代 though。但名词若为单数可数名词，移至句首时，原有的不定冠词 a 或 an 一定要省略。

例：Though / Although | he is a nice boy, I dislike him.
S be n.

→ A nice boy | as / though | he is, I dislike him. (×)

→ Nice boy | as / though | he is, I dislike him. (√)

（虽然他是个好孩子，我还是不喜欢他。）

Though / Although | they are nice boys, I dislike them.
S be n.

→ Nice boys | as / though | they are, I dislike them.

（虽然他们是好孩子，我还是不喜欢他们。）

c. though 引导的状语从句中有副词时，可将副词移至句首，此时 though 亦可用 as 取代。

例：Though he studied hard, he failed to pass the exam.
adv.

→ Hard | as / though | he studied, he failed to pass the exam.

= As hard as he studied, he failed to pass the exam.

（虽然他努力学习，还是未能通过考试。）

Though she sings well, she can't dance.

adv.

→ Well | as / though | she sings, she can't dance.

= As well as she sings, she can't dance.

（她虽然歌唱得好，却不会跳舞。）

d. though 引导的状语从句若无副词时，可在句首添入副词 much（很），再接 as 或 though 即可。

例: Though he loves me, I dislike him.

无副词

→ Much | as / though | he loves me, I dislike him.

= As much as he loves me, I dislike him.

（他虽然很爱我，但我就是不喜欢他。）

Though he wanted to see her, he didn't have the courage.

无副词

→ Much | as / though | he wanted to see her, he didn't have the courage.

= As much as he wanted to see her, he didn't have the courage.

（他虽然很想见她，却没有勇气。）

e. though 引导的状语从句有助动词 may 时，其后原形动词可置于句首，再接 as 或 though 即可。

例: Though you may try, you still can't make him change his mind.

= Try as you may, you still can't make him change his mind.

（即使你会尝试，仍无法令他改变心意。）

2. as 表"因为"的用法：

as 若置于句首，则表示"因为"之意，是副词性连词，等于 because。

例: As he is nice, I like him.

= Because he is nice, I like him.

（因为他人好，所以我喜欢他。）

但 as 引导的从句若为“主语 + 一般动词”的结构，且为肯定句时，可有下列变化：

例: As he lives here, he may have ample chances to view the beautiful scenery.
一般动词

→ Living here as he does, he may have ample chances to view the beautiful scenery.
（由于他住在这里，因此会有很多机会欣赏美丽的景色。）

其步骤为：

第一步：将 as 从句中的动词移至句首，变成现在分词;

第二步：再于主语之后按人称与时态变化添加助动词 do、does 或 did。

例: As he works hard, he is sure to succeed.
一般动词

第一步：将 works 移至句首，改为现在分词 working；

第二步：由于 works 是动词的第三人称单数形式，故主语之后，应加 does。

即　成：Working hard as he does, he is sure to succeed.
（因为他努力，所以一定会成功。）

*只是此类变化较少见，通常不被使用，此处提出来仅供同学们参考，不必模仿。

EXERCISE

I. 请选出一个正确的答案：

1. On the other side of the fence ______.
   (A) a man stood with black hair　(B) had a man with black hair
   (C) stood a man with black hair　(D) were a man with black hair
2. Under this roof ______ gathered today the most distinguished names of the country.
   (A) are　(B) be　(C) is　(D) being
3. Only when a person has read much English poetry ______ Shakespeare.
   (A) he can understand　(B) can he understand
   (C) can he understood　(D) can we understand
4. Nowhere ______ to be found.
   (A) can the missing book　(B) is the missing book
   (C) the missing book is　(D) the missing book can
5. At the gate ______.
   (A) waiting the beggar　(B) waited the beggar
   (C) the beggar waiting　(D) did the beggar wait
6. Only when we give happiness to others regardless of any reward ______ we achieve happiness ourselves.
   (A) as　(B) may　(C) so　(D) that
7. She didn't come yesterday, ______ come tomorrow.
   (A) nor she will　(B) nor she does
   (C) nor will she　(D) nor does she
8. ______ satisfied with what he had.
   (A) Never had he　(B) Never he was
   (C) Never he had　(D) Never was he

9. An order was given, and ______.

(A) away they dashed (B) away dashed they

(C) dashed they away (D) away dashed them

10. Only after Norman acquired considerable facility in speaking _____.

(A) did he learn to read and write

(B) finally comes reading and writing

(C) then he learned reading and writing

(D) he learned to read and write

11. Hardly had she seen her husband ______ she ran to him.

(A) when (B) than (C) as (D) that

12. Not for a moment ______ the truth of your story.

(A) he has doubted (B) he doubts

(C) did he doubt (D) he did doubt

13. ______ succeed in doing anything.

(A) Only by working hard we can (B) By only working hard we can

(C) Only by working hard can we (D) Only we can by working hard

14. Not only ____ a promise, but he also kept it.

(A) did he made (B) he made

(C) did he make (D) he makes

15. Nowhere in the world ______.

(A) travelers can buy so much beauty for so little money as in Hawaii

(B) no one can buy so much beauty for so little money as Hawaii

(C) so much beauty can be bought for so little money in Hawaii

(D) can travelers buy so much beauty for so little money as in Hawaii

16. Never before in similar circumstances ______.

(A) a British Prime Minister had refused to step down

(B) did a British Prime Minister have refused to step down

(C) a British Prime Minister have refused to step down

(D) had a British Prime Minister refused to step down

17. ______ received law degrees as today.
(A) Never so many women have (B) Never have so many women
(C) The women aren't ever (D) Women who have never

18. Flying demands a much greater supply of energy ______ other forms of transportation.
(A) than do most (B) most than do
(C) than most do (D) do than most

19. On the right ______.
(A) Mr. Fleming saw the foremost lines of the students
(B) saw Mr. Fleming the foremost lines of the students
(C) were seen by Mr. Fleming the foremost lines of the students
(D) the foremost lines of the students were seen by Mr. Fleming

20. Not far from the upper ford ______.
(A) they met an old friend of theirs
(B) met they an old friend of theirs
(C) was met by them an old friend of theirs
(D) there was met an old friend of theirs by them

21. "Have you ever been to Europe before, Martha?" "______."
(A) Never I have been there before (B) Never did I been there before
(C) Never have I been there before (D) I have been never there before

22. "Is Conrad always on time, Pierre?" "______."
(A) Seldom does he comes on time (B) Seldom is he on time
(C) Seldom he is on time (D) He seldom come on time

23. "Can you understand what the old man says, Harry?"
(A) Hardly can I understand what does he say.
(B) I can hardly understand what does he say.
(C) Can I hardly understand what he says.
(D) Hardly can I understand what he says.

24. "Did you see Liza make any mistake, Harry?" "______."
(A) Rarely have I seen her make any mistake
(B) Rarely I have seen her make any mistake
(C) Rarely have seen I her make any mistake
(D) I have seen her making any mistake rarely

25. "Does Lewis come here to see you very often, Nina?" "______."
(A) Scarcely does he come here to see us
(B) Scarcely has he come here to see us
(C) He scarcely come here to see us
(D) Scarcely is he come to see us

26. One of the walls of his room was lined with cupboards and bookcases; on the other ______.
(A) hung pictures of men and places
(B) pictures of men and places hanged there
(C) he hanged many pictures of men and places
(D) was hung pictures of men and places

27. Close behind the entrenchment ______.
(A) they came upon dozens of soldiers
(B) came they upon dozens of soldiers
(C) dozens of soldiers were come upon by them
(D) they had came upon dozens of soldiers

28. On the northwest side of the island ______.
(A) have signs of the incessant influence of the wind and sea
(B) there have signs of the incessant influence of the wind and sea
(C) are signs of the incessant influence of the wind and sea
(D) is signs of the incessant influence of the wind and sea

29. With the economic boom ______.
(A) a boom in education has come along with it
(B) has came a boom in education with it
(C) has come a boom in education
(D) there has a boom in education

30. Meg opened the box. Inside ______.
    (A) a diamond ring was there
    (B) a diamond ring lies there
    (C) was a diamond ring
    (D) a diamond ring was found

标准答案

1. (C)	2. (A)	3. (B)	4. (B)	5. (B)	6. (B)	7. (C)	8. (D)	9. (A)	10. (A)
11. (A)	12. (C)	13. (C)	14. (C)	15. (D)	16. (D)	17. (B)	18. (A)	19. (A)	20. (A)
21. (C)	22. (B)	23. (D)	24. (A)	25. (A)	26. (A)	27. (A)	28. (C)	29. (C)	30. (C)

习题解说

1. 主语 + 不及物动词 + 介词短语
→ 介词短语 + 不及物动词 + 主语
2. 主语 + be + p.p. + 介词短语
→ 介词短语 + be + p.p. + 主语
3. only when（只有当……）或 only after（只有在……之后）引导的状语从句置于句首时，该主句须倒装。
4. 否定副词置于句首，该句须倒装。
   若选 (A)，则空格之后的 to 应删除。
5. 与第 1 题同理。
6. 与第 3 题同理。
7. ..., nor will she come tomorrow.
= ..., and neither will she come tomorrow.
= ..., and she will not come tomorrow, either.
8. 与第 4 题同理。
9. 地点副词置于句首时，若该主语为代词，则主语与动词不可倒装。
10. 与第 3 题同理。

11. 主语 + had hardly + p.p. + when 引导的一般过去时从句
= Hardly had + 主语 + p.p. + when 引导的一般过去时从句
一……就……
12. 否定副词短语置于句首时，该句须倒装。
13. 与上题同理。
14. 与上题同理。
15. 与上题同理。
16. 否定副词（Never）置于句首，该句须倒装。
17. 与第 16 题同理。
18. ...than most other...do
= ...than do most other...
此处的 do 原应置于句尾，但因主语过长，故与之倒装。
19. 介词短语置于句首时，若该句动词为及物动词，则不可与主语倒装。
20. 本句中的主语 they 为代词，动词 met 为及物动词，故该句虽有地点副词短语置于句首亦无须倒装。
21. 否定副词（Never）置于句首，该句须倒装。
22. 与第 21 题同理。
23. 与第 21 题同理。
24. 与第 21 题同理。
25. 与第 21 题同理。
26. ...; on the other wall hung pictures of men and places.
= ...; on the other hung pictures of men and places.
本句因介词短语置于句首，动词 hung 为不及物动词，故形成倒装。原句中的 wall 因与前面重复，故予以省略。
27. 与第 9 题同理。
28. 与第 1 题同理。
29. 与第 1 题同理。
30. 地点副词置于句首时，主语必须与不及物动词倒装。

第十章　比较结构

概述

约 30 年前，赖老师在中学阶段学英语的时候，不是个很用功的学生。当时喜欢穿喇叭裤，不时将高中大盘帽的两侧往内挤压，看起来像顶希特勒式的军帽。有事没事，嘴里嚼着一片口香糖，轻哼着西洋歌曲，自认洋派得很。旁人总以为赖老师的英语好得很，但赖老师心里有数，因为在班上的英语成绩排名总是最后几名。

有一天，英语老师正巧教授比较结构的形成及用法，赖老师没专心听（因为觉得太过复杂），就被老师狠狠揍了一顿（当时是可以体罚的）。赖老师个性硬，心一横，就誓言不再听英语课了。而从此以后，赖老师的英语成绩也就变成了个位数。

现在赖老师写比较结构时，心中真有无限的感慨，30 年后的今天，比较结构对赖老师而言实在易如反掌。但赖老师毕竟走了好长的一段学习路程。为使同学们在短短几天内学得赖老师的累积经验，赖老师执笔本章时，尽量以简洁易懂的笔调撰写。只要有耐心，你一定会弄懂比较结构的。在看本章之前，请同学们先看下列的句子，即使不懂亦没关系。

比较结构要靠两种副词性连词形成：than、as。

基本句型有两种：

1. 原级比较：as

例: He is as diligent as Peter.

副词（as）　副词性连词（as）

（他和彼得一样勤奋。）

He doesn't study so hard as Peter.

副词（so）　副词性连词（as）

（他没有彼得那样用功。）

2. 一般比较：than

例: He is more diligent than Peter.

副词（more）　副词性连词（than）

（他比彼得勤奋。）

He doesn't study harder than Peter.

副词（harder）　副词性连词（than）

（他没有比彼得用功。）

第一节　一般比较结构

一般比较结构，一定要使用副词性连词 than。

1. 造句方式：

a. 先造一个含有形容词或副词的句子；

例: He is prudent.
adj.
（他很小心。）

He works enthusiastically.
adv.
（他工作很热心。）

b. 再将句中的形容词或副词变成比较级，即：

more | + | adj.	（比较……）；
less | | adv.	（比较不……）

例: He is more prudent.
（他比较小心。）

He works less enthusiastically.
（他工作比较不热心。）

c. 再设定比较对象，并在该比较对象之前置副词性连词 than，即告完成。

例: He is more prudent than Peter.
比较对象
（他比彼得小心。）

He works less enthusiastically than Peter.
比较对象
（他不如彼得工作热心。）

2. 理论基础：

than 之后原本并非单一的比较对象，而是与主句结构完全相同的状语从句。该状语从句修饰主句中的比较副词 more 或 less。

即：He is more prudent than Peter is prudent.
S be 比副 adj. 副连 S be adj.
（than Peter is prudent：状语从句，修饰“比副”more）

He works less enthusiastically than Peter works enthusiastically.
S vi. 比副 adv. 副连 S vi. adv.
状语从句

但：为了避免重复，than 引导的状语从句结构中仅保留比较对象，相同的陈述部分（即动词及动词以后的词）均予以省略，而成：

He is more prudent than Peter.

He works less enthusiastically than Peter.

3. than 引导的状语从句结构变化：

than 引导的状语从句结构中，若有 be 动词，可将其保留；若有助动词（can、will、shall、have、has 等）亦可保留；若有一般动词，则应以 do、does、did 代替。当然这些 be 动词、助动词或 do、does、did 均可予以省略。

a. be 动词

例: He is less responsible than you (are).

（他没有你负责任。）

b. 助动词

例: He can sing more beautifully than you (can).

（他唱得比你悦耳。）

c. 一般动词

例: He worked more carefully than you (did).

（他工作比你更仔细。）

4. 形容词及副词的比较级：

绝大多数的副词或形容词（特别是三音节以上的副词或形容词），被 more 修饰时，均保留原级形态，但双音节的副词或形容词则是不规则变化（或改变词尾，或用 more 修饰），至于单音节的形容词和副词则几乎都采用词尾变化，而甚少用 more 修饰。

例: 三音节: She is more beautiful than Mary.

（她比玛丽漂亮。）

双音节: He is more prudent than Peter.

（他比彼得小心。）

但: 双音节: He is more clever than Peter. (口语)

→ He is cleverer than Peter. (✓)

（他比彼得聪明。）

单音节: He runs more fast than Peter. (×)

→ He runs faster than Peter. (✓)

（他跑得比彼得快。）

注意

有些词变成比较级时，甚至连原来的样子都改变了。

例: He speaks English well.
（他英语说得很好。）

→ He speaks English better (非 more well) than John.
（他英语说得比约翰说得好。）

He is bad.
（他很坏。）

→ He is worse (非 more bad) than John.
（他比约翰坏。）

因此，副词或形容词形成比较级时，我们应注意其是否为规则变化或不规则变化，一般词典或普通的参考书中均有列出来。由于这些词类变化非技术性的东西，赖老师不打算列出来乱凑篇幅，浪费本语法书的宝贵空间。相信同学们肯查词典，多看文章，自己就会了解的，而赖老师亦是这样学出来。

5. less 之后的副词或形容词均使用原级：

例: He is less hardworking than John.
（他没有约翰勤奋。）

He visits us less often than John.
（他没有约翰那么常来看我们。）

He does things less carefully than John.
（他做事没有约翰小心。）

6. 与本身作比较：

比较结构中通常比较对象是不同的人或物，但亦有与自己作比较的情形发生。

例: He studies harder than he did before.
(= studied hard)
（他比从前用功。）

She looks younger than she is (young).
（她看起来比实际年轻。）

注意

a. 自行作比较时，句中的时态若不同（即主句为一般现在时，than 从句为一般过去时），则 than 之后的主语以及其后之一般过去时 be 动词、助动词或一般动词变成的 did 不可省略。

1) be 动词

例: He is healthier than he was.

不同时态

（他比以前健康。）

2) 助动词

例: He can sing better than he could.

不同时态

（他比从前唱得好。）

3) 一般动词

例: He works harder than he did.

(= worked hard)

不同时态

= He works harder than he used to (work hard).

不同时态

（他比以前努力。）

b. 此类不同时态的自行比较结构中，若主句及 than 从句均有对等的介词短语，或 than 从句有另一 when 引导的状语从句修饰时，than 之后的主语及动词或助动词部分可以省略。

1) 介词短语

例: He is happier with Mary than he is (happy) with Jane.

= He is happier with Mary than with Jane.

（他和玛丽在一起比和简在一起快乐。）

He is more interested in English than he is (interested) in Japanese.

= He is more interested in English than in Japanese.

（他对英语比对日语有兴趣。）

注意

介词短语对等时，第二个短语中的介词千万不可省略，否则会造成对象的错误比较。

例: He is more interested in English than he is in Japanese. (✓)

He is more interested in English than Japanese. (劣)

上列第二句中，than 之后的 Japanese 变成主语，译成“日本人”，整句则成了下列不合逻辑的译文：

他比日本人对英语更有兴趣。

不过有时候我们亦会在一般文章中见到这种错误的比较，勉强可以接受，但我们应本着严谨的语法规则避免此种语病。

2) when 从句

例: He is much thinner than (he was) when I saw him ten years ago.
状语从句

→ He is much thinner than when I saw him ten years ago.
（他比我十年前看见他时瘦多了。）

He is much thinner than I saw him ten years ago. (×，比较对象错误)

理由:
本句成了 He 与 I 在作比较，而非 He 与十年前的 he 作比较。

7. 比较结构中相同动词的化简：

比较结构中，若主句为“主语 + 及物动词 + 宾语”，而 than 从句亦为“主语 + 及物动词 + 宾语”，且两个及物动词均相同时，than 从句的动词可用 do、does、did 取代。

例: I love you more than he loves you.
相同动词

= I love you more than he does you.
（我比他更爱你。）

I love you more than I love Mary.
相同动词

= I love you more than I do Mary.
（我爱你比爱玛丽多。）

千万不要造这样的句子：

I love you more than Mary.

理由:

本句可能有两个意思：

→ I love you more than Mary loves you.
（我比玛丽爱你。）

→ I love you more than I love Mary.
（我爱你比爱玛丽多。）

因此，语意模棱两可，故应改为：

I love you more than Mary does. (does 不宜省略)
（我比玛丽更爱你。）

或:I love you more than I do Mary.
（我爱你比爱玛丽多。）

8. 数量形容词的比较级变化:

数量形容词 much、little、many、few 变成比较级时，有下列变化:

a. much（很多的）及 little（很少的）修饰不可数名词:

原级	比较级	最高级
much	more	the most
little	less	the least

例: 原级: He has very much money. (可)
He has a lot of money. (佳)
（他有很多钱。）

不可说: He has much money. (×)

理由:
肯定句中应使用 very much 或 a lot of，否定句中则使用 much。
He doesn't have much money. (✓)
（他并没有很多钱。）

比较级: He has more money than John (does).
（他比约翰有钱。）

最高级: He has the most money of all.
（他是所有人中最有钱的。）

原级: He has little time.
（他的时间很少。）

比较级: He has less time than I (do) for the job.
（他做这工作的时间比我的少。）

最高级: He has the least time of all.
（他的时间最少。）

b. many（很多的）及 few（很少的）修饰可数的复数名词:

例: 原级: He has many friends.
（他有很多朋友。）

比较级: He has more friends than John.
（他的朋友比约翰的多。）

最高级: He has the most friends of all.
（他的朋友最多。）

原级: He has few friends.

（他的朋友很少。）

比较级: He has fewer friends than John.

（他的朋友比约翰的少。）

最高级: He has the fewest friends of all.

（他的朋友最少。）

9. 避免错误比较:

“主语 + 介词短语”或“所有格 + 主语”极易形成对象的错误比较，应予避免。

例: The apples in this basket are sweeter than the table. (×)

主语 介词短语

理由:

The apples 是水果， the table 是桌子，属性不同，故形成对象的错误比较。

改正:

→ The apples in this basket are sweeter than those on the table. (✓)

主语 介词短语 主语 介词短语

（这个篮子里的苹果比桌子上的那些要甜。）

His car is better than his friend. (×)

所有格 主语

理由:

car 为物， his friend 为人，比较对象错误。

改正:

→ His car is better than | his friend's. | that of his friend. |

所有格 主语

（他的车比他朋友的好。）

注意

使用 that 或 those 作代词时， that 代替单数名词（或不可数名词）， those 则代替复数名词。

例: I have found that John's interest in English is greater than that of his classmate Jim.

单数 n.

＊上句画线的 that 等于 the interest。

（我发现约翰对英语的兴趣比他同学吉姆的还高。）

The stamps he has collected are more valuable than those Peter has collected.
复数 n.

＊上句画线的 those 等于 the stamps (which)。
（他收集的邮票比彼得收集的还值钱。）

10. 本身已有最高级意味的形容词：

有些形容词（包括由其演变过来的副词），本身就有“至极”或“最高级”的意味，不能使用在比较级结构中。这些词常用的有：perfect（完美的）、sublime（卓越的）、noble（高贵的）、extreme（极度的）、superb（极好的）、excellent（特优的）等。

例: He speaks English more perfectly than John. (×)

理由:

perfectly 既已表“完美无缺”，故无比较级。

11. 本身已有比较级意味的形容词：

某些 -ior 结尾的形容词本身已具有比较级的意味，不可用“more...than...”或“less...than...”修饰，而要与介词 to 连用。

常用的此类形容词一共有四个：

be superior to...　比……优越的
be inferior to...　比……差劲的
be senior to...　比……年长的；比……地位高的/资深的
be junior to...　比……年轻的；比……地位低的/资浅的

例: I really doubt John's competence; it seems quite obvious that he is inferior to his friend David.
（我真怀疑约翰的能力，很明显地，他比他朋友大卫差劲。）

Even though he is superior to most of his classmates, he is not arrogant.
（虽然他比他大多数的同学优秀，但他并不高傲。）

Mary is senior to her husband in the company.
（在公司里，玛丽的职位比她先生高。）

其他类似的词类：

prior to + n.　在……之前（指时间）
= before + n.

例: Prior to the war, he was a teacher.
（在战前他是位老师。）

12. 注意同范围及不同范围的比较：

a. 同范围：

某人或某物属于同一团体或种类，写作者欲将之与该团体或种类的其他所有份子作比较时，采用下列句型，以避免将该人或该物形成重叠比较：

人：John is better than	any other student all the other students all the others anyone else	in his class. 同范围

（约翰比他班上其他学生优秀。）

物：Tokyo is bigger than	any other city all the other cities	in Japan. 同范围

（东京比日本的其他城市要大。）

b. 不同范围：

写作者欲将某人或某物与不同的团体或种类的所有份子作比较时，any 或 all 之后无需加 other 一词。句型如下：

人：John is better than	any student all the students anyone 代 all 代	in Mary's class. 不同范围

（约翰比玛丽班上所有的同学优秀。）

物：Shanghai is bigger than	any city all the cities	in Nepal. 不同范围

（上海比尼泊尔的任何城市都要大。）

13. be getting more and more + adj.　　变得越来越……
= be getting 比较级 adj. + and + 比较级 adj.
= be getting increasingly + adj.

例：Life over there is getting	more and more difficult. increasingly difficult.

（那儿的生活越来越不容易。）

The boy is getting more and more fat. (×)
adj.

理由:
fat 的比较级形态应为 fatter，无 more fat 的用法。
改正:
→ The boy is getting | fatter and fatter. / increasingly fat. |
（那个男孩越来越胖了。）

注意
increasingly 等于 more and more，之后不必再接比较级。
例: The sick man is getting | weaker and weaker. / increasingly weak. |
（那名生病的男子越来越虚弱了。）
The weather is getting | hotter and hotter. / increasingly hot. |
（天气越来越热。）

14. 修饰比较级的副词:

用来修饰比较级副词或形容词的有以下六个副词，置于被修饰的副词或形容词之前:
far、much、a lot、a great deal、still、even

例: This question is | far / much / a lot / a great deal / still / even | more difficult than that one.
（这个问题比那个要难多了/甚至更难。）
He studies much harder than anyone of them.
（他比他们之中任何一个都用功得多。）

注意

a. 上列六个副词中，以 far、much 及 a lot 最常用，亦可用以修饰 superior、inferior、senior、junior。

例: This car is | far / much / a lot | superior to that one.
（这辆车比那辆好太多了。）

b. far、much 及 a lot 亦可修饰副词 too。

例:

He is	far much a lot	too old to do the work.

（他太老了，无法做这项工作。）

The price is much too high for me.

（这个价钱对我来说实在太高了。）

This question is far too hard for my teacher to answer.

（这问题实在太难了，连我的老师也答不出来。）

15. 最高级副词：

最高级副词有两个：most 及 least，可用以修饰句中的形容词、副词或动词。

a. 形容词

例: She is the most beautiful girl (that) I've ever seen.

adj.

（她是我见过最美的女孩。）

Of the three girls, she is the least beautiful.

adj.

（三个女孩之中，她最不好看。）

b. 副词

例: He treats people most politely.

adv.

（他待人最有礼貌。）

c. 动词

例: I need you most.

vt.

（我最需要你。）

I least expected to see you here.

vt.

（我绝没想到会在这里见到你。）

注意

某些副词或形容词由于不规则变化的关系，变成最高级时并不需要 most 或 least 修饰，即可自成最高级的副词或形容词。

原级	比较级	最高级
good (adj.) 好的	better	best
hot (adj.) 热的	hotter	hottest
bad (adj.) 坏的	worse	worst
hard (adj.) 硬的；难的	harder	hardest
hard (adv.) 努力地	harder	hardest

赖老师不打算一一列出来，以免占篇幅。同学们在平常阅读文章、查词典时均可看得到这些词。

例: She is the best student of all.
（她是全部学生中最好的一个。）

Of the five students here, she studies (the) hardest.
（在这五个学生中，她最用功。）

16. 最高级的比较对象一定是三者以上：

使用最高级副词或形容词所形成的比较对象一定是三者或以上，通常出现在下列两个结构中：

a. of (among)	the three the four ⋮ ⋮ all	...	在	这三个 这四个 ⋮ ⋮ 所有	……之中

例: Of the five books, I like that one best.
(like: vt.; best: adv.)

（这五本书中，我最喜欢那本。）

He is the best student of all.
(best: adj.; student: n.)

（他是所有学生中最好的一个。）

注意

of the two 则使用比较级。

例: Of the two students, John is the better.

adj.

（这两个学生中，约翰比较好。）

Of the two books, I like that one better.

adv.

（这两本书中，我比较喜欢那本。）

b. 最高级形容词 + n. + 关系代词 that（不可使用 who、whom、which）+ 定语从句完成时

例: John is the most responsible man (that) I've ever known.

最高级 adj.　　定语从句完成时

（在我所认识的人中，约翰是最有责任感的一位。）

He is the best student (that) I've ever taught.

最高级 adj.　　定语从句完成时

（在我教过的学生中，他是最好的一位。）

That's the greatest idea that has ever occurred to me.

最高级 adj.　　定语从句完成时

（那是我所想到过最棒的点子。）

17. the 与最高级的关系：

最高级副词修饰动词或副词时，不一定要加定冠词 the，但最高级形容词修饰名词时，则须加 the。

a. 副词

例: Of the four students, he treats people (the) most politely.

最高级 adv.　adv.

（这四个学生中，他待人最有礼貌。）

b. 动词

例: Of all the people I know, I respect him (the) most.

vt.　　最高级 adv.

（我所认识的人中，我最尊敬他。）

He studies (the) hardest of all.

vi. 最高级 adv.

（他是所有人中最用功的一个。）

c. 名词

例: He is the best student of all.

最高级 adj. n.

（他是所有学生当中最好的一个。）

I find Mary the most beautiful girl in her class.

最高级 adj. n.

（我觉得玛丽是她班上最美的女孩。）

18. the + 最高级形容词:

最高级形容词修饰名词时，前面因为加了定冠词 the，而 "the + adj." 可做代词用，故之后的名词可省略。

例: She is the most beautiful girl of all.

adj. n.

= She is the most beautiful of all (the girls).

代词

（她是所有女孩中最美的一个。）

Of all the boys, he is the cleverest (boy).

（所有男孩中，他最聪明。）

19. 最高级的结构替换:

例: He is the best student of all.

= No one else / No (other) student | is | better than / as good as / so good as | he.

（他是所有学生中最好的一个。）

He studies hardest of all.

= No one (else) studies | harder than / as hard as / so hard as | he.

（他是所有人中最用功的一个。）

20. most 亦可做 very（很）解：

加形容词修饰名词时，不必于 most 之前加定冠词。

例：She is really a | most / very | beautiful girl.

（她真是个很美的女孩子。）

21. by far 可修饰最高级：

带有 the 的最高级副词或形容词，可被 by far 及 much 两个副词修饰，其中以 by far 较为常用。

例：She is | by far / much | the most beautiful girl in town.

（她是镇上最美的女孩子。）

I find him | by far / much | the best student of all.

（我发觉他是所有学生中最棒的一个。）

第二节 原级比较结构

原级比较结构出现在含有“as...as...”（和……一样地……）的结构中。

1. 造句方式：

a. 先造一个含有形容词或副词的句子；

例: He is prudent.
adj.
（他很小心。）

He runs fast.
adv.
（他跑得快。）

b. 再于句中的形容词或副词之前置 as 一词；as 为副词，译成“一样地”。

例: He is as prudent.
adv. adj.
（他一样地小心。）

He runs as fast.
adv. adv.
（他跑得一样快。）

c. 再设定比较对象，并在该比较对象之前置副词性连词 as 即告完成；此 as 译成“和”。

例: He is as prudent as John.
一样地 和
（他和约翰一样小心。）

He runs as fast as John.
一样地 和
（他跑得和约翰一样快。）

2. 理论基础：

上列例句中，第二个 as 为副词性连词，之后应有一个与主句完全一样的结构，即 as 引导的状语从句，修饰第一个 as（此为副词，表“一样地”）。

即：He is as prudent as John is prudent.
S be adv. adj. 副连 S be adj.

（一样地） （和）状语从句

He runs as fast as John runs fast.
S vi. adv. adv. 副连 S vi. adv.

（一样地）（和）状语从句

但为了避免重复，as 从句仅保留比较对象，相同的部分（即动词和动词以后的词）均予以省略，而形成：
He is as prudent as John.
He runs as fast as John.

3. as 从句的变化：

a. be 动词

例: He is as prudent as John (is).
（他和约翰一样小心。）

b. 助动词

例: He can sing as well as John (can).
（他唱得和约翰一样好。）

c. 一般动词

例: He runs as fast as John (does).
（他跑得和约翰一样快。）

4. as 从句或 than 从句亦可采用倒装结构：

这种倒装结构常出现在 as 从句或 than 从句之后有定语从句时。

例: He is as prudent as John is, who is a good friend of mine. (×，who 之前无先行词 John)
→ He is as prudent as is John, who is a good friend of mine. (√)
（他和我的好友约翰一样谨慎。）

He is more prudent than is John, who is a good friend of mine. (√)
（他比我的好友约翰谨慎。）

He studies as hard as Mary does, who is my sister. (×，who 之前无先行词Mary)

→ He studies as hard as does Mary, who is my sister. (√)

（他和我妹妹玛丽一样用功。）

He studies much harder than does Mary, who is my sister. (√)

（他比我妹妹玛丽用功多了。）

5. "as...as..."用于肯定句或否定句，而"so...as..."则只用于否定句：

例：肯定句：He studies so hard as Mary. (×)

→ He studies as hard as Mary. (√)

（他和玛丽一样用功。）

He is so thin as a rail. (×)

→ He is as thin as a rail. (√)

（他和栏杆一样瘦。—— 他瘦极了。）

否定句：He doesn't study as / so hard as Mary.

（他没有玛丽用功。）

He isn't as / so polite as John.

（他不像约翰那样有礼貌。）

第三节　其他有关 as / than 的重要用法

1. “as...as...” 可与单数可数名词连用：

造句方法：

a. 先造一个含有形容词的单数可数名词的句子；

例: He is a handsome boy.

adj.　n.

b. 再将第一个 as 置于动词之后；

即：He is as a handsome boy. (×)

由于 as 是副词（一样地），并非修饰不定冠词 a，故须将形容词 handsome 与 a 互换位置，使 handsome 紧接 as 之后，以供其修饰。

即：He is as handsome a boy.

adv.　adj.

c. 再将第二个 as 置于 a boy 之后，然后接比较对象，即告完成。

即：He is as handsome a boy as John.

（他和约翰一样是英俊的男孩。）

同理：I have as fancy a car as that one.

（我有一辆车和那辆一样炫。）

注意

1) 类似此种只能与单数名词连用的结构尚有：

so...that...　　如此……以至……

too...to...　　太……而不……

how...　　多么地……

a) so...that...

例:He is so good a boy that I like him very much.

= He is such a good boy that I like him very much.

（他是个这么好的男孩子，因此我非常喜欢他。）

b) too...to...

例:He is too old a man to do it.
（他年纪太大，没法做此事。）

c) how...

例:How great a man he is!
= What a great man he is!
（他真是个伟大的人物！）

2) what 与 such 之后可修饰单复数或不可数名词。

例: What a great man he is!
单数 n.
（他真是个伟大的人物！）

What beautiful music it is!
不可数 n.
（这真是好听的音乐！）

What good boys they are!
复数 n.
（他们真是好孩子！）

He is such a good boy that I like him.
单数 n.
（他是个这么好的孩子，因此我喜欢他。）

They are such good boys that I like them.
复数 n.
（他们是这么好的孩子，因此我喜欢他们。）

It is such good music that I enjoy it.
不可数 n.
（这音乐这么好，因此我很欣赏。）

注意

这类只能与单数可数名词连用的结构可通过下列一句中文牢记下来：
从前有个书呆子（so...that...），他有两个朋友，一个叫阿西（as...as...），一个叫土土（too...to...），三人相聚时，最爱说一个字：“好！”（how...）。

2. as...as one can 尽可能地……
= as...as possible

a. 造句方法：

1) 先造一个含有形容词或副词的句子；

例: You must study hard.
adv.
（你一定要用功。）

He remained quiet.
adj.
（他保持沉默。）

2) 在 hard 或 quiet 之前置入第一个 as（做副词，中文译为“一样地”）；

即： You must study as hard.
He remained as quiet.

3) 句尾添入 as one（you，he...）can 或 possible，即告完成。

即： You must study as hard | as you can. / as possible. |
（你要尽可能地用功。）
He remained as quiet | as he could. / as possible. |
（他尽可能地保持安静。）

b. 理论基础：

1) as one can 之后省略了与前面主句中相同的部分，以避免赘述。

例: You must study as hard as you can study hard.
重复
→ You must study as hard as you can. (✓)
He remained as quiet as he could remain quiet.
重复
→ He remained as quiet as he could. (✓)

2) as possible 是由 as it is / was possible 化简而成，it 是代词，代替前面相同的部分。

例: You must study as hard as it is possible.
= You must study as hard as studying hard is possible.
动名词（做主语）
He remained as quiet as it was possible.
= He remained as quiet as remaining quiet was possible.
动名词（做主语）

由于经常使用的关系，as it is / was possible 中的 it is / was 已被省略而形成 as possible 的固定短语。

即：You must study as hard as possible.
He remained as quiet as possible.

3. as...as any 与任何人一样……

例: He is as happy a man as any.
（他和任何其他人一样快乐。）

4. as...as ever 与往常一样……

例: Though it has been a long time since I parted from him, he is as young as ever.
（虽然我和他分开已久，但他还是和以前一样年轻。）

5. as...as ever lived 古今最……之一
= one of the + 最高级 ... that ever lived

例: He is as great a hero as ever lived.
= He is one of the greatest heroes that ever lived.
（他是古今最伟大的英雄之一。）

6. 两个形容词的相互比较：

"more...than" 结构中，若为两个形容词相互比较，则这两个形容词一律使用原级。

例: He is more good than bad.
adj. adj.
= He is not so bad as good.
= He is good rather than bad.
（他好的成分大过坏的成分——与其说他坏，倒不如说他好。）

但:He is more good than John. (×)
→ He is better than John. (√)
（他比约翰好。）

7. 倍数词造句法：

a. 本结构一共有四种：

1) 倍数词 + as...as... 是……的几倍
2) more than + 倍数词 + as...as... 是……的几倍还不止
3) 倍数词 + the（或所有格）+ 名词 是……的几倍

4) more than + 倍数词 + the（或所有格）+ 名词　　是……的几倍还不止

例: He is three times as heavy as I.
（他的体重是我的三倍。）

He is more than three times as heavy as I.
（他的体重是我的三倍还不止。）

He is three times my weight.
= He is three times as heavy as I.
（他的体重是我的三倍。）

He is more than three times my weight.
= He is more than three times as heavy as I.
（他的体重是我的三倍还不止。）

b. 倍数词 + as...as...　　是……的几倍

本结构因含有“as...as...”的短语，故句中必须有形容词或副词，才能使用本结构。造句的步骤如下：

译: 他的用功程度是我的三倍。

第 一 步：先译“他用功。”
He studies hard.
*句中有副词 hard。

第 二 步：再译“他和我一样用功。”
He studies as hard as I.

第 三 步：将倍数词 three times（三倍）置于“as...as...”之前，即完成整句的翻译。
He studies three times as hard as I.
倍数词　副词
（他的用功程度是我的三倍。）

注意

上句是以副词 hard 为依据，而完成倍数词的结构。我们亦可用形容词 diligent（勤奋的、勤勉的）译出意思相同的句子：

第 一 步：先译“他勤奋。”
He is diligent.
*句中有形容词 diligent。

第 二 步：再译“他和我一样勤奋。”

He is as diligent as I.

第 三 步：将倍数词 three times 置于“as...as...”之前，而完成整句的翻译。

He is three times as diligent as I.

倍数词　　形容词

（他比我勤奋三倍。）

由此得知，只要有副词或形容词，就可使用本结构。

译: 我的年纪是他的三倍。

第 一 步：I am old.

第 二 步：I am as old as he.

第 三 步：I am three times as old as he.

c. more than + 倍数词 + as...as...　　是……的几倍还不止

本结构与 b. 中的结构大致一样，只是在倍数词之前加 more than，表“还不止”之意。

译: 他的用功程度是我的三倍还不止。

第 一 步：He studies hard.

第 二 步：He studies as hard as I.

第 三 步：He studies three times as hard as I.

第 四 步：He studies more than three times as hard as I.

注意

more than + 倍数词 + as...as...

= 倍数词 + more...than...

故：He is more than three times as diligent as I.

= He is three times more diligent than I.

He studies more than three times as hard as I.

= He studies three times harder than I.

I am more than three times as old as he.

= I am three times older than he.

d. 倍数词 + | the
that
his
those
these
所有格 | + 名词　是……的几倍

＊本结构必须要与名词连用。

译: 他的钱是我的两倍。

第 一 步：先译“他有我的钱。”
He has my money.
（句中有所有格 my）

第 二 步：再将倍数词置于所有格之前，即完成整句的翻译。
He has twice my money.
倍数词 所有格

同　理：这条河的长度是淡水河的十倍。
The river is ten times the length of the Tamsui River.
倍数词
= The river is ten times as long as the Tamsui River.

e. more than + 倍数词 + the（或所有格）+ 名词　是……的几倍还不止

本结构与 d. 中的结构大致一样，只是在倍数词之前加了 more than，表示“还不止”的意思。

译: 他的钱是我的两倍还不止。

第 一 步：He has my money.
第 二 步：He has twice my money.
第 三 步：He has more than twice my money.
同　理：The river is more than ten times the length of the Tamsui River.
（这条河的长度是淡水河的十倍还不止。）

f. 下列词类均可视为倍数词：

one-third	三分之一
two-thirds	三分之二
⋮	⋮

⋮	⋮
three-fourths	四分之三
⋮	⋮
⋮	⋮
one-fifth	五分之一
two-fifths	五分之二
⋮	⋮
⋮	⋮
twice	二倍
three times	三倍
four times	四倍
⋮	⋮
⋮	⋮

例: I am half as old as you.
（我的年龄只有你的一半。）

I study only one-third as hard as he.
（我的用功程度仅及他的三分之一。）

She is twice my weight.
（她的体重是我的两倍。）

g. 特殊结构:

1) twice as...as... (常用)　　是……的两倍
= as...again as... (少用)

例: He is twice as old as I.
= He is as old again as I.
（他的年纪是我的两倍。）

He has twice as much money as I.
= He has as much money again as I.
（他的钱是我的两倍。）

2) one and a half times as...as... (常用)
= half as...again as... (少用)　　是……的一倍半

例: He is eight years old, and I am one and a half times as old as he.
（他 8 岁，我 12 岁。）

3) as many as + 数词 + 复数名词　　多达……

例: As many as one hundred people were killed in the air crash.
（这次空难中多达 100 人丧生。）

There are as many as five apples on the table.
（桌上的苹果有 5 个之多。）

但:He has as many as fifty dollars with him. (×)
→ He has as much as fifty dollars with him. (√)
（他身上有 50 块钱之多。）

理由:
fifty dollars 固然为复数名词，但其集合名词为 money，是不可数名词，修饰 money 要说 much money，而非 many moneys。故使用“as...as...”时，亦要用“as much as + 金钱名词”。

例: Building costs ran up to as much as $20 million.
（建筑费用涨到高达 2000 万美元。）

同理:
as long as + 数词 + 名词　　长达……
as wide as + 数词 + 名词　　宽达……
as high as + 数词 + 名词　　高达……
as early as + 数词 + 名词　　早在……
as late as + 数词 + 名词　　迟至……

例: I have been learning English (for) as long as 25 years.
（我学英语已有 25 年之久。）

The river is as wide as 100 meters.
（这条河宽达 100 米。）

I mailed the letter as early as Friday.
（我早在星期五就把信寄了。）

He came home as late as two in the morning.
（他迟至凌晨两点才回家。）

8. not so much...as...　与其说是……倒不如说是……
not so much as...　甚至都不……

a. 表“与其说是……倒不如说是……”，共有四种用法:

1) be not so + | adj. adv. | + as | adj. adv. |

由于原级形容词或副词不能以 much 修饰，故不可用“not so much + adj. /

adv. + as”，而要用“not so + adj. / adv. + as”的结构。

例: She is not so beautiful as charming.
　　　　　　　　形容词　　　形容词

= She is charming rather than beautiful.
（与其说她美，不如说她迷人。）

2) be not so much + n. + as + n.

例: He is not so much a writer as a scholar.
　　　　　　　　　　　名词　　　名词

= He is more of a scholar than a writer.
（与其说他是个作家，不如说他是个学者。）

He is not so much a thinker as an orator.
　　　　　　　　　　名词　　　名词

= He is more of an orator than a thinker.
（与其说他是思想家，不如说他是演说家。）

3) not so much + | 介词短语
不定式短语 | + as + | 介词短语
不定式短语 |

例: Success lies not so much in luck as in hard work.
　　　　　　　　　　　　　介词短语　　介词短语

= Success lies more in hard work than (in) luck.
（与其说成功在于运气，不如说在于辛勤努力。）

Our success was attributed not so much to your help
　　　　　　　　　　　　　　　　　　　介词短语

as to our cooperation.
　　介词短语

= Our success was attributed more to our cooperation than to your help.
（我们的成功与其说是归功于你的帮忙，不如说是归功于我们的合作。）

The great use of a school education is not so much to teach you things
　　　　　　　　　　　　　　　　　　　　　　　　　　　不定式短语

as to teach you the art of learning.
　　　　不定式短语

= The great use of a school education is to teach you the art of learning more than to teach you things.
（学校教育的最大用处，与其说是教你东西，不如说是教你学习的方法。）

4) not so much + 动词 + as + 动词

例: The oceans do not so much divide the world as unite it.

动词　　动词

= The oceans do not divide the world so much as unite it.

= The oceans unite the world more than they divide it.

（与其说是海洋分割这个世界，不如说是统合这个世界。）

b. not so much as...　甚至都不……

= not even...

> **注意**
>
> 使用本短语时，要置于助动词之后，即：
>
> cannot so much as + 原形动词　甚至……都不能……
>
> do not so much as + 原形动词　甚至……都不……
>
> have not so much as + 过去分词　甚至……都没有……

例: He cannot so much as write his own name.

= He cannot even write his own name.

（他甚至连自己的名字都不会写。）

He did not so much as thank me.

= He did not even thank me.

（他甚至没谢我。）

He has not so much as written a single word yet.

= He has not even written a single word yet.

（他甚至连半个字都还没写。）

> **注意**
>
> 介词 without 之后亦可采用类似短语，即：
>
> without so much as + V-ing　连……都没有
>
> = without even + V-ing

例: He went away without so much as saying goodbye.

= He went away without even saying goodbye.

（他连声“再见”都没说就走了。）

9. the + 比较级..., the + 比较级...　越……就越……

a. 句型分析：

The older he grew, the weaker his memory became.
(1) (2)

（他越老，记忆力就越差。）

(1) 为状语从句。此处的 The 是副词性连词，引导状语从句，The 不具任何意义，故不必译出，但 The 亦兼副词，修饰其后的比较级形容词 older。

(2) 为主句。此处的 the 则是副词，亦不具任何意义，修饰其后的比较级形容词 weaker。

b. “越……就越……”的造句法：

由于“The..., the...”均为副词，故使用本句型的先决条件为：句中要有副词或形容词。

译: 你越用功，你就越能成为一个好学生。

第一步：加入 The..., the...，并于 The 及 the 之后预留空格，即：
The ______..., the ______....

第二步：将中文句子中的“越”去掉，而成：
你用功，你就能成为一个好学生。
You study hard, you'll become a good student. (×)

第三步：将第二步中的英语句子置于第一步中的空格后，即成：
The _____ you study hard (副词), the _____ you'll become a good (形容词) student.

第四步：将第三步句中的形容词或副词移位到空格中，并变成比较级。若形容词之后有名词，该名词也要移位，而原有冠词 a 或 an 则删除，即：
The _____ you study hard (副词), the _____ you'll become a good (形容词) student (名词).

→ The harder you study, the better student you'll become. (✓)

为了使同学们能够牢记这种造句法，赖老师特别设计了下列公式：

1) 加 The ______, the ______；
2) 造句子；
3) 在空格之后填上句子；
4) 副词或形容词往前移入空格中；若形容词之后有名词，也往前移，但名词若有冠词则要删除。

译: 你越谨慎，你犯的错就越少。

____

第 一 步 : The _______..., the _______...

第 二 步 : 你谨慎，你犯的错就少。

You are careful, you'll make few mistakes. (×)

第 三 步 : The _____ you are careful, the _____ you'll make few mistakes.

形容词 形容词 名词

第 四 步 : The more careful you are, the fewer mistakes you'll make.

C. 使用"越……就越……"的结构时，要注意两点：

1) 若句中无副词或形容词，则在 The 或 the 之后置副词 more 或 less。

译 你越爱我，我就对你越好。

____

The ______ you love me, the ______ I'll be nice to you.

无形容词或副词 形容词

→ The more you love me, the nicer I'll be to you. (√)

2) 若句中的主语为一般名词，而非代词（he、it、you、they 等）或专有名词（John、Mary 等），且后面的动词为 be 动词时，该 be 动词可省略。

例: The better the boy (is), the more I like him. (√)

一般名词

（这男孩越好，我就越喜欢他。）

The better	you, （代词） John, （专有名词）	the more I like	you. him.	(×) (×)

→ The better you are, the more I like you. (√)

（你越好，我就越喜欢你。）

→ The better John is, the more I like him. (√)

（约翰越好，我就越喜欢他。）

故:The colder the weather (is), the more active the penguins (will be).

一般名词 一般名词

即:The colder the weather, the more active the penguins.

（天气越冷，企鹅就越活跃。）

d. 比较级 + and + 比较级　　越来越……

例: It is getting warmer and warmer every year.
（气候每年变得越来越暖和了。）

The girl became more and more beautiful.
（这女孩变得越来越漂亮了。）

The law student studied harder and harder.
（这名法律系学生越来越用功。）

e. all the + 比较级 + | for + N / because 从句 |
即使……却更加……；就是因为……却更加……

本短语中的 for 为介词，之后接名词做宾语。because 则为副词性连词，引导状语从句。for 及 because 原本表“因为”，但在此句型中，译成“即使”，更吻合英语的意思。

例: I like him very much.
　　　　　　　　副词

→ I like him all the better | for his stubbornness. / because he is stubborn. |
（即使他固执，我却更喜欢他。／我就是因为他固执而更加喜欢他。）

The children are rebellious.
　　　　　　　　形容词

→ The children are all the more rebellious | for their parents' strictness. / because their parents are strict. |
（正因为他们的父母严格，那些孩子反而更加叛逆。）

He studied hard.
　　　　副词

→ He studied all the harder | for his failure. / because he had failed. |
（正因为他失败了，所以他更加努力学习。）

She is beautiful.
　　　形容词

→ She is all the more beautiful | for her shabby clothing. / because her clothing is shabby. |
（即使她衣衫褴褛，却显得更加美丽。／就因为她衣衫褴褛，她显得更加美丽。）

f. none the + 比较级 + | for + N / because 从句 | 即使……却一点儿也不……

例: His health is not good.
形容词

→ His health is none the better | for his exercise. / because he exercises. |

（即使他运动，他的健康状况却一点儿也不好。）

She is not beautiful.
形容词

→ She is none the more beautiful because she wears a fancy dress.

（即使她身穿时髦裙装，却一点儿也不美丽。）

g. none the less + | adj. / adv. | + | for + N / because 从句 | 即使……却仍然……

none the less 为副词，原意为“一点儿也不少”，译成“仍然”，可修饰动词、形容词或副词。

1) 修饰动词，置于该动词之后。

例: I love him none the less because he is poor.
及物动词

（即使他穷，我还是一样爱他。）

2) 修饰形容词，置于该形容词之前。

例: She is none the less beautiful for her shabby clothing.
形容词

（即使她衣衫褴褛，却依然美丽。）

3) 修饰副词，置于该副词之前。

例: He studied none the less hard because he had failed the exam.
副词

（即使未考试及格，他仍然努力学习。）

10. no more...than... / no less...than...:

no more...than... ……不是……正如……不是……

no less...than... 和……一样……

a. 此类结构一共有四种：

1) no more...than... ……不是……正如……不是……

例: He is no more a student than I (am).

（他不是学生，正如我也不是学生一样。）

2) no less...than... 和……一样……

例: He is no less good at English than John (is).

（他和约翰一样精通英语。）

3) not more...than... 没有比……更……

例: She is not more beautiful than Mary (is).

（她没有比玛丽更漂亮。）

4) not less...than... 至少与……一样……

例: She is not less beautiful than Mary (is). (罕)

（她至少与玛丽一样美。）

b. no more....than... ……不是……正如……不是……

本结构是由下列句型演变而成：

译: 他不会唱歌，正如我也不会唱歌一样。

---

1) He cannot sing, just as I cannot sing. (✓)

2) He cannot sing not any more than I cannot sing. (×)

没有比……多（即：与……一样/正如……）

但：

a) 因为在“He cannot sing”一句中已有 not，故 not any more than 中的 not 要省略，以避免双重否定，而成 any more than，仍译成“与……一样”或“正如……”。

b) than 之后的相同词类要省略，故 than I cannot sing 中的 not 要省略，而成 than I can sing，由于 He cannot sing 中已有 sing，故 than I can sing 中的 sing 要省略，而成 than I (can)。

即：He cannot sing ~~not~~ any more than I cannot sing.

→ He cannot sing any more than I (can). (✓)

3) 在“He cannot sing any more than I (can).”的结构中，any more 可移位至 cannot 之后，any 与 not 结合，而形成 no，后面再接 more。

即：He cannot any more sing than I (can).

not any 结合成 no

→ He can no more sing than I (can). (✓)

（他不会唱歌，正如我也不会唱歌一样。）

换言之，下列三句意思均相同：

He cannot sing, just as I cannot sing.
= He cannot sing any more than I (can).
= He can no more sing than I (can).
译: 鲸鱼不是鱼， 正如马不是鱼一样。

A whale is not a fish ~~not~~ any more than a horse is ~~not~~ a ~~fish~~.
（同词类要省略）

整理：
A whale is not a fish any more than a horse is. (√)
= A whale is no more a fish than a horse is.
= A whale is not a fish, just as a horse is not a fish.
（鲸鱼不是鱼， 正如马不是鱼一样。）

注意

a) 在 “no more...than” 或 “not...any more than” 的结构中， 若 than 之后的词类不同于前面的词类时， 则不可省略。
他不会唱歌， 正如我不会跳舞一样。
He cannot sing, just as I cannot dance. (√)
→ He cannot sing any more than I can~~not~~ dance.
整理：
He cannot sing any more than I can dance. (√)
= He can no more sing than I can dance.
他不是学生， 正如我不是老师一样。
He is not a student, just as I am not a teacher. (√)
→ He is not a student any more than I am ~~not~~ a teacher.
整理：
He is not a student any more than I am a teacher. (√)
= He is no more a student than I am a teacher.

b) happy、good、clever 等形容词以及 well、hard、fast 等副词， 在比较级中会形成不规则变化， 而成为 happier、better、cleverer 或 better、harder、faster。故置于 no more 或 not any more 之后时， 不可写成：

no more happy	not any more well
no more good	not any more hard
no more wise	not any more fast
⋮	⋮
⋮	⋮

而要写成：

no happier	no better
no better	no harder
no wiser	no faster
⋮	⋮
⋮	⋮

他跑不快，正如我一样。

He cannot run fast, just as I cannot run fast. (√)

→ He cannot run any ~~more fast~~ than I can.

faster

= He cannot run any faster than I can. (√)

他的英语不好，就像我一样。

He is not good at English, just as I am not good at English. (√)

= He is not good at English any more than I am.

= He is no ~~more good~~ at English than I am.

better

c. no less...than... 和……一样……

= as...as...

由于 no less...than...就等于 as...as...，故 no less 之后可置副词或形容词以供修饰。

1) 副词：

例：He studies no less hard than John.

副词

= He studies as hard as John.

（他和约翰一样用功。）

2) 形容词：

例：He is no less good at English than John.

形容词

= He is as good at English as John.

（他和约翰一样精通英语。）

d. not more...than... 没有比……更多……

= at best as...as... 最多只是和……一样……

本结构较为简单，在 more...than...（比……更……）之前加上 not 即可。

例：She is more beautiful than Mary.

（她比玛丽美。）

→ She is not more beautiful than Mary.

= She is at best as beautiful as Mary.

（她不比玛丽美丽——顶多只是和玛丽一样美。）

e. not less...than... 没有比……更少……

= at least as...as... 至少与……一样……

例: She is not less beautiful than Mary.

= She is at least as beautiful as Mary.

（她至少和玛丽一样美。）

f. 兹整理本单元句型如下：

例: He can no more drive than I.

= He cannot drive any more than I.

= He cannot drive, just as I cannot drive.

（他不会开车，就如我一样。—— 两人都不会开车。）

He is no less handsome than I.

= He is as handsome as I.

（他和我一样英俊。）

He is not more handsome than I.

= He is at best as handsome as I.

（他不比我英俊。—— 顶多跟我一样英俊。）

He is not less handsome than I.

= He is at least as handsome as I.

（他至少跟我一样英俊。）

11. no more than... / no less than...：

no more than + 数词 最多不超过……

= not more than + 数词

no less than + 数词 至少/不少于……

以上短语均为修饰数词的副词短语，句型如下：

a. no more than + 数词 + N 最多不超过……

adv. adj.

= at most + 数词 + N

例: It takes no more than ten minutes to get there on foot.

（从这儿走到那儿只需 10 分钟。）

b. not more than + 数词 + N　　最多不超过……

adv.　　　adj.

= at most + 数词 + N

例: I'll stay here not more than three days. (罕)

= I'll stay here no more than three days. (常用)

（我在此停留的时间最多不超过 3 天。）

c. no less than + 数词 + N　　至少/不少于……

adv.　　　adj.

= as least + 数词 + N

例: No less than seventy thousand people attended the concert.

= At least seventy thousand people attended the concert.

（去听那场演唱会的人数至少有 7 万。）

That lawyer earns no less than 500,000 dollars a year.

= That lawyer earns at least 500,000 dollars a year.

（那位律师的年收入至少有 50 万美元。）

> **注意**
> 根据上述，得知"no more than + 数词"等于"not more than + 数词"，均表"最多不超过"；而"no less than + 数词"则表"至少/不少于……"之意，理论上等于"not less than + 数词"的用法。

12. at most / at best:

a. | at most / not more than | + 数词　　最多不超过……

例: He is at most ten years old.

（他最多只有 10 岁。）

b. at best...　　充其量/只不过是……

= nothing but...

例: He is at best a second-rate musician.

= He is nothing but a second-rate musician.

= He is but a second-rate musician.

= He is only a second-rate musician.

（他只不过是个二流的音乐家。）

13. much less... 更不用说……

例: The child can't even walk, much less run.
（那孩子连走路都不会，更别说跑了。）

注意

表“更不用说……”有“肯定”与“否定”之别。

a. 肯定句:

例: She can drive a truck, | to say nothing of (driving) a car. / not to mention (driving) a car. / not to speak of (driving) a car. |

（她会开卡车，更不用说开轿车了。）

b. 否定句:

例: She cannot drive a car, | not to mention (driving) a truck. / not to speak of (driving) a truck. / to say nothing of (driving) a truck. / let alone (drive) a truck. / much less (drive) a truck. / still less (drive) a truck. |

（她连开轿车都不会，更别说开卡车了。）

注意

由此得知，not to mention、not to speak of 及 to say nothing of 可用于肯定句与否定句中，而 let alone、much less 及 still less 只能用于否定句中。且因 not to mention、not to speak of 及 to say nothing of 分别含有及物动词 mention 及介词 of，故其后须接名词或动名词做宾语，而 let alone、much less 及 still less 则因其具有连词的作用，故其后应置与其前相同的词类。故在上列否定句中，“She cannot drive a car”中的 drive 是原形动词，因此 let alone、much less、still less 之后亦应接原形动词。

同理：

He isn't interested in singing（动名词）, | let alone / much less / still less | dancing（动名词）.

（他对唱歌没兴趣，更别说跳舞了。）

EXERCISE

请选出一个正确的答案：

1. He is ______ than the two boys.
   (A) better (B) more good (C) the better (D) the best
2. He is ______ of the two boys.
   (A) better (B) more good (C) the better (D) the best
3. He is ______ boy than Tom.
   (A) better (B) a better (C) the better (D) the best
4. Your knowledge is greater than a ______.
   (A) specialist (B) specialist's (C) specialists (D) specialists'
5. My watch is more expensive than ______.
   (A) you (B) your (C) yours (D) yourself
6. Mary is ______ than her sister.
   (A) less kinder (B) kind (C) less kind (D) more kinder
7. Smith is not so ______ as you are.
   (A) strong (B) stronger (C) strongest (D) the strong
8. Jean is taller than ______ in her class.
   (A) all girls (B) all the girls (C) any other girl (D) any girl
9. New York City is larger than ______ city in the U.S.
   (A) any (B) all (C) any other (D) all the other
10. New York City is larger than ______ city in China.
    (A) any (B) all (C) any other (D) all the other
11. Helen is ______ than her sister.
    (A) more proud (B) proud (C) prouder (D) the proudest
12. Helen is ______ than vain.

(A) more proud (B) proud (C) prouder (D) the proudest

13. John seems to be ______ than wise.
(A) clever (B) cleverer (C) more clever (D) the cleverer

14. Knowledge is the most useful thing. = ______
(A) No thing is so useful as knowledge.
(B) Knowledge is more useful than most things.
(C) Nothing is more useful than knowledge.
(D) Knowledge is more useful than all things.

15. To talk too much is sometimes ______ than useful.
(A) worse (B) bad (C) more bad (D) much worse

16. I did not run so fast as he. = ______.
(A) He ran faster than I. (B) I ran most fast.
(C) He ran fastest than I. (D) He ran fast than I.

17. Mary knows electronics ______ than any of her classmates.
(A) well (B) better (C) best (D) betterly

18. Most of us work ______ in the morning than in the afternoon.
(A) efficient (B) efficiently
(C) more efficient (D) more efficiently

19. Minneapolis is now ______ of these two competing cities.
(A) the largest (B) the large (C) the larger (D) larger

20. Sound travels ______ air.
(A) faster through water than through
(B) faster than through water and
(C) through water faster and
(D) where it is faster through water than through

21. Few of the people who live on the cooperatives ______ than they were as laborers.
(A) is well off financial (B) financially well off
(C) are better off financially (D) financial better off

22. The photographs of Mars taken by satellites are ______ than those taken from the Earth.
(A) clearest　(B) the clearest　(C) much clearer　(D) more clearer

23. Adams now maintains that it is less important to save the nation ______.
(A) had alerted them to a perilous future
(B) from alerting it to a perilous future
(C) as to alert them to a perilous future
(D) than to alert it to a perilous future

24. I think Alice's ______ than unfriendly.
(A) shy　(B) shyer
(C) more shy　(D) more shy rather

25. Microwave oven thermometers are ______ than other kinds of oven thermometers.
(A) more cost　(B) more costly　(C) more costlier　(D) less cost

标准答案

1. (A)　2. (C)　3. (B)　4. (B)　5. (C)　6. (C)　7. (A)　8. (C)　9. (C)　10. (A)
11. (C)　12. (A)　13. (C)　14. (C)　15. (C)　16. (A)　17. (B)　18. (D)　19. (C)　20. (A)
21. (C)　22. (C)　23. (D)　24. (C)　25. (B)

习题解说

1. 一般的比较级用法。
2. the + 比较级 + of + 两者　　两者中较……的
3. boy 为可数名词，故 better boy 之前应加 a。
4. Your knowledge is greater than a specialist's knowledge.
= Your knowledge is greater than a specialist's.
5. My watch is more expensive than your watch.
= My watch is more expensive than yours.

6. less之后必须加原级形容词。

7. as + 原级形容词 + as...　　和……一样……

not so + 原级形容词 + as...　　没有比……更……

= less + 原级形容词 + than...

John is as tall as you.

（约翰和你一样高。）

John is not so diligent as you.

= John is less diligent than you.

（约翰没有你用功。）

8. Jean 和其班级作比较时，必须将自身与班级分开，故指班上的女生用 any other girl in her class。

9. New York City 本身是美国的都市之一，故与美国其他都市比较时，必须用 any other city in the U.S.。

10. New York City 并非中国的都市之一，故与中国的都市比较时，不必加入 other。

11. 一般的比较结构。

12. 表本身性质的形容词作比较时，一律用“more + 原级形容词”。

more A than B　　与其说是 B，不如说是 A

= less B than A

= not so A as B

John is more lazy than stupid.

= John is less stupid than lazy.

= John is not so stupid as lazy.

（说约翰笨，不如说他懒。）

13. 与上题同理。

14. Knowledge is the most useful thing.

= Nothing is	as useful as more useful than	knowledge.

= Knowledge is more useful than	all the other things. any other thing.

15. 与第 12 题同理。

16. not so + 原级副词 + as　　没有比……更……

= less + 原级副词 + than

17. 此处 better 是副词 well 的比较级，修饰 knows。

18. 空格前有动词 work（工作），故空格内应置入比较级的副词 more efficiently，以修饰 work。
19. 与第 2 题同理。
20. Sound travels faster through water than it does through air.
 = Sound travels faster through water than through air.
21. well off 是形容词短语，表“境况佳的”，空格之后因有 than，故 well of 应改成比较级 better off。
22. cleverer 已是比较级，故不可再用 more 修饰，而应以 much、far、a lot 修饰。
23. ...it is less important to save...than it is to alert...
 = ...it is less important to save...than to alert...
24. 与第 12 题同理。
25. costly（昂贵的）的比较级为 more costly。

A Quick Note

第十一章　代词

1. it 做形式主语：

a. 代替不定式短语

例：It is good to study.

（学习有益。）

但不定式本身可做主语，故上句可改为：

To study is good.

It is necessary to read these books.

= To read these books is (非 are) necessary.

（这些书必须看。）

注意

上列最后一句中，books 虽为复数，然而并非主语，主语乃整个不定式短语，故动词仍用单数。

b. 代替 that 从句（名词性从句）

例：It is good that he wants to study.

= That he wants to study is good.

（他想学习，这是件好事。）

∗名词性从句本身具有名词的功能，故可做主语。

He can study is good. (×)

∗He can study 是句子，非名词性从句，因 He 之前无连词，不能构成名词性从句，故不能做主语。

c. 代替动名词

这种用法只有与极少数名词连用。

例：It is | no use / no good | reading novels all day long.

= There is no use (in) reading novels all day long.

（整天看小说是没用的。）

It is no use to read novels all day long. (×)

但: It is | of no use / useless | to read novels all day long. (√)

2. it 做形式宾语:

即 it 做不完全及物动词之宾语，代替不定式短语或 that 从句。

a. 动词若加宾语意思很完整，而无须补充说明时，叫做完全及物动词。

例: I love him. (love 为完全及物动词)

（我爱他。）

但动词虽加宾语，意思却不完整，而需要补充说明，叫做不完全及物动词，其补充语一定是名词或形容词（包括分词变成的形容词）。

例: I consider him. (×)

（我认为他。）

上面例句意思残缺，故需补充语。

→ I consider him good. (√)
adj.

（我认为他人很好。）

→ I consider him a good man. (√)
n.

（我认为他是个好人。）

但: I consider her beautifully. (×)
adv.

→ I consider her beautiful. (√)
adj.

（我认为她很美丽。）

b. 不定式或 that 从句有名词的功能，可做主语，亦可做宾语。

例: I want to go.
宾语

To study abroad has always been my dream.
主语

I think that he is good.
宾语

That he doesn't study is true.
主语

但两者却不能直接做不完全及物动词之宾语，必须用 it 代替。

例: I think that he is good true. (×)
宾语 补语

→ I think it true that he is good. (√，think 译成"认为……是……")
不完全 vt.

（我认为他人不错，这是事实。）

I think to get up early good. (×)
宾语 补语

→ I think it good to get up early. (√)

（我认为早起很好。）

I think (that) it is true that he is good. (√，think 译成"认为")
完全 vt. 名词性从句做 think 的宾语

注意

以下是常用的不完全及物动词：

think	认为……是……
consider	认为……是……
deem	认为……是……
believe	相信……是……
find	发现……是……

例: I consider / think / deem / believe / find it necessary to exercise on a daily basis.

（我认为/认为/认为/相信/发现每天运动是有必要的。）

3. it 用以强调主语或宾语：

例: I love him.

→ It is I who (或 that) love him.
（爱他的是我。）

His words made me angry.

→ It was his words that (或 which) made me angry.
（使我生气的是他说的话。）

I am in need of your help.

→ It is your help that (或 which) I am in need of.
（我需要的是你的帮助。）

4. it 亦可用以强调介词短语或状语从句：

It is / was + | 介词短语
状语从句 | + that 从句

例: It was in 1974 that I began to study English.
（我是在 1974 年开始学英语的。）

It was because he was lazy that he failed.
（他是因为懒惰而失败的。）

5. 数量代词的用法：

most all some half part the rest one-third two-thirds none	of + the（或 my, your...）+	不可数名词 + 单数动词 复数名词 + 复数动词

例: Most of the money was stolen. (money 不可数，故用 was)
（大部分的钱都被偷了。）

The most of the money was stolen. (×)
∗此类代词前不得加冠词。

Some of the students are here. (students 为复数名词，故用 are)
（部分学生在这儿。）

All of students are here. (×，缺少 the)

→ All of the students are here. (√)
（所有学生都在这儿。）

All of his students are here. (√)
（他所有的学生都在这儿。）

One third of the students has passed the test. (×，students 为复数)

→ One third of the students have passed the test. (√)
（有三分之一的学生通过了测验。）

Seventy percent of the water is contaminated. (✓，water 是不可数名词)
（70% 的水被污染了。）

Seventy percent of the students have failed the test.
（70% 的学生考试不及格。）

6. almost、most、all 之关系：

almost 为副词，表“几乎”不能作代词。

most 为形容词（大多数的，最多的）、副词（最），亦可做代词，表“大多数”。

all 为形容词（所有的），亦可做代词（全部），可用 almost 修饰。

例: Almost of the students are here. (×)

→ Most of the students are here. (✓)
代词
（大多数学生在这儿。）

All of the students are here. (✓)
代词
（所有的学生都在这儿。）

Almost all of the students are here. (✓)
（几乎所有的学生都在这儿。）

Most students love music. (✓，不可写成“Most the students...”)
形容词
（大多数学生都喜欢音乐。）

All students love music. (✓，可写成“All the students...”)
形容词
（所有学生都喜欢音乐。）

7. 人称代词：

	主格	形容词性物主代词（后加名词）	宾格	名词性物主代词（后不加名词）	反身代词
第一人称	I we	my our	me us	mine ours	myself ourselves
第二人称	you（你） you（你们）	your your	you you	yours yours	yourself yourselves

	主格	形容词性物主代词（后加名词）	宾格	名词性物主代词（后不加名词）	反身代词
第三人称	he she it they	his her its their	his her it them	his hers (its) theirs	himself herself itself themselves

例: He is a student. (主语，用主格)
（他是学生。）

I like him. (宾语，用宾格)
（我喜欢他。）

She killed herself. (主语和宾语若为同一人，则宾语用反身代词)
（她自杀了。）

Her books are interesting. (形容词性物主代词 + 名词)
（她的书很有趣。）

Her books are as interesting as mine. (为避免重复，名词性物主代词 mine，等于my books)
（她的书和我的一样有趣。）

8. 反身代词的强调用法:

例: He himself did it. (强调主语)
= He did it himself.
（他亲自做这件事。）

I want to see the boss himself.（强调宾语）
（我要见老板本人。）

Himself did it. (×)
＊反身代词不能单独做主语。

9. that、those 代替出现过的名词:

that（表单数）、those（表复数）代替前面所提到的名词，以避免重复。

例: The plants on the other side of the fence are greener than the plants in my garden. (劣)
→ The plants on the other side of the fence are greener than those in my garden. (佳)
（篱笆那边的花草要比我花园里的绿。）

The color of the door is more beautiful than the color of the window. (劣)
→ The color of the door is more beautiful than that of the window. (佳)
（这扇门的颜色比那扇窗的好看。）

10. a friend of mine / this book of hers 的用法：

a / an	+ 名词 + of	mine	或 of	my own
any		yours		your own
some		his		his own
this		theirs		their own
these		⋮		⋮
that		⋮		⋮
those		Peter's		Peter's own
which		Mary's		Mary's own
a few				

例：He is a friend of me. (×)
→ He is a friend of mine. (√)
（他是我的一位朋友。）

This friend of you is good. (×)
→ This friend of yours is good. (√)
（你的这位朋友是个好人。）

注意

上述结构使用到“of + 所有格代词”时，均可与不定冠词（a、an）、指示代词（this、that、these、those、which）或数词（some、a few、ten、many、most 等）连用，但不可与定冠词 the 连用，换言之，无下列用法：

例：He is the best friend of mine. (×)
→ He is my best friend. (√)
（他是我最好的朋友。）

或：He is one of my best friends. (√)
（他是我最好的朋友之一。）

11. ...those who / ...those whom：

...those	who whom	... (√)
...them	who whom	... (×)

例：Tell those who are late to come and see me. (√)
（叫那些迟到的人来见我。）

Evan's paintings are interesting to them who believe in nihilism. (×)

→ Evan's paintings are interesting to those who believe in nihilism. (✓)

（虚无主义者对伊凡的画感兴趣。）

12. every man and woman 与代词（所有格）的关系：

Every man and woman should do their（或 his or her）best to protect their country.

（不论男女每个人都应尽力保卫自己的国家。）

One should do one's (美语中可用 his) duty.

（人人都应克尽己责。）

13. each other / one another：

a. each other （两者彼此）

one another （三者或三者以上彼此）

例: The two students like each other.

（这两位同学彼此都很喜欢对方。）

The five students hate one another.

（这五位同学彼此互相讨厌。）

> **注意**
>
> each other 与 one another 在美语中已无区别，渐可通用，均可表示两者或三者以上的彼此。

b. one after the other （两者相继地）

one after another （三者或三者以上相继地）

例: He raised his hands one after the other.

（他相继地举起左右手。）

All the students came in one after another.

（所有学生一个接一个地进来。）

14. either、neither、both、all、any、none 做代词的用法：

either（两者中任一） any（三者或以上任一）

neither（两者皆不） none（三者或以上皆不）

both（两者皆） all（三者或以上皆）

例: I don't care whether you serve coffee or tea; either will do.

（你上咖啡也好，茶也好，我都不在乎，随便哪样都行。）

I don't like any of the four chairs.

（这四把椅子没有一把是我喜欢的。）

Neither of the two books is good.
（这两本书都不好。）

None of the three students is (或 are) diligent.
（三个学生中没有一个是用功的。）

Both of the two students are lazy.
（那两个学生都懒惰。）

All of the five apples are rotten.
（这五个苹果都烂掉了。）

15. one...the other...　一个……另一个……（限定的两者）

例: He has two sons. One is a teacher, and the other is a soldier.
（他有两个儿子。一个是老师，另一个则是军人。）

16. one...another...the other...　一个……一个……另一个……（限定的三者）

例: He has three sons. One is a teacher, another is a soldier, and the other is a lawyer.
（他有三个儿子。一个是老师，一个是军人，另一个则是律师。）

17. one...another...　一个……另一个……（非限定的两者）

例: Hobbies vary with people. One may enjoy swimming, while another may love hiking.
（喜好因人而异。某甲可能喜欢游泳，某乙则可能喜欢远足。）

18. some...others...　一些……另一些……（非限定的两群）

例: Hobbies vary with people. Some may enjoy swimming, while others may love hiking.
（喜好因人而异。有些人可能喜欢游泳，有些人则可能喜欢远足。）

19. some...others...still others...　一些……一些……另一些……

例: Hobbies vary with people. Some may enjoy swimming, others may be fond of bungee jumping, and still others may love hiking.
（喜好因人而异。有些人可能喜欢游泳，有些人可能喜欢蹦极，也有些人则喜欢远足。）

20. 明确数词...the others / the rest...　若干……其他/其余……

例: Only two students in my class passed the test. The others failed.
（我班里只有两个学生通过考试，其余全不及格。）

EXERCISE

I. 请选出一个正确的答案：

1. I guess James didn't have a chance to win the election. ______ the people in the city voted for his opponent.
   (A) Almost all of (B) Most all of
   (C) Most of all (D) Almost the whole of
2. Wagner and Strauss were such good friends that they frequently exchanged gifts with ______.
   (A) each one (B) each other (C) the other (D) another
3. The beginning course in algebra was very easy, but ______ one is certainly not.
   (A) which (B) this (C) some (D) no
4. She is very forgetful and cannot recognize her grandchildren from one visit to ______.
   (A) next one (B) other one (C) the other one (D) the next
5. Even though Africa game preserves have saved many animals, there are ______ that will not be saved.
   (A) some more (B) all others (C) many more (D) much more
6. Some of our wedding vows were taken from the traditional ceremony, and some of them were written by ______.
   (A) my husband and I (B) my husband and my
   (C) my husband and me (D) my husband and mine
7. The principal responsibility of managing the dormitory rests with the students ______.
   (A) itself (B) of itself (C) themselves (D) their selves
8. John behaved so strangely today; I thought he wasn't acting like ______.
   (A) him (B) himself (C) he would (D) he does

9. I don't take John's pen because I don't like ______.
(A) that pen of his (B) that his pen
(C) his that pen (D) that pen of him

II. 请选出错误的画线部分:

10. As one nears the bridge, you come to a narrow rocky valley, the site of several historic battles.
(A) As one nears (B) rocky (C) the site (D) historic

11. Many modern skyscrapers, though visually pleasing, they have heating and cooling systems that require closed windows and consequently waste energy.
(A) visually pleasing (B) they have (C) closed (D) waste

12. Each member of the team bought themselves a new car with the money earned in the championship game.
(A) bought (B) themselves (C) earned (D) in

13. The functions performed by individual members of a colony of bees are determined by chemical substances transferred from a bee to another.
(A) performed (B) individual (C) are determined (D) a

14. They asked us, Henry and I, whether we thought that the statistics had been presented fairly and accurately.
(A) I (B) thought (C) had been presented (D) fairly

15. He is familiar with the most of calculus equations, but he wants to study them again before the examination.
(A) familiar with (B) the most of (C) to study (D) before

16. Whoever inspected this radio should have put their identification number on the box.
(A) Whoever (B) this (C) should have (D) their

17. Most early settlers provided for themself before sharing their surplus with
(A) (B) (C) (D)
others.

18. Computers are indispensable in data processing, but some people are afraid
(A)
that its impersonal solutions might do harm to mankind in the long run.
(B) (C) (D)

19. Maria has long had the desire to become a famous writer even though the
(A) (B)
study of it would require years of sacrifice on her part.
(C) (D)

20. Every man and woman should vote for the candidate of her choice.
(A) (B) (C) (D)

21. In order to get married in this state, one must present a medical report
(A) (B)
along with your identification.
(C) (D)

22. If we finish all of our business as planned, Helen and me will leave for New
(A) (B) (C)
York on Monday morning.
(D)

23. William the Conqueror built the Tower of London to protect himself from
(A) (B)
them he had conquered.
(C) (D)

24. When science, business, and art learn something of each others' methods and
(A) (B)
goals, the world will have come closer to cultural harmony.
(C) (D)

25. She wore clothes that were better than that of the other girls.
(A) (B) (C) (D)

26. It is often easier to select a particular tool than to use them correctly.
(A) (B) (C) (D)

27. It was her who represented her country in the United Nations and later
(A) (B) (C) (D)
became ambassador to the United States.

28. The speaker announced that there was a small fire and directed them nearest
(A) (B) (C)
the door to leave first.
(D)

29. While some of lawyers would endorse the opposite view, most would
(A) (B) (C)
probably agree that freedom of the press is not absolute.
(D)

30. The good statesman, like all sensible human beings, always learns more from
(A) (B) (C)
their opponents than from his supporters.
(D)

标准答案

1. (A)	2. (B)	3. (B)	4. (D)	5. (C)	6. (C)	7. (C)	8. (B)	9. (A)	10. (A)
11. (B)	12. (B)	13. (D)	14. (A)	15. (B)	16. (D)	17. (B)	18. (B)	19. (C)	20. (D)
21. (D)	22. (B)	23. (C)	24. (B)	25. (C)	26. (D)	27. (B)	28. (B)	29. (A)	30. (D)

习题解说

1. almost all of the...　几乎所有的……
2. each other　彼此（两者）
   one another　彼此（三者以上）
3. a. 空格前有连词 but，故空格内置入指示代词 this（这个）即可。
   b. 关系代词 which 本身可做定语从句的关系代词，其前面不可再加连词 but。
   I have a book, which is good. (✓)
   I have a book, and which is good. (×)

I have a book, and it is good. (✓)

故 (A) 不可选。

4. from one visit to the next

= from one visit to another

5. animals 为可数名词，故其前不可用 much more，而要用 many more。

6. 做 by 的宾语，故用宾格 me。

7. students 为复数形式，其反身代词为 themselves。

8. himself 为 he 的反身宾格。

9. 所有格不可和指示代词（this、that、these 等）并置于名词前。

his that pen (×)

→ that pen of his (✓)

他的那支笔

10. As one nears 应改为 As you near 使主语一致。

11. (B) they have 应改为 have，因 have 已有主语 Many modern skyscrapers。

12. (B) themselves 应改为 himself 或 herself，因主语 Each member 是单数。

13. (D) a 应改为 one (one...another)。

14. (A) I 应改为 me，因 Henry and me 是 They asked us 之宾语同位语，故用宾格。

15. (B) the most of 应改为 most of the，或 most（做形容词用），修饰 calculus equations。

16. (D) their 应改为 his，因 whoever = any one who，恒做单数用。

17. (B) themself 应改为 themselves。

18. (B) its 应改为 their，因 computers 为复数。

19. (C) it 应改为 writing，因 it 不可能代替 a famous writer。

20. her 应改为 their 或 his or her。

21. (D) your 应改为 his（美语）或 one's（英语），因主语是 one。

One should love one's country.（较严谨）

= One should love his country.

22. (B) me 应改为 I，做主语。

23. (C) them 应改为 those，因其后有定语从句修饰，...those (whom) he had conquered。

24. (B) each others' 应改为 each other's，因 each other 恒无复数。

They like each other. (✓)

They like each others. (×)

25. (C) that 应改为 those = the clothes。
26. (D) them 应改为 it，it = this tool。
27. (B) her 应改为 she，It was...who 用来强调主语 she。
28. (B) them 应改为 those，those nearest... = those who were nearest...。
29. (A) some of 应改为 some of the 或 some。
30. (D) their 应改为 his，因主语 The good statesman 是单数。

A Quick Note

第十二章　复合形容词

概 述

复合形容词就是两个以上的词加连字符形成的形容词，通常置于名词之前，用以修饰该名词。一般而言，复合形容词有下列几种形式：

a. 数词 + 名词

例：The government has just mapped out a five-year plan to improve our secondary education.
（政府刚刚拟定一项改善中等教育的五年计划。）

b. 数词 + 名词 + 形容词

例：The ten-year-old boy is regarded as a child prodigy.
（这个 10 岁的男孩被视为神童。）

c. 名词 + 现在分词

例：The heart-breaking story made everyone cry.
（大家听到这个伤心的故事都哭了。）

d. 副词 + 现在分词

例：John is easy-going, which makes him quite popular.
（约翰很随和，这使他很受大家的欢迎。）

e. 名词 + 过去分词

例：The heart-broken man committed suicide.
（那个心碎的男子自杀了。）

f. 形容词 + 名词变成的过去分词

例：Everyone likes that kind-hearted old man.
（每个人都喜欢那个好心的老伯伯。）

g. well / ill + 过去分词

例: This is a well-organized company.
（这是一家很有组织的公司。）

兹分项说明如下：

1. 数词 + 名词：

a. 数词修饰名词时，该名词一定是可数名词，数词若为 one，名词一定是单数，但数词若为 two 以上时，则名词一定是复数。

例: This program will last one year, but that program will last five years.
（这个计划会持续一年，但那个计划则会持续五年。）

b. 数词若为 zero（零）时，由于为无限大，故之后应置复数名词。

例: It's zero degree Celsius. (×)
→ It's zero degrees Celsius. (√)
（现在气温是摄氏零度。）

c. 如何将"数词 + 名词"变成复合形容词？

1) 保留数词；
2) 在数词之后置入连字符，再接名词。不论数词是 one 或 two 以上，之后的名词恒为单数。

例: This five-years plan may take more than five years to carry out. (×)
→ This five-year plan may take more than five years to carry out. (√)
（这项五年计划执行起来得超过五年。）

The zero-degrees temperature is unbearable. (×)
→ The zero-degree temperature is unbearable. (√)
（零度的气温让人受不了。）

2. 数词 + 名词 + 形容词：

a. 此类结构中，"数词 + 名词"视为副词，修饰之后的形容词，数词若为 one，之后名词应为单数，数词若为 two 以上，则之后的名词应为复数。

例: John is five years old. (√)
（约翰 5 岁了。）
上列例句中，数词 five years 是副词，修饰形容词 old。

The road is three miles long. (√)
（这条路有 3 英里长。）

上列例句中，three miles 是副词，修饰形容词 long。

b. 如何将“数词 + 名词 + 形容词”变成复合形容词？

这种复合形容词仅限于与年龄有关：

1) 保留数词；
2) 在数词之后置入连字符，再接单数名词，该名词之后亦置入连字符，再接形容词 old 即告完成。

例: John is a five-years-old boy. (×)
→ John is a five-year-old boy. (✓)
（约翰是 5 岁的男孩。）

但其他“数词 + 名词 + 形容词”的结构，变成复合形容词时，原有的形容词一定要省略。

例: The three-miles-long road leads to my village. (×)
→ The three-mile road leads to my village. (✓)
（这条 3 英里长的路直通我的村落。）

3. 名词 + 现在分词：

此类结构形成的复合形容词一律由主动语态的定语从句化简而成。

a. 主动语态的定语从句

例: Mary is a girl who likes to break boys' hearts.
vt. (break)　o. (hearts)
（玛丽是个喜欢伤男孩子心的女孩。）

上列例句中，“who likes to break boys' hearts”是定语从句，及物动词 break 之后有宾语 hearts，属主动语态。

b. 如何将主动语态的定语从句变成复合形容词？

1) 找出做宾语的名词，并将该名词一律变作单数，之后置入连字符；
2) 将宾语前的及物动词变成现在分词，置入连字符之后，所形成的复合形容词置于被定语从句修饰的名词之前即告完成。

例: Mary is a girl who likes to break boys' hearts.
vt. (break)　o. (hearts)

a) 找出宾语 hearts，并将 hearts 变成单数 heart，之后置入连字符，即成 heart-；
b) 将宾语前的及物动词 break 变成现在分词 breaking，置入连字符之后，即成 heart-breaking（主动伤人心的），再将 heart-breaking 置于 girl 之前即告完成。故上句亦可改写如下：
Mary is a heart-breaking girl.
（玛丽是个会伤人心的女孩。）

c. 试将下列定语从句改为“名词 + 现在分词”的复合形容词结构：

1) This is an animal that eats men.
2) They are people who abide by the law.

解答：

1) This is a man-eating animal.
（这是个会吃人的动物。）
2) They are law-abiding people.
（他们是守法的人。）

d. 有些复合形容词因为常用的关系，日久就省略了连字符，成为一个词了。如 heart-breaking 早已改成 heartbreaking（伤人心的），blood-curdling 亦已改成 bloodcurdling（令人毛骨悚然的）。

4. 副词 + 现在分词：

主动语态的定语从句中的动词若为不及物动词，且有副词修饰时，该定语从句亦可化简为复合形容词，原则如下：

1) 找出定语从句中的副词，之后置入连字符；
2) 将从句中的不及物动词变成现在分词，置入连字符之后，即形成复合形容词，置于被定语从句修饰的名词之前即告完成。

例: The area which lay low was flooded.
定语从句
（这块低洼地区淹水了。）

a) 找出副词 low，之后置入连字符，即成 low-；
b) 将不及物动词 lay（lie 的过去式）变成现在分词 lying，置入连字符之后，即成 low-lying（地势低的），再将 low-lying 置于 area 之后即告完成。故上句亦可改写为：
The low-lying area was flooded.
（这块低洼地区淹水了。）

5. 名词 + 过去分词：

此类结构形成的复合形容词一律由被动语态的定语从句化简而成。

a. 被动语态的定语从句

例: I feel sorry for the boy whose heart is broken.
主语　被动语态
（我为那个心碎的男孩子感到难过。）

上列例句中，“whose heart is broken”是定语从句，主语 whose heart 之后有 is broken，是“be + 过去分词”形成的被动语态。

b. 如何将被动语态的定语从句变成复合形容词?

1) 找出做主语的名词，并将该名词一律变作单数，之后置入连字符；
2) 将被动语态的过去分词置入连字符之后，所形成的复合形容词置于被定语从句修饰的名词之前即告完成。

例: I feel sorry for the boy whose heart is broken.
　　　　　　　　　　　　　主语　被动语态

1) 找出做主语的名词 heart，之后置入连字符，即成 heart-；
2) 将被动语态的过去分词 broken 置入连字符之后，即成 heart-broken（心被打碎的），再将 heart-broken 置于 boy 之前即告完成。

故上句亦可改写如下：
I feel sorry for the heart-broken boy.
（我为那个心碎的男孩感到难过。）

6. 形容词 + 名词变成的过去分词:

a. 此类结构形成的复合形容词均与身体部位的器官或组织有关。

例: Who is that big-cycd girl?
（那个大眼睛的女孩子是谁？）

上列结构中，big 是形容词，eyed 是名词 eye 变成的现在分词。

b. 如何形成“形容词 + 名词变成的过去分词”之类的复合形容词?

在定语从句中，若有表“身体部位的器官或组织”的名词，之前有形容词修饰时，可在该形容词之后置入连字符，再将该名词变成过去分词置于连字符之后即成复合形容词。

例: a girl who has big eyes → a big-eyed girl
adj. n.　（大眼睛的女孩）

a soldier who has only one leg → a one-legged soldier
adj. n.　（独腿的战士）

a snake that has two heads → a two-headed snake
adj. n.　（两头蛇）

a boy who has a broken heart → a broken-hearted boy
adj. n.

或: a boy whose heart is broken → a heart-broken boy
被动语态　（伤心的男孩）

7. well 及 ill 如何形成复合形容词：

well 及 ill 之后亦可置连字符，再接过去分词，形成复合形容词。常用的此类复合形容词如下：

well-behaved	很守规矩的
well-bred	很有教养的
well-built	体格很棒的
well-chosen	慎选的
well-done	表现很棒的；（牛排）全熟的
well-dressed	穿着体面的
well-known	很出名的
well-mannered	彬彬有礼的
well-read	书读得很多的，饱读诗书的
well-traveled	去过很多地方的，老马识途的
ill-bred	没有教养的
ill-considered	考虑不周的
ill-fated	命运不好的，不幸的
ill-gotten	用不正当手段获得的
ill-judged	判断不当的
ill-mannered	态度不好的
ill-natured	心地不好的，本性坏的
但：good-natured	本性善良的（非 well-natured）

以上形容词可置于 be 动词之后做表语；亦可置于名词前，修饰该名词。

例：I like the child because he is well-behaved.
（我喜欢这孩子，因为他很乖。）

The ill-fated young man committed suicide in the end.
（这位命苦的年轻人最后自杀了。）

EXERCISE

请选出一个正确的答案：

1. David was brought up in a ______ country.
   (A) tearing-war (B) torn-war (C) war-torn (D) war-tearing
2. I live in a ______ building.
   (A) five-story (B) five-stories (C) five-story-high (D) five-storied
3. Who is that ______ man talking to John over there?
   (A) gray-hair (B) gray-hairy (C) gray-hairs (D) gray-haired
4. The president will step down because of the scandal, ______ sources said today.
   (A) well-informing (B) well-inform
   (C) well-informed (D) well-information
5. Mary's miniskirt is indeed ______ in the picture.
   (A) eye-caught (B) eye-catching
   (C) catching-eye (D) eyes-catching

标准答案

1. (C) 2. (A) 3. (D) 4. (C) 5. (B)

习题解说

1. war-torn a. 被战争撕裂的，饱受战争摧残的
2. five-story a. 五层楼高的（数词 + 单数名词）
3. gray-haired a. 白发苍苍的（hair 为身体组织，故用过去分词）
4. well-informed sources 消息灵通人士（新闻用语）
5. eye-catching （主动）引起注意的

A Quick Note

第十三章　介词的用法

第一节　at

1. at + 建筑物（邮局、车站、银行、学校等）　在某建筑物（可能在其内或其外面）

at the post office / station / bank　在邮局/车站/银行（之内或之外）

例: We're going to meet at the station.
（我们将在车站碰面。）

注意

a. 城市、国家等则与介词 in 连用。

in the city / my hometown / the United States
在城市里/我的故乡/美国

例: There's a famous temple in my hometown.
（我的故乡有一座有名的寺庙。）

b. 若强调“在某建筑物内”则介词仍须使用 in。

in the post office / station / bank　在邮局/车站/银行里

例: My husband works in this office building.
（我先生在这栋办公大楼上班。）

2. at + 人　对某人（尤指近距离，常与 yell、point、shout、laugh 等动词连用。此处 at 表“朝向”）

yell / shout at 人　对某人吼叫/咆哮

laugh at 人　嘲笑某人

point at 人　指着某人

例: The man always shouts at his wife when he is angry.
（那个男人生气时总是对他的太太咆哮。）

Don't laugh at the poor beggar, Johnny.
（约翰尼，不要嘲笑那个可怜的乞丐。）

The teacher pointed at him and said, "I saw you cheat on the test."
（老师指着他说：“我看到你考试时作弊。”）

比较:

point to...　　指着远处的……

例: He pointed to the house on the hilltop and said, "It's my house."
（他指着山顶上的房子说："那是我的家。"）

3. at 与下列名词连用，表"从事某活动"：

be at work　　上班, 做事

be at church　　做礼拜

be at school　　上学

be at rest　　休息

例: Selena is at work now; don't bother her.
（赛琳娜正在工作，不要打扰她。）

A: Where's Jack?

B: He's at church.

（A：杰克在哪里？）
（B：他去做礼拜。）

A: Is Frank at home?

B: No, he's at school.

（A：弗兰克在家吗？）
（B：不在，他在学校。）

You can go ask the manager now; he's at rest in the lobby.
（你现在可以去问经理；他正在大厅里休息。）

4. at 亦与度数/程度/价格/年龄等与数词有关的名词连用：

at the price / cost / expense of + 数词　　以……的价格

at the age of + 年龄　　在……的岁数时

at the speed of + 速度　　以……的速度

例: I bought the portable CD player at the price of $450.
（我以 450 美元的价格买了这台 CD 随身听。）

Sandy had her first child at the age of 32.
（珊蒂在 32 岁时生了第一个小孩。）

She drove at the speed of 28 miles an hour.
（她当时以时速 28 英里的速度开车。）

第二节 by

1. 表“在……旁边”，相当于 beside：

by the window 在窗边
by the door 在门边
by my side 在我旁边

例: The woman always sat by the window and stared into the distance.
（那位女士总是坐在窗边，凝视着远方。）

He came over and stood by my side.
（他走过来站在我旁边。）

2. 表“凭借”：

judge A by B 通过 B 来评鉴、判断 A
tell A by B 通过 B 知道是 A

例: Don't judge a person by his or her looks.
（不要以貌取人。）

I can tell by his action that he is a naughty boy.
（从他的行为我可以判断他是一个调皮的男孩。）

3. by 与下列表“抓”的动词连用，仍表“通过”：

catch / grab / grasp / hold / seize / take + 人 + by the + 身体部位或衣物的部分
抓住某人的……

例: The man seized him by the collar and told him to shut up.
（那个男人抓住他的衣领叫他闭嘴。）

注意

此句型中 by 之后只可接 the，不可接所有格。

I caught him by the hand.
（我抓住了他的手。）

不可说 I caught him by his hand. (×)

4. by 亦表“经过”之意：

pass by my house 经过我家
drive by my house 开车经过我家
walk by my house 走路经过我家

例: I passed by my house and didn't walk in.
（我经过家门而没有走进去。）

5. by 亦表“差距”之意，尤用于下列用法：

be older than + 人 + by two years 比某人大两岁
be younger than + 人 + by two years 比某人小两岁

例: She is older than I by five years.
（她比我大 5 岁。）

We beat the other team by two points.
（我们以两分之差赢了另一个队。）

6. by 亦表“按照”：

例: They sell eggs by the dozen.
（他们论打卖鸡蛋。）
*上句中，by 之后置 the，再置度量单位名词，如 by the box（论盒）、by the yard（论码）。

It is five twenty by my watch.
（我的表现在是 5 点 20。）

7. by 亦表“取道”：

come back by way of Hong Kong 取道香港回来
= come back via Hong Kong

例: We went to Beijing by way of Hong Kong.
（我们取道香港前往北京。）

8. by 亦表“乘坐（交通工具）”：

come back by bus / train / ship / air / bicycle / motorcycle
乘公交车/火车/船/飞机/（骑）自行车/（骑）摩托车回来

例: He goes to work by taxi every day.
（他每天乘出租车上班。）

注意

a. 以上句型中交通工具不可与冠词或所有格连用。
*不可说 by the train、by a car、by my taxi。
b. 表“步行”时则应使用“on foot”。

例: He came back on foot.
（他是走路回来的。）

9. by 亦用于被动语态，表“被……”：

be + 过去分词 + by...

例: He was killed by a car.
（他被车撞死了。）

10. by 亦可用于主动语态：

by + 动名词　　用/通过……

例: He succeeded by working hard.
（他通过努力取得成功。）

The old woman makes a living by selling fruit.
（那个老太太以卖水果为生。）

11. by + 时间　　最迟不超过某时间

例: Come back by ten.
= Come back no later than ten.
（10 点以前要回来。）

第三节 for

1. 与表“动身”之意的动词连用，表“前往（某地）”：

set out / set off / depart for + 地点	动身前往某地
head for / to + 地点	朝某地前进
leave A 地 for B 地	离开 A 地前往 B 地

例: She set out for America last night.
（她昨晚动身前往美国。）

We headed for / to the pub after the movie.
（看完电影后我们就前往酒吧。）

He left Australia for New Zealand yesterday.
（他昨天离开澳大利亚前往新西兰。）

2. 表“为……的目的”：

do it for you	为了你做这件事
for the sake of...	为了……的缘故

例: Don't blame him. After all, he did it for you.
（不要责怪他。毕竟，他这件事是为你做的。）

He does everything for the sake of money.
（他做每件事都是为了钱。）

3. 表“赞成”：

be for + 事　　赞成某事
= be in favor of + 事

例: Are you for his idea?
= Are you in favor of his idea?
（你赞成他的想法吗？）

4. 表“为了……的原因”：

reward + 人 + for + 事　　因为某事而奖励某人

例: The villagers rewarded him for saving the girl.
（村民报答他救了那个小女孩。）

5. 表“当做……”：

use A for B　　把 A 当做 B 使用

take A for B (误)把 A 当做 B

例: The natives use some insects for food.
(那些原住民以一些昆虫为食。)

I took John for a girl because he wears long hair.
(我把约翰误当作女孩子,因为他留长发。)

6. 表"找寻":

be hard pressed for time 时间不够用(而需寻找时间)

look for... 寻找……

例: The lady wears many hats. She is always hard pressed for time.
(那位女士扮演多重角色。她的时间总是不够用。)

7. 表"持续(一段时间)":

例: I have learned Japanese for three years.
(我已经学了 3 年日语了。)

I haven't seen John for a long time / for ages.
(我好长一段时间没见到约翰了。)

8. for 亦用于下列句型中:

It is + 非表人之本性或气质的形容词 + for sb to + 原形动词...

对某人来说(做)……是……的。

例: It is necessary for you to study English.
(学英语对你来说是有必要的。)

比较:
It is + 表人之本性或气质的形容词(如 kind、cruel、stupid)+ of sb to + 原形动词...
某人做某事实在很……。

例: It is very kind of you to help me.
(你能帮我真是太好了。)

9. 表"开往(某地点)(的交通工具)":

例: The flight for Chicago will depart at two thirty.
(往芝加哥的班机将在 2 点30 分起飞。)

10. 表"以……价格":

例: I bought the book for only $10.
(这本书我 10 元就买到了。)

第四节 from

1. 表“从……”：

from A to B 从 A 到 B

from Macao to Hong Kong 从澳门到香港

from what he said 从他所说的话

go from bad to worse 每况愈下

例: It takes more than an hour to fly from Shanghai to Hong Kong.
（从上海飞往香港要花一个多小时。）

I couldn't figure out what he meant from his words.
（从他的话中我无法了解他的意思。）

Their business has gone from bad to worse since that incident.
（从那次事件后，他们的生意就每况愈下。）

be made from... 由……做的（成品不能还原成原料）

例: This wine is made from grapes.
（这酒是葡萄酿造的。）→ 酒不能还原成葡萄

比较:

be made of... 由……做的（制成的成品其原料本质不变）

例: This table is made of wood.
（这张桌子是用木头做的。）→ 木头制成桌子后本质仍不变

2. 表“戒除”：

refrain from + 动名词 戒除/控制……

例: Jeff could not refrain from laughing.
= Jeff could not help laughing.
（杰夫忍不住大笑。）

3. from 亦可与表“禁止、阻止、保护”的动词连用，此处 from 表“免于”：

ban / prohibit / restrict / restrain sb from + 动名词 禁止某人（做）……

prevent / stop / keep sb from + 动名词 阻止某人（做）……

protect sb from + 动名词 保护某人免于……

例: He was prohibited from smoking in the lobby.
（他被禁止在大厅里抽烟。）

The woman came in time to prevent her son from killing himself.
（那位女士及时赶来阻止了她的儿子自杀。）

The prince protected the princess from being attacked by the bandit.
（王子保护公主免受盗匪攻击。）

比较:

forbid sb to + 原形动词　　禁止某人（做）……

例: Our teacher forbids us to bring comic books to school.
（我们老师禁止我们带漫画书到学校。）

不过亦有将 forbid 与 from 连用，形成下列的用法：

Our teacher forbids us from bringing comic books to school.
（我们老师禁止我们带漫画书到学校。）

*考试时，仍以"forbid sb to + 原形动词"为准。

第五节 in

1. 表“在……之内”，如建筑物、空间、书、文件、公司等：

in the house	在房子里
in the park	在公园里
in the magazine	在杂志里
in this company	在这家公司里

例: Your dog is in the house, not in the backyard.
（你的狗在房子里，不在后院。）

The kids are playing in the park.
（孩子们正在公园里玩。）

There's a report about this superstar in the current issue of *Time*.
（这一期的《时代》杂志中有一篇关于这位超级巨星的报道。）

Eighty percent of the workers in this company are female.
（这家公司有 80% 的员工是女性。）

2. 表“穿/戴着……”：

be dressed in...　　身穿/戴着……
= wear...

例: Who is the girl that is dressed in red?
= Who is the girl that is wearing a red dress?
（那个穿着红衣服的女孩是谁？）

比较:

put on 指“穿”的动作

例: She put on her coat before going out.
（她出门前穿上她的外套。）

3. “in + 一段时间”表“在一段时间之后”，相当于“一段时间 + later”，亦可表“在一段时间之内”，此时 in 相当于 within：

例: I'll be back in two minutes.
= I'll be back two minutes later.
（我两分钟后就会回来。）

I think I can finish the work in two minutes.

= I think I can finish the work within two minutes.
（我想我在两分钟内就可以完成这项工作。）

4. 表"以……（颜料、工具等）"：

write the letter in ink / pencil　　用墨水/铅笔写信
write the word in chalk　　用粉笔写字

注意

pencil 当不可数名词，指"铅笔的颜料"，若当可数名词，则指"铅笔"要用"with a pencil"（用一支铅笔）。chalk 原指"滑石粉"，亦是粉笔的原料，是不可数名词，表"用一支粉笔"要用"with a piece of chalk"（非 with a chalk）来表示。

write the words in ink　　用钢笔写字
= write the words with a pen
write the words in pencil　　用铅笔写字
= write the words with a pencil
write the words in chalk　　用粉笔写字
= write the words with a picce of chalk

例: She wrote a letter to me in ink.
（她用钢笔给我写了一封信。）

The professor wrote some words in chalk on the blackboard.
（教授用粉笔在黑板上写了几个字。）

5. 表"按……次序"：

in alphabetical order　　按字母顺序
keep...in order　　将……整理好/整齐

例: He put the papers in the folders in alphabetical order.
（他把文件按照字母顺序放入档案夹中。）

Keep your room in order before the guests come.
（客人来之前把你的房间整理好。）

6. 表"以……语言/声音"：

write in Chinese　　用中文写
speak in a low voice　　低声说话
talk in a bitter tone　　以尖刻的语调说话

例: It's surprising that the foreigner can write in Chinese.
（这老外会写中文，真令人惊讶。）

Kate is speaking to her friend in a low voice.
（凯特正低声在和她的朋友说话。）

My mother stared at Tim and talked in a bitter tone.
（我母亲凝视着提姆，并以尖刻的语调说话。）

比较:

with a heavy Japanese accent　带有浓重的日本口音

例: The man spoke with a heavy Japanese accent.
（那个男子说话带有浓重的日本口音。）

第六节 on

1. 表“接触在某物体的表面上”：

on the table　　在桌上

on the roof　　在屋顶上

例: The maid put the dishes on the dining table.
（女仆把碗盘放在餐桌上。）

There are two cats on the roof.
（屋顶上有两只猫。）

2. 与表“距离”的名词连用：

go on a trip / journey　　去旅行

go on an expedition　　去探险/远征

go on an excursion　　（尤指团体）去远足

例: My husband likes to go on a trip to Japan at this time of the year.
（我先生喜欢在每年的这个时候去日本旅行。）

Those explorers went on an expedition to the Sahara.
（那些探险家去撒哈拉沙漠探险。）

The students in the sixth grade are going on an excursion today.
（六年级的学生今天要去远足。）

3. 与表“差遣”的名词连用：

be on an errand　　跑腿，办差事

be on a mission　　身负使命

例: A: Where's Johnny?
B: He's out on an errand.
（A：约翰尼在哪里？）
（B：他出去办点差事。）

The soldiers were sent to the front on a mission.
（那些军人被派往前线作战。）

4. 与表“约会”的名词连用：

be on a date with sb 跟某人约会

例: Were you on a date with the man over there last night?
（你昨晚和那边那位男士约会了吗？）

5. 与表“特别饮食”的名词连用：

be on a diet 节食

例: Cindy won't eat these cakes. She's on a diet.
（辛蒂不会吃这些蛋糕的。她正在节食。）

6. 与 run、go 等名词连用，表“持续的动作”：

be on the run 到处流窜

be on the go 忙碌（= be busy）

例: The three wanted men have been on the run for six months.
（那三名通缉犯已经逃亡六个月了。）

My eldest sister is always on the go.
（我大姐总是忙个不停。）

7. 与表“平地”或“大陆”的名词连用：

on campus 在校园内

on the mainland 在大陆

on the farm / ranch 在农场/牧场上

例: The club held many activities on campus this week.
（该社团这星期在校园里举办了许多活动。）

Life on Hainan is different in many ways from life on the mainland.
（海南岛居民的生活和大陆的居民在很多方面不同。）

They rear cattle and sheep on the ranch.
（他们在牧场上饲养牛羊。）

比较:

off campus 在校外

例: Students should behave themselves even off campus.
（学生即使在校外也应该守规矩。）

8. 与表“线状 / 线条”意味的名词连用：

live on that street	住在那条街上
walk on the beach	在海滩散步（海滩为线状）
on the coast	在海岸上
on the brim / edge / verge of...	在……的边缘
on the frontier	在边境

例: The Green family live on that street.
（格林家住在那条街上。）

I like to walk on the beach with my boyfriend.
（我喜欢和男友在海滩散步。）

The village is located on the coast.
（那个村子位于海岸上。）

The entrepreneur is on the verge of bankruptcy.
（那位企业家正濒临破产的边缘。）

Many rare animals are on the edge of extinction.
（很多稀有动物濒临绝种。）

There are few people living on the frontier.
（边境地区很少有人居住。）

9. 表“凭，靠”之意：

on foot　　步行（非 by foot）

例: Do you go to school on foot every morning?
（你每天早上都是走路上学吗？）

10. 表“根据、遵照”：

act on one's advice	按照某人的建议行事
act on one's order	遵照某人的命令行事

例: I'll act on your advice and try to achieve the goal.
（我会按照你的建议行事，试着去达成目标。）

Don't ask too much. Just act on my order.
（不要问太多。只要遵照我的命令行事就对了。）

11. 与表有关“无线电器材”之名词连用：

on / over the telephone　在打电话
on television　在电视屏幕上（非 on the television）
on / over the radio　在广播中

例: Steven is talking on the telephone.
（史蒂文正在打电话。）

I saw your daughter perform on television last night.
（我昨晚看到你女儿在电视上表演。）

We heard the news on the radio this afternoon.
（今天下午我们在广播中听到这个消息。）

12. 与表“赞美、恭贺”的名词连用，表“为了/因为……”：

congratulate sb on（代）名词/动名词　因……而恭贺某人

例: His family congratulated him on passing the exam.
（他的家人恭喜他通过了考试。）

13. 与“日子”连用：

on Sunday　在星期天
on December 11　在 12 月 11 日

例: Emile goes to church on Sundays.
（埃米尔星期天都上教堂。）

We're going to celebrate Leon's birthday on December 11.
（我们将在 12 月 11 日庆祝利昂的生日。）

注意

in the morning / afternoon / evening　在早上/下午/傍晚
at night　在晚上

但 morning / afternoon / evening 如与日子连用时，介词用 on。

on the afternoon of August 16　在 8 月 16 日下午
on Monday morning　在星期一早上
on Saturday night　在星期六晚上

例: The famous singer got together with his fans on the afternoon of August 16.
（那位著名歌手在 8 月 16 日下午和他的歌迷聚会。）

We always have a meeting on Monday morning.
（我们总是在星期一早晨开会。）

14. 表“请客”：

例: Everything is on me.
（一切我请客。）

＊但 be on the house 表“主人请客”之意。

We had a drink on the house last Saturday.
（上星期六主人招待我们喝酒。）

15. on 的其他重要用法：

on call　随时待命

on duty　值班/上班时间中

例: The firefighters are on call for emergencies.
（消防队员随时为紧急情况待命。）

The guard is on duty from 7:00 a.m. to 9:00 p.m.
（警卫的值班时间是从早上 7 点到晚上 9 点。）

第七节 to

1. 通常表“到达、往”之意：

go to the station 到车站去

turn to the right 右转

= turn right（非 turn to right，因为 right 之前无 the 时，是副词）

be moved to tears 感动得落泪

up to + 数词 多达（若干数词）

例: What time are you going to the station?
（你几点要去车站？）

Turn to the right at the next crossroads.
= Turn right at the next crossroads.
（在下一个十字路口右转。）

He was moved to tears by the movie *Titanic*.
（他被《泰坦尼克号》这部电影感动得落泪。）

He makes up to $ 50,000 per month.
（他每个月赚将近 5 万美元。）

2. 与“人”连用，表“对某人而言”：

be everything to sb 是某人的一切

例: Her children are everything to her.
（她的子女是她的一切。）

3. 与下列名词连用，形成固定用法，表“针对”之意：

the key to success 成功的关键
（非 the key of success）

the answer to the question 问题的答案
（非 the answer of the question）

the solution to the problem 解决问题之道
（非 the solution of the problem）

例: The key to success is diligence.
（成功的关键就是勤奋。）

The answer to this question is unknown.
（这个问题的答案没人知道。）

She brought forward a solution to the problem.
（她提出了一个解决这个问题的方法。）

4. 表“附加”之意：

the annex to the building	这栋大楼的附属建筑物
the amendment to the constitution	宪法修正案

例: The old man lives in the annex to the building.
（那个老人住在这栋大楼的附属建筑物里。）

The amendment to the constitution is still under discussion in the parliament.
（这项宪法修正案仍在国会讨论中。）

5. to 亦与情绪名词连用，形成“To one's + 情绪名词，……”（令某人……的是，……），通常置于句首：

To one's surprise,...	令某人惊讶的是，……
To one's joy,...	令某人高兴的是，……
To one's satisfaction,...	令某人满意的是，……
To one's dismay,...	令某人沮丧的是，……
To one's astonishment,...	令某人惊奇的是，……

例: To my surprise, he left without saying anything.
（令我惊讶的是，他什么也没说就离开了。）

To our joy, he passed the entrance exam and entered a good university.
（令我们高兴的是，他通过了入学考试，进入一所好大学就读。）

To their satisfaction, this new product sells well.
（令他们满意的是，这款新产品卖得很好。）

To his dismay, he found his car was gone.
（令他沮丧的是，他发现他的车不见了。）

To the audience's astonishment, the magician appeared again after the fire disappeared.
（令观众惊奇的是，火焰消失后魔术师再度出现。）

注意

表“就某人所知”亦与介词 to 连用。

例: To my understanding / knowledge, John moved to Hong Kong early this month.
（就我所知，这个月初约翰已经移居香港了。）

6. 表“配合（音乐、曲调、节拍等）”：

dance to the music	随着音乐跳舞
*不可说 dance with the music	抱着音乐一起跳舞 (×)
dance to the melody	随着旋律跳舞

例: The teacher had the music on and everyone started to dance to the music.
（老师放音乐后，大家便开始随着音乐跳舞。）

比较:

dance with sb　　与某人跳舞

例: I'd like to dance with you.
（我想和你跳舞。）

7. “be up to + 事”表“从事某事”，通常指令人怀疑或不好的事，常用于疑问句：

例: What are you up to?
（你在搞什么鬼？）

但“It's up to sb.”则表“由某人做决定。”

例: A: Should I do it?
B: It's up to you!
（A：要不要由我来做这件事？）
（B：由你决定吧！）

第八节　with

1. 表“使用（某物）”之意：

cut it with a knife　　用刀切它
do it with care　　以谨慎的心做这件事

例: Mom cut the potato with a knife.
（妈用刀子切马铃薯。）

She does everything with care.
（她谨慎地做每一件事。）

2. 与“人”连用，表“跟随（某人），和（某人）”：

do it with me　　跟我一起做这件事

例: Come with me. I'll show you something.
（跟我来。我给你看一样东西。）

3. with 亦可放句首，表“有……；随着……”：

例: With your help, I have nothing to worry about.
= Having your help, I have nothing to worry about.
（有你的帮忙，我没什么好担心的。）

With the passing of time, he's getting older.
（随着时间的流逝，他的年纪越来越大。）

注意

with 表上述之意时不一定要置于句首，亦可置于名词之后。

a girl with big eyes　　一个（有）大眼睛的女孩
rise with the sun　　随着太阳升起而起床

例: He is a man with a big nose.
（他是个有大鼻子的人。）

Abigail Van Buren, the writer of the column *Dear Abby*, rose with the sun every day.
（《艾比信箱》专栏的作者艾比盖尔·凡·布伦每天在太阳升起的同时便起床。）

4. with 也可形成复合结构，通常为大动作附带小动作时，大动作以本动词表示，小动作则使用 with 复合结构，其结构为：

with + 宾语 + 形容词/介词短语/分词/副词（做宾语补语）

例: He was sitting there with his arms folded.
（当时他双臂交叉着坐在那里。）
＊上句中“坐”为主要动词，“双臂交叉”为附带动作，故后者使用“with his arms folded”。

He was talking to me with a pipe in his mouth.
（当时他嘴里含着烟斗跟我说话。）
＊上句中“讲话”为主要动词，“嘴里含烟斗”为附带动作。

注意
在该结构中，若为“with + 宾语 + 介词短语”时，可将该结构中的 with、冠词及所有格予以省略，保留名词，故上句亦可写成“He was talking to me pipe in mouth.”。

5. with 亦可与表“疾病”之意的名词连用：

with + 疾病	因某疾病而病倒了
be ill with + 疾病	生了某疾病
come down with + 疾病	患了/得了某疾病
be infected with + 疾病	感染某疾病
= contract + 疾病	
be attacked with + 疾病	因某疾病而病倒了

例: Her father fell ill with lung cancer last month.
（她父亲上个月因肺癌病倒了。）

Many students in the class were infected with the flu.
（这个班有很多学生得了流行性感冒。）

6. with 亦表“因为”，与 what 连用：

例: What with his laziness and illness, he was fired.
= Partly because of his laziness and partly because of his illness, he was fired.
（一方面因为懒惰，另一方面因为生病，所以他被开除了。）

7. with 的其他常态用法：

leave sth with sb	将某物留给某人
compare A with B	将 A 与 B 作比较
be popular with + 一群人	受某一群人欢迎
be wrong with sb	某人出了差错

= be the matter with sb

例: His parents left a fortune with him after they died.
（他的父母死后留给他一笔财富。）

Most parents like to compare their kids with other kids.
（大多数的父母喜欢拿他们的孩子和别的小孩比较。）

The humorous professor is popular with his students.
（这位幽默的教授很受他学生的欢迎。）

Something's wrong with her.
（她有点不对劲。）

What's the matter with you?
（你怎么了？）

第九节 about

1. 表“环绕”之意，相当于 around：

sit about the campfire　　坐在营火边

= sit around the campfire

turn about　　向后转（= turn around）

beat about / around the bush　　说话兜圈子

例: Stop beating about the bush and get to the point.
（说话别再兜圈子了，快说重点。）

When she heard someone calling her, she turned about to see who it was.
（她听到有人叫她时，转过头去看是谁。）

2. 表“有关”，相当于 on / concerning / regarding：

write an article about air pollution　　写一篇有关空气污染的文章

= write an article on / concerning / regarding air pollution

例: He wrote an article about astrology.
（他写了一篇有关占星术的文章。）

We'll have a meeting about environmental protection.

= We'll have a meeting on / concerning / regarding environmental protection.
（我们将开一个有关环保问题的会议。）

但 about 多为口语用法，on 则在文字中使用，通常与书或文章题目连用。

a book on the Renaissance　　一本有关文艺复兴的书

第十节　after

1. 表“在（一段时间）之后”：

after three years　　3 年后

例: The man came back to his hometown after three years.
（那名男子3 年后回到了他的故乡。）

2. 表“追逐”，通常与动词连用：

be after 人　　追逐/追捕某人
= run after 人
= chase (after) 人

例: The police are still after the thief.
= The police are still running after the thief.
= The police are still chasing (after) the thief.
（警方仍在追缉这名小偷。）

但 chase (after) 亦可指“追求异性”。

例: He is chasing (after) Mary.
（他正在追求玛丽。）

3. 表“像，模仿”：

take after...　　像……
= resemble...
= look like...

例: He takes after his father.
= He resembles his father.
= He looks like his father.
（他长得像他爸爸。）

This is a picture after van Gogh.
（这是一幅模仿梵高画风的画。）

第十一节　toward

1. 表“朝向”：

toward sb　　朝某人的方向

toward the station　　朝车站的方向

toward evening　　快傍晚时

例: The girl ran toward him with a bright smile.
（那个女孩带着灿烂的笑容跑向他。）

比较:

forward　　往前 (adv.)

backward　　往后，倒退 (adv.)

wayward　　任性的；四面八方的 (adj.)

例: The little child is toddling forward.
（那个小孩正摇摇晃晃地向前走。）

The students were asked to run backward.
（学生们被要求倒退着跑。）

She is a wayward girl, who never thinks about others.
（她是个任性的女孩，从不会为别人着想。）

2. 表“对于”：

one's attitude toward / to...　　某人对……的态度

例: What's your attitude toward mercy killing?
（你对于安乐死的看法如何？）

第十二节　except

1. 表“除了……之外”，通常与涵盖性完全的形容词（all、every、any、no）连用，并可以 save 取代 except，但 save 为古老用法：

例: All except him will go.
= All save him will go.
（除了他之外，所有的人都会去。）

＊不可说“Most people except him will go.”，因为 most 不是涵盖性完全的形容词。

I like any kind of fruit except guavas.
（除了番石榴之外，任何水果我都喜欢。）

Everybody can do it except Peter.
（除了彼得之外，每个人都可以做这件事。）

＊不可说“Many people can do it except Peter.”，因为 many 不是涵盖性完全的形容词。

He enjoys nothing except music.
（除了音乐之外，他什么都不喜欢。）

＊但“nothing except”亦可用“nothing but”取代，故上句亦可写成“He enjoys nothing but music.”。

2. except 之后亦可接 that 从句或“for + 名词”，表示“只可惜……”或“只不过是……”：

例: He is quite nice except that he is bad-tempered.
= He is quite nice except for his bad temper.
（他人蛮不错，只不过脾气不好。）

第十三节 behind

1. 表"在……之后"：

behind 表此意时与 after 用法不同，after 通常与动词连用，表动态的"追逐"之意，尤与动词 run 连用，形成"run after..."（追逐……）的固定短语。behind 则为静态。

例: There is a tree behind the house.
（房子后面有一棵树。）

*上句不可说"There is a tree after the house."。

He is sitting behind me.
（他正坐在我后面。）

She is standing behind the door.
（她正站在门后面。）

2. 表"落后"：

behind schedule　比预定时间落后

例: He always finishes his work behind schedule.
（他总是比预定时间落后完成工作。）

比较:

on schedule　按预定时间

ahead of schedule　比预定时间提前

例: We'll try to keep everything running on schedule.
（我们会尽量使每件事按预定时间进行。）

The train arrived ahead of schedule.
（火车比预定时间提前到达。）

第十四节　into

1. 通常与动态动词连用，表“进入”：

walk into the classroom　　走进教室
run into the room　　跑进房间

例: As soon as the teacher walked into the classroom, the class became quiet.
（老师一走进教室，全班立刻变得很安静。）

My sister ran into the room and told me the good news.
（我妹妹跑进房间告诉我这个好消息。）

注意

“run into + 人”表“与某人巧遇”，等于“bump into + 人”。

例: I ran into an old friend on the street yesterday.
= I bumped into an old friend on the street yesterday.
（我昨天在街上巧遇一位老朋友。）

2. 表“转变成”：

change / transform / turn A into B　　将 A 转变成 B
translate A into B　　将 A 翻译成 B

例: The witch transformed herself into a little girl.
（那个女巫把自己变成一个小女孩。）

Our homework today is to translate a Chinese article into English.
（我们今天的作业就是把一篇中文文章翻译成英语。）

3. 与 be 动词连用，形成“be into”的短语，表“热衷于……”：

例: He is into classical music.
（他热衷于古典音乐。）

第十五节 within

1. 表“在……之内”，尤指在某空间或某时间之内，相当于 in：

within the country　　在这个国家之内
= in the country
within an hour　　在一小时之内
= in an hour

例: There's no desert within the country.
= There's no desert in the country.
（这个国家没有沙漠。）

I believe he can finish it within an hour.
= I believe he can finish it in an hour.
（我相信他能在一小时内完成。）

但 in an hour 亦可指“在一小时之后”。

例: He finished the work in an hour.
（他在一个小时之后完成了工作。）

2. 亦可指范围，表“在……范围内”：

act within the law　　在法律范围内行事

例: A law-abiding citizen should act within the law.
（守法的公民应该依法行事。）

第十六节　without

1. 表“没有/无……”：

coffee without sugar　　无糖的咖啡
without his help　　没有他的帮助

例: Robert likes to drink coffee without sugar.
（罗伯特喜欢喝无糖的咖啡。）

I couldn't have succeeded without his help.
（若没有他的帮助，我当时就无法成功。）

2. 与 without 有关的短语：

can do without...　　没有……也行
cannot do without...　　没有……就不行
It goes without saying + that 从句　　不用说，……。

例: I can do without money, but I can't do without your love.
（我可以没有钱，但不能没有你的爱。）

It goes without saying that money can't buy everything.
（不用说，金钱不能买到每一样东西。）

第十七节 above

1. 表“在……之上”，通常指空间、离开地面或某物体表面之上，相当于 over：

例: Some birds are flying above the city.

= Some birds are flying over the city.

（有几只鸟正在城市上空飞翔。）

2. 表“地理位置在……的上方”：

例: Keelung is located above Taipei on the map.

（在地图上，基隆位于台北的上方。）

3. 表“超过/超越”，与数词连用：

例: No one above the age of twenty-six can stay in the youth hostel.

（年龄超过 26 岁的人不能入住这家青年旅社。）

4. 在下列短语中，above 表“不屑”之意：

be above + 动名词　　不屑/不愿（做）……

例: He is above cheating.

（他不屑于欺骗别人。）

但 be not above + 动名词　　愿意（做）……

例: He is not above asking questions.

（他总是不耻下问。）

第十八节　over

1. 表“在……之上”，但通常为悬空的状态，相当于 above：

be over the city　　在城市上空
= be above the city

例: An eagle is flying over the mountaintop.
（有一只老鹰正在山顶上空飞。）

2. 表“覆盖在……之上”，为有接触物体的状态：

put one's hands over one's face　　把某人的手放在某人的脸上

例: He put his hands over her face, telling her not to worry.
（他把手放在她的脸上，告诉她不要担心。）

3. 表“（悬空）掠过”，尤与动词 jump 连用：

jump over the wall　　跳过这座墙

例: The thief jumped over the wall and ran down the street.
（那名窃贼跳过墙跑到街上去了。）

4. 与地点名词连用，表“在某地方的另一头”：

somewhere over there　　在那儿的某处

例: I live over the road.
（我住在马路那头。）

5. 与数词连用，表“超过”之意：

over + 数词　　超过某数词
= more than + 数词

例: Over twenty people were seriously injured in the traffic accident.
= More than twenty people were seriously injured in the traffic accident.
（在这场车祸中有超过 20 个人受了重伤。）

6. 与表“驾驭”同义之名词或动词连用：

have authority / control / power over...　　有支配、指挥……的权力
rule over...　　统治……

例: The president has authority over the army.
（总统有权指挥军队。）

The king has ruled over the people for ten years.
（这个国王已经统治人民 10 年了。）

7. 与咖啡、茶、三餐等连用，表“吃/喝……了一段时间”，常与 talk 连用：

例: We talked over a cup of tea.
（我们谈了一杯茶的光景。）

They talked over dinner.
（他们聊了一顿晚饭的时间。）

词辨

a. 当描述某物的位置高于另一物时，above 与 over 均可使用。

例: There is an attic above the house.
= There is an attic over the house.
（房子上方有一个阁楼。）

b. 但若表“从某物的一边移动到另一边”之动态动作，则只可用 over。

例: The child threw the ball over the wall.
（那个小孩把球丢到墙外。）

c. 另外 above 与 over 均可表“超越”，但 above 多与表示最小等级或一固定点之名词连用，over 则与数词、时间、年龄、金钱等连用。

例: Mt. Jade is 3952 meters above sea level.
（玉山的高度为海拔 3952 米。）

The boy is above average height for his age.
（这个男孩身高超过同龄的其他小孩。）

The man is over thirty.
（这个男人 30 多岁了。）

I spent over five hundred dollars buying this book.
（我花了 500 多元买这本书。）

第十九节 below

1. 表“在（某物体）的下方”：

write below the line　　写在横线下方

例: There is a supermarket below the department store.
（这家百货商店下面有一家超市。）

There is a waterfall far below the bridge.
（桥下的远处有个瀑布。）

2. 表“（数量等）少于……；（地位等）低于……”：

例: He is a man below fifty.
（他是个不到 50 岁的男子。）

A lieutenant is below a captain.
（上尉的军衔低于上校。）

第二十节 beneath

1. 表“在（某空间）之正下方”：

例: They live beneath the same roof.
（他们住在同一个屋檐下。）

2. 表“（身份、地位、智力等）低于……”，相当于 below：

例: Frank is far beneath Daniel in intelligence.
（弗兰克的智力远不及丹尼尔。）

3. 表“与……不相称；不值得”：

It is beneath sb to + 原形动词...　　从事……有失某人的身份。

marry beneath oneself　　与身份或社会地位比自己低的人结婚

例: It is beneath you to do this kind of thing.
（做这种事有失你的身份。）

She doesn't mind marrying beneath herself.
（她不介意与一个社会地位比自己低的人结婚。）

第二十一节 under

1. 表"在（某物体）的下面"：

under the tree　　在树下

under the bed　　在床下

例: The high school student sat under the tree with his girlfriend.
（那名高中生和他的女友坐在树下。）

I found my turtle under the bed.
（我在床底下找到我的乌龟。）

2. 表"低于……；少于……"：

under seven years old　　7 岁以下

例: People under twenty-one are not allowed to buy alcohol in America.
（在美国，21 岁以下的人不可以买酒。）

He is an officer under a commander.
（他是一名军衔低于中校的军官。）

3. 表"在……支配/控制/影响下"：

under the president　　由总统统治

under the influence of drugs　　在药物的影响下

例: The country is now under a benevolent queen.
（这个国家现在由一位仁慈的女王所统治。）

He told the truth under the influence of wine.
（他在酒醉后吐露了实情。）

4. 表"承受着（重担、压力等）；在……的情况/状态下"：

under the heavy pressure of work　　在沉重的工作压力下

under any circumstances　　在任何情况下

under construction　　施工中

例: She collapsed under the burden of debts.
（她在背负债务的重担下崩溃了。）

Don't tell others the secret under any circumstances.
（在任何情况下都不要告诉别人这个秘密。）

The bridge is still under construction.
（这座桥仍在施工中。）

5. 表“接受（考验、刑罚、手术等）”：

under an eye operation　　接受眼部手术
under penalty　　受到处罚

例: He is under an eye operation at that hospital.
（他在那家医院接受眼部手术。）

People who disobey the regulations will be under penalty.
（凡是违反规定的人就会受到处罚。）

6. 表“以……的名义/形式；假借……”：

under a false name / a pseudonym　　以假名
under the guise of a woman　　假扮成女人

例: She writes novels under the pseudonym of George Eliot.
（她以乔治・艾略特作为笔名来写小说。）

The man always steals cosmetics under the guise of a woman.
（那名男子总是假扮成女性去偷化妆品。）

7. 表“依照/根据（约定、法令等）”：

例: All people are equal under the U.S. constitution.
（根据美国宪法，人皆生而平等。）

8. 表“属于……项目”：

例: Novels come under literature.
（小说属于文学类。）

第二十二节 underneath

表“在……之下”，相当于 under 或 beneath：

underneath the table　　在桌子下

= under the table

= beneath the table

例: The cat is sleeping underneath the table.

= The cat is sleeping under the table.

= The cat is sleeping beneath the table.

（那只猫正在桌子底下睡觉。）

第二十三节 against

1. 表“对抗、抵制、反对”：

be against a plan　　反对一个计划

例: All members were against the plan he brought forward.

（所有成员都反对他提出的计划。）

2. 表“顶着”：

lean against the wall　　靠墙站

例: Be careful of the man leaning against the wall.

（小心那个靠墙站着的男子。）

3. 表“以……为背景”：

例: That color looks good against your skin.

（那个颜色在你皮肤的衬托下看起来不错。）

第二十四节 along

1. 表“沿着……”：

walk along the river　　沿着河走

例：Walk along the street and you'll see many bookstores.
（沿着街走，你会看到很多书店。）

2. 表“顺畅”：

get along with 人　　与某人相处得很好

例：Cynthia gets along with her classmates.
（辛西亚和她的同学们相处得很好。）

3. 与介词 with 连用，形成 along with，表“以及”之意，相当于 together with：

例：He, along with me, enjoys music.
= He, together with me, enjoys music.
（他和我都喜欢音乐。）

第二十五节 before

表“在……之前”，之后可接表空间或时间的名词：

stand before the car　　站在车前
before June　　在 6 月之前

例：The boy standing before the black car is my brother.
（站在那辆黑色汽车前的男孩是我哥哥。）
Elly will come back from Japan before December.
（艾莉在 12 月之前会从日本回来。）

第二十六节 beyond

表“超越”之意：

be beautiful beyond description	美得难以形容
beyond one's imagination	超乎某人的想象
beyond one's expectation	出乎某人意料之外

例: The scenery there is beautiful beyond description.
（那里的风景美得难以形容。）

He is so smart beyond our imagination.
（他的聪明超乎我们的想象。）

Jenny won the competition beyond everyone's expectation.
（珍妮出人意料地赢得了比赛。）

第二十七节 during

表“在（一段时间）期间”：

during his stay here	在他待在这里期间
during the two months	在这两个月中

例: Rebecca went shopping in Causeway Bay every weekend during her stay in Hong Kong.
（瑞贝卡待在香港期间每个周末都去铜锣湾逛街。）

I won't be here during the two months.
（这两个月期间我都不会在这里。）

第二十八节　through

1. 表“经过”：

walk through the crowd　走过人群

例: The singer walked through the crowd and left.
（那位歌手穿过人群离开了。）

2. 表“取道/通过”：

travel through Hong Kong　取道香港去旅游

例: We went to Canada through Hong Kong.
（我们取道香港去加拿大。）

3. 表“凭借”：

through one's help　凭借某人的帮助

through the magazine　通过这本杂志

例: Gina got the job through Linda's help.
（吉娜凭借琳达的帮助而获得这份工作。）

I knew Tom through the magazine.
（我是通过这本杂志认识汤姆的。）

4. 表“从（活动、场合等）开始到结束”：

through the whole meeting　从会议开始到结束

例: The manager didn't say a word through the whole meeting.
（从会议开始到结束经理一句话都没说。）

5. 表“整段时间”：

through the day　一整个白天

through the night　一整个晚上

例: He wandered around on the street through the day.
（他白天一整天都在街上游荡。）

Did you cram for the test through the night?
（你一整个晚上都在为考试临时抱佛脚吗？）

第二十九节 besides

表"除了……之外"，相当于"in addition to"：

besides +（代）名词/动名词　　除了……之外

= in addition to +（代）名词/动名词

例: Besides basketball, he also enjoys tennis.

= In addition to basketball, he also enjoys tennis.

（除了篮球，他也喜欢网球。）

Besides swimming, he can also roller-skate.

= In addition to swimming, he can also roller-skate.

（除了游泳，他也会滑冰。）

第三十节 till / until

表"直到……"：

till 与 until 可互通使用，不过 until 较 till 正式。

stay here till ten　　在这里待到 10 点

= stay here until ten

until 另常与 not 连用，形成：

not...until...　　直到……才……

例: He didn't come until nine o'clock.

= Not until nine o'clock did he come.

（他直到 9 点才来。）

till 有时与 from 连用，形成：

from...till...　　从……到……

= from...to...

例: We watched the movie from eight till ten.

= We watched the movie from eight to ten.

（那场电影我们从 8 点看到 10 点。）

第三十一节 since

表"自从……"，通常与完成时连用：

since + 时间名词/动名词　　自从……

例: He has been ill since Tuesday.
（他从星期二就开始生病了。）

Since graduating from college, she has been working in this company.
（自从大学毕业之后，她就一直在这家公司工作。）

第三十二节 beside

1. 表"在……之旁"，相当于 by 之意：

sit beside me　　坐在我旁边
= sit by my side

例: Come and sit beside me, Karen.
= Come and sit by my side, Karen.
（凯伦，过来坐在我旁边。）

2. 表"与……相较"，相当于"compared with"或"in comparison with"：

例: Beside him, I'm nothing.
= Compared with him, I'm nothing.
= In comparison with him, I'm nothing.
（跟他相比，我便微不足道了。）

EXERCISE

请选出一个正确的答案:

1. She would by no means marry ______ herself.
   (A) before (B) after (C) beneath (D) below
2. Stop yelling ______ him. He didn't do anything wrong.
   (A) to (B) for (C) at (D) against
3. John is attentive whenever he is ______ work.
   (A) on (B) in (C) over (D) at
4. John left home ______ the age of 18 and didn't come back until he was fifty.
   (A) at (B) for (C) in (D) on
5. Never judge a book ______ its cover.
   (A) to (B) by (C) on (D) at
6. He took me ______ the hand and said, "I love you."
   (A) by (B) on (C) in (D) with
7. We beat the team ______ five points.
   (A) with (B) for (C) over (D) by
8. When did they set out ______ Hawaii?
   (A) to (B) for (C) on (D) over
9. Quit smoking now ______ the sake of your health.
   (A) with (B) for (C) at (D) by
10. John wears his hair long, so people often take him ______ a girl.
    (A) as (B) for (C) with (D) by
11. It's very nice ______ you to say so.
    (A) with (B) for (C) of (D) by

12. The watch is really a bargain. I bought it ______ only NT$200.
(A) in (B) with (C) at (D) for

13. It's not a good idea to buy your child toys made ______ plastic. Plastic can be poisonous, you know.
(A) of (B) from (C) in (D) with

14. We should do something to prevent him ______ drugs.
(A) to take (B) of taking (C) from taking (D) not to take

15. Who is that lady ______ green?
(A) dressing in (B) dressing on (C) dressed in (D) dressed on

16. The room is a mess. Keep it ______ order.
(A) in (B) at (C) on (D) with

17. He talked to me ______ a low voice for fear someone else might hear us.
(A) with (B) in (C) on (D) under

18. We're planning to go ______ an expedition to the Sahara.
(A) in (B) for (C) on (D) over

19. You're too fat. You need to go ______ a diet immediately.
(A) on (B) in (C) for (D) at

20. Why is it that you are always ______ the go?
(A) in (B) on (C) for (D) along

21. I was born ______ the morning of July fourth, the same day the United States was founded.
(A) in (B) on (C) for (D) at

22. Dad won't be home until nine. He is ______ duty today.
(A) at (B) with (C) on (D) over

23. Peter came up with a good solution ______ the problem.
(A) for (B) of (C) on (D) to

24. Much ______ my surprise, the man turned out to be a woman.
(A) in (B) against (C) at (D) to

25. Let's dance ______ this song; it's so beautiful.
(A) with (B) to (C) on (D) by

26. ______ everything done, I closed the door and left for the station.
(A) On (B) With (C) For (D) By

27. Stop beating ______ the bush and tell me exactly what you want.
(A) at (B) down (C) around (D) over

28. Don't you think that the baby boy really takes ______ his father, especially when he smiles?
(A) on (B) for (C) after (D) over

29. I don't like his attitude ______ life. He is a little too pessimistic.
(A) in (B) toward (C) of (D) for

30. Generally speaking, he is not bad ______ that he is a little too lazy.
(A) except (B) in (C) so (D) for

31. Thanks to your timely help, we finished our project right ______ schedule.
(A) on (B) with (C) along (D) at

32. Being ______ music, I go to concerts quite often.
(A) by (B) into (C) over (D) under

33. We should all act ______ the law, or we could be in trouble.
(A) along (B) for (C) within (D) over

34. It goes ______ saying that honesty is the best policy.
(A) by (B) for (C) without (D) before

35. John is inquisitive and is never ______ asking questions.
(A) under (B) above (C) over (D) beneath

36. We talked ______ a cup of tea and came up with many good ideas as to what we should do next.
(A) in (B) at (C) over (D) for

37. What did you have ______ breakfast this morning?
(A) for (B) at (C) in (D) as

38. The view of the valley is really beautiful ______ description.
(A) beyond　(B) within　(C) by　(D) for

39. This letter was written in Chinese. Can you translate it ______ English?
(A) to　(B) into　(C) for　(D) as

40. All the doctors and nurses are ______ call for rescue missions.
(A) in　(B) by　(C) for　(D) on

标准答案

1.(C)	2.(C)	3.(D)	4.(A)	5.(B)	6.(A)	7.(D)	8.(B)	9.(B)	10.(B)
11.(C)	12.(D)	13.(A)	14.(C)	15.(C)	16.(A)	17.(B)	18.(C)	19.(A)	20.(B)
21.(B)	22.(C)	23.(D)	24.(D)	25.(B)	26.(B)	27.(C)	28.(C)	29.(B)	30.(A)
31.(A)	32.(B)	33.(C)	34.(C)	35.(B)	36.(C)	37.(A)	38.(A)	39.(B)	40.(D)

A Quick Note

第十四章　反意疑问句

1. 反意疑问句的使用规则：

陈述句为肯定时，接否定疑问句，陈述句为否定时，接肯定疑问句。

a. 陈述句有 be 动词，反意疑问句沿用 be 动词。

例: He is nice, isn't he?

（他人不错，是不是？）

I wasn't sick, was I?

（我没病，是不是？）

b. 陈述句有助动词，反意疑问句沿用助动词。

例: He will come, won't he?

（他会来，是不是？）

They can't do it, can they?

（他们不能做这件事，是不是？）

You have done it, haven't you?

（你做完了，是不是？）

（have 为助动词，其后之 done 才是主要动词）

c. 陈述句有一般动词，反意疑问句则使用 do、does、did。

例: He came, didn't he?

（他来了，是不是？）

（came 为一般过去时，故用 didn't）

He gets up early, doesn't he?

（他起得很早，是不是？）

（gets up 为一般现在时，故用 doesn't）

He didn't come, did he?

（他没来，是不是？）

He has money, doesn't he?

（他有钱，是不是？）

（has 为动词，其后有宾语 money）

d. 与祈使句使用时，反意疑问句一律用 will you。

例: Come here, will you?

（来这里，好不好？）

Stop smoking, will you?

（别抽烟了，好不好？）

e. 与祈使句 “Let's...” （咱们……）句型使用，反意疑问句一律用 shall we。

例: Let's go, shall we?

（咱们走吧，好不好？）

Let's not do it, shall we?

（咱们别做那件事，好不好？）

但: Let	us them him ⋮ John	go, will you? (祈使句)

（请你让我们/他们/他/……/约翰走吧，好不好？）

2. 句中有否定副词：

陈述句含有 scarcely、hardly、rarely、no doubt、little、never、by no means 等否定副词，陈述句视为否定句，须接肯定反问句。

例: Michael	scarcely ever hardly ever rarely	smokes,	does he? doesn't he?	(✓) (×)

（迈克尔很少抽烟，是不是？）

He is no doubt a good boy, is he?

（毫无疑问他是个好孩子，是不是？）

3. 句中有助动词短语：

陈述句含有 would rather、had better 等助动词短语，反意疑问句中用其第一个词。

例: You would rather go,	wouldn't you? wouldn't rather you?	(✓) (×)

（你宁愿去，是不是？）

You had better do it, hadn't you?

（你最好做这事，是不是？）

注意

但陈述句中的助动词短语若为 ought to 时，反意疑问句中须用 shouldn't。

例: He ought to come, | shouldn't he? | (√)
　　　　　　　　　　| oughtn't he to? | (×)
（他应当来，是不是？）

4. 否定反意疑问句中 not 的位置:

例: He is bad, | isn't he? | (√)
　　　　　　| is he not? | (√)
　　　　　　| is not he? | (×)
（他很坏，是不是？）

He left, | didn't he? | (√)
　　　　| did he not? | (√)
　　　　| did not he? | (×)
（他离开了，是不是？）

5. 反意疑问句须用人称代词:

反意疑问句一定要用人称代词，但陈述句句首为 There is / are / was / were 等时，则须用 there。

例: John is fine, isn't John?	(×)
→ John is fine, isn't he?	(√)
This is not good, is this?	(×)
→ This is not good, is it?	(√)
That is good, isn't that?	(×)
→ That is good, isn't it?	(√)
These are not good, are these?	(×)
→ These are not good, are they?	(√)
Those are good, aren't those?	(×)
→ Those are good, aren't they?	(√)
但: These is a man there, isn't it?	(×)
There is a man there, isn't there?	(√)

（那里有个人，是不是？）

6. “I + 表意见的动词 + that 从句”的反意疑问句:

陈述句中，主语若为第一人称单数 I 表示意见或观点时，不可能对自己反问，应以其后的 that 从句形成反问。

例: I think that David is nice, don't I? (×)
（我认为大卫人不错，我不是这样想的吗？）

I think that David is nice, isn't he? (√)
（我认为大卫人不错，是不是？）

I believe that we've met before, haven't we?（√）
（我认为我们以前见过面，是不是？）

I guess that Helen will come, won't she?（√）
（我猜想海伦会来，是不是？）

注意

1) 但主语若为 I 以外的主语，则反意疑问句仍是以主句为依据而形成的。

例: We think that the new teacher is nice, don't we?（√）
（我们认为这个新老师很好，是不是？）

They think that the new teacher is nice, don't they?（√）
（他们认为这个新老师很好，是不是？）

2) "I think that David is nice, isn't he?" 此句若改为 "I don't think that David is nice." 则反意疑问句就要改为 "I don't think that David is nice, is he?"

例: I don't believe that we've met before, have we?
（我不相信我们以前见过面，是不是？）

7. need 做一般动词及助动词的反意疑问句:

need 可做一般动词，也可做为助动词（仅限于否定句，须与 not 并用，无论第几人称 need 之后都不加 s）。

例: He needs to go, doesn't he?（此处 need 是动词，to go 为不定式短语，做其宾语）
（他需要过去，是不是？）

He doesn't need to go, does he?
（他不需要过去，是不是？）

He need not go, need he?（此处 need 与 not 并用，是助动词）
（他不需要过去，是不是？）

8. 助动词不止一个时如何反问:

陈述句中的助动词若不止一个的时候，反意疑问句中则使用第一个助动词。

例: But for his accident, he might have been a wonderful pianist, mightn't he?
= If it had not been for his accident, he might have been a wonderful pianist, mightn't he?
（当初要不是因为车祸，他本来可能成为一位很棒的钢琴家，是不是？）

EXERCISE

请选出一个正确的答案：

1. He's going to call us back, ______?
   (A) won't he (B) didn't he (C) doesn't he (D) isn't he
2. We had to wait a long time to get our visas, ______?
   (A) don't we (B) didn't we (C) couldn't we (D) shouldn't we
3. She's already made her reservation for next Saturday, ______?
   (A) hasn't she (B) isn't she (C) doesn't she (D) hasn't it
4. They don't seem to answer their phone whenever I call. There isn't anyone at home, ______?
   (A) isn't there (B) is there (C) is it (D) isn't it
5. John isn't a diligent student, for it is the third time he has been late, ______ ?
   (A) wasn't it (B) hasn't it (C) isn't it (D) hasn't he
6. You haven't seen Mary, ______ ?
   (A) have you (B) haven't you (C) has she (D) hasn't she
7. You have very little to eat in the morning, ______ you ?
   (A) do (B) don't (C) have (D) won't
8. On this busy road bus drivers ought to be especially careful, _____ ?
   (A) ought it (B) shouldn't they (C) oughtn't they to (D) ought they
9. Help me with this box, ______ ?
   (A) will you (B) shall we (C) shall you (D) don't you
10. Let's start early, ______ ?
    (A) will you (B) won't you (C) shall we (D) will we
11. Let me go home, ______ ?
    (A) will you (B) shall you (C) shall I (D) will I

12. Let us go to the movies, ______?
(A) shall we (B) will we (C) will you (D) won't we

13. You have a cold bath every morning, ______ you ?
(A) have (B) haven't (C) do (D) don't

14. You'd better go now, ______ you ?
(A) wouldn't (B) hadn't (C) would (D) didn't

15. This is the pen my father gave you, ______ ?
(A) isn't this (B) didn't he (C) didn't you (D) isn't it

16. That's where I used to live when I was a child, ______?
(A) isn't that (B) isn't it (C) didn't I (D) wasn't I

17. But for his accident, he might have been a wonderful pianist, _____ ?
(A) might he (B) mightn't he (C) didn't he (D) wasn't it

18. He never used to get up early, ______ he ?
(A) did (B) didn't (C) does (D) doesn't

19. You can hardly expect me to lend you money again, ______ you ?
(A) can (B) can't (C) do (D) don't

20. Mary seldom goes out in the evening, ______ ?
(A) does she (B) doesn't she
(C) does Mary (D) doesn't Mary

21. There's been no man in this house since you left, ______ ?
(A) hasn't there (B) isn't there (C) has there (D) isn't it

22. I think John has left, ______ ?
(A) don't I (B) has he (C) doesn't he (D) hasn't he

23. I needn't bring my books here tomorrow, ______ I ?
(A) need (B) do (C) shall (D) needn't

24. They need to be reminded of it, ______?
(A) needn't they (B) need they (C) don't they (D) doesn't it

25. I take it you won't be coming then, ______?
    (A) don't I　(B) doesn't it　(C) will you　(D) shall I

标准答案

1. (D)	2. (B)	3. (A)	4. (B)	5. (C)	6. (A)	7. (A)	8. (B)	9. (A)	10. (C)
11. (A)	12. (C)	13. (D)	14. (B)	15. (D)	16. (B)	17. (B)	18. (A)	19. (A)	20. (A)
21. (C)	22. (D)	23. (A)	24. (C)	25. (C)					

习题解说

1. 陈述句中有 be 动词，反意疑问句中沿用 be 动词。
2. had to（必须）在此视为一般动词，故反问部分用 didn't we。
3. She's 是 She has 的缩写，has 是完成时助动词，故用 has 形成反问。
4. 陈述句中有 there is / there be，反意疑问句中沿用 there。
5. 与第 1 题同理。
6. 与第 3 题同理。
7. 因 You have very little to eat. = You have almost nothing to eat. 是否定句，故反问部分应为肯定 do you。
   比较：You have a little to eat, don't you?
8. 陈述句中有 ought to 时，习惯用 should 反问。
9. 祈使句之后的反意疑问句一律用 will you。
10. "Let's..." 句型之后的反意疑问句一律用 shall we。
11. 此为一般祈使句，故用 will you。
12. 此亦为一般祈使句，故用 will you。
13. have 在此为一般动词，故用 don't 作反问。
14. You'd better = You had better，反问部分采用 hadn't。
15. 陈述句中的主语为 this，在反意疑问句中须改为 it。
16. 与第 15 题同理。
17. 陈述句中的助动词若不止一个，反意疑问句中用第一个助动词。

18. 此处 used 视为一般动词，之前有否定副词 never，故之后采用肯定反问，did 应为正选。
19. hardly 为否定副词。
20. seldom 为否定副词。
21. There's been = There has been
22. “I think + that 从句”中以 that 从句来形成反问。
23. need 用于肯定句是一般动词，用于否定句则是助动词，无论第几人称均不加 s。

He needs to go, doesn't he?

（他需要去，不是吗？）

He need not go, need he?

= He doesn't need to go, does he?

（他不需要去，是吗？）

24. 见上题解答。
25. I take it (that) ... = I think (that) ...

附 录（一）

第一章 句子的形成		
动词的种类	完全不及物动词（简写 c.vi.）	Something **happened**. 有事发生了。
	不完全不及物动词（简写 i.vi.）	He **looks** happy. 他看起来很快乐。
	完全及物动词（简写 c.vt.）	He **wrote** a book. 他写了一本书
	不完全及物动词（简写 i.vt.）	I **made** him wash the car. 我叫他洗车。
	授予动词（简写 d.v.）	Please **lend** me your book. 请把你的书借我。
五大句型	主语 + 完全不及物动词（谓语）	He went away. 他走了。
	主语 + 不完全不及物动词（谓语）+ 表语	He became a good student. 他变成好学生了。
	主语 + 完全及物动词（谓语）+ 宾语	They enjoy dancing. 他们喜欢跳舞。
	主语 + 不完全及物动词（谓语）+ 宾语 + 宾语补语	He made me happy. 他让我很开心。
	主语 + 授予动词(谓语)+ 间接宾语(授予对象）+ 直接宾语（被授予的东西）	I told him a lie. 我跟他说了谎。

第二章 两句的连接方法		
连接符号	破折号“—”	He is trash—he is good for nothing. 他是废物——他什么都不行。
	冒号“：”	He has made his goal known: he wants to be a scientist. 他已经让大家知道他的目标了：他要当科学家。
	分号“；”	He is a man of principle; we all respect him. 他是有原则的人，因此我们都尊敬他。
并列连词	单一连词：and, or, but	He is kind **and** handsome. 他心地好，人又帅。
	连词短语：both...and...; not only...but also...;as well as; rather than 等	He is happy **rather than** sad. 他很快乐，不是伤心。
副词性连词	because, if, once, as soon as, however, in addition, while, as 等	**Once** I am free, I will take a trip abroad. 我一旦有空就会出国旅行。

第三章　关系词		
关系代词	who, whom, which, that	He is not the man **that** he once was. 他已不是当年的他了。
关系代词所有格	whose（= the...of which = of which + the +...）	This is a fancy car, **whose** color I like very much. 这是一辆漂亮的车，我非常喜欢它的颜色。
关系副词	where, when, why, how	This is the city **where** I met Mary. 这就是我与玛丽相遇的城市。
复合关系代词	whoever, whomever, whichever, whatever, however	**Whatever** he says, I don't believe him. 不论他说什么，我都不相信他。
准关系代词	than, as, but	He has as much money **as** I (do). 他的钱和我的一样多。

第四章 非谓语动词		
不定式	原形不定式	You should help him **study** the lesson. 你应该帮他学这一课。
	to+ 动词原形	He refused **to study** the lesson. 他拒绝学这一课。
分词	现在分词：与被修饰词之间是主谓关系，表示动作与谓语动作同时发生	The **retiring** teacher walked into the classroom. 这位即将退休的老师走进教室。
	过去分词：与被修饰词之间是被动关系，表示动作发生在谓语动作之前，现已经完成或只表示状态	The **retired** soldier died last month. 那位退役军人上个月去世了。
动名词	通常指被修饰词的用途，无逻辑上的主谓关系	**Losing** his fortune drove him mad. 失去财富使他发疯了。

第五章　助动词及易用错的动词		
助动词	be, have, do, shall, will, can, may, must, ought to, need, dare, used to 等	He **used to** live in Taiwan. 他以前住在台湾。
易用错的动词	lie/lay; sit/set/seat; rise/raise/arise/arouse; take/bring 等	Don't **lie** to me. 别对我说谎。

第六章　时态及语态			
1、一般现在时	表示现在状态或习惯性的动作。	主动：主语 + 一般现在时动词 被动：主语 + am/is/are + 过去分词	Everyone **loves** him. He **is loved** by everyone. 人人都喜欢他。

2、一般过去时	表示过去的动作或状态。	主动：主语 + 一般过去时动词 被动：主语 + was/were+ 过去分词	I **saw** him yesterday. He **was seen** by me yesterday. 我昨天看见了他。
3、一般将来时	表示将来发生的动作或状态。	主动：主语 + will + 原形动词 被动：主语 + will be + 过去分词	He **will finish** the work in an hour. The work **will be finished** in an hour. 这项工作一个小时后完成。
4、现在完成时	表示到现在为止完成的动作。	主动：主语 + have/has + 过去分词 被动：主语 + have/has been + 过去分词	He **has turned** the light off. The light **has been turned** off by him. 他把灯关了。
5、过去完成时	表示截止到过去某时为止所有完成的动作或经历。	主动：主语 + had + 过去分词 被动：主语 + had been + 过去分词	He **had done** it. It **had been done** by him. 他已经做完了这件事。
6、将来完成时	表示到将来某时为止所有完成或仍在继续的动作或经历。	主动：主语 + will have + 过去分词 被动：主语 + will have been + 过去分词	When you come, I **will have finished** everything. When you come, everything **will have been finished**. 你来的时候，每一件事将已全部完成。
7、现在进行时	表示现在正在做的动作。	主动：主语 + is/am/are + 现在分词 被动：主语 + is/am/are + being + 过去分词	He **is writing** a letter now. A letter **is being written** by him now. 他现在正在写信。
8、过去进行时	表示过去某时正在做的动作。	主动：主语 + was/were + 现在分词 被动：主语 + was/were + being + 过去分词	He **was cleaning** my car at nine yesterday morning. My car **was being cleaned** by him at nine yesterday morning. 昨天早上 9 点他正在洗我的车。
9、将来进行时	表示将来某时将进行的动作。	主动：主语 + will be + 现在分词 被动：主语 + will be + being + 过去分词	They **will be doing** the experiment here at this time next Monday. The experiment **will be being done** by them here at this time next Monday. 下周一的这个时候他们会在做实验。
10、现在完成进行时	表示一直继续到现在且仍将继续下去的动作。	主动：主语 + have/has been + 现在分词 被动：主语 + have/has been + being + 过去分词	He **has been punishing** the thief for what he had done. The thief **has been being punished** by him for what he had done. 他已经因为这个小偷的行为而处罚了他。

11、过去完成进行时	表示一直继续到过去某时，而当时仍在继续进行的动作。	主动：主语 + had been + 现在分词 被动：主语 + had been + being + 过去分词	He **had been writing** a letter for two hours. A letter **had been being written** by him for two hours. 这封信他已经写了两个小时了。
12、将来完成进行时	表示一直继续到将来某时，而仍将继续进行的动作。	主动：主语 + will have been + 现在分词 被动：主语 + will have been + being + 过去分词	I **will have been teaching** the boy for ten years by the end of this year. The boy **will have been being taught** English for ten years by the end of this year. 到今年年末，我已经教这个男孩 10 年英语了。

第七章　虚拟语气		
纯条件虚拟语气（真实条件句）	从句：If + 主语 + 一般现在时动词 主句：主语 + will/情态动词 + 动词原形	If he **is** here, I **will beat** him. 如果他在这里，我会打他。
非真实条件句	与现在事实相反： 从句：If + 主语 + 一般过去时动词 主句：主语 + should/would/could/might/ought to + 动词原形	If I **were** rich, I **would help** you. 我要是有钱，我会帮助你。
	与过去事实相反： 从句：If + 主语 + had + 过去分词 主句：主语 + should/would/could/might /ought to + have + 过去分词	If I **had arrived** earlier, I **could have met** him. 如果我早到一会儿，我可能会遇到他。
	与将来事实相反： 从句：If + 主语 + should/were + to + 动词原形 主句：主语 + should/would/could/might /ought to + 动词原形	If you **should fall** ill, the meeting **would be put** off. 如果你生病，会议会被取消。
省略 if 的虚拟条件句	将虚拟条件从句中的 were、had、should 放到主语之前，构成主谓倒装	**Had he done** it, he would have felt sorry. =If he had done it, he would have felt sorry. 如果他做了，他会感到难过的。

第八章　副词		
副词的功能	修饰动词、形容词、副词或全句	**Evidently**, this answer is right. 这个答案显然是对的。
副词的位置	一般情况位于 be 动词及助动词之后或动词之前。（特殊情况详见正文。）	They **often** go fishing. 他们常去钓鱼。

第九章 倒装结构		
部分倒装	否定倒装：never，hardly, rarely, seldom, little, by no means, in no way, on no account, not until..., only when..., only after...	**Hardly can he** move. 他几乎不能动。
	so...that /such...that 倒装	**So late did he** come **that** he missed the train. 他到得太晚了，没有赶上火车。
完全倒装	there, here, in, out, down, up off 等（主语是名词时倒装）	**In walked** a boy. 一个男孩走了进来。
	形容词 + be 动词 + 主语	**Happy is he** who is content.（正常语序：He who is content is happy.） 知足者常乐。

第十章 比较结构		
一般比较	比较级：两者间作比较 表示一方超过另一方时，用“比较级（+ than）” 表示一方不及另一方时，用“less + 原级 + than”的结构表示。	He worked more carefully **than** you (did). 他做事比你细心。 He is less responsible **than** you(are). 他没有你负责任。
	最高级：三者或三者以上作比较 of / among...；最高级形容词 + n. + 关系代词 that + 定语从句完成时	He is the best student **that I've ever taught**. 在我教过的学生中，他是最好的一位。
原级比较	as...as...“和……一样地……” not so (as)...as...“和……不一样地……”	He runs **as** fast **as** John. 他跑得和约翰一样快。 He **doesn't** study **as (so)** hard **as** Mary. 他没有玛丽用功。
倍数的表达	倍数词 + as...as...“是……的几倍”	He studies **three times as** hard **as** I. 他的用功程度是我的三倍。
	more than + 倍数词 +as...as...“是……的几倍还不止”	He studies **more than three times as** hard **as** I. 他的用功程度是我的三倍还不止。
	倍数词 + the（或所有格）+ 名词 “是……的几倍”	The river is **ten times the length of** the Tamsui River. 这条河的长度是淡水河的十倍。
	more than + 倍数词 + the（或所有格）+ 名词 “是……的几倍还不止”	He has **more than twice** my money. 他的钱是我的两倍还不止。

第十一章　代词（略）

第十二章　复合形容词（略）

第十三章　介词的用法（略）

第十四章　反意疑问句		
使用规则	主句是肯定句，反问部分用否定形式；主句是否定句，反问部分用肯定形式。	He **gets up** early, **doesn't he**? 他起得很早，是不是？
	陈述句中含有否定副词（如：scarcely, hardly, rarely, no doubt, little, never, by no means 等），陈述句视为否定句，后接肯定反问句。	Michael **hardly** ever smokes, **does he**? 迈克尔很少抽烟，是不是？
其他	“I + 表意见的动词 + that 从句”的反意疑问句以其后的 that 从句形成反问	**I think** that **David** is nice, **isn't he**? 我认为大卫人不错，是不是？ 注意：**I don't think** that **David is nice, is he**?
	“主语非 I + 表意见的动词 + that 从句”的反意疑问句以主句为依据形成反问句	**We think that** the new teacher is nice, **don't we**? 我们认为这个新老师很好，是不是？

附 录（二）

台湾、大陆语法用语对照表	
文　法	语　法
单　字	单　词
片　语	短　语
主词补语	表　语
虚受词	形式宾语
虚主词	形式主语
真主词	真正主语
真受词	真正宾语
主　词	主　语
受　词	宾　语
受　格	宾　格
代名词	代　词
介系词	介　词
地方副词	地点副词
不定词	不定式
不定词片语	不定式短语
直接受词	直接宾语
间接受词	间接宾语
对等连接词	并列连词
指示形容词	指示代词
关系指示形容词	关系指示代词
句　构	结　构
形容词子句	定语从句
名词子句	名词性从句
副词子句	状语从句
主要子句	主　句
子　句	从　句
句　构	结　构
分词构句	分词结构

命令句	祈使句
长划符号	破折号
并　用	连　用
逗　点	逗　号
连字号	连字符
授与动词	授予动词
句　点	句　号
情状介词片语	with 复合结构
完成进行式	完成进行时
现在完成式	现在完成时
过去完成式	过去完成时
未来完成式	将来完成时
现在进行式	现在进行时
过去进行式	过去进行时
未来进行式	将来进行时
现在完成进行式	现在完成进行时
过去完成进行式	过去完成进行时
简单式	一般时
现在式	一般现在时
过去式	一般过去时
未来式	一般将来时
进行式	进行时
未　来	将　来
假设语气	虚拟语气
数字词	数　词
所有格代名词	名词性物主代词
反问句	反意疑问句
动状词	非谓语动词
字	词
限定修饰	限制性定语从句
连接词	连　词
非限定修饰	非限制性定语从句